# THE RAVINE OF MEMORY

# THE RAVINE OF MEMORY

Babyn Yar Between the Holocaust
and the Great Patriotic War

**SHAY A. PILNIK**

Foreword by
NATAN SHARANSKY

**PURDUE UNIVERSITY PRESS • WEST LAFAYETTE, INDIANA**

Copyright 2025 by Purdue University. All rights reserved.
Printed in the United States of America.

Cataloging-in-Publication Data is available from the Library of Congress.
978-1-62671-092-4 (hardback)
978-1-62671-093-1 (paperback)
978-1-62671-094-8 (epub)
978-1-62671-095-5 (epdf)

*Cover:*
The improvised sign, hung by a group of young Jews on the occasion of the twenty-fifth anniversary of the Babyn Yar Massacre. Courtesy of the Central Archives for the History of the Jewish People; Emmanuel Diamant.
The crowd at the first Babyn Yar commemoration since 1944, September 29, 1966. Courtesy of the Central Archives for the History of the Jewish People.

*In memory of my mother, Rachel (Hazanovsky) Pilnik z"l,
daughter of a Holocaust survivor and a Red Army officer*

# CONTENTS

| | |
|---|---|
| *Foreword* | *ix* |
| *Preface* | *xiii* |
| *Acknowledgments* | *xvii* |
| Introduction: Babyn Yar Unearthed | 1 |
| 1. Early Responses | 21 |
| 2. The Thaw and the Memory of Babyn Yar | 31 |
| 3. The Second Thaw | 56 |
| 4. Babyn Yar Set to Music | 80 |
| 5. Documentary in Content, Fictional in Form: Anatoly Kuznetsov | 91 |
| 6. "Their Memory Is Alive": Babyn Yar on the Soviet Yiddish Literary Scene | 108 |
| 7. "Let Us Go There by Foot": Itsik Kipnis | 133 |
| 8. A Lullaby to Babyn Yar: Shike Driz | 145 |
| 9. Between Marranos and Conversos: The Next Generation of Kyiv Yiddish Writers | 153 |
| Epilogue | 183 |
| *Notes* | *189* |
| *Bibliography* | *227* |
| *Index* | *239* |
| *About the Author* | *253* |

# FOREWORD

SHAY PILNIK'S *THE RAVINE OF MEMORY* OFFERS A COMPREHENSIVE AND ILLUMInating study of a subject that for me, as for most Jews living in the post-Holocaust Soviet Union, remained an enigma for decades. It was a memory black hole, a taboo subject on which one may have had some vague knowledge, but upon which one also knew to stay silent.

I was born in 1948 in the city of Donetsk, known during those years as Stalino. Not unlike my Jewish peers, I grew up surrounded by killing fields from the days of World War II, by pits, ravines, and anti-tank trenches where the remains of my neighbors and relatives were buried. As children, signs of the Great Patriotic War were all around us. They were constant references at home, at school, on the radio, and on the street to the Soviet Union's long, painful, bloody victory over Adolf Hitler and the Nazis. We often attended ceremonies celebrating the Soviet Union's victory over Nazi Germany. We romped on abandoned rusting tanks that hung around our town for many years. We constantly played war games, competing for the honor of "belonging" to the noble Red Army, the forces of light who defeated the Nazi forces of Darkness.

Yet while talking incessantly about the war, we could not talk about the war against the Jews. Official documents mentioned Jews far down the long list of victims, after Soviet soldiers, Soviet partisans, Soviet prisoners of war, innocent Soviet civilians, and Romani. Only decades later did I discover that we were living—and playing—near monstrous proof of the Holocaust that officially never happened. Our playgrounds were some of the bloodiest sites in Jewish history—in human history.

Donetsk was infamous for having the second largest pit after Babyn Yar, where over 75,000 murdered Jews were buried. Many of them were children who were thrown alive into the pit. And I knew nothing of it. It was near these ravines and pits that I played war games with my childhood friends, reenacting our parents' defeat of the Nazis, bragging about the decorations and medals they brought from the battlefields. We did not know anything about the tragedy that befell our mothers, sisters, grandparents and other relatives right there. Even worse, we knew nothing of the two million Soviet Jews who were victims of the Final Solution. While the shaft in the Rykovskaya mine in the Donetsk region was the closest one to my home, thousands of these mass grave sites had dotted the western part of the Soviet Union.

The one that came to epitomize these mass graves, to emerge as a symbol of the Shoah in the Soviet Union or *The Holocaust by Bullets* was Babi Yar, as the site is known in Russian, or Babyn Yar, as it is known in Ukrainian. It was a symbol for the brutality demonstrated by the Nazi Einsatzgruppen (mobile killing units) and local collaborators, where the first phase of the Nazi Final Solution plan to exterminate European Jews was implemented. Babyn Yar was, first and foremost, a name associated with a Nazi crime. With the fall of Hitler, however, this terrifying name became the grounds for a new crime, now a Soviet one. After the Nazis killed their Jewish victims and later destroyed all evidence of the genocide they committed, it was the task of the Soviet liberators—of Ukraine, Belarus, the Baltic States, and other areas, to continue the memory erasure work that the Nazis had begun. Babyn Yar, thus, became the symbol of the Soviet crime of attempting to wipe the memory of the Holocaust on Soviet soil from the face of the earth. By turning the ravine into a park with a stadium on top, Moscow's target was to make the most painful chapter in Jewish history, right under our noses, completely disappear.

To me, as a young Soviet Jew, nothing could be more puzzling than this Soviet policy. Why? In Dante Alighieri's punctual portrayal of the different stages of hell, one cannot find a description gruesome enough to correspond to the reality of Babyn Yar, where layer upon layer of humans, Jewish mothers and their children, young and old, lay shot, mostly dead but some still moving, taking their last breaths, inside an enormous ravine turned mass grave. I was baffled by the shrouds of secrecy in which Babyn Yar and other sites were enveloped. Why, I wondered, did the regime that defeated the Nazis force the Holocaust by bullets into the shadows of history and memory? I was only later to understand that what motivated Moscow to form this new unwritten policy, observed from 1944 into the next four decades, could be summarized in one word: antisemitism.

Growing up Jewish in the Soviet Union offered nothing positive: no Jewish tradition, no Jewish institutions, no Jewish culture, no Jewish history, no Jewish holidays, no Jewish books. Nor did we celebrate circumcisions, bar mitzvahs, or Jewish language. The only real Jewish experience I had was facing antisemitism. In stripping away Jewish identity, Jewish history, and Jewish literacy, the state also deprived us of knowledge about the Holocaust, which had occurred only a few years before and in our own backyards. While the persecution of Jews peaked in 1953 with the arrest of Jewish doctors (an attack thwarted by Stalin's passing weeks before the trial and certain execution of the arrestees), the Soviet policy toward Jews—of discriminating against and demonizing the Jews and the Jewish state—persisted till the very last years of communism. One key aspect of Soviet antisemitism was to not recognize the Nazi systematic slaughter of the Jews. The Shoah, therefore, simply didn't exist. Indeed, antisemitism itself was deemed nonexistent.

For a moment, it seemed as though the Soviet regime may revisit this clear policy, adding insult to the injury of genocide that had taken place in our midst. I remember when, finally, the words "Babyn Yar" appeared in the newspaper, when my father, with trembling hands and voice, came to me reading the poem "Babi Yar" by the poet

Yevgeny Yevtushenko. My father showed me the poem and sighed with relief—"Now we can finally talk about it." Yet he was wrong. His joy was premature. The next day a campaign against the poem and the poet was launched. Yevtushenko was forced to change some of its most daring, truth-evoking verses. The fate of Dmitri Shostakovich's symphony *Babi Yar* was not different. The Soviets decided to ban it right after its Moscow premiere.

Today, when there is no longer a Soviet Union or Nazi Germany, some observers may wonder what relevant lessons we may be able to draw from a mid-twentieth-century site such as Babyn Yar. My answer to them is very simple. Although humanity succeeded in defeating these two evil and murderous regimes, weakening the danger of antisemitism and repercussions of hatred toward Jews and other minorities around the globe, we must remember that those who encourage hate toward Jews are not interested in showing their audiences how far the virus of antisemitism may reach and how lethal it may be. *What starts with Jews never ends with Jews.* Therefore, it is the task of scholars, Holocaust museums, civil leaders, politicians—all of humankind—to preserve these dark memories that remind us of the dangers of Jew-hatred and its consequences: of how, when left unchecked, it may destroy the very foundations of our society, of humanity. We must be ready to confront our past but also the Jew-haters of today, whether they be the leaders of the Islamic Republic of Iran, Hamas, ISIS, or the new generation of neo-Nazis, far-right extremists, or progressives demanding to liberate Palestine from the river to the sea—all those wishing to perpetrate a new Holocaust in the twenty-first century.

This is why the memory of Babyn Yar as the symbol of the Holocaust in the Soviet Union is so important today. It is a symbol of a catastrophe that defies the imagination. But it is also a symbol of the call to make the world better and safer, to bring antisemitism—and the senseless violence, terrorism, and war that has been engulfing us in recent year, first in Ukraine, and now in Israel—to a swift end.

*Natan Sharansky*

# PREFACE

> *Bronye has been lying in this mass grave for almost two decades; she shared the bitter fate of the other 16,000 innocent people, who were murdered on October 10, 1941, in the "trenches" [okopes]. Every city, in which the German fascists were present, had its own "Babi Yar." In Vilna—this was Ponary, in Kharkov—Kholodnaya Gora, and in my hometown of Azovsk we [simply] call them "trenches."*
> TEVYE GEN, "IN DER HEYMSHTOT: TOGBUKH,"
> SOVETISH HEYMLAND

IF I WERE TO LOOK FOR A WORD, PLACE, CONCEPT, METAPHOR, OR SPACE THAT would encapsulate the Holocaust in the Soviet Union—as distinct from the implementation of the Final Solution elsewhere in Europe—the ravine would be the first one that comes to mind. In the ravines of Ukraine are buried dreams, lives, hopes, and memories. In these ravines lie the memories of the murdered and murdered memories. Humans were efficiently murdered by German bullets, and memories were murdered, albeit far less efficiently, by suffocation in the hands of the Germans' Soviet rivals, turned allies, turned archenemies. The ravines are the places toward which all the stormwater flows; the ravines are the "ground zero" of both the surrounding landscape and of collective memory: They are the places where both local topography and humanity reached their lowest point. They are the places where the mass murder of infants, women, men, children, and the elderly—accused of the crime of being Jewish—took place. They are also a memory marker for the many non-Jews buried in Babyn Yar. No wonder that Holocaust historian Wendy Lower chose to entitle her searing study of open-air massacres in Ukraine simply *The Ravine*.[1]

Metaphorically, the ravines of the western frontiers of the Soviet Union also comprise the confluence point of two narrative streams: the Holocaust and the Great Patriotic War. The latter is the narrative produced by the Soviet government and embraced by millions of Soviet citizens of a great war, a great triumph, and a great sacrifice—a narrative of the struggle against the German occupation that was shared by the Russian majority and the many Soviet ethnic minorities.

The story of the ravines of the Soviet western frontiers is dark and complex. In the physical landscape, charting out the terrain and the streams leading into the ravine is the topographer's task. When mapping the landscape of memory, though, the streams intersect, draw apart from one another, and then pour back into the ravine, becoming indistinguishable. The dead are all buried in the same ravine, but the meanings of their death are many. These meanings may coexist, and they may even conflict, buried as they are in the pit's very depths.

While the ravines of the Soviet frontiers were many, the streams flowing into Babyn Yar were of different natures and shapes: the ravine on the outskirts of Kyiv was the place where the Jewish and Soviet memories of the Shoah and the Great Patriotic War converge; where dissent in its soft form, as a potential crime, and dissidence, as a dangerous criminal offense, met; where the recent past of genocide streamed into a Jewish future of national revival in the wake of the Six-Day War; and where the major Russian and the minor Yiddish literature within the Soviet multinational polity echoed the victims' screaming and the deadly silence of the massacre's aftermath. This is the story of the ravine known internationally during the Cold War by its Russian name, Babi Yar, and of a city known back then as Kiev, the capital of Soviet Ukraine: the ravine and the city were hailed as such by the international and scholarly communities, but today they are known by their respective Ukrainian names—Babyn Yar and Kyiv. It is also the story of Russian literature during a critical point in its twentieth-century history, a time known as "Khrushchev's Thaw." And, no less importantly, it is the story of Jews as a minority within the Soviet ethnopolitical structure in the years following World War II and up until the mid-1970s. It is a complex, convoluted story, one that seeks to excavate the existential core of what it meant to be a writer, artist, and intellectual in the Soviet Union—and also of what it meant to be a Soviet Jew. Unlike the postwar West, it was an experience of persecution, discrimination, and dissent: a modern incarnation of the early-modern-era Marrano.

In the study offered here, Babyn Yar emerges as a complex web of narratives flowing in and out of each other during the reign of three Soviet leaders: Joseph Stalin, Nikita Khrushchev, and Leonid Brezhnev (or more precisely, from the first reactions to Babyn Yar in 1944, through the Thaw period, our periodical focal point, and up until the unveiling of the official Soviet memorial in the ravine's vicinity in 1976). As a scholar trying to place the memory of Babyn Yar and the literature that this vast memory hole engendered in its proper historical and cultural context, I offer a close reading of the varied and complex literary texts. When I set out on this journey into Babyn Yar's different memory streams back in 2006, the ravine and the struggle to commemorate it were an important yet neglected subject in Western scholarship. Although the story of Babyn Yar, of the ravine's memory formation in the Russian literary sphere, was already established as a significant chapter in the history of Russian culture during the post-Stalin era, little had been written and known, let alone published, about Babyn Yar and באבי יאר—that is, about the crystallization of the ravine's memory in the Soviet Ukrainian and Yiddish spheres, respectively.

At that point, to offer the ultimate, all-encompassing study of Babyn Yar in three literary spheres was an ambitious task, the scope of which seemed still within reach. But with Babyn Yar's recent emergence as a hot news item, and with the renewed interest by scholars from a variety of countries who now wish to study it from a variety of perspectives and explore its literary legacies in a variety of languages, the scope of my itinerary had shifted: from writing the encyclopedic monograph on Babyn Yar to a more focused comparative study on the Russian and Yiddish spheres in order to explore how Babyn Yar's crystallization in Soviet memory differed between a major literary sphere and a minor one—that is, between the celebrated creative effort of key non-Jewish writers and the invariably obscure works of far-less-known Jewish ones. And while referencing a few works belonging to the Ukrainian sphere—also authored by both Jews and non-Jews, stories and poems in which reactions of shock and despair blended with reminisces of prewar cordial neighborly relations—and with the more recent, inconvenient, and haunting memories of Ukrainian collaboration with the German occupiers—the present study does not emphasize the canon of works on Babyn Yar in the Ukrainian language that have recently been treated in depth in works like Ostap Kin's *Babyn Yar: Ukrainian Poets Respond*.[2]

As a community leader, as someone who has had the fortune of helping to give shape to Holocaust memory—first as the director of the Nathan and Esther Pelz Holocaust Education Resource Center in Milwaukee and later as the head of the Emil A. and Jenny Fish Center for Holocaust and Genocide Studies at Yeshiva University in New York—I strive to simplify the story. It has to be simple, lest the moral obligation resting on my shoulders weaken. On the countless occasions on which I presented the story of Babyn Yar told in this book to teachers, students, and lay leaders, I did my best to find a way to make it a quintessential Holocaust story. As a grandson of three Holocaust survivors, I was afraid that Babyn Yar's many subtleties would obscure the underlying, terrifying fundamental message.

When all was said and done, it was my desire to view Babyn Yar as the site of murder and suffocation—of humans and of their memory alike—the former successful, the latter abortive. But as will be further elaborated and explicated in this study, when dealing with ravines—with the physical and metaphysical, the historical and the cultural—simplicity is only wishful thinking. The story starts to stream on its own, and the portrayal of Babyn Yar unfolding in this book, while not offering the quintessential guide to the ravine—no study of Babyn Yar can claim to encompass the event from all angles, as is evident by the exponential growth of both scholarly and artistic publications on Babyn Yar in recent years—*does* help explain, in no simple terms, just how complex the ravine is.

When reflecting on the twentieth century and the first two decades of the twenty-first, it became clearer to me that with the growing number of studies dedicated to the ravine and the foundation of the Babyn Yar Holocaust Memorial Center, the struggle over Babyn Yar—the struggle underlying both ethnic conflict and the individual effort to make sense of the ravine—is far from over. What Michael Berenbaum wrote about the Holocaust—namely, that "the more distant we stand from the event, the larger the event looms"[3]—resonates strongly in the case of Babyn Yar. That in late 2022 the ravine looms larger and larger is both a propitious sign and a testimony to our misfortune. For along with the renewed interest in Babyn Yar by scholars, artists, and the public at large, there has also been renewed interest in old conflicts and, even worse, in their resumption and in the desire to resolve them via brute force by committing war crimes and the murder of civilians, and by violating international laws.

When I began my research on Babyn Yar more than a decade ago, I had every reason to believe that my investigation was about a sealed chapter in the history of Soviet literature and culture. As I write and edit the very last words in this book, however, new times of trouble have engulfed us. The war in Ukraine has sent us all a chilling reminder that in the annals of humankind, tragically, ethnic conflicts of whatever sort can never be so easily sealed. And while so different from the context of the current war, I hope that the story told in this book may guide us in our search for truth, for the proper way to honor the dead, for a lasting peace between rival nations predicated on mutual respect, the reconciliation of dark memories, and the affirmation of the infinite value of life.

# ACKNOWLEDGMENTS

WRITING ONE'S FIRST BOOK IS A LONG JOURNEY, AND MANY PEOPLE HAVE SUPported me since I embarked on it. This started with a final paper for a course on the history of Soviet Jewry that was triggered by an encounter back in 2006 with the recording of Dmitri Shostakovich's Thirteenth Symphony at the Lincoln Center music store in New York. A small project transformed into a PhD dissertation, and now, at long last, it has finally become a book. After spending close to twenty years reading, speaking, writing, and thinking about Babyn Yar, I had the fortune of meeting and working with friends and colleagues who kept challenging me to think and rethink this meaningful site and the commemoration of the Holocaust in the Soviet Union as a complex, multifaceted phenomenon, and to view this book as just the beginning of a much wider exploration of the subject.

The list of credits is long but must begin with the inspiration for writing this book: my late grandparents Mikhael and Fruma Hazanovsky and Anshel and Sara Pilnik. The four of them met and married in postwar Vilnius, where they gave birth to my parents and decided to immigrate to Israel about ten years later—twenty years before I was born. Their Jewish upbringing, though unique for each of them; their experiences before and after the Holocaust; the life-changing decisions they made; and the countless conversations I had with them about these decisions have touched every section of *The Ravine of Memory*.

As for those who offered inspiration and those who offered assistance, I must begin with two close colleagues and friends: Steven Fine, who welcomed me to Yeshiva University and, without delay, asked to read my dissertation and immediately said, "There is a book here, my new friend." Without his mentorship, encouragement, and boundless patience, this book would have remained in dissertation form. I am also deeply grateful to Glenn Dynner, without whose wisdom, determination, redaction tips, and navigation guidance through the maze of academic publishing this book would not have become what I really wanted it to be. I will always be grateful to them for their knowledge, their support, and, most of all, their friendship.

I would like to thank Gennady Estraikh, Mikhail Krutikov, and Arkady Zeltser for taking the time to read a draft of this manuscript and offering valuable insights related to the commemoration of Babyn Yar within the context of Soviet history and culture. In correspondence and through Zoom calls and in-person meetings, these three scholars—born and raised in the Soviet Union and possessing an intimate familiarity with postwar Soviet culture—helped illuminate many aspects of this study. Together with them, I am indebted to Zvi Gitelman, whose feedback on my work when it was still in embryonic form was invaluable, and whose work has provided me with foundational knowledge and countless insights on the unique universe of Soviet Jewry.

I am especially grateful for President Ari Berman, Provost Selma Botman, Dean Daniel Rynhold, Joshua Karlip, Jess Olson, Karen Shawn, Ronnie Perelis, Joseph Angel, Stuart Halpern, and Joshua Zimmerman, my colleagues at Yeshiva University. Since the winter of 2020, I have had the privilege of assuming the position of the director of the Emil A. and Jenny Fish Holocaust and Genocide Studies Center at one of the most consequential Jewish educational institutions in the world. I thank my new colleagues at YU, who have provided me with an ideal intellectual home and a smooth transition from the nonprofit world to the academic one.

I have been blessed to know the generous, philanthropic visionary behind the Fish Center, who over the last four years has become one of my closest friends, Mr. Emil Fish. Mr. Fish was liberated from the infamous Nazi concentration camp Bergen-Belsen at the age of ten and has partnered with me on building an educational institute of the highest caliber for the study of the Holocaust. He has ensured that his experiences, those of his parents and sister and his relatives, those of the community, and those of the entire Jewish people will continue to be taught and studied by posterity.

Research is often done in solitude, but it cannot be done without a good team of archivists and librarians whose advice and patience make this labor much easier and more productive. I thank Zvi Erenyi and Tina Weiss from YU's Mendel Gottesman Library, who have worked closely with me on the completion of this book and addressed my many library needs and bibliographical questions. And to the helpful staff at so many institutions—to Vadim Altskan from the United States Holocaust Memorial Museum archives, Anastasia Glazanova and Benjamin Lukin from the Central Archives for the History of the Jewish People, Vital Zajka from the YIVO Institute for Jewish Research archives, Edward Serotta from Centropa (Central Europe Center for Research and Documentation), and Bettina Malka-Igelbusch and Emanuel Saunders from the Yad Vashem Archives. Their amazing work helped make mine possible.

My next thanks go to Emmanuel Diamant for sharing with me his personal experiences as a young Jewish nationalist activist in late-1960s Kyiv as well as some invaluable materials both in our conversations and via correspondence. I also thank Anna Sharogradskaya, my Russian language and culture teacher from the two summer courses I attended at Indiana University more than a decade ago. I have been blessed to have had the opportunity to learn about the Thaw era from someone who lived through it and about dissent—and the courage as well as intellectual honesty that it entails—from a true and inspiring practitioner of it. My heartfelt gratitude also goes out to Eugene Orenstein, the man who gave me my first and ultimate guided tour of Yiddish literature and culture at McGill University in Montreal more than twenty years ago, and who turned me into a lifelong student of East European Jewish civilization.

Because this is a book based on a dissertation submitted in fulfillment of a PhD program in modern Jewish studies, I am indebted to my two original mentors, David Fishman and David Roskies, for helping me with *The Ravine of Memory* at a time when the project had a different title and was still taking its first steps. It is their dedication to the study of modern Jewish history and literature and their commitment to excellence in the field that have made them both mentors and role models for me. Together with them, I am indebted to another mentor from the days of graduate school, Catherine Nepomnyashchy, the Ann Whitney Olin Professor of Russian Literature at Barnard, who noticed my unusual interest in the Soviet universe and reassured me that the input of outsiders, "those who know Russian grammar pretty well but would still look up words in the dictionary for the rest of their lives," is critical in this unique and often forgotten field.

I would like to offer thanks to Hodaya Blau, the Fish Center's dedicated assistant director. I did my best not to bother her too much with matters related to the production of this book. However, knowing that I could rely on her guidance on any technical issue and trusting that the students in our different programs were all taken care of in her more-than-capable hands gave me the peace of mind I needed while I was busy with the book's revisions and final edits.

Thank you to Michael Helfield and Kelley Kim, my loyal book editors, for helping to polish and ready my English writing for prime time and for paying attention to both the big picture and the slightest of details. Thanks also go out to Andrea Gapsch and her team at Purdue University Press for supporting this project as soon as they learned about my quest for a suitable home for it. I could not have wished for a more patient, caring, and professional team.

I would like to express my gratitude to the colleagues and friends who shared a keen interest in this project and were ready to contribute with publishing and translation tips, or with factual, conceptual, or editorial comments and suggestions. I am grateful to Dan Haumschild, Steve Russek, Itay Zutra, Leyzer Burko, Michael Jasinski, Elissa Bemporad, Pavel Bortnovsky, Tal Magen Goldstein, Iryna Irchak, and Alyssa Quint.

My warmest and deepest gratitude goes out to my close family. Some of them have, in fact, not been so close geographically for the past twenty years, but with the aid of boundless love (and also up-to-date technology) they deserve credit for helping me to turn my dream into a reality. Thank you to Rachel and Israel Pilnik—my mother of blessed memory, to whom this book is dedicated, and my father—for love that knew, and still knows, no boundaries. And thank you to my parents-in-law, Rachel and Reuben Hauser, who kept telling me that the light at the end of the tunnel was there, even when this light seemed greatly distant.

And finally, I thank my wife, Orlee Hauser, my most loyal and ardent reader, commentator, and line editor, who assumed these roles after we met in Montreal in the summer of 2003. Orlee means "my light" in Hebrew, and, during both brighter and darker periods, with all the different stops and starts on our journey—including the beautiful family we have created with our two children, Mikhael and Dina—it is Orlee who has illuminated both my path and hers and has made them the most marvelous ones I could have possibly imagined.

# INTRODUCTION: BABYN YAR UNEARTHED

A T BABYN YAR, AS IN NUMEROUS LOCATIONS ACROSS THE SOVIET FRONtiers, Jews young and old were led to forests, ravines, or anti-tank ditches located near their hometowns, ordered to strip off their clothes, line up, and wait their turn (sometimes at the pit's edge; at other times while lying on their stomachs) to be shot from a short distance by the Nazis and their collaborators.[1] In Kyiv, those Jews who obeyed the decree that had been posted on September 28 throughout the city, calling on all who remained there to turn up the following morning at the corner of Mel'nikovskaya and Doktorskaya Streets, were marched to an enormous ravine outside the city named Babyn Yar (the Women's Ravine). Karel Berkhoff, in his history of Ukraine under Nazi rule, describes the long march: Jewish "men, women and small children—along with non-Jewish husbands, wives and other dear ones, walked to the designated street corner in Kyiv's Lukianivka district." He cites L. Nartova, a Russian middle-aged teacher:

> Moving in an endless row, overflowing the entire street and sidewalks. Women and men are walking, young girls, children, old people, and entire families.... They walk in silence, quietly. How awful.... It went on like this for very long, the entire day and only in the evening did the crowd become smaller.[2]

Believing rumors that they would be transported elsewhere and that they were *not* about to be shot, the victims—mainly women, children, and the elderly (most able-bodied men had already been mobilized into the Red Army)—were first ordered to part with their food and belongings. Historian Lucy Dawidowicz describes what happened afterward:

The Germans began shoving the Jews into new narrower lines. They moved very slowly. After a long walk, they came to a passageway formed by German soldiers with truncheons and police dogs [these were the members of Sonderkommando 4A, an advance unit of Einsatzgruppe C, one of the "special-duty units," who were entrusted with the task of murdering by bullets the Jews of the Soviet Union, among other "undesirable elements," as they were advancing on the heels of the Wehrmacht]. The Jews were whipped through. The dogs went at those who fell.... Bruised and bloodied, numbed by the incomprehensibility of their fate, the Jews emerged on a grassy clearing.... Ukrainian militiamen, supervised by Germans, ordered the Jews to undress. Those who balked, who resisted, were assaulted, their clothes ripped off.... The Germans led small groups away from the clearing toward a narrow ledge along the ravine.... When the ledge contained as many Jews as it could hold, the Germans gunned them down. The bodies toppled into the ravine, piling up layer upon layer. Where once a clear stream flowed, now blood ran.[3]

Indeed, Babyn Yar surpassed in significance all the other mass graves scattered throughout the western frontiers of the USSR for several reasons. First, the city of Kyiv, the capital of the Soviet Ukrainian Republic with a Jewish population of 224,000 in 1939, was the first European capital to become *Judenrein*.[4] The massacre at Babyn Yar, which began in late September 1941, commenced when the Nazis shifted their anti-Jewish policies from social exclusion and ghettoization to genocide.[5] With Babyn Yar, along with the parallel operations of mass shooting perpetrated across the western frontiers of the USSR, the Nazis launched their murderous grand plan to annihilate European Jewry.

Portrait of four-year-old Malvina Babat and her three-year-old sister, Polina, who were murdered at Babyn Yar. (Photo courtesy of the United States Holocaust Memorial Museum: Babyn Yar Organization, Kyiv, Ukraine.)

Second, what made Babyn Yar tower above all other Holocaust sites of the Soviet Union was the unprecedented pace of the killing. The Nazis would later come to the realization that perpetrating a "Holocaust by Bullets" was not the most effective method of mass murder. But as Lucy Dawidowicz notes, the killing of 33,771 Jews (according to official Nazi secret reports) at Babyn Yar within thirty-six hours on September 29–30, 1941, set a record that made even the high efficiency of Auschwitz pale in comparison, with its cremation capacity of 6,000 persons a day at its peak.[6]

Third, what stood out at Babyn Yar was its death toll. Though considered higher—the number often referenced during much of the Cold War was over 100,000 people killed at Babyn Yar throughout the city's German occupation, among them 90,000 Jews—more recent estimates established by a group of researchers commissioned by the Babyn Yar Holocaust Memorial Center set the total number of victims at 65,000: 40,000 Jews and 25,000 non-Jews.[7] These figures, the debate over which seems likely to continue,[8] for Jews murdered at gun point, helped further render Babyn Yar the centerpiece of the Holocaust in the USSR.

Just as important, however, was Babyn Yar's strange afterlife—a convergence of state-imposed forgetting and defiant artistic remembering. It may seem strange that the tens of thousands of Jewish dead should pose any threat to the mighty Soviet Union, but the Great Patriotic War narrative, summed up as a common struggle against fascism by members of *all* nations, had no room for Jewish victimhood of such magnitude, for to acknowledge it would be to acknowledge Jewish difference. To be sure, the regime inadvertently enhanced Jewish difference through its own various forms of discrimination and suppression. But the intention remained assimilation, and nothing defied assimilation like targeted mass-murder of Jews on a colossal scale. Many writers resorted to coded references. Some proved willing to speak the open truth. But the current book recounts more than simply two versions about Babyn Yar—the one promoted by the state and the other by courageous individuals. It is, rather, an account of a multiform literary negotiation over the most iconic Holocaust event in the Soviet Union, a complex, grueling negotiation during which works of searing artistic beauty rose irrepressibly from the deep ravine of memory to confront a massive historical trauma, some furtively and some boldly.

# THE HISTORIOGRAPHICAL CONTEXT

In 2009, two decades after the conclusion of the Cold War, a geographical transition in the landscape of Holocaust historiography and memorialization was more apparent than ever. The Holocaust's center of gravity was shifting from west to east; and from the ghettos, labor and transit camps, and extermination centers to the Nazi mass shooting *Aktionen* on the western frontiers of the Soviet Union. The pendulum was moving swiftly from an almost exclusive focus on the figure of the desk murderer and the metaphor of the death factory, in the not so recent past, to the specters of the spontaneous, sporadic, and chaotic brutalities that often took place at gunpoint by the Einsatzgruppen, the German special killing squads, and their local collaborators.

Among the flood of publications underscoring this tectonic historiographical shift, two books and one article are of note. With the publication of Yitzhak Arad's first major monograph dedicated to the subject, *The Holocaust in the Soviet Union*,[9] the more popular circulation of Patrick Desbois's *The Holocaust by Bullets: A Priest's Journey to Uncover the Truth Behind the Murder of 1.5 Million Jews*,[10] and the advent of the article "The Holocaust: The Ignored Reality" by Timothy Snyder heralding the publication of his transformative study *Bloodlands* two years later, a new historiographical era was ushered in.[11] It seemed as though at this point, with the Iron Curtain being fully dismantled, a new generation of students of Soviet, Eastern European, Jewish, and Holocaust history were ready to take a fresh and nuanced look, having freed themselves from key biases permeating the historiography of the Cold War era.

This new outlook would, no doubt, have far-reaching implications for the study of these fields for the next decade, not only placing the Holocaust in the USSR in a new light, but also calling for the reconsideration of the Holocaust itself within the broader context of World War II, totalitarianism, and mass violence in twentieth-century Europe. This was a new perspective on events that took place during the first half of the twentieth century without some of the key biases of the second half. As we will see in greater detail in the coming chapters, this new evaluation purported to achieve multiple goals. First, it brought the crimes of the Nazis and Soviets closer to each other, making it easier for scholars to both compare and equate them. Although this was not an entirely new trend—credit must go to the pioneering work of Hannah Arendt in *The Origins of Totalitarianism*,[12] who insisted on studying these two grand tyrannies in conjunction—it had never truly loomed large in Holocaust scholarship. Second, it geographically contextualized the Holocaust not as an all-European program, but rather as a far more focused chain of atrocities taking place within the specific zone covering Ukraine, Belarus, eastern Poland, and the Baltic states, the region defined by Snyder as the "bloodlands." Third, and chiefly due to the high civilian toll that World War II had witnessed in those bloodlands as opposed to countries in Western or Northern Europe, this new perspective on the events that took place in the years 1941–1945 in that part of Europe allowed scholars to reexamine the Holocaust. It was now viewed in conjunction with the Great Patriotic War, the official Soviet coinage for the grand military theater pitting Nazi Germany against the Soviet Union, which broke out with the onset of Operation Barbarossa on June 22, 1941.[13]

This new perspective, offering a retrospective account of a bloody half-century on blood-drenched soil, resembled another rendition of the twentieth century's first half, one offered by the Russian poet and Noble laureate Boris Pasternak in his early 1958 poem "After the Storm":

> *The memories of half a lifetime's age*
> *Recede now with the passing of the storm:*
> *This century outgrows its tutelage*
> *To clear the way for all the years to come.*
> *It is not some upheaval or uprising*
> *Can lead us to the new life we desire—*
> *But open truth and magnanimity*
> *And the storm within a soul afire.*[14]

Needless to say, a great deal of important works have been written on the perpetration of the Holocaust on Soviet soil as the first phase in the implementation of the Final Solution plan and the shift in Nazi policy from indirect extermination to mass murder. But for the first time, a grand call was made to bring the ignored reality of mass murder at gunpoint from the shadows of Holocaust history, collective memory, and education into the public limelight. This was a loud and clear call for Pasternak's "open truth and magnanimity," situating those war crimes at the very heart of both scholarly and public Western perceptions of the Holocaust.[15] As Timothy Snyder puts it, paraphrasing the title of *Dark Continent* by Mark Mazower: "If Europe was ... a dark continent, Ukraine and Belarus [then] were the heart of darkness."[16] In the ravines large and small that became mass graves, some containing the bodies of a few dozen and some of a few dozens of thousands, we are made to peer into twentieth-century Europe's heart of darkness.

## A SOVIET JEWISH REALM OF MEMORY

As one of the largest World War II mass murder sites, where, as noted above, the Holocaust's most rapid mass execution took place, Babyn Yar has gained an iconic stature for what it represented during the war and its aftermath, and for its history under both the Nazis and the Soviets. It is this symbolic dimension, embedded in the quote by Tevye Gen in the preface "Every city ... had its own 'Babi Yar,'" that calls for the study offered here, for a new, post–Cold War understanding of Babyn Yar's evolution, of the many ways in which its memory crystallized in Soviet culture, literature, and collective memory within the multiethnic and multilingual Soviet ecosystem. As David Shneer points out: "As the largest burial pit, ravine and trench, Babi Yar, more than Auschwitz, Majdanek or other concentration camps came to symbolize the Soviet experience of Nazi atrocities."[17] Indeed, since the end of World War II Babyn Yar has come to symbolize the very essence of the Holocaust in the USSR, though it has also emerged as a representation of so much more. It became the inspiration for some of the most poignant Holocaust poetry and fiction, a foundational trope within Soviet literature during the Thaw period (1953–1966), a mnemonic signifier for the disastrous collapse of the Red Army at the beginning of the Nazi–Soviet War, and, last but not least, a rallying cry for the nascent Jewish nationalist movement in the USSR in the years preceding and following the Six-Day War.

What exactly made Babyn Yar a symbol for so many different phenomena and imagined communities? To begin sorting this puzzle, let us acquaint ourselves with another Eastern European capital and another Holocaust site; let us travel for a moment to the Warsaw Ghetto Uprising Memorial. And let us imagine ourselves on an ordinary spring day at the pavilion lying between the celebrated memorial and POLIN, the Museum of the History of Polish Jews, a space packed with visitors from near and far, both local and foreign. Staring at the massive relief, carved by sculptor Nathan Rappaport in the socialist-realist style, exploring and deciphering both its explicit and more subtle messages, let us consider how difficult it would be for anyone slightly familiar with what the monument stands for to avoid the linking of one memory to another, one time and place to another. It would be difficult, somewhat impossible to avoid, because this is what "good" or "effective" monuments are all about: they facilitate this temporal as well as spatial interaction, conjuring up a scenario befitting any good stream of consciousness novel. It is a serene, quiet spring day as another Israeli tourist group walks by, a busload filled with museum visitors arrives, and an old lady with a basket and cane donning a red, flowery dress passes by on her way to the grocery store. It is a moment in space and time that instantaneously and inevitably correlates to another one, one in early May of 1943. The Warsaw Ghetto has been set ablaze, and the sky filled with black clouds of smoke. Screams and the staccato of machine gun salvos are heard all over; Mordechai Anielewicz and his comrades, heroes of the Jewish Fighting Organization, are about to make their last charge, ready to sacrifice their lives ... and ... we go back to an ordinary spring day, to now. It is the present day; you are back to where you started; you are experiencing an ordinary moment at the Warsaw Ghetto Uprising Memorial soon to be forgotten.

No doubt, this transition from one specter to another requires some historical knowledge and a creative mind. The two different components of collective memory according to Jan Assmann are employed here, complementing and feeding each other: "communicative memory"—unofficial fragments of memory transmitted from parent to child, from teacher to student, and through numerous conversations, images, and references—and "cultural memory"—the officially sanctioned memory generated by the state or municipality, the typical commissioner of public memorials.[18] Between these two modes and between past and present stands the sculptor's artistic design. Without it, these two images—of the past and present, the social and the individual, the official and unofficial—would never intersect or interact. It certainly would not happen in the minds of so many and at the same time. As Jeffrey Olick reminds us, spelling out the not-at-all-obvious, "memory"—the phenomenon to which we so commonly refer and that so much constitutes an indispensable part of our life—while taking place in the minds of individuals, is a social phenomenon.[19] The past becomes memory when more than one human being can give form, in the present moment, to a past event. Indeed, this transition is characteristic of every memorial, not only those commemorating Holocaust sites and events. What distinguishes the Holocaust monument from other kinds of monuments is its details: the chronological time frame, the European geographical context, and the horrors, of course—the conceptualization and visualization of evil and horror in their extreme. It is an image prompting us to imagine the unimaginable.

The description above thus becomes a simple formula for the creation of a solid, proper Holocaust monument. For what is a Holocaust monument in a nutshell? It is the filling of a presence in lieu of an absence, all too often by way of referring to the presence of the absence. "Look," the monument calls out, "here stood the center of European Jewish life before World War II. Here stood the largest ghetto in German-occupied Europe. On this very soil the ZOB (the Jewish Fighting Organization) David dared to challenge the Nazi Goliath." How pleased, how satisfied would Nathan Rappaport be, we may surmise, had he known that one black granite wall, his masterpiece, has attracted so many and has communicated so much at the end of the twenty-first century's second decade?

The centrality of monuments as the memory capsules of our age has already been deftly observed by key memory studies scholars like French philosopher Pierre Nora, a pioneer in the field, who has pointed out in his "Between Memory and History: Les Lieux de Mémoire" that modern society's preoccupation, perhaps obsession, with its own history—with archiving, the production and construction of historiographical works, public commemorations, museums, and monuments—is a testimony not to wealth, but to dearth. This overproduction of history, leading to an inflation of memorials and history books, is merely a manifestation of a shortage in our memory. It points to how collective amnesia governs life in the modern world. These artifacts, according to Nora, "mark rituals of a society without rituals; integral particularities in a society that levels particularity; signs of distinction and of group membership in a society that tends to recognize individuals only as identical and equal."[20] Why have so many monuments mushroomed across our landscape? Not because of any commemorative aptitude on our part, Nora would argue, but because of our helplessness in attempting to hold on to a past that is fading away at a pace greater than ever before: our "hopelessly forgetful modern societies ... organize the past."[21] For Nora, any discussion like our momentary tour of the Polish capital, of an "effective memorial," or of a "successful artist" would amount to a naïve, superficial, and misleading understanding of memory in modern times. The phrase "effective monuments" in the modern era, in particular, is an oxymoron.

James Young, who applied Nora's insights to his seminal study of Holocaust memorials from around the world, including the previously mentioned masterpiece, made a similar observation in his introduction: "The more memory comes to rest in its exteriorized forms, the less it is experienced internally.... For once we assign monumental form to memory, we have to some degree divested ourselves of the obligation to remember. In shouldering the memory-work, monuments may relieve viewers of their memory burden."[22]

When a monument turns over time into an indispensable part of its surroundings and "grows as natural to the eye as the landscape in which it stands,"[23] its effectiveness as a bearer of a memory of a past event may be seriously diminished. In other words, Young, following Nora, expresses a concern that it is precisely the best constructed monument, carrying the clearest, most communicative message, attaining fame and, eventually, wholesomely blending into the environs in which it was placed, that could lead over time to the undoing of the very purpose for which it was created—namely, the *obligation* to remember.

As right as Young is in observing that exteriorized formation can undermine the true, profound, and internal process of memorialization, that monuments carved in stone may blend in with their surroundings and run the risk of becoming, with time, transparent, the story of Babyn Yar illustrates how much truer his observation is when the opposite occurs: when a monument is absent. For what happened to Babyn Yar is exactly what did not happen with other Holocaust monuments. Ours is a story of the most effective memorial one could think of—albeit not one made out of stone, but rather of words—calling its memory-bearers to act rather than simply to recall, galvanizing a literary, social, and national movement to revolve around it. And why was the Babyn Yar monument so effective and for decades? Because from 1945 through 1966, or, as some would argue, till 1976, or, as others would insist, till 1991, this powerful memorial, placing the brunt of memory on living humans rather than on its own inanimateness, simply did not exist.

## TWO TALES OF ONE RAVINE

From a state of total neglect in the immediate years after World War II, through the deliberate attempts to flood it in the early 1960s and the first small obelisk laid there in 1966 to herald great things to come, to the erection of the first lasting monument at the site in 1976—a gigantic granite slab that contained no reference at all to the Jewish ethnic identity of most of its victims—Babyn Yar was throughout much of the Cold War a "memory black-hole."[24] "There are no memorials over Babi Yar" is the iconic first line in Yevgeny Yevtushenko's poem dedicated to the ravine. It was penned by a Russian, non-Jewish poet who was by no means a solitary voice representing Babyn Yar in Soviet literature.

Over the years, and in a large part due to the worldwide reception of Yevtushenko's "Babi Yar," the ravine was remembered as a site standing for two contrasting vectors: the duty never to forget and the tendency of neglect and chronic amnesia. To be sure, such "memory black-holes," or, more aptly, "memory ravines," are invariably epitomized by such inner tension, where two irreconcilable narratives clash. One narrative, often held by the powerless, identifies a particular locus as connected to a meaningful historic event of a traumatic or heroic nature. The other, held often by the powerful—namely, by the state apparatus—perpetuates its erasure by striving forcefully, and at times even violently, to blur, reject, or even totally efface any possible thread on the ground that could potentially link the site to the awesome tragedy.

The case of Babyn Yar, however, does not correspond to this black-and-white paradigm, compelling as it may be. This dualist view of Babyn Yar—and, by extension, of the whole treatment by the Soviet regime of the Holocaust of European Jewry—was firmly in place and hardly ever called into question throughout much of the Cold War. When carefully examined and broadly explored, however, the memory of Babyn Yar emerges as a kaleidoscopic entity, consisting not of two contrasting colors, but rather of multiple shades of gray, each relating to the memory of the site in its own way. While some components of Babyn Yar's memory were indeed shaped and owned by Soviet official bodies, others were formed by individuals who in one way or another were touched by its symbolic resonance. The present study will illustrate how, despite the ideological gaps between these two groups, the attempt to set a clear demarcation line between them is an almost impossible task.

During the Cold War, whenever Babyn Yar was brought up in the context of the repression of Soviet Jews by the Soviet government, a strong reaction of identification with the former and fury about the heartless attitude of the latter was evoked. Several Westerners were moved to view Babyn Yar as the focal point of a grand "battle of histories" waged between Soviet Jews, joined by some bold dissidents, and Moscow, the Soviet regime's officials.[25] Such confrontations, in fact, did occur and gained momentum from the mid-1960s onward, ever since the anniversary of the main massacre at Babyn Yar on September 29 became the occasion of grassroots ceremonies at the site, which were often followed by clashes between Soviet Jews and the local police.[26] Yet this Manichaean portrayal of Babyn Yar as a battle between the powerful Soviet government and its powerless subjects—Jews and non-Jews alike—reflects only a part of the history of Babyn Yar's memory, whose evolution was the outcome of both conflict and collaboration.

In American scholarship on Babyn Yar, this dualistic framework continued to reverberate long after the Cold War's end. Two articles in particular, one by Edith Clowes and one by Jeff Mankoff, are good cases in point. For Clowes, the underlying drama of the Babyn Yar Memorial was a generational struggle waged between the establishment ideologues of the Communist Party and the younger generation of Soviet intellectuals coming of age in the late 1950s and early 1960s. For Mankoff, Babyn Yar's memory is anchored in another polarized paradigm: he views its construction in Foucauldian terms as the outcome of a grand conflict between the memory of Soviet officialdom and the counter-memory of Jewish dissidents.[27] Yet between these two poles of government officials and Jewish dissidents stood a whole spectrum of opinions and reactions formed by political activists, writers, poets, and composers, both Jewish and non-Jewish.

The absence of a clear barrier between the Soviet state and the writers who decided to dedicate themselves to the memory of Babyn Yar, while shaped by many factors, was primarily the result of the unique way in which World War II unfolded in the USSR. In both popular memory and historiography, this site lies at the intersection of two master narratives: the Holocaust of European Jewry and the theater of war waged between Nazi Germany and the Soviet Union known in Soviet history as the Great Patriotic War or the Great Fatherland War (*velikaya otechestvennaya voina*). Uniquely, Babyn Yar is among the only sites within the interwar boundaries of the USSR that plays a pivotal role in these two very different grand historical narratives. The former was downplayed by the Soviet authorities. The latter, in sharp contrast, gradually emerged as the legitimating myth of the Soviet state. By signifying both of them, the memory of Babyn Yar crystallized as a complex aggregate of divergent memories, defying the schemes often used to explain it during the Cold War.

## THE BABYN YAR MASSACRE AND ITS AFTERMATH

The Jews who inhabited the western frontiers of the Soviet Union, and among them, the Jews of Kyiv, fell victim to the Final Solution plan in its initial phases. Before the deportations of Central and Western European Jews to concentration camps and extermination facilities took place, the Nazis had in store a different murderous end for Soviet Jews.[28] They became the first group to be targeted for annihilation by the Nazis. With the onset of Operation Barbarossa on June 22, 1941 (the code name for the Nazi invasion of the USSR, viewed by Adolf Hitler as a total war between two ideological archenemies), and on the heels of the advancing Wehrmacht, special squads known as

Einsatzgruppen, or mobile killing units, roamed the villages, small towns, and cities of the frontiers with the intent of searching for, identifying, and killing the local civilian Jewish population. This was precisely the key moment in the history of the Holocaust, or the Shoah, when Nazi policy shifted from indirect extermination (through the process of ghettoization) to mass murder by shooting, which is commonly known today as the "Holocaust by Bullets."

Notwithstanding the centrality of the Babyn Yar massacre, it is important to point out that the anti-Jewish genocide that took place on September 29–30, 1941, was not the only example of the sheer and utter brutality of the German Nazi war machine. While in the West the Holocaust is often viewed as the nadir of humanity in the modern era (we may conjure up Michael Berenbaum's reference to the Holocaust as the "gold standard of evil"), the mass murder of Jews on Soviet soil took place in a different context—that of total war. Notably, the systematic killing of Soviet Jews was simultaneous with other war crimes and atrocities targeting both military personnel and civilians from the non-Jewish population. From a cold, analytical point of view it may be possible to agree that the Nazi war crimes against the Soviet POWs and some specific targeted groups were not on par with the Holocaust on the scale of evil because the latter was a comprehensive genocide targeting a totally defenseless population. However, for the Soviet population, particularly for those who experienced the German occupation firsthand, these nuanced distinctions hardly mattered. From the perspective of the Soviet regime, and much of the Soviet population, too, the apocalyptic dimensions of the violence they had experienced during the war years made any comparison between one type of extreme violence and another irrelevant.

What kind of evil can even come close to resembling the murderous plan to wipe European Jewry from the face of the earth? This is a question that the uninitiated student, who is less familiar with Soviet history and the grand theater on the Eastern Front, may be wondering. The Red Army's defeat in Kyiv is a good example of a simultaneous cataclysmic event that would later rival the memory of the Babyn Yar massacre itself. The unprecedented massacre of the Jews was carried out in the midst of one of the greatest debacles in military history. By heeding Joseph Stalin's command to defend the Ukrainian capital at all costs, rather than pursue a strategic withdrawal from the city, the commanders of the Red Army led their men to the slaughter: the Soviet troops were subsequently encircled and wiped out. That battle cost the Red Army a total of over half a million soldiers, who were either among the casualties or captured as POWs.[29] The Soviet defeat was accompanied by gruesome cycles of mass execution carried out by the Nazis, targeting both civilians and POWs. From the figures gathered by the Extraordinary State Commission, the Soviet body set up in Ukraine upon its liberation and in other localities in order to investigate the crimes against the local population perpetrated by the Nazis, an approximate total of 195,000 victims of World

War II were believed to be buried in the vicinity of Greater Kyiv, a figure that includes both Babyn Yar's death toll and victims buried elsewhere.[30]

While estimates of the exact ratio of Jews to non-Jews murdered in Babyn Yar vary, it is agreed by most accounts that a significant minority, a minimum of 10,000 non-Jews, among them Russians, Ukrainians, and Roma, were buried at the site.[31] These victims, together with the Jewish dead, were regarded by the Soviet regime as victims of the Great Patriotic War, the Soviet generic term referring to the USSR's war against Hitler's armies. These non-Jewish victims died for a variety of reasons. The majority were fighters: POWs, members of the underground, and partisans. Others were members of the Communist Party or other Soviet functionaries. Still others were factory workers and ordinary civilians.[32] In addition to the presence of victims from a variety of backgrounds, complicating matters further was the fact that, among the Ukrainian victims buried in Babyn Yar, some were members of the Organization of Ukrainian Nationalists (OUN), a paramilitary group that in the early stages of the war sided with the Nazis and that prior to its own targeting by the Nazis had taken active part, inter alia, in the annihilation of Soviet Jews.[33] In short, Babyn Yar was a memory space associated with a number of catastrophic collective memories that could not—and cannot—be so easily reconciled.

Babyn Yar's position, if we imagine it geometrically, was in the overlapping area between two nonconcentric circles, each standing as a twentieth-century master narrative of victimhood and sacrifice: the Great Patriotic War, with a death toll reaching an estimated figure of 27 million Soviet citizens, and the Holocaust, with the destruction of 6 million European Jews. Yet most of the players responsible for shaping its memory during the Cold War were oblivious to this crucial, central fact. The first party to display this ignorance was the Soviet regime itself. For reasons that we should further explore, the Soviet regime, for the most part, came to view the Soviet victims of the Holocaust as totally merged into the staggering figure of 27 million dead Soviet citizens. Why single out any one group? As for the treatment of the Final Solution beyond the boundaries of the USSR, Moscow tended, for the most part, to either downplay or ignore it. This helped to consolidate the Soviet Union's legitimating myth, exhibiting the degree of evil embodied in both Nazism and fascism, two political systems that could not be defeated without the Red Army's might and tremendous sacrifice. More than anything, any linkage between the Final Solution and the destruction of Soviet Jewry by mass shootings and gas vans irked the Soviet regime, bringing into high relief the fear that the particularistic tragedy of the Jewish people might overshadow the noble sacrifice made by millions of Soviet citizens in the Soviet Union's life-or-death war against Nazi Germany. Ironically, the state's suppression of the Jewish dimension to the tragedy may have done just that.

The treatment of the Holocaust by the Soviet regime has been a subject of fascination for Soviet Jewish historians, for the attempts to silence the story of Babyn Yar (as we shall see) were a part of an official Soviet policy that was never written or clearly formulated. As Zvi Gitelman notes, no work could be found in the Soviet Union that would treat the Holocaust as sui generis or make use of the term "Holocaust," a coinage that appeared in the West during the 1950s and is laden with theological implications that would have not easily been received in the USSR, the first atheist state in history. Surrogate terms referring to the annihilation of Soviet Jews did exist, among them *katastropha* (catastrophe) and *unichtozhenie* (annihilation).[34] Critics of Moscow's approach to Babyn Yar and, by extension, to all Holocaust-related atrocities, discerned an antisemitic underpinning, a set of biases that emerged before the conclusion of the war and persisted with many vicissitudes up until the era of glasnost (*glasnost'*, lit. "openness"). From Moscow's standpoint, the Holocaust was viewed as a legal "gray zone" in a way that would permit a limited number of publications on the Holocaust to appear, during the war and its aftermath, and a few monuments commemorating the Jewish dead to be erected following the war's conclusion.[35]

This intricate Soviet attitude did not only affect literary works. Karel Berkhoff has illustrated how the Soviet reluctance to speak about anti-Jewish atrocities also found expression in the sphere of journalism and war reportage. "Inconsistency" is the term he chooses to best describe the regime's treatment of the subject in the media.[36] The reason for it was simple: while Stalin, who had become aware of the German Nazi plan to annihilate Soviet Jews no later than August of 1941, was fairly persistent—beginning in the following winter—in stripping the Soviet Jewish victims of their Jewish identity, he decided to never issue his underlings any specific directives to this effect. A Soviet policy on the Holocaust, thus, in the arenas of both real-time journalistic reporting and, later, of literature and public commemoration, never existed in the Soviet Union, neither in the days of Stalin nor in those of his successors. This combination—of a regime plagued by antisemitism from its bottom rungs all the way up to the top, during the late Stalin years but under his successors too, coupled with a lack of any clear direction from above—led to the Holocaust being consigned to a state of limbo, regarded as neither a taboo nor an acceptable topic. To put it another way, whereas antisemitism played a key role in our story, it never constituted a single factor. The Soviet Union was an autocratic regime in which not every policy was legally spelled out.

In addition to the regime's antisemitic nature, Moscow had a good reason to downplay the large proportion of Jews among the Soviet victims of Nazism.[37] As noted above, it viewed all the Soviet dead in the war as victims of the Great Patriotic War, supporting another Soviet master narrative: *druzhba narodov*, the brotherhood of all Soviet peoples. The notion of Soviet society as a multiethnic empire, where all nations were bonded together through their love and dedication to one Soviet motherland, was at odds with both the clear link between Nazi atrocities on Soviet soil and the destruction of Jews elsewhere, and the most inconvenient truth emerging from the Holocaust: namely, the deep complicity of some segments of the Soviet population—primarily ethnic Ukrainians, Lithuanians, Latvians, and Estonians—in the destruction of Jews on Soviet soil. Moscow and Kyiv thus felt compelled to treat the years of German occupation with caution, seeking out a usable past that would help consolidate, rather than shake, the multiethnic foundation upon which Soviet society was resting—a universalizing impulse that is recognizable in attempts to subsume the Holocaust under the rubric of genocide studies today.

## WESTERN PREJUDICES

If the Soviet regime's refusal to acknowledge the linkage between Babyn Yar and the occurrence of genocide targeting its Jewish civilians in the midst of the war was laden with a great amount of cynicism, prejudice, and insensitivity, then the West's refusal to acknowledge the converse linkage—namely, between Babyn Yar and the Great Patriotic War—seems far more innocent. In the face of a regime that tended to downplay and at times completely ignore the Holocaust, it is easy to understand why key Jewish leaders and culture-makers formed a stance toward Babyn Yar that invariably ignored the non-Jewish dead at the ravine, victims of the Great Patriotic War. It is not clear, though, how deliberate this effort was. Perhaps it was an error committed subconsciously as a reaction to the negative attitude of the Soviet regime to the Holocaust. Or maybe this was a result of what Alan Mintz views as the "exceptionalist" response to the Holocaust, the view of it as a "radical rapture in human history that goes well beyond notions of uniqueness."[38] We may also surmise that this was an aspect of what Timothy Snyder called the "ignored reality": in a Western world so laser-focused on the liberation of Buchenwald, Bergen Belsen, and Dachau, or on attentively listening to the witness accounts of Auschwitz survivors like Elie Wiesel, Primo Levi, and Viktor Frankl, the Great Patriotic War's victims were not mendaciously forgotten. The space to remember them, rather, was highly narrow, as they were overshadowed by the horror stories of planet Auschwitz and its extensive network of labor camps, the scorched earth of the Warsaw Ghetto, and the unprecedentedness of German Nazi extermination centers like Sobibor, Belzec, and Treblinka.

Either way, during the late years of the Cold War, when such Western observers as Korey, Dawidowicz, and Wiesel visited the theme of Babyn Yar, their gaze was always exclusively fixated on the Babyn Yar massacre, the murder of 33,771 Jews at Babyn Yar, perpetrated on September 29–30, 1941. To cite only one example of many, we may recall Wiesel's official visit to Babyn Yar, conducted in 1979 in his capacity as the chairman of the President's Commission on the Holocaust appointed by Jimmy Carter. Confronted by the new face of Babyn Yar, by the memorial to the Soviet POWs erected there three years earlier, Wiesel spoke of a deep feeling of frustration, shame, and rage that the Soviet government chose to perpetuate the memory of Babyn Yar's victims without being willing to even slightly recognize the fact that "the men and women buried in this ravine, were murdered for being Jewish!... While still alive, the Jews of Babyn Yar were abandoned, and now their memory is being betrayed."[39] No doubt, Wiesel did not mean to claim that no Soviet POWs were killed in Babyn Yar, or that the ravine was the burial ground of Jews only. But for him and for Dawidowicz and Korey, the war crimes committed against prisoners, partisans, and underground members were not a part of the *essence* of Babyn Yar's symbolic meaning. As a response to a Soviet government that was actively downplaying and erasing that essence from memory, it is easy to understand Wiesel's motives. Still, what the legacy of the Cold Warriors on both sides of the Iron Curtain is leaving us with is the marginalization of the Holocaust's Jewish victims in the Soviet bloc and, vice versa, the downplaying of the Great Patriotic War's Soviet non-Jewish victims by Western observers.

While the validity of Wiesel's words still stands, his was the voice not only of the belligerent West but also, first and foremost, of the Holocaust survivors and, by extension, of the Jewish people as a whole. However, the recent, unprecedentedly broad and meticulous study of the site of Babyn Yar's history and topography conducted by the Ukrainian scholar Vitalii Nakhmanovich seriously challenges Wiesel's statements. As Nakhmanovich's study compares the multiple testimonies describing the sequence of events that took place at the ravine, it exposes the many contradictions among the plethora of official reports, personal testimonies, and historiographical works written on Babyn Yar before and after the collapse of the Soviet Union. One of the main conclusions he draws is that mass shootings at Babyn Yar, as a part of which both Jews and non-Jews were targeted, while never coming close to the tempo reached during September 29–30, began about a week earlier, soon after the Nazis entered Kyiv, and lasted until mid-November of that year.[40] Parallel to this conclusion, Nakhmanovich challenges another commonly held view: that only following the massacre of September 29–30, after the main liquidation of Kyiv Jews came to a conclusion, did Babyn Yar turn into a site that, inter alia, was chosen for the execution of non-Jews. By arguing that the first massacres at the site were those of POWs, shot on the day following the Germans' arrival, Nakhmanovich places the incident of mass shooting known as "the Babyn Yar massacre" in the context of a sequence of mass executions. He thus further complicates any tendency to magnify and isolate the thirty-six hours of horror, in the course of which the majority of the civilian Jewish population remaining in Kyiv was murdered.[41] We now realize that a variety of factors—political, ethical, cultural, and also purely historical-factual—based on the analysis of the reality of a series of violent acts in the sprawling vicinity of Babyn Yar compel us to reconsider the bipolar, zero-sum-game conception of Babyn Yar's victimhood, so prevalent during the Cold War.

## ON THE EVOLUTION OF MEMORY

What I shall do in the following chapters, while focusing entirely on the murder of Jews at Babyn Yar, is to pursue in the realm of literature what Nakhmanovich has achieved on the ground: to see how the reality transpiring in the physical space of Babyn Yar, the reality of multiple massacres—more seamlessly connected than previously imagined—found a parallel manifestation in Soviet literary works dedicated to Babyn Yar. Since Babyn Yar will interest us as a memory-site only insofar as it was a site of forgetting, the chronological framework of our discussion will not go beyond 1976, the year when the first permanent monument was finally erected. When considering the representation of Babyn Yar from the conclusion of the war until 1976, it is apparent that two main factors greatly complicated the memory of the site in Soviet literature. The first is purely historical: the occurrence of atrocities related to the Great Patriotic War and the Holocaust in the vicinity of Babyn Yar, which took place concurrently, gave rise to two overlapping and necessarily contradictory narratives, as we have seen. The second is more historiographic: in addition to the competition between the two master narratives at the same site, each of these master narratives, if examined individually, emerges as a complex phenomenon.

In a study of Holocaust literature's genesis and evolution, David Roskies illustrates the extent to which the current, "authorized" memory of the Holocaust, embedded in belletristic works in a number of countries, was the product of a long, reciprocal process involving a variety of participants: members of political parties, communal organizations, writers, and artists. Together, these players gave the current, authoritative Holocaust memory its final shape "at the intersection of the private and public spheres."[42] Similarly, Arkadi Zeltser shows that, for the most part, the 733 monuments erected by Soviet Jews in the decades that followed the war's conclusion were the outcome of a compromise between the desire of the Jewish relatives of the Holocaust's victims and what the Soviet authorities deemed permissible. The result was the erection of memorials blending Soviet imagery and language with traditional Jewish imagery and language.[43]

Roskies's view of the literary representation of the Holocaust as a multiphase process has its parallel in the evolution of the memory of the Great Patriotic War. As both Nina Tumarkin and Catherine Merridale argue, the myth of the Great Patriotic War also evolved over time, transitioning from the war patriotism during the heat of battle to silence in the immediate postwar years.[44] During the last years of Stalinism, the publishing of books and the release of films that mentioned the war amounted to a trickle, as Stalin was well aware of the subversive potential of a memory of a colossal trauma as well as of the threats embodied in the greater freedoms and sense of self-assertion that many Soviet citizens had experienced during the war.[45] As Tumarkin notes, in 1946, on

May Day, Stalin signaled that the war was over and there was no need to talk about it too much, and that the focus should rather be on the new war—the Cold War. From the years of silence, the master narrative of the Great Patriotic War started to gradually emerge during the era in Soviet history known as "Khrushchev's Thaw" (1953–1966)[46] and reached its zenith in the Brezhnev era as a full-blown cult of World War II.[47] For the new generation of Soviet citizens who were too young to remember or witness the October Revolution, the Great Patriotic War was meant to function as a new and compelling legitimating myth.[48] It could be utilized by Moscow as a raison d'être for a political system that, albeit lagging behind the West technologically, economically, and in many other respects, could boast about having defeated fascism.

Curiously, Zeltser's view of the Holocaust commemorative process in the USSR as a product of negotiation is paralleled by the recent studies of the evolution of the official memory of the Great Patriotic War.[49] In a study focusing on the Siege of Leningrad, Lisa Kirschenbaum illustrates how the public and the individual memories of the war overlapped.[50] If individual writers such as Ilya Ehrenburg or Olga Berggolts, among many others, helped forge the official memory of the war, individual Soviet citizens managed to make sense of their personal, and often traumatic, war experiences by drawing upon "ready-made" slogans and clichés transmitted to them by the Soviet media.[51] Thus, for both Kirschenbaum and Zeltser, attempting to draw the line between passive individuals and the active state as bearers of memory is a very difficult if not impossible task.

Once we interweave all the threads, we will be ready to identify and analyze a select number of works dedicated to Babyn Yar. Some are famous and have brought their authors national and international notoriety; others are rather obscure and are brought to light here for the first time. These key parameters help clear the fog clouding Babyn Yar, making it easier to recognize the site's literary representation as a matrix formed through a multiphase process in which two vectors intersected: the Great Patriotic War and the Holocaust, and the Soviet state versus individual Soviet writers, Jewish and non-Jewish. Throughout our exploration of the literary works in which Babyn Yar was represented, we will see how each of these may be placed as a product of a negotiation process between the attention that writers needed to give to the Holocaust versus the Great Patriotic War, and between the desires and values of Soviet writers and the Soviet state, the controller of all means of literary and artistic production in the country.

Chapter 1 provides an overview of Babyn Yar's evolution as a literary memorial from the end of the war by exploring the very first works written on the subject in Russian, Yiddish, and Ukrainian, and the political context in which they were written. In looking at Soviet literature as one integrated system, we will follow two trajectories: historical and literary. The first ranges from the last years of Stalinism to the early Thaw era; the second ranges from the relative freedom of nationalist sentiments during the war years to the almost complete silencing of Babyn Yar memory during the Zhdanovshchina and the campaign against "rootless Cosmopolitans." In the Russian-focused section, we will focus on a critical epoch in Soviet history that was given form, among other factors, by the memory of Babyn Yar—the Thaw period, which spanned the years 1953–1966. This part will be devoted to the work of three key players in the commemoration of Babyn Yar, three Russian writers who were joined at some point by a world-renowned composer.

Chapter 2 is dedicated to the oeuvre of the Russian writer Viktor Nekrasov and his exceptional, pioneering preoccupation with the memory of Babyn Yar. The juxtaposition of his published works and documents found in the KGB archive will help flesh out his idiosyncratic position on Babyn Yar and the heavy personal price he paid for it. Special attention in this chapter is given to purely political matters. As we explore the suppression of Babyn Yar on the ground, it will become clear that one of the key players in determining the fate of Babyn Yar, both as a physical space and as a literary phenomenon, was Nikita Khrushchev, the man who succeeded Stalin as the ruler of the Soviet state.

After assessing the impact of the Soviet premier on the attempts to consign Babyn Yar to oblivion, chapters 3 and 4 shift attention to the last years of the Thaw period and analyze the worldwide response to the poem "Babi Yar" by Yevgeny Yevtushenko, and assess the impact that the poem had once it was set to music as part of the Thirteenth Symphony by Dmitri Shostakovich, subtitled *Babi Yar*. Chapter 5 explores the novel by the Russian writer Anatoly Kuznetsov, who toward the very end of the Thaw period rendered his own account of the atrocities at the site in two different versions, a censored one and an expanded one, the latter appearing in the West following Kuznetsov's defection to England.

The next set of chapters turns to the younger and more fragile sister of Soviet Russian literature—that is, to works published on Babyn Yar in the Soviet Union in the Yiddish language. In marked contrast to the case of Russian works dedicated to Babyn Yar, the Yiddish ones were hardly ever given critical attention. Beyond the need to rescue some of them from oblivion, the juxtaposition of Yiddish and Russian works on Babyn Yar, augmented by several key Ukrainian works, will elucidate the different role that Babyn Yar as a trope played in each sphere. If in the Russian one it acted as a symbol constantly defining and redefining the shifting bounds of the permissible, marking, in other words, Soviet culture's general level of openness, in the Yiddish sphere Babyn Yar's role was reversed. Alluded to in many cases only obliquely, sometimes without even calling the ravine by its name, the site emerges in the Yiddish sphere as the marker of what is regarded as taboo.

Chapter 6 is dedicated to a broad historical overview of Babyn Yar's representation in Yiddish literature from the conclusion of the war up until 1976. It presents the Kyiv circle of Yiddish writers, the group that more than any other in the Yiddish sphere bore the impact of the Babyn Yar massacres. As a prelude to the Brezhnev years, the period during which the representation of Babyn Yar reached its peak, the chapter also briefly analyzes two works, the poem "The Mother Rachel" by Aron Kushnirov and "War" by Peretz Markish. Chapters 7 and 8 explore the two most important works on Babyn Yar written in Yiddish: an essay-story by Itzik Kipnis and a poem by Shike Driz, which both carry the title "Babi Yar." Through our close reading of both texts, we will gain an appreciation of how these two writers, each in his own way, turned Babyn Yar into a Jewish space, aligned his vision of Babyn Yar with the master narrative of the Holocaust, yet obliquely in order to pass the hurdle of censorship. Chapter 9 is dedicated to Yiddish poetry dealing with Babyn Yar written both during the Thaw era and the decade that succeeded it. Through an analysis of works on the ravine by the Kyiv circle poets Motl Talalayevsky, Dore Khaykine, and Shloyme Cherniavsky, we will be able to characterize the narrow boundaries of the permissible in the Soviet Yiddish sphere and come to perhaps the most striking realization of this study: that it was Soviet Jewish writers, for whom the language of expression was a Jewish tongue, who tended to view Babyn Yar as a Great Patriotic War site. Whether they did so out of choice or coercion—and the effects that such a decision had on their Jewish consciousness—we may be able to surmise once we explore these poems against the background of the modest Yiddish literary apparatus that existed in the USSR beginning in 1961, which was headed by the poet Aron Vergelis, who was also the editor of the sole Yiddish literary periodical to appear in the country at that time.

This study pays careful attention not only to the literary artifacts themselves, but also to their specific time and place, and idiosyncratic conditions that help unlock the many meanings embedded in them. Our reading will help us to realize the delicate interplay between the two different master narratives, the individual writer and the state, and between the major Russian literary system and the minor Yiddish one. This contextualist methodology will perforce affect the image of Soviet Jewish identity that emerges from our exploration of Babyn Yar, the ravine that, though being only one World War II site in the Soviet Union among many, encapsulates in many ways the story of Soviet Russian culture and Soviet Yiddish culture in the postwar era. As we shall see, the story of Babyn Yar is neither one of cultural freedom nor one of suppression, neither one of a "thin" Jewish identity, to borrow Zvi Gitelman's term, nor one of a fertile ground for unlimited opportunities to develop a viable Soviet Jewish culture.

Babyn Yar, in the broader framework of Soviet culture in general, and Soviet Jewish culture in particular, emerges as a boundary marker helping to dispel two common assumptions. First, it helps illustrate that what was previously assumed in the West to be a subject placed under strict taboo—references to the Holocaust in Soviet Russian literature—gradually emerged, in fact, during the Thaw years as a fairly benign zone for free expression. And conversely, what was projected by Moscow outwardly and often perceived by Western observers as a proof of some form of limited freedom of artistic expression—the existence of a state-funded Yiddish literary sphere in the USSR—will turn out, upon a closer examination of oblique references to one ravine on the outskirts of Kyiv, to be the product of a long process of cultural self-censorship. But let us "begin at the beginning," soon after the massacre on the outskirts of Kyiv and while World War II was still raging, with the first literary monuments erected for Babyn Yar.

# 1

# EARLY RESPONSES

> *This woman I had never met.*
> *My dearest child! My rosy blushes!*
> *My countless relatives, my own!*
> *From every gorge your summons rushes:*
> *You plead with me, beseech and moan.*
> *We'll gather all our strength and rise,*
> *Our bones will clatter as we wend—we'll haunt*
> *the towns still left alive,*
> *Where bread and perfumes waft their scent.*
> *Your candles sputter. Flags rip out their seams.*
> *We've come to you. Not we—but the ravine.*
> ILYA EHRENBURG, "BABI YAR"[1]

THE URGE OF THE LIVING SPEAKER TO BECOME ONE WITH THE DEAD; THE HARrowing, haunting mood of a city that has been invaded by the mass graves surrounding it; the veiled reference to its murdered Jews were already present in "Babi Yar" by Ilya Ehrenburg (1891–1967), published in the Soviet periodical *Novy mir* in January 1945. This poem, one of the first literary works in the Russian language to address this theme, was written by a Soviet Jewish author who played a major role in conveying the latest events of World War II to the Soviet public.[2] Together with another great Soviet Jewish writer, Vasily Grossman, Ehrenburg compiled *The Black Book*, a collection of reports on Nazi anti-Jewish atrocities, the publication of which was ultimately banned.[3] As a native of Kyiv, and known as a leading Russian intellectual, a mouthpiece of Soviet Jews, and a leading wartime journalist who reported on the Nazi genocidal operations on the Soviet western frontiers, Ehrenburg, appropriately, was the first to erect a literary memorial to Babyn Yar. Over the next two decades, his poem would spawn more literary monuments of great artistic merit.

Ehrenburg's "Babi Yar" is a landmark work of Holocaust poetry on several levels. It is one of the first works in Holocaust literature to reflect on the grand transition that took place in the immediate aftermath of the war—from activism to passive reflection and from vengeance to commemoration. While we will get back to the theme of vengeance below, suffice it for now to mention David Shneer's remark that this poem by Ehrenburg shifts from preoccupation with revenge to a more reconciliatory attitude toward the German people, as the latter were facing defeat and surrender. This tendency would only intensify in the postwar period with the partition of Germany and the foundation of the German Democratic Republic, a Soviet satellite state.[4] The poem constitutes the first work on Babyn Yar to appear in a major publication. It is an excellent point of departure for a process of commemoration that spanned the late Stalin years, the Khrushchev era, and a part of the Brezhnev era—from the time of the massacres of Babyn Yar through the erection of the first permanent monument at the site.

The poem was written by a beloved son of Jewish Kyiv, a man who in the wake of the Holocaust was sent a chilling reminder about his Jewish identity. In a speech delivered in Moscow about a month before the Babyn Yar massacre, Ehrenburg had famously exclaimed: "I grew up in a Russian city. My mother tongue is Russian. I am a Russian writer. Like all Russians, I am now defending my homeland. But the Nazis have reminded me of something else: My mother's name was Hannah. I am a Jew. I say this proudly. Hitler hated us more than anyone else."[5] As the poem reveals, upon his return to Kyiv, Ehrenburg transformed into a ghost, belonging neither to the world of the postwar Ukrainian capital that had been bereft of its Jewish population, nor to the domain of the charred bones of his dead relatives and friends, who now resided outside Kyiv and threatened to encroach upon and hover over the city of the living.

This is where our literary journey begins. But in order to portray an accurate trajectory of Babyn Yar's representation in Soviet literature, we should begin with "Avraham," a poem published by the Ukrainian Jewish writer Sava Holovanivsky prior to the Soviet takeover of Kyiv and fully two years before Ehrenburg's poem.[6] His poem differs in one crucial respect from Ehrenburg's far more celebrated work. Whereas Ehrenburg refers to the victims of Babyn Yar as Jews only implicitly by alluding to friends and relatives, to children and mothers, Holovanivsky does it more explicitly, featuring the character of an old man, whose name and sense of isolation from his environment as he marches to Babyn Yar, while his non-Jewish neighbors watch him passively, brings to mind the biblical prototype of another lonely man of faith. When juxtaposed to each other as the first two Soviet literary responses to Babyn Yar, one is struck by the fact that what for Holovanivsky is a painful truth that must be openly discussed—the Jewish identity of the victims—is for Ehrenburg a no less tormenting truth that must be carefully concealed. Indeed, the comparison reveals a literary transition that is both a reflection and a product of a historical reality. For it was in the winter of 1944, between the publication dates of these two poems, that the excision of the Jews from the official memory of Babyn Yar began. If with the outbreak of Operation Barbarossa Ehrenburg could feel safe, refer to himself as a Jew, and go as far as expressing his Jewish pride, three-and-a-half years later any prudent Soviet Jewish writer would most definitely refrain from such exclamations.

What led to that dramatic change, where the primary victims of the Soviet Union's archenemy could no longer freely and securely refer to their own Jewish identity? In theory (and in Marxism–Leninism, we must bear in mind, theory matters), these competing narratives of the Holocaust and the Great Patriotic War stood a good chance, at least initially, of sharing a great deal of common ground. From a purely logical standpoint, this actually makes a lot of sense. For example, did Adolf Hitler, for whom the equation between Judaism and Bolshevism was an ideological cornerstone, not order a total war against the Soviet system, an unprecedented attack against the entire Soviet civilian population, and a special, historically unparalleled war of extermination targeting Soviet Jews first and later expanding it to encompass Jews from all over Europe? And Holovanivsky's "Avraham" shows that it was indeed possible to think along these lines. Ehrenburg—and, as we shall see, the many Jewish writers that followed in his footsteps—was destined to despairingly realize that doing so would become not only difficult and uncomfortable, but indeed well-nigh impossible and even quite dangerous.

There are quite a few signs that at the beginning of the war, for the Soviet regime and especially for its Jewish leadership, the tendency to reconcile, rather than distinguish and divide, was the one to gain currency. Karel Berkhoff, who studied the Soviet media during the war, carefully traced the evolution of Jewish identity in the press from a revealed to a concealed one. Like with Holovanivsky's poem, the first steps taken by the Soviet leadership were those of inclusion. In July and August of 1941, Stalin received the first NKVD report about atrocities in the occupied Soviet territories and became aware of the plan to kill all Soviet Jews. A few months later, in November, he made his first and last reference to Jews being victims of the German Nazis in his October Revolution Day speech.[7] In the specific case of Babyn Yar, it was his minister of foreign affairs, Vyacheslav Molotov, who reported the murder of 52,000 people in Kyiv.[8] Hoping to garner the support of the foreign governments in the Soviet war effort, the communiqué, issued in January of 1942, admitted that this was a Nazi attack overwhelmingly targeting Soviet Jewish citizens.

Berkhoff not only illustrates how with time the open references to Jews as primary targets of the German Nazis in general, and the Nazis in Kyiv in particular, gave way to an increasingly colder attitude toward any specific references to Jewish victims, he also tracks down the exact turning point and identifies Stalin himself as the orchestrator of this shift. Nonetheless, and as noted above, as befitting an ideological "gray zone," what characterized the Soviet media's policy with regard to Hitler's Jewish victims more than anything else was inconsistency. For instance, if a public reference to those deported to and gassed in Treblinka[9]—the overwhelming majority of them Jewish—could overtly refer to Jews, this identity mark would often be excised from many other publications.

Sometimes, Soviet Jews managed to insert the word "Jew" into an article and see it published.[10] In other cases, they failed to do so. This inconsistency was a result of two trends. On the one hand, things were orchestrated from above: Stalin was certainly reluctant to openly speak about the destruction of European Jews and, among them, Soviet Jews. On the other hand, neither Stalin nor his immediate inferiors were ever interested in developing a clear, unequivocal policy in this respect.[11] As Ehrenburg's poem shows, whenever it was ideologically "imprudent" for the Soviet authorities to openly write about Jewish victims they refrained from doing so. Babyn Yar was certainly a good case in point when this kind of prudence was warranted.

While the trajectory in the Russian media was that of a turn from plainly evoking Jewish suffering to toning it down, the Yiddish media of the war and immediate postwar years operated under different unwritten rules. Parallel to Molotov's candid report of the Nazi atrocities at Babyn Yar, the single official body representing Soviet Jews during the war, the Jewish Anti-Fascist Committee, also began to place the emerging narrative of the Nazi anti-Jewish genocide within the framework of Russia's "holy war" against the invading fascists. In October 1942, the JAFC published its first report on Babyn Yar in its Yiddish organ *Eynikayt*.[12] Its author was none other than Ilya Ehrenburg. His report, translated from Russian, like the note by Molotov, explicitly mentioned the fact that the majority of the victims shot at the ravine were Jewish. If Molotov intended to enlist foreign support, then Ehrenburg intended to do so not only by appealing to a Yiddish readership abroad, but also by enlisting support for the war on the home front by helping to mobilize Soviet Jews into the ranks of the Red Army so as to join the desperate effort to drive the German Army out of the country and take vengeance on them. Nothing epitomizes more clearly the porous boundaries in the early stages of the war between what began to crystallize as the narratives of the Holocaust and the Great Patriotic War than the title of Ehrenburg's call: "Gebentshte erd" (Sanctified land or Blessed earth). If Ehrenburg's "Babi Yar," written two years later, would portray the ravine as so daunting a place that it would even eclipse the city itself, his article of October 1942 concluded by shifting the meaning of "sacred earth" from Babyn Yar to the battlefield. The early response, then, of both the Soviet regime and its official body representing its Jewish citizens was similar: they both realized that the Nazis were carrying out a monstrous scheme devised to annihilate Jews, one that stood out but one that was still embedded within the framework of the general war effort.[13]

As Arkadi Zeltser notes, whereas a tendency to tone down the Holocaust and downplay it was already discernible, no complete ban on the mentioning of Babyn Yar's Jewish victims was in place.[14] This window of opportunity when both master narratives about Babyn Yar could have coexisted was open for only a very short while. As early as March 1944, about four months after the Soviet takeover of Kyiv, a Soviet-created Ukrainian Extraordinary State Commission was set up to investigate Nazi atrocities

Jewish Anti-Fascist Committee signing an appeal to the Jews of the world to join the fight against Hitler, 1940. In the photo are Ilya Ehrenburg (front right) and Perets Markish (second from left). (Sovfoto/UIG / Bridgeman Images.)

perpetrated during the German occupation. The commission—chaired by Nikita Khrushchev, who assumed the role of first secretary of the Ukrainian party organization at that time—began to refer to the "thousands of peaceful Soviet citizens" who were shot in Kyiv while collecting data in the city.[15] What prompted this turn toward euphemism was the wave of pogroms then engulfing Ukraine, the chief target of which were Ukrainian Jews who had survived the Holocaust and were now returning to their previous homes. It was in this climate that Khrushchev warned the returning Red Army not to alienate the local Ukrainian population by underlining either the anti-Jewish genocidal character of Nazi atrocities or the Ukrainian complicity in those crimes. Additionally, the commission was instructed "to suppress the extent of Ukrainian collaboration with the Germans and particularly with the SS in the mass shooting of Jews."[16] Khrushchev, who succeeded Joseph Stalin and would later play a central role in the suppression of Babyn Yar, left no ambiguities in this early postwar report about the reason for this tectonic shift in the Soviet regime's attitude toward Babyn Yar. He declared: "Here is the Ukraine and it is not in our interest that the Ukrainians should associate the return of Soviet power with the return of the Jews."[17]

The report compiled by the Ukrainian Extraordinary State Commission is a convenient point of reference to mark the watershed between the Soviet acknowledgment of Babyn Yar as a site of a tragedy with a distinctly Jewish nature, apparent during the years 1942–1944, and the suppression of this historical fact that marked much of the postwar era up until the collapse of the Soviet Union. Yet if a clear demarcation line may be drawn between these two eras with regard to the Soviet Union's official statements, an exploration of Soviet culture would show that for a regime that controlled all channels of publication and enjoyed a monopoly in the realms of literature and the arts, the Soviet cultural sphere often reflected a lack of ideological clarity in the attitude of the Soviet regime to Babyn Yar. If the immediate years following the massacre witnessed the publication of "Avraham" by Holovanivsky and "Babi Yar" by Ehrenburg, this trend was not cut short in the wake of the Extraordinary State Commission's investigation, but, rather, gained momentum with the appearance of several more works.

In spite of an increasingly antisemitic environment and the suppression of Jewish writers and artists that was characteristic of the late Stalin era, the works on Babyn Yar that followed those of Holovanivsky and Ehrenburg proved capable of passing the scrutiny of the Soviet censors. These works included the poem "Babi Yar" by the Russian Jewish poet Lev Ozerov, appearing in the journal *Oktiabr'* in 1948,[18] the first as well as second novel by Ilya Ehrenburg dedicated to the Great Patriotic War, *The Storm* (1948) and *The Ninth Wave* (1952), the symphony *Babi Yar*, composed after the war by the Ukrainian Jewish composer Dmitry Klebanov,[19] and the film *Nepokorennye* (The unvanquished) by the Odessa-born Jewish director Mark Donskoi (1945), based on a novel bearing the same title by Boris Gorbatov, which was shot in Kyiv and featured the procession of Jews to Babyn Yar. A review of it published in *Pravda* harshly criticized Donskoi for concentrating on passive victims who were submissively walking to their death, a behavior disparaged by official Soviet dogma as being antiheroic.[20]

No doubt, these works constituted the exception to the rule of silence about the Holocaust and Babyn Yar. They came into being at a time when the Soviet regime's relative tolerance toward artists, characteristic of the war period, came to an end and a new wave of artistic suppression and terror was about to begin. It was then that a new tide of persecutions was set in motion, launched through the wide publication of the August 1946 speech by Stalin's ideological spokesman, Andrei Zhdanov; this new campaign aimed at further narrowing Soviet intellectual discourse and severing Soviet society from all foreign influences and ties. Now, with the war behind him and with no need to be mindful of the international community's support, Stalin began to target some of the more free-thinking and less party-line-oriented Soviet cultural figures.[21] Known as the Zhdanovshchina, this campaign turned in 1948, after the death of Zhdanov and the establishment of the State of Israel, into a virulent, violent attack against "rootless Cosmopolitans." Carrying a distinctively antisemitic character, the campaign at that point included official denunciations in the party organ *Pravda* as well as arrests. It reached its nadir with the execution of some of the most prominent Yiddish writers and cultural activists in the Soviet Union.[22]

The Zhdanovshchina and the ensuing campaign against "rootless Cosmopolitans" made it dangerous for Soviet Jewish writers to mention the Holocaust in general and

Babyn Yar in particular. As Benjamin Pinkus notes, these writers became increasingly aware of the Zhdanovites' new policies and forced upon themselves a complete silence with respect to any Jewish themes.[23] While a universal taboo on the Holocaust was never in effect in the Soviet Union, the years 1949–1953 were a time when a policy of silence was put in place; all mention of Jewishness was erased from existing Great Patriotic War memorials.[24] It was during this period, also known in Soviet Jewish historiography as the "Black Years," that the silencing of the Babyn Yar massacre in all spheres of Soviet life, even though never formulated as a specific ordinance, became a comprehensively enforced practice.

Even in this reality, which was least auspicious for the publication of works dealing with Babyn Yar, a Soviet writer of prominent stature like Ilya Ehrenburg dared to briefly touch upon the theme in two of his novels—*The Storm* (1947) and its sequel, *The Ninth Wave* (1952)—which appeared in the two major literary journals *Novy mir* and *Znamya*, respectively. The latter novel, significantly, came out only a year before the first announcement of the "Doctors' Plot," the alleged scheme of mostly Jewish physicians to poison Stalin, a libel orchestrated by the increasingly paranoid tyrant in January 1953. While in both novels Ehrenburg had to pay lip service to anti-Western and anti-Zionist propaganda, both of which were rampant at that time, he did allow mention of some aspects of the Babyn Yar massacre deemed by the Soviet regime to be strictly taboo. In the novels, Ehrenburg explicitly refers to the Jewish identity of his hero, Osip, and his loved ones, who were killed at Babyn Yar, an allusion to the ethnic identity of Babyn Yar's victims that he avoided in his earlier poem. Furthermore, when his novels' protagonist, Osip, revisits the postwar city of Kyiv to see for himself the streets in which his wife and daughters marched to their death in Babyn Yar, Ehrenburg describes the antisemitic reactions that Osip encounters from the locals.

Ehrenburg's engagement with the theme of Babyn Yar indicates (and we have seen the same characteristic feature in the Soviet press above) that this topic—insofar as the Stalin years are concerned—ought not to be presented as a trajectory of constant decline leading up to a point of complete silence. A mood of extreme antagonism toward Jews and the Holocaust did prevail following the Zhdanovshchina and the anti-Cosmopolitan campaigns, yet it did not result in an effectively imposed silence with regard to the Babyn Yar massacre. Observing, outside of literature, the way that the Babyn Yar massacre was commemorated by Soviet Jews in other realms, we arrive at a similar picture of a suppressed yet persisting engagement with the memory of the tragedy. As the Soviet Jewish history scholar Mordechai Altshuler notes in his work dedicated to the role played by the synagogue—the last vestige of officially sanctioned Soviet Jewish institutions—during the late Stalin era the Kyiv synagogue became, around the High Holidays, a magnet for the Kyiv Jewish crowds, who attended services not out of a feeling of religious duty but rather as a manifestation of their sense of belonging to the Jewish people and its fate. Indeed, the 1951 Yom Kippur services were endowed with special significance because they coincided with the tenth anniversary of the Babyn Yar massacre.[25]

The new historical data gleaned from the archives of the former Soviet Union by Altshuler describing Jewish life in Kyiv during the Black Years, combined with Ehrenburg's depiction of the Babyn Yar massacre as an event with a distinct connection to Soviet Jews, calls into question the frequent tendency of scholars to divide the commemoration of Babyn Yar into two opposing periods: the Stalin years as a period of harsh suppression versus the ensuing years, known as "Khrushchev's Thaw," as a period in which the memory of Babyn Yar resurfaced. Edith Clowes, for example, summarizes the literary responses to Babyn Yar of the late Stalin years as lacking a strong statement of Jewish identity or bearing a passive memory of the tragedy that might ultimately "help to bury and to consign it to oblivion" rather than manifest resistance to Soviet repression.[26] This dichotomy between the Stalin era and the Thaw era is underscored by parallel ethnic and generational divides. According to this scheme, such Soviet Jewish writers as Holovanivsky, Ozerov, and Ehrenburg responded immediately to the Babyn Yar massacre in a voice that was, for the most part, hesitant and unripe, while the theme of Babyn Yar was subject to the audacious, probing attention of a new generation of Soviet artists only later and under the new and far more propitious circumstances that were created in the country following the death of Stalin.[27]

The issue at stake here concerns more than an evaluation of who was bolder, the generation of Soviet Jewish writers who dared to assert their Jewishness and agony over the Babyn Yar massacre while under the yoke of Stalin or the new group of artists who embraced the cause of Babyn Yar in their battle against Stalin's successor. The debate here is also over the question of whether the story of Babyn Yar's commemoration in Soviet literature and art can be accurately presented by drawing a strict dividing line between the silence of the Stalin years and the outspoken battle to commemorate it during the Thaw era. A closer look at the representation of Babyn Yar in the Russian cultural arena during the Thaw years reveals, on the contrary, that the beginning of the epoch of relaxation and increasing tolerance that Soviet society underwent soon after the death of Stalin marked the nadir of the silence enforced in the Soviet Union with regard to the memory of the Babyn Yar massacre.

## *OTTEPEL'*: THE THAW (1953–1966)

The Thaw period and the many vicissitudes that characterized this era in the history of the Soviet Union left an indelible imprint on the evolution of the memory of Babyn Yar as both a locus and symbol. When the Thaw period began, Babyn Yar was a neglected mass grave where the incinerated bones of the murdered lay scattered amidst heaps of garbage, a focal point for dubious characters who would often hang out in its vicinity, digging for any valuable item they could unearth.[28] By the time this thirteen-year period ended, Babyn Yar had been transformed into one of the most celebrated symbols of the nascent Soviet dissident movement, attracting to it thousands of dissidents, Jews and non-Jews alike, who would come to the ravine to attend the annual memorial ceremonies there and protest Soviet antisemitism and ethnic discrimination.[29] Scholars who point to the impact of the events that took place in the Soviet cultural arena during the Thaw invariably refer to four cultural figures who shaped the discourse about Babyn Yar during this period: Viktor Nekrasov, Yevgeny Yevtushenko, Dmitri Shostakovich, and Anatoly Kuznetsov. These artists, all of them non-Jewish Russians, turned the memory of the massacre from the concern of a small group of local Kyiv residents into an issue that preoccupied the wider Soviet Jewish community, the Soviet intelligentsia, and, later, the international community as well.

Given the fact that the Thaw period began after the death of Stalin in March 1953, it must be noted that the reactions offered by these artists to the Soviet suppression of Babyn Yar's memory came quite late. They happened only when the process of liberalization that so typified the Thaw era was already in full swing in the late 1950s and early 1960s. Students of Soviet cultural history and literature who emphasize the interconnectedness between the commemoration of Babyn Yar and the atmosphere of the Thaw tend to concentrate on these works, and thereby also focus on the later years of this period. This tendency, though, leaves one under the impression that, contrary to the Stalinist suppression of Babyn Yar, the years of Stalin's successor, Khrushchev, were radically different. If we carefully examine the entire span of the Thaw period, however,

Uncovered bones in the vicinity of Babyn Yar, 1961.
(Photo courtesy of the Central Archives for the History
of the Jewish People; Emmanuel Diamant.)

we discover that at no other time was the policy of suppression and neglect of Babyn Yar as effectively enforced as during the years of the early Thaw, the exact same time when the "Ice Age" (i.e., formed as a result of decades of Stalinist totalitarian rule) afflicting so many other spheres of Soviet life came to an end. It is perhaps one of the many ironies of Soviet history that in its early years the Thaw period, with its promise of recovery from decades of oppression and terror and its promise of greater tolerance and openness for the expression of opinions that might deviate from the party line, brought little change in the Soviet government's attitude toward Jewish culture, and brought hardly any discernible change in Soviet official policy vis-à-vis the commemoration of the Babyn Yar massacre.

In reality, it took more than six years from the death of Stalin for the silence over Babyn Yar to be broken. Two developments marked this change: the republication of Ehrenburg's "Babi Yar" in 1959 and the appearance in September of that year of a new figure on the Russian literary and political scenes, the Kyiv-born and resident Soviet Russian writer Viktor Nekrasov. Remarkably, Nekrasov's work was not an attempt to undo the silencing of Babyn Yar imposed by Stalin but was rather aimed at Nikita Khrushchev, the man who came to prominence as the leader of the Soviet Union in the wake of the death of Stalin and who would become the most influential figure in Russian politics and culture up until his forced retirement in October 1964. Admittedly, Khrushchev's role was instrumental in bringing the witch hunt for Jewish intellectuals and physicians to a halt, as exemplified by the arrest of Stalin's butcher, Lavrentiy Beria, and in the release from prison of thousands of gulag inmates, among which were many Jews.[30] But his coming to power and his political career as the First Secretary of the Communist Party were also characterized by equivocation and political zigzagging as he found a need to constantly test the boundaries of the permissible in the sphere of Soviet culture. To better understand how the theme of Babyn Yar came to play a crucial role in this process when Soviet public and cultural discourses were constantly tested, let us briefly survey the historical background of the Thaw period and assess the way in which it transformed Soviet culture.

# 2

# THE THAW AND THE MEMORY OF BABYN YAR

*No, it's impermissible!*
VIKTOR NEKRASOV, "WHY HAS IT NOT BEEN DONE?"

DURING THE FIRST THIRTEEN YEARS AFTER STALIN'S DEATH, SOVIET SOCIETY underwent a process of liberalization and cultural revitalization that it had not experienced since the early years of Communism and would not recover until the Glasnost of the latter half of the 1980s. Beginning with the news of the death of the tyrant on March 5, 1953, and reaching its conclusion during the Brezhnev era with the trial of the writers Andrei Sinyavsky and Yuli Daniel in February 1966, this remarkable era in Soviet history was named "Ottepel'" (the "Thaw") after a short novel by Ilya Ehrenburg that was published in early 1954.¹ Featuring as its central protagonist an autocratic, Stalin-like character, the work offered a remarkably unflattering portrayal of Stalinism. Ehrenburg's negative attitude toward the Soviet past was already apparent in the novella's title. The term "thaw" meant that, contrary to the Soviet propaganda of the late Stalin era, which claimed that era to be a "hot" time of dynamism and rapid progress, the death of the tyrant left Soviet society in the midst of a long and freezing winter that could, now that Stalin was dead, possibly thaw.²

In this work, Ehrenburg gave voice to the demand, supported by a growing number of Soviet intellectuals who survived the Stalinist purges, to introduce radical changes to both the social and the literary spheres of Soviet life. He called on ordinary citizens to transform the entire fabric of Soviet society, to cast aside the web of fears, suspicions, and rigidity that had become entrenched after decades of terror and, instead, warm up to each other and foster a new climate of mutual empathy.³ No less importantly, *The Thaw* was also a cultural manifesto, a call to the new Soviet leadership to do away with the Stalinist dogmatic interference with the work of writers and artists. This interference was first and foremost evident in the strict enforcement of socialist realism, the artistic theory endorsed by Stalin. Socialist realism had functioned since its proclamation at the First Congress of the Soviet Writers' Union as the only legitimate prescription for the composition of artistic works in the USSR. According to its chief tenets, artists and writers were obliged to compose pieces that would comply with the Communist Party of the Soviet Union (CPSU) party line, render a present-day, optimistic portrayal of Soviet society and the working class, and capture them in their "revolutionary development."

Ehrenburg, in fact, was not the first to criticize the Soviet leadership or raise an objection to socialist realism and thereby spawn this new trend of de-Stalinization in Soviet culture. The first manifestations of mild dissent came, in fact, in the immediate aftermath of Stalin's death in the form of production novels. These novels were part of a series that appeared in *Novy mir*, which was soon to become the Soviet Union's primary platform for the expression of dissonance. These were novels where voice was given for the first time to the criticism of irrational economic planning, the chaotic bureaucracy, incompetent management, and the corruption that is usually endemic to the first three.[4] While still retaining the façade of bona fide socialist-realist works due to their focus on industrial and agricultural themes, these novels were followed by other publications that contained even sharper criticisms of the Soviet system.

These new essays and stories, appearing in *Novy mir* beginning in December 1953, did not limit their censure to flaws in the Soviet bureaucracy and economy—criticism that was overall well received by the new leadership—but rather chose as their targets some of the premises upon which the Soviet ideological edifice rested. The first prominent work of this new wave of dissent was the essay by Vladimir Pomerantsev titled "On Sincerity in Literature." Voicing concerns invoked later by Ehrenburg in *The Thaw*, the essay alludes to the dire straits of Russian literature in the Soviet era. In the essay, Pomerantsev regards socialist realism as the chief cause for the turning of Soviet literature, the inheritor of the canon of nineteenth- and early twentieth-century Russian literature, from its glorious stature into a monotonous entity almost completely irrelevant to the lives of its readers.[5] Pomerantsev asserts that writers must write with honesty and let only their sincerity and conscience guide them, rather than any theoretical dogma imposed upon them from above. In his bleak review of the havoc wrought by socialist realism on the Russian literary tradition, Pomerantsev contends that for a literature to be worthwhile and not perceived as a hodgepodge of hackneyed socialist clichés, its writers must be gifted and present Soviet life with candor as it really is.

The call for a new literature that aimed to engage its readers and portray the harsh reality that Soviet citizens faced at that time continued to run like a thread in the Soviet literature of the ensuing years. A growing number of works followed in the footsteps of Ehrenburg and Pomerantsev, calling into question not only the credibility of socialist realism but of many other aspects of the Soviet system, all of which were the legacy of decades of Stalinism. Yet Babyn Yar would remain conspicuously absent from this artistic reckoning.

If in the first three years of the Thaw no prominent Soviet artists touched upon the theme of Babyn Yar (except for the reprint of Ehrenburg's poem), the most pivotal event of the era, the decision made by Nikita Khrushchev to openly denounce Stalin and his cult of personality at the Twentieth Party Congress in February 1956 brought virtually no change with respect to the treatment of Babyn Yar in Soviet literature. One would imagine that, together with other key features of the Stalin era, the suppression of the Babyn Yar massacre, one facet among many of Stalinist antisemitism, would have been openly addressed by the more liberal wing of the Soviet intelligentsia. The opposite, however, was true: it is evident from the silence about Babyn Yar in Soviet literature of the early Thaw, and no less importantly from the actions taken by the local Ukrainian authorities at the same time to eradicate the ravine, that no room for a process of "thawing" was considered by the new regime with respect to the memory of Babyn Yar.

A glimpse into the condition of the site of Babyn Yar and the attitude of the Kyiv City Council toward it (an attitude endorsed by the Ukrainian government) illustrates how the Soviet literary sphere and the posture of the Soviet authorities vis-à-vis Babyn Yar went hand in hand at that time. As much as the last years of World War II saw the gradual withdrawal of the theme of Babyn Yar from the Russian literary scene, a parallel process took place on the ground. At first, as early as 1945, the Kyiv City Council approved a memorial project to commemorate the Babyn Yar massacre, putting Kyiv's chief architect A. Vlasov and the artist B. Ovchinnikov in charge of the monument's design for "the victims of the fascist terror at Babi Yar." This was a part of a five-year plan for the construction of a number of monuments in the city.[6] By 1949, it was clear that a commemorative project of this sort would simply not be allowed. The plan for the memorial was thus shelved, and in its stead the Kyiv City Council decided to transform the topography of the site altogether by flooding the ravine with pulp and mud, so as to level it with the surrounding area. While the decision to flood the area was made in 1950, it is striking that the ravine's eradication started to be carried out only four years later, during the early Thaw.[7]

Officially, the Ukrainian government, backed by Moscow, argued that the flooding of Babyn Yar was a necessity because the leveling of the area was part of a larger plan to reconstruct the postwar Ukrainian capital and connect its center to the suburbs. But this argument could hardly withstand critical examination; after all, the Ukrainian authorities could have found other ways to help turn Kyiv into a modern metropolitan center without manifesting utter disrespect toward the burial place of tens of thousands of its citizens. It was also striking that, while insisting on the eradication of Babyn Yar, the Soviet regime encouraged the construction of Great Patriotic War monuments at other sites throughout the Soviet Union where Nazi atrocities had taken place.[8] If one expected the plan to eradicate Babyn Yar, as a vestige of Stalinism, to be overturned in the wake of Khrushchev's Secret Speech, the attitude toward the site shown by the new head of the Ukrainian Central Committee, Nikolai Podgorny, a Khrushchev loyalist, dispelled any such hopes. After a renewed discussion of the possibility of erecting a monument at the site, the committee, under Podgorny, decided in 1957 to take the last steps in Babyn Yar's eradication process. It rejected the proposal for a monument and, at the same time, approved a plan to lay out a stadium and a park on top of the mass grave.[9]

The shelving of the plan to construct a monument at the site for the second time, coupled with the implementation of the resolution to flood the ravine, indicated that the "freeze" decreed on the commemoration of Babyn Yar in the immediate aftermath of World War II remained intact, as if the Thaw period and the process in which Stalinist practices were openly renounced and overturned had never happened. While a general overview of the attitude of the new regime toward Jewish culture will be provided in the second part of this study, it is worth noting that during the early years of the Thaw the new leadership of the Soviet Union did take some courageous steps in bringing the virulent Stalinist persecution of Jews to a halt. Whereas implicit antisemitism pervaded many segments of the Soviet bureaucracy during the Thaw years as much as it did during the Stalin era, the acquittal and release of the imprisoned Jewish physicians by the new leadership in April 1953 and the later release and the posthumous rehabilitation of many other Jewish victims of the Stalinist repressions were courageous moves, indicating that the new regime deemed antisemitism, to a certain extent, to be a sinister, ingrained aspect of Stalinist totalitarianism.[10] That Khrushchev was willing to take this route was indicative that, at least to some degree, he wished to dissociate himself from the rabidly antisemitic rule of his predecessor. However, while the Soviet dictator was dead, the admittance and reversal of such antisemitic Stalinist crimes had the potential of implicating some of Stalin's immediate subordinates, who were by now members of the newly formed Presidium, the governing body of the CPSU. These moves were therefore not easy to make.

One may question, given the comprehensive nature of the process of de-Stalinization, which engaged for several years both the Soviet leadership and the intelligentsia, why the memory of Babyn Yar was so sternly suppressed. Why could no one among the Soviet literati of the early Thaw period—and even a towering cultural figure such as Ilya Ehrenburg, who had addressed the memory of the Babyn Yar massacre in his earlier works—publicly express any objection to the flooding of the ravine? Indeed, the root causes of this silence over the memory of Babyn Yar observed by both intellectuals and politicians are identical. Two of them merit a close examination.

The first cause of the general neglect of Babyn Yar during the early Thaw is quite simple. In view of the plethora of challenges that both the Soviet government and the intelligentsia faced during this time of postwar recovery, the concern over the question of how Babyn Yar needed to be commemorated must have seemed rather marginal. At a time when the residents of Moscow were experiencing severe shortages of the most basic food supplies, when the country was still run by a war economy and its economic raison d'être depended on the slave labor of an army of 2.5 million prisoners,[11] it is hardly surprising that the memory of Babyn Yar and the moral implications of the plans to flood the site did not capture the minds of any influential figures. The ravine's memory, in a fashion similar to other topics begging a serious historical revision of Stalinism, must have seemed at that time to have little immediate and practical repercussions. Hence, it was cast aside and postponed for the more distant future. The Khrushchev–Malenkov duumvirate, not unlike the Soviet intellectuals of that era, was eager initially to halt—and later, as early as the Twentieth Party Congress, to begin to revisit—the crimes perpetrated by the Soviet regime itself. A discussion of how the crimes of Nazi Germany needed to take shape in official Soviet memory was, in this respect, quite understandably an issue relegated to a much lower priority.

That such rational considerations guided the Soviet elite, intelligentsia, and bureaucracy of the post-Stalin era in the marginalization of Babyn Yar during the very early years of the Thaw was true. But this was by no means the whole picture, for the neglect of Babyn Yar was not merely a by-product of a wish to put off the debate about how the site was supposed to be commemorated and wait for a more propitious time. On the contrary, it was a direct result of active attempts to completely erase the ravine and the surrounding area from the face of the earth. Why was the post-Stalin era Soviet regime so loyal to the plan to destroy Babyn Yar, and why did none of the Soviet intellectuals who so critically appraised the legacy of Stalinism make any serious attempt to hinder it?

In order to penetrate the second and more profound cause of the neglect of Babyn Yar during the early Thaw, we must dwell on the unique role that Nikita Khrushchev played, first from Kyiv and later from the Kremlin, in consigning Babyn Yar to oblivion. Due to the immense influence that Khrushchev had on shaping the Russian culture of the Thaw period, a discussion of his stance toward Babyn Yar should not be overlooked. Let us consider it more closely.

## NIKITA KHRUSHCHEV AND BABYN YAR

The Soviet historian of the Thaw period Rudolph Pikhoya notes that, despite the popular view of Khrushchev as a courageous reformer, the chief ideologue of de-Stalinization, and the man who in the days immediately following the death of Stalin gave the process of liberalization and relaxation from terror its first thrust, the reality in which the Thaw came into being was a great deal more complex. Despite his later tendency to portray himself as its initiator, Khrushchev approached the nascent process of de-Stalinization with ambivalence. He had a good reason to do so, knowing that he was no less complicit in the Stalinist crimes than his colleagues in the post-Stalin Presidium: Beria, Malenkov, Kaganovich, and Molotov.[12] As Khrushchev started to gain power and eclipse his colleagues (at the outset of the Thaw period, he ranked only fifth in the Presidium and was the least likely among its members to become the next Soviet leader),[13] he realized the potential of de-Stalinization as a means of securing and strengthening his position. While the death of Stalin was at first met by the majority of the Soviet population with despair and anxiety, Khrushchev, with his down-to-earth political savvy and tactical maneuvering, realized how de-Stalinization was gaining currency and how identifying himself with this trend might greatly work to his advantage.

Viewed from this perspective, de-Stalinization was not simply the comprehensive unraveling of any policy associated with Stalin's crimes. Rather, it was a selective, deliberate process, and by February 1955, when Nikita Khrushchev became the leader of the Soviet Union, it was he who was in the position to orchestrate it.[14] While no one can deny the moral underpinnings that prompted Khrushchev to launch his campaign, his ulterior motives must not be overlooked. At first, he laid the blame for Stalin's tyranny on Lavrentiy Beria; he then turned to exposing the complicity of Malenkov in the Doctors' Plot and the Leningrad Affair; and in 1957 he felt secure enough to attack all of his rivals—Malenkov, Molotov, and Kaganovich, the plotters of the so-called anti-party coup—portraying them as neo-Stalinist and the enemies of progress. Khrushchev pursued de-Stalinization as a means to eliminate anyone who stood in his way of becoming and remaining the head of the Soviet state.[15]

Evidently, Khrushchev could overturn Stalinist policies with relative ease and openly condemn those crimes from the Stalin era in areas that were far removed from his direct involvement. But this was certainly not the case concerning Babyn Yar and its memory. Here Khrushchev, who had spent much of his career in Ukraine, could not escape his own close involvement in the attempts to eradicate the ravine. As Stalin's appointee for first secretary of the Communist Party during the late 1930s and the immediate postwar years,[16] Khrushchev was the one to reject, in 1949, the Vlasov–Ovchinnikov proposal for a monument at the site.[17] As in the Katyn massacre of 22,000 Polish officers in 1940, another instance and symbol of Stalinist repression in which Khrushchev was closely involved,[18] the best course of action for Khrushchev to take—in view of the fact that here there was no one to associate Stalinism with but himself—was to continue the Stalinist policy of silence.

This was exactly the path Khrushchev chose. When the question of whether Babyn Yar deserved public commemoration was brought up for discussion in 1957, it was Khrushchev's associate Nikolai Podgorny who, as noted above, after a review of another proposal for a memorial, decided that this plan, like the previous one, would be shelved.[19] In March 1960, already from his office in Moscow, Khrushchev vetoed a decision made earlier in December 1959, according to which a park and an obelisk would be erected to commemorate the victims of Babyn Yar who had died there in 1941.[20] Even though this was essentially a proposal to erect a memorial stone for the overwhelming majority of those murdered at Babyn Yar in the course of 1941, who were Jews, the inscription for the bottom of the obelisk was to speak of the "Soviet citizens tormented by the Hitlerites in 1941." This vague formulation, however, did not keep Khrushchev from actively interfering with the affairs of the Ukrainian authorities and, from Moscow, thwarting the construction of a monument.

The involvement of the Soviet premier in shaping the unwritten and unofficial Soviet policy vis-à-vis Babyn Yar does not stand in the way of placing responsibility for the ravine's neglect on the shoulders of his many underlings in Ukraine, and particularly those in Kyiv. This local dimension of the attempts to thwart the public commemoration of Babyn Yar is highlighted by Victoria Khiterer, who views the Ukrainian Soviet Socialist Republic (and particularly its capital) as characterized by exceptionally rampant antisemitism, a sentiment that harkens back to wartime Ukrainian collaboration and the chagrin of many Ukrainian non-Jews at the encounter with Jewish survivors of the Holocaust who returned to the city at the war's end.[21] The validity of these local factors notwithstanding, the invisible hand of Khrushchev was apparent enough in shaping the Soviet stance toward Babyn Yar. The Soviet premier must have realized that, though having the power to revise his predecessor's almost absolute silence with respect to Babyn Yar, this change of direction could bring him only harm. In official statements, Khrushchev was careful to toe the old party line of his predecessor, and he categorically dismissed the two foundations upon which the Soviet silence over Babyn Yar rested: the antisemitism ingrained in the Soviet system and the identification of Babyn Yar as an inherently Jewish mass grave. In a meeting with a group of Russian intellectuals that took place on December 17, 1962, in response to the publication of Yevgeny Yevtushenko's poem "Babi Yar" and the performance of Dmitri Shostakovich's Thirteenth Symphony (which I will discuss in chapter 4), Khrushchev dismissed both accounts:

> This is a very important question—the fight against antisemitism.... I was raised in the Donbas. I was a witness to a pogrom as a child in Yuzovke, and I can say one thing—that the great majority of the miners—even the miners—were opposed to that pogrom. And after the pogrom, when [the region] was swept by a wave of strikes, who were the majority of the orators [who instigated] those strikes? The Jews. They were admired. They were respected. And here comes "Babi Yar." I used to work in Ukraine and went to that Babi Yar. Many people perished there. But comrades, Comrade Yevtushenko, not only Jews were killed there. Gypsies were exterminated there, and next came the turn of the Slavs.... And if we do the math [and

figure out] how many were killed in greater numbers—Jews or Slavs—then those who claim that [this is all based on antisemitism]—would realize that more Slavs were killed [in Babi Yar] than Jews. That is certain. So why divide, why generate this kind of discord? What are the goals of those who raise this question? And why? I think that it is wrong.[22]

Khrushchev's egregious distortion of victim identities and his categorical dismissal of antisemitism as the cause of Babyn Yar's neglect, were, undoubtedly, fully in line with Soviet ideology and its modus operandi: denial that Jew-hatred exists, on the one hand, and the espousal of anti-Jewish discriminatory policies, on the other.[23]

Beyond the Soviet premier's personal prejudices and biases, it was in his best interest to maintain the silencing of Babyn Yar, as the site not only reminded passersby of the dark days of Stalinism but also alluded to the antisemitic prejudice of the person who came to succeed him. Thus, when seen within the context of Khrushchev's highly selective politics of de-Stalinization, it is easier to understand why it took Soviet intellectuals so long to criticize the attempts to destroy Babyn Yar, an eradication process that reached its peak in 1960, when a new dam designed to facilitate the waters flooding into the ravine was constructed near the site.[24] The reticence of the Soviet intelligentsia was revealing—it indicated that they understood Khrushchev's complicity all too well. The present Soviet premier—they all seemed to have received the memo—could not be so easily divorced from the crimes of the Stalinist past, and especially when those crimes persisted in the present. Khrushchev, therefore, had to be exempted from this kind of critical examination.

How are we to account, then, for this very delicate and carefully measured criticism made by Soviet writers and artists against the Soviet regime during this era of relative freedom? Dina Spechler, in her study of the most central intellectual platform of the Thaw period, the periodical *Novy mir*,[25] where literary works containing criticism of the Soviet system under Stalin appeared, contends that the practice of what she calls "permitted dissent" was the fruit of the mutual support that the Soviet intelligentsia and leadership bestowed upon each other. They did so, knowing that their society was in grave need to shift from the path of totalitarianism to a more tolerable, party-centered mode of dictatorship.[26] This process was gradual, convoluted, and fragile and was affected by developments not only within the USSR but outside as well. It was fairly clear that an open discussion of an irritable subject such as Babyn Yar, with its potential of casting a shadow on the image of the Soviet premier, had to be postponed to a distant future. This moment came, at last, in October 1959, toward the Thaw's zenith, when the first attack on the Soviet stance vis-à-vis Babyn Yar was finally launched. It took the form of a short polemical essay published in the literary organ of the Soviet Writers' Union, *Literaturnaya gazeta*, which candidly criticized the

Soviet Ukrainian authorities' attempts to level the site of Babyn Yar and bring about its complete effacement.

As we shall see, while this critical work may neatly fall into the category of permitted dissent, as it was meant to engage rather than confront the Soviet authorities, one could recognize in it the buds of a new development. The essay's author, the Russian writer Viktor Nekrasov, signaled in it that he wished to broaden the boundaries of the permissible and explore a new theme that could potentially shed a negative light on Khrushchev and the post-Stalinist Soviet regime. This was, in other words, still a piece of constructive criticism, yet it was a great deal more audacious than anything that had come before. Over the next two decades, Nekrasov would become one of the most prominent cultural figures of the late Thaw period to uphold the banner of Babyn Yar's memory and turn it into a focal point for Soviet dissent.

As evident from the KGB's[27] archival records, which were culled and published by journalist Liubov Khazan, of all the Soviet Russian intellectuals who saw Babyn Yar as an ideological bone of contention and fought for its commemoration, believing that the Soviet people could not be reformed while ignoring the thousands of dead lying underneath them, Nekrasov was the one to pay the highest personal price: the banning of his works, constant harassment by the KGB, and, since 1974, exile. These records, conjoined with Nekrasov's own statements and those of his peers, portray a picture of a hunted man. The harassment of Nekrasov included random searches in his apartment by KGB agents, who left it in a state of chaos as though after a burglary, interrogations for six days in a row, and constant pressure to betray some of his close friends.[28] It is the image of a man who, under these toxic, coercive conditions, decided to leave the motherland that he had defended as a Red Army captain more than thirty years earlier in Stalingrad, only to find out later, from his exile in Paris, that his Soviet citizenship had been revoked and that he would never see his beloved country and city again.[29] Nekrasov's essay—what is, essentially, an op-ed, not a work of art—had a pioneering quality. It would act as a harbinger for the work of other non-Jewish Russian artists who would give the debate over Babyn Yar in the Russian cultural sphere its ultimate shape.

## FROM THE TRENCHES OF STALINGRAD TO THE COLD WAR FRONT

In the wake of the Hungarian Revolution in October 1956, the dawn of de-Stalinization came to a halt. It was now time for the Soviet government to resort to repression in the handling of writers and artists. That this popular uprising, which took place in a Soviet satellite country, was endorsed and encouraged by a group of Communist intellectuals served only to alarm the Soviet leadership about the perils of intellectual freedom when harnessed against the Soviet regime itself. Khrushchev, in a bid to ensure that these developments would not spill into his own country, during a conversation with writers at the beginning of 1957 warned his guests that in the eventuality of a similar situation in the USSR he "would know what to do with them, and his hand would not tremble."[30] Two years later, however, during the Third Congress of Soviet Writers in 1959, Khrushchev's curtailment of literary freedom seemed to be toning down. The quelling of the anti-CPSU coup that had been plotted against him and the launching of the first Sputnik in 1957 managed to restore his confidence in the policy of de-Stalinization, which he seemed to have lost in the aftermath of the Hungarian Crisis. The conquering of space signaled to the Soviet leadership (and to many Soviet citizens too), once again, that a great future awaited the empire under Khrushchev's rule.[31]

During the second half of the 1950s, the Soviet political and literary scenes were in a state of limbo: on the one hand, Khrushchev, who toward the end of the decade saw his country's economy and industry slowly recovering from the devastation wrought by the war, was no longer feeling in dire need of the support of either the scientific or the artistic intelligentsia. The mass popularity he had enjoyed in the wake of the Secret Speech no longer seemed as crucial to his political survival as before. The Hungarian Crisis only reinforced his conviction that the previous campaign of relaxation and benign liberalism must be decelerated. On the other hand, it was clear to Khrushchev and his apparatchiks in charge of ideology and the arts—as much as it was to the Soviet intellectual elite—that the days of the Stalinist harassment, imprisonment, and assassination of artists were already behind them and that the process of de-Stalinization was by now unstoppable.[32]

Against the background of this fluctuation between liberalization and repression, there appeared, on October 10, 1959, a short essay by the Russian writer Viktor Nekrasov titled "Why Has It Not Been Done?" Its aim was laser-focused: it protested the Kyiv City Council's attempts to flood Babyn Yar, fill it with mud, and later lay out on its territory a park and a stadium.[33] Published by a Russian writer who had established himself already as one of the leading members of the post-Stalin era Soviet intelligentsia, this essay constituted the first overt act of protest against the Soviet attempts to suppress the memory of Babyn Yar.[34] Up until the appearance of this essay, the various references to the massacre at the ravine, as we recall, were meant only to sustain Babyn Yar's memory in the public consciousness—they were not meant to directly raise any objection to the measures taken at that time by the Soviet regime. In his essay, Nekrasov was the first to seek the latter course of action and protest the Soviet attempts to destroy Babyn Yar that were then only gathering momentum. With Nekrasov's essay, Babyn Yar became, for the first time, not only a symbol for the Holocaust in the Soviet Union, but, no less importantly, one of the tropes of dissent within the Soviet Union,

Soviet Russian writer Viktor Nekrasov. (Photo from the Central Archives for the History of the Jewish People; Emmanuel Diamant.)

signaling both internally and externally that the Soviet cultural sphere was not an ideological monolith.

The essay was well received: two months later, in response to it, a group of residents living in the Babyn Yar vicinity sent a letter to *Literaturnaya gazeta* endorsing Nekrasov's demand for a monument dedicated to the victims of fascism to be built. They had but one reservation, which was that no objection to the construction of a park over the site be considered, as Babyn Yar could not simply be left intact and its incorporation into the postwar greater Kyiv area was inevitable.[35] Thereafter, the vice chairman of the Executive Committee of the Kyiv State Council of Workers' Deputies, T. Skirda, announced a decision made in December 1959 to erect an obelisk at Babyn Yar with a plaque noting that the site functioned in 1941 as a Nazi mass murder site. Although the plan was vetoed later on by Khrushchev, the pressure that Nekrasov and the other Russian intellectuals who followed in his footsteps exerted on the Soviet government led to the ultimate placement of an obelisk at Babyn Yar in 1966.

Markedly, the obelisk included an inscription fully aligned with the official Soviet position that Babyn Yar was a Great Patriotic War and not a Holocaust site. As it turned out, however, its erection helped turn Babyn Yar into a focal point for memorial assemblies and rallies. Attended by those who came to protest the Soviet stance toward Babyn Yar and commemorate it as a distinct tragedy of Soviet Jews, these rallies were precisely where Soviet dissent of the late 1960s and the Soviet Jewish nationalist movement intersected. Not coincidentally, Nekrasov became one of the key figures to propel these efforts since 1966.[36] We shall see below, though, that while he was a key leader of this grassroots movement, Nekrasov was not a lone actor. And we shall see that the question of who initiated these unauthorized commemorations has more than one answer.

The first monument at Babyn Yar, erected in 1966. (Photo from the Central Archives for the History of the Jewish People; Emmanuel Diamant.)

In its format, while squarely criticizing the Kyiv City Council's plan to turn the site into a recreational center, Nekrasov's essay of late 1959 had all the features of a piece of permitted dissent. It came out, after all, through official Soviet publication channels and must have been endorsed to a certain extent by the Soviet censor. Nevertheless, in the essay Nekrasov approached the neglect of Babyn Yar in a fashion bolder than ever before. Evidently, the three years that had passed since the Hungarian Crisis and the pronouncements made by Khrushchev hinting that a new wave of liberalization was imminent gave both Nekrasov and the editors of *Literaturnaya gazeta* the confidence they needed to openly address a topic that was hitherto completely covered up. If these signals of an approaching relaxation enabled the publication of the essay, what gave it a sense of urgency was the ongoing flooding of the ravine that would play a decisive role in the history of Babyn Yar.

Nekrasov's essay was more than an expression of disagreement over a specific wrongdoing by a certain municipality in the vast Soviet empire. The essay raised, rather directly, the moral repercussions of Soviet postwar urban reconstruction efforts. This process, according to Nekrasov, was morally flawed because it involved erasing any traces that alluded to the horrific toll that the German occupation had taken on the country. The Russian author was the first to point to the character of postwar Kyiv as a city having a "memory black hole" in its midst as a city mendaciously attempting to recover from the trauma of Nazi ruin by completely turning its back on its past.[37] Appalled by this attitude, he argued that ethical, farsighted considerations must guide the Kyiv City Council, rather than the immediate, practical need for new roads to connect Babyn Yar to the greater Kyiv area. In the last two paragraphs of his essay, Nekrasov points out that the city's natural expansion drive must not come at the expense of the basic human need to remember and honor the dead:

> Is that possible? Who could think of that? To fill a ravine 30 m deep, and to make merry and play football where the greatest tragedy took place.
> No, it's impermissible!
> When a man dies, he is buried, and a monument is placed on his grave. Can it be that such a token of respect is not deserved by the 195,000 people of Kyiv brutally shot in Babi Yar, Syrets, Darnitsa, the Kirillov Hospital, the Monastery, the Lukyanoka Cemetery?![38]

In the introduction to our study, we observed a number of representations of Babyn Yar's memory characteristic of the Cold War and looked at how the ravine was approached as a zero-sum game as either a Holocaust or a Great Patriotic War site. Perhaps the most conspicuous detail transpiring from the quotation above is what seems at first to be Nekrasov's reiteration of what we have seen already: Soviet officialdom's tendency to ignore the anti-Jewish nature of the German Nazi genocidal policies and regard all victims of Nazism as Great Patriotic War casualties. To put it another way, what no reader of the essay, either a contemporary or current one, can avoid is the following question: What exactly was the policy—and by extension the mentality—that Nekrasov stood against?

On the surface, it seems as though, first and foremost, Nekrasov was protesting not the Soviet government's suppression of the Holocaust but rather its suppression of the Great Patriotic War. By citing the figure of 195,000 dead, a number corresponding to the Extraordinary Commission's report on the total number of fascism's victims in the entire vicinity of Kyiv (more on the work of the Extraordinary Commission in chapter 5), Nekrasov's concern was both all-Soviet and universal as he presented the Nazi victims monolithically. Upon closer examination, and once we juxtapose the essay with Nekrasov's unpublished work of the same period together with his other published work, his stance turns out to have been a great deal more complicated. Since Nekrasov was constrained by the limitations of the Soviet censor and since he was acting within the bounds of permitted dissent, it stands to reason that for Nekrasov a specific reference to Jews in his *Literaturnaya gazeta* essay was not really in the cards. Yet, a comparative reading of the Russian writer's censored versus uncensored work reveals a very different Nekrasov, one concerned with a variety of Soviet offenses, not the least of which was the blatantly antisemitic obliteration of Babyn Yar.

## BETWEEN NAZI DESTRUCTION AND SOVIET REPRESSION

When offering a close reading of "Why Has It Not Been Done," we must first pay attention not only to what was left out but, no less importantly, to what was quite strikingly kept in, albeit in the most implicit fashion. Although Nekrasov in his essay zeroed in on merely one issue of contention, those who could read between the lines were able to recognize the condemning subtlety hinted at in the essay—the juxtaposition of the brutal Nazi handling of the Soviet civilian population and the Soviet disregard for their memory. In the Soviet Union in 1959, these were perilous waters to tread, although Nekrasov was not the only Soviet cultural figure to make this analogy. When another great Russian writer, Vasily Grossman, equated the criminal nature of the Nazi and Soviet regimes a year later in his epic novel *Zhizn' i Sud'ba* (*Life and Fate*), his manuscript was promptly confiscated by KGB agents.[39] In later years, first from his Kyiv residence and later from his exile in Paris, Nekrasov would become increasingly explicit about this analogy. Iryna Zakharchuk observes that this became a key feature of his worldview. He was one of the first prominent Soviet culture-makers to realize, imply, and later, while in exile, loudly pronounce that the massacres that took place at Babyn Yar and the destruction of the Jewish cemetery by the German Nazis and later by the Soviets, which led to the spatial effacement of Babyn Yar, were all manifestations of the captive mind in the age of totalitarianism.[40] Needless to say, in order to be published in *Literaturnaya gazeta*, Nekrasov could only draw such parallels in the most oblique fashion.

The recent publication of *Arrested Pages*, a collection of Nekrasov's unpublished work, together with illuminating comments about his oeuvre, dissident activities—among them the struggle to commemorate Babyn Yar—and his constant quest for a truthful life in the midst of what he recognized as a system built on lies, helps us understand Nekrasov's motivations to publish "Why Has It Not Been Done?" In a remarkable essay titled "A Stone over Babi Yar" (the stone is a reference to the 1966 obelisk), written in 1973, a piece Nekrasov never thought he could publish through official Soviet channels (the piece was later confiscated during one of the aforementioned searches to which his apartment was subject), he goes back in time to the late 1950s, the same period when "Why Has It Not Been Done?" was written. Here, in this short essay, Nekrasov makes the reason of his preoccupation with Babyn Yar crystal clear: Soviet antisemitism, which was one of the ailments of Soviet society and which formed the basis for Moscow's unwritten stance toward Babyn Yar.

Interestingly, for Nekrasov the proof for the ubiquity and profundity of antisemitism in shaping Soviet policy is embodied not so much by the ravine itself. After all, Babyn Yar, as Nekrasov acknowledges in "A Gravestone over Babi Yar," was the mass grave containing the bodies of both Soviet Jews and non-Jews.[41] Rather, Nekrasov turns his attention to the old Jewish cemetery adjacent to Babyn Yar, the last station on the path that led the Babyn Yar massacre's victims to their death. In this essay, Nekrasov recalls that by the end of the war the cemetery was in terrible shape: it was vandalized and neglected with broken gravestones lying everywhere. For some reason, he notices that the Nazis, who had no respect for either living or dead Jews, left a large portion of the cemetery intact. When revisiting the site in the late 1950s, he could not believe the specter of havoc that appeared before his eyes of thousands of gravestones that were now razed, upturned, and scattered all over. His reflection on how the Soviet crimes seamlessly succeeded the Nazi crimes merits citation:

> This sacrilege was started by the Germans. With their methodical [precision], they destroyed all gravestones in the main alley. The next alleys the Hitlerites did not reach [for some reason], so tens of thousands of other gravestones were left untouched....
>
> What further unfolded is inexplicable. I cannot tell when that happened, but when I happened to stop by the cemetery in the late 1950s, I could not believe what my eyes first saw: the cemetery had been fully destroyed. Fully, that is, not a single gravestone had been left intact. All of these [gravestones], I repeat, no less than tens of thousands of them, were [now] turned upside down, shattered... there were no exceptions. This destructive force of inertia touched all gravestones, not even one had been spared.
>
> As I was standing beside these ruined gravestones, I asked myself: Who did it? And what kind of hate could have led a person to this degree of vandalism? I wrote "person," yet in order to commit this sacrilege, hundreds of hands were needed; you cannot manage [to do so] with a handful of shovels.... I could imagine with some difficulty [how] some punks and hooligans, armed with whatever heavy tools [were] at their disposal, in a frenzy of drunkenness, could crush anything that would come their way, left and right. But with this kind of hefty force, losing all measures of shame, these boors could have destroyed [perhaps] ten, twenty, fifty gravestones. But who destroyed the rest? And with what destructive means? With bulldozers? Tractors? TNT? And when did it happen? During the day, at night? And how long did it take— a week, two, a month?[42]

In addition to this recently published piece revealing Nekrasov's motivations to write the October 1959 essay, a short autobiographical story that he wrote in late 1974 while in Paris (it had been, in fact, rejected for publication by *Novy mir*) titled "Zapiski zevaki" (Notes of a bystander) echoed the same sentiments underlying "A Gravestone over Babi Yar." In it, Nekrasov begins by making a reference to the infamous Aktion (Operation) 1005, the code name for the Nazi campaign to erase all evidence of the mass extermination of European Jewry launched in June 1942 that ran until late 1944:[43]

> And then the Nazis left. They were trying to conceal the traces of their own crimes. But how can you conceal.... They forced the prisoners of war to incinerate the bodies; to gather them into piles and burn [them]. But you cannot burn all of them.
> Then [they] flooded the ravine.[44]

According to Nekrasov, it was exactly the short episode in these autobiographical sketches dealing with Babyn Yar, including in the quotation above, that resulted in the rejection of "Notes of a Bystander" by *Novy mir*. Nekrasov further relates that his attempt to submit it to another journal, the less liberal *Moskva*, was followed not only by the story's rejection, but also by his exclusion from the Communist Party, another step in the deterioration of his standing vis-à-vis the Soviet regime that would later lead to his emigration.[45]

All that happened later, when the atmosphere of relative liberalism ran its course and gave way to the coming to power of Brezhnev and Kosygin, who, together with other conservative, neo-Stalinist elements in the government and party apparatus, brought the Thaw period to an abrupt end. In "Notes of a Bystander" and "A Gravestone over Babi Yar," Nekrasov sheds light on what drove him to protest the flooding of Babyn Yar in his 1959 essay. From this intertextual reading, the ideological motivation underpinning the essay becomes clearer: the Russian author's protest of the Soviet regime's efforts to make all evidence of the death of tens of thousands of its own people wholly evaporate. It was a practice that had been started by the Nazis but that was resumed by the Soviets.

Nekrasov was the first to dwell on the moral implications that underlay the actions of the local Kyiv authorities. "Why Has It Not Been Done?" was also unprecedented in other respects. It was the first time that precise details about the September 29–30 events were given to the Soviet public after fifteen years of silence. If mentioning the silenced massacre was not enough, Nekrasov told his audience that the Soviet regime, while communicating to the entire world the news about the atrocities at the site only a few months after they had taken place, overturned in the wake of the war its own proposal to construct a monument at the site. By mentioning the rejected sketches proposed by Vlasov and Ovchinnikov, Nekrasov suggested that it was not a passive process of forgetting that led to the neglect of Babyn Yar but, on the contrary, a highly active one.

Moreover, Nekrasov hinted that the events at Babyn Yar were all well-orchestrated by none other than the first secretary of the CPSU, Nikita Khrushchev himself. True, Nekrasov did not mention Khrushchev by name. But it did not require much effort to identify the culprit of the crime committed against Babyn Yar. The appearance of the essay in a Moscow journal, rather than a local, Ukrainian one, also alluded to the fact that Nekrasov's concern for Babyn Yar's neglect was nothing short of an attack leveled at the very top of the Soviet hierarchy. It suggested that this matter had to be resolved, not by the Kyiv City Council but by an entity higher up the chain. Inasmuch as the man who had headed the CPSU during the conclusion of World War II was now the head of the entire USSR, Nekrasov, by sending his essay to *Literaturnaya gazeta*, showed his awareness of the fact that when it came to Babyn Yar, Moscow and Kyiv politics were completely intertwined. As we shall see, this step made by Nekrasov would later be emulated by other Russian writers. Like Nekrasov, they would also pursue the turning of Babyn Yar from a minor, local matter into an issue that had to resonate beyond the realms of the Ukrainian Soviet Socialist Republic's capital, and ultimately attract the attention of the international community.

## BABYN YAR DE-JUDAIZED?

How can one account for this sudden appearance of this first protest of the Soviet treatment of Babyn Yar's memory that, despite its obliqueness, was extraordinary and unprecedented at the time of its publication? While some signs that changes for the better in Khrushchev's relationship with the intelligentsia were noticeable toward the turn of the new decade, it was, as we saw earlier, not simply a matter of timing that facilitated the publication of Nekrasov's "Why Has It Not Been Done?" but also a key omission. For without taking the word "Jews" out of the essay, it is highly unlikely that the piece would have seen the light of day. Readers of the essay on both sides of the Iron Curtain could not pass over the fact that nowhere in it did Nekrasov make any reference to the fact that it was, overwhelmingly, Jews who were murdered at Babyn Yar on September 29–30, 1941, as well as in the subsequent killing operations that took place at the site. Instead of speaking about Jews, Nekrasov only asserted that "on September 29, 1941, the Hitlerites drove here some tens of thousands of peaceful people who were guilty of no crime and shot them mercilessly."[46]

This omission, of course, was not a coincidence, especially if one considers the predicament of Soviet Jewry in the late 1950s. While, as we noted above, this period could be seen, in hindsight, as a fitting time for the appearance of permitted dissent, of works like Nekrasov's essay, the same period also witnessed the deterioration of the Soviet state's relationship with its Jewish citizens. This trend, taking place as part of a general anti-religious campaign that was launched between the years 1957 and 1964, underpinned the degree of freedom Nekrasov had to associate Jews with Babyn Yar. Although this campaign targeted Soviet religious institutions across the board, it took a marked toll on Jewish synagogues and cemeteries.[47] Together with the closure of synagogues, which remained during those years the last vestige of Jewish communal life, the campaign was accompanied by virulent attacks against Jews both in the media and on the street. Only six days before Nekrasov's essay appeared, a synagogue and the home of the Jewish cemetery warden were burned in the town of Malakhovka, which was known as the "Jewish capital of the Moscow region." This attack, leading to the death of the warden's wife, was the culmination of a malicious campaign launched by a local gang that had named itself "Beat the Jews and Save Russia" after the slogan of the notorious antisemitic group of the czarist era, the Black Hundreds.[48] Against this backdrop, it is easier to understand why Nekrasov's particularistic concerns about Jewish memory found no expression in his *Literaturnaya gazeta* essay.

There were some who, in response to the carefully chosen wording by Nekrasov, contended that by referring to the September 29–30 massacre without mentioning the Jews the Russian writer helped reinforce the Soviet reluctance to admit that Babyn Yar was a site of a distinctly Jewish tragedy. Jeff Mankoff, for instance, has argued that the essay was "one of the first attempts to both acknowledge the importance of Babyn Yar and reject the centrality of its Jewish narrative."[49] Instead of countering the official Soviet posture, so the argument goes, Nekrasov, a leading member of the intelligentsia, only gave it approbation. He did so most conspicuously by drawing upon the data that had first appeared in the March 1, 1944, *Pravda* report about Nazi atrocities in the Kyiv area, compiled by the Extraordinary Commission, and even more so by using its terminology—that is, by mentioning "peace-loving Soviet citizens" rather than "Jews."

Nekrasov's essay was in agreement with this earlier report not only in this respect. As noted, by relying on the statistical figures of the dead gleaned by the Extraordinary Commission, the essay placed the Babyn Yar massacre in the context of other Nazi war crimes, thereby downplaying its distinct character. In the excerpt cited above, Nekrasov plainly refers to the number of dead whose memory deserved the attention of Soviet officials: 195,000 victims. A glimpse into the details provided by Nekrasov as he cites the findings of the Extraordinary Commission shows that these figures amounted to the total number of victims of Nazism in the city: the 100,000 who died at Babyn Yar, added to the 68,000 POWs and citizens who were shot in the Darnitsa labor camp, the 25,000 POWs and citizens who were shot near the Syretsky camp, and, finally, a smaller number of victims from other Nazi massacres.[50] The fact that the victims buried in Babyn Yar amounted to only half of those whose murder Nekrasov called on his comrades never to forget, and that among them were not only Jews but Russians and Ukrainians as well, may indicate that the memory of the Jews was not Nekrasov's single concern in his essay. There were, therefore, some who assumed that Nekrasov's mention of Jews and non-Jews, soldiers and civilians, in one breath reflected a desire to call for the commemoration of all of those who fell victim to fascism during the German occupation of Kyiv, irrespective of their ethnic affiliation, reiterating thus a quite widespread Soviet policy (not applied to Babyn Yar, though, which was condemned by Moscow to complete neglect). According to this account, what underscored "Why Has It Not Been Done?" was the highlighting of the Great Patriotic War casualties at the expense of the German Nazis' Jewish victims.

If we look for evidence from his *tamizdat* work, the following scene from Nekrasov's autobiographical "Notes of a Bystander" helps highlight his Universalist, rather than Jewish, concerns. Consider how he wraps up his discussion of Babyn Yar, asserting:

> Stop and bow your head.
> People were shot here.
> One hundred thousand.
> By the fascists.
> The first salvo was fired on September 29, 1941.

Here Nekrasov, free of the need to refer to the death of the Jews in a circumlocutory manner, decides to characterize them as "people." It follows from this assertion that Nekrasov viewed the victims of the Babyn Yar massacre as civilian casualties of one of the most horrific events of the Great Patriotic War. This comparative reading suggests that it was not the concern for the commemoration of the Holocaust in the Soviet Union that preoccupied him but rather the Soviet cult of the Great Patriotic War: a cult that took shape following the death of Stalin and that revolved around Soviet war heroism and left in the shadows the war's victims, the helpless civilians together with the POWs.

An examination of Nekrasov's earlier career only further reinforces this one possible reading of Nekrasov's essay. The novel *In the Trenches of Stalingrad*, with which Nekrasov made his literary debut in 1946 and which won him the Stalin Prize the following year, already took issue with the Soviet myth of Stalingrad. In the eyes of Nekrasov, as an ordinary officer who participated in that consequential battle that ushered the beginning of the Third Reich's doom, the postwar Stalingrad myth was far removed from the hardships experienced by the rank-and-file soldiers. The novel offered a rare, candid account of combat during World War II based on Nekrasov's own experience as a commander of a battalion positioned in the beleaguered city. In addition to *In the Trenches of Stalingrad*, another work by Nekrasov, titled "Hometown" (1954), also elaborated on the ordeals facing Red Army soldiers now discharged from their duty and returning home, emotionally and physically scarred and unable to find an honorable place in a society that sought only war heroes and that labeled the invalid veterans, or those bearing the emotional scars of war, as "deviants" or "cowards." These works thus help to highlight the fact that Nekrasov, the veteran writer of World War II, was first and foremost concerned in his essay with a Great Patriotic War cult that had no room whatsoever for the memory of nearly 200,000 Kyiv residents who lost their lives during its course. This leading Soviet writer's criticism of the Soviet government for its disrespect of the victims of fascism was certainly a bold step. But was such criticism tantamount to accusing the Soviet regime of being antisemitic, of denying for decades that the large-scale mass murder that had taken place on the outskirts of Kyiv was an anti-Jewish genocide? Those offering a Universalist reading of the essay would respond that it was certainly not.

"Notes of a Bystander" provides us with another piece of evidence that may help us confirm Nekrasov's Universalist position. Dwelling in this piece on the difference between the Darnitsa prison camp for POWs, the Warsaw Ghetto, and Babyn Yar, Nekrasov concludes that the future monument for the victims of Babyn Yar must underscore the site's distinctiveness. He presents a view of the Babyn Yar massacre as unique, but does not portray the ravine as a uniquely Jewish site:

> The monument at the Warsaw Ghetto is a monument for an uprising, for the struggle against death; the [proposed] monument at Darnitsa for the soldiers, fighters, people who fell captive and had been murdered in a beastly manner... for people, who were for the most part strong, young. But Babyn Yar, this is a *tragedy* of the helpless, the old.[51]

This comparison of the ravine with the other two World War II sites is very telling. Rather than linking Babyn Yar to the Warsaw Ghetto Uprising and the fate of European Jewry, Nekrasov deems the Babyn Yar massacre a universal symbol, exceeding the context of the Jewish people's tragedy. In his eyes, it stands for the degradation of humankind, reaching its nadir when the well-armed soldiers of Europe's mightiest army targeted an innocent civilian population on a scale hitherto unimaginable.

Thus far we have found quite enough evidence for the image of the Universalist Nekrasov to emerge through a work published within the Soviet Union, a *samizdat* short sketch, and a *tamizdat* autobiographical story.[52] But here is exactly where things get a lot more complicated. For when we study the work of Nekrasov through the methodology of cultural history—in the specific historical context in which it was written—the Russian writer emerges as the ultimate champion of the particularistic Jewish view of Babyn Yar. In his writings, in his social activism, and, most importantly, in the price he was willing to pay by putting Babyn Yar at the very top of his agenda, first as a practitioner of permitted dissent and later as an anti-Soviet émigré and a full-blown dissident, Nekrasov emerges as the first non-Jewish champion of the battle to keep the memory of Babyn Yar as a Holocaust site alive. As his friend Venyamin Smekhov noted, Nekrasov never raised an objection when he was accused of being a Jew (an accusation embedded in the next literary work that we will carefully read: Yevgeny Yevtushenko's "Babi Yar"). Nekrasov would always shrug off these attempts to label him: "Don't [the Soviet leaders] call Jewish anyone who is against them, who doesn't agree with them?" he would respond.[53]

There were, therefore, those who took "Why Has It Not Been Done?" to constitute a courageous, unprecedented effort to confront the Soviet regime for its suppression of Babyn Yar as an indispensably Jewish site. Richard Sheldon and Benjamin Pinkus, while noticing Nekrasov's omission of the Jews from his article, could not but credit the Russian writer for bringing up an issue that at a time when Soviet antisemitism was on the rise was very unlikely to receive any attention.[54] The two scholars viewed the essay as primarily concerned with the antisemitic bias that underlay the Soviet silence over Babyn Yar, even though it had to resort to the use of the Aesopian language of "peaceful Soviet citizens" when alluding to the Jewish victims. To support this argument, Edith Clowes refers to the fact that the essay opens with a statement that Babyn Yar is adjacent to the ancient Jewish cemetery of Kyiv by way of hinting obliquely at Babyn Yar as a site of a Jewish tragedy.[55] Clowes, like other proponents of this view, believes that Nekrasov, being unable to do otherwise, used the terminology of the Extraordinary Commission not in order to agree with its anti-Jewish bias but to counter it.

This account of Nekrasov's essay as one concerned with Babyn Yar as a Jewish site may also be supported by the Russian author's testimony offered in his later autobiographical work. In "Notes of a Bystander," Nekrasov goes to great lengths to underscore the fact that the innocent people who had been killed in Babyn Yar were Jewish. On a personal note, he relates that his mother, who had many Jewish friends, warned them not to heed the Nazi command to show up at the assembly point on the morning of September 29, and to run away; she even offered them refuge in her own home.[56] Moreover, while even at this late date Nekrasov still seems ambivalent about how Babyn Yar ought to be commemorated, he leaves no doubt that an antisemitic bias was the true reason behind the Soviet neglect of the site over the decades since the war.[57]

Yet, the most forceful case for the view of Nekrasov as taking immense interest in the fate of the Jews comes from the confiscated "A Gravestone over Babi Yar." We have seen above the categorization of victimhood according to Nekrasov: Darnitsa was the symbol of resistance by a mighty military, the Warsaw Ghetto Uprising was the work of fully isolated, barely armed individuals, and Babyn Yar was the story of the helpless—helpless *people*. In "A Gravestone over Babi Yar," Nekrasov explains why the memory of defenseless civilians is intrinsically a Jewish one:

Babi Yar is a unique, perhaps unprecedented site. They ordered [us] to forget it. They didn't even order it, but rather something was said by somebody: "A monument? Why monument? For those who voluntarily went to their death? Without any resistance, without protest? We do not erect monuments for cowards." When this was said and by whom are not really important; one can only guess, though the grain has fallen onto a fertile soil. In different circumstances, by different people, mostly those with power and influence, I have heard the following words: "They didn't resist." The word "Jews" was never uttered. It would have been considered rude for people to pronounce it, speaking like that was [considered inappropriate], but this is [exactly] what was implied.[58]

Without being aware of its clear Soviet context, one may have thought that this paragraph was written upon a reflection of Yehuda Bauer, the Israeli dean of Holocaust history, who framed the Shoah as "unprecedented but not unique," or as the response of the Warsaw Ghetto Uprising deputy commander Yitzhak Zuckerman, or some of the Eichmann trial witnesses who endeavored to help a young generation of Israelis understand why Hitler's Jewish victims would often go to their death in complete submission. It turns out that the "tragedy of the helpless, the old" was for Nekrasov very clearly the tragedy of the Jewish helpless, the Jewish old.

## MULTIDIRECTIONAL MEMORY

Two salient conclusions may be inferred from Nekrasov's dedication to Babyn Yar. If we presented the relationship between the two meta-narratives of the twentieth century under discussion, the Holocaust and the Great Patriotic War, as two overlapping nonconcentric circles, Nekrasov presents a different layout—namely, that of two concentric circles, one (the Great Patriotic War) subsuming the other (the Holocaust in the Soviet Union). According to Kiril Feferman in his study of the Soviet regime's unofficial and unwritten policy vis-à-vis the Holocaust, Nekrasov's conception of the two events was not so different from Moscow's. According to Feferman,

> the Soviet policy rested on two pillars—the latter's Jewish character and its being part and parcel of the Soviet World War heritage.... During the period under study coinciding with Stalin's and Khrushchev's rulership, the Holocaust theme was in fact never totally suppressed.... Once brought to the fore either as a result of tangible Soviet propaganda efforts or in the wake of developments tolerated by the regime, the latter (Khrushchev) made an attempt to subsume it into what the Soviets viewed as the country's war legacy. Thus, the unique qualities of the Jewish tragedy were not highlighted but rather expanded to include the entire Soviet people.[59]

Feferman, who does not overtly dismiss antisemitism as an underlying factor shaping Soviet policy, diverges here from the "Cold Warrior" scholars and critics that we have observed so far, minimizing the notion of antisemitism in Soviet society and across many echelons of the Soviet bureaucracy having a preponderant impact on the Soviet approach to the Holocaust. For Feferman, the casting of a shadow on the Holocaust—on Soviet soil, and by extension, beyond its boundaries too—was done on reasonable grounds, given the horrendous circumstances of the Nazi onslaught in the east, the death of more than 24 million Soviet civilians and military personnel, and the havoc wrought across the vast expanses of the Soviet western frontiers, an Armageddon-like cataclysm of which the mass murdering of Jews was only one facet.

A whole different understanding of the relationship between two of the twentieth century's most powerful meta-narratives, however, emerges from our reading of Nekrasov. We may imagine the Russian writer's response to the observation above as follows: "Yes, in theory, the legacy of Russia's war could encompass the Holocaust on Soviet soil and, as part of the greater war against fascism, the Holocaust of European Jewry as a whole. But in practice," Nekrasov would argue, "this did not happen because of Soviet antisemitism with its long-standing persistence, social ubiquity, and toxic inhumanity."

What we have here are two opposing interpretations of Nekrasov's essay. As we turn from Nekrasov to the next Soviet culture-maker to put Babyn Yar on the public's agenda, and as we turn from the late 1950s to the early 1960s, it may be worthwhile to pause for a moment and take a deeper glimpse into both readings: Is there really an innate contradiction between the two? Can we not reconcile the view correlating Babyn Yar with the Great Patriotic War and the ravine's conception as a Holocaust site? The truth of the matter is that Nekrasov's original essay, its ambiguous language notwithstanding, seems to criticize the Soviet regime on multiple issues and sets for itself goals that are not necessarily contradictory. From the standpoint of Nekrasov, the implicitly antisemitic suppression of the Holocaust and the overly patriotic Great Patriotic War cult were two policies employed to achieve the same goal: the glorification of the Soviet people and the Red Army during the war as the legitimating myth of the Soviet system. This myth, no matter how useful it was, was something the Russian author found objectionable, if not repulsive. He understood all too well how this myth came at the expense of a candid process of reckoning with the harsh realities of World War II—that is, of enormous civilian casualties, of major military blows, and, yes, of genocide too: the mass murder of Soviet Jews on Soviet soil.

Of all the writers and culture-makers surveyed in our study, the work of Viktor Nekrasov best embodies the nature of collective memory as multidirectional. As Michael Rothberg, the one who coined the term, contends, multidirectional memory is a framework resisting the otherwise common tendency to construe the interaction between the collective memories of different ethnic groups in a multicultural society as a "zero-sum game over scarce resources." In its stead, Rothberg calls for a new and more optimistic understanding of this interaction as a "productive, intercultural dynamic."[60] He adds that "it is often difficult to tell whether a given act of memory is more likely to produce competition or mutual understanding—sometimes both seem to happen simultaneously."[61] Thus, the conception of Babyn Yar offered by Nekrasov brings multidirectional memory from theory into practice. It demonstrates that Moscow's postulate—namely, that the memory of the war and the sacrifice made by Soviet citizens stand in complete contrast with the Jewish narrative—was only one possibility among many others. In Nekrasov's work, one finds an alternative stance, which views both narratives as harmonious and Babyn Yar as a connecting trope rather than a dividing one. In other words, Moscow's silence on Babyn Yar emblematized its inhumanity toward *both* its Jewish population *and* its general population along with its ignorance of the way in which both the Holocaust and the Great Patriotic War should have been remembered.

The view of Nekrasov's work as containing two conflicting messages that simply cannot coexist therefore fails to take into account the historical and cultural context in which the debate about Babyn Yar's memory took place. As we have seen, this debate was an indispensable part of the evolution of permitted dissent, the process through which new voices began to emanate from post-Stalinist Russia and went as far as mildly criticizing specific Soviet policies while manifesting overall support for the Communist enterprise. In this sense, we may summarize the legacy of Viktor Nekrasov by highlighting two of his main accomplishments. The first was his ability to delineate the contours of the public debate about Babyn Yar as it took shape during the Thaw period. As we shall see later in this study, the Russian artists who later joined Nekrasov would also criticize the Soviet policy vis-à-vis Babyn Yar in a moderate fashion, leaving some leeway for ambiguity as they would not draw a clear dichotomy between the memory of Babyn Yar as a Holocaust site and a Great Patriotic War one. Curiously, they would all approach Babyn Yar as outsiders to the collective of its victims and their relatives and descendants, as they, like Nekrasov, did not have a Jewish background. Each of them in their own unique way would practice permitted dissent but, at the same time, would keep pushing against the boundaries of the permissible. Nekrasov's second accomplishment, which is no less important, was the identification of the Babyn Yar massacre—and by extension the Holocaust on Soviet soil—as an indispensable part of what the *true* narrative of the Great Patriotic War represented. This is why the two views presented here, while seen as contradictory for some Cold Warriors, were in clear harmony both in Nekrasov's eyes and the eyes of many Soviet citizens, among them Soviet Jews.

From the publication of "Why Has It Not Been Done?" onward, the clamor over Babyn Yar's neglect would make headway and gradually intensify. In the next stage, a new work, no doubt the most famous to have been written about Babyn Yar, would appear in the Russian literature of the Thaw period: the poem "Babi Yar" by Yevgeny Yevtushenko. Its author, while approaching the ravine's memory with no less ambiguity than Nekrasov, would now deviate from his fellow Russian writer on a critical issue. Casting aside the "peace-loving Soviet citizens" referred to by Nekrasov, Yevtushenko would proclaim in the very first stanza of his poem that Babyn Yar was a Jewish site. And he will go ahead to present a new vision of Babyn Yar, linking it not only with the fate of Soviet Jewry during World War II but with the Jewish people as an entity transcending time and space.

# 3

# THE SECOND THAW

*For that reason I am a true Russian.*
YEVGENY YEVTUSHENKO, "BABI YAR"

THE SOVIET CULTURAL SCENE HAD TO AWAIT POLITICAL CHANGES BEFORE A more candid and open discussion of the true reasons behind the ravine's neglect could take place. It was only later, at the beginning of the new decade, that a substantial change in the regime's attitude toward the arts and intellectual freedom became evident. This shift of policy brought about a period of two years of relaxation of the harsh censorship and the suppression of writers, a period commonly referred to as the "Second Thaw."[1] Two major factors—unrelated to each other—underlay this shift in the Soviet cultural atmosphere: Khrushchev's change of heart toward the expression of dissent, and the coming to the fore of a young, dynamic, and vocal group of intellectuals—a new generation with whose demands for artistic freedom Khrushchev and his old-guard conservative associates soon needed to reckon.

Once he established himself in power as the unassailable leader of the Soviet Union and was able to keep in check the political unrest within the Soviet satellite states, Khrushchev decided to seize the opportunity presented by the occasion of the convening of the Twenty-Second Party Congress, held in October 1961, to return, now in full vigor, to the course of de-Stalinization that he seemed to have abandoned in the wake of the Hungarian Revolution. Khrushchev's denunciation of Stalin in his speech addressing the congressional delegates was part of a broader move on his part: for the first time after the Secret Speech, he seemed to be back again on the side of the liberal, left-leaning wing of the Soviet intelligentsia, signaling that his regime would welcome the greater involvement of this group in politics and allow the publication of their works.[2]

Khrushchev now allowed works that offered a far more profound exploration of the Stalinist past. For the first time, the detachment of Khrushchev himself from the crimes of the Stalinist past, a sentiment that he had attempted to instill in Soviet public consciousness ever since he had come to power, was called into question. Most representative of these works were Alexander Solzhenitsyn's *One Day in the Life of Ivan Denisovich* (in which the Soviet public was given, for the first time, a glimpse into the degradation of innocent Soviet citizens in the Stalinist prison-camp system), Ilya Ehrenburg's memoirs (where Ehrenburg shared his recollections of the Great Terror, implying that if he himself had known that innocent people, loyal Communists, were being arrested and executed at that time, Khrushchev must have also fully been aware of this),[3] and, as we shall explore in great detail below, the poem "Babi Yar" by Yevgeny Yevtushenko.

How is one to make sense of this move back to the course of de-Stalinization on the part of Khrushchev after several years in which artistic and intellectual freedom were strictly curtailed? Though it is not difficult to hypothesize about why Khrushchev wanted to keep playing the card of de-Stalinization both domestically and abroad, the reason for his change of heart most relevant to our discussion may be found not in any immediate political considerations but rather in his temper. As Peter Kenez remarks, Khrushchev was the last Soviet leader to be loyal to the Marxist-Leninist ideology and revolutionary spirit. He espoused policies that he believed would turn the Soviet Union into the mightiest, most prosperous, and technologically as well as culturally advanced civilization on earth even at the price of current crises and instability.[4] When it came to the cultural arena, this proclivity on the part of Khrushchev for change, experimentation, and risk-taking was best reflected in the Communist Party's new program, which he adopted in June 1961, only three months after Yuri Gagarin became the first man to orbit the earth, signaling to the whole world that the Soviet way of life was synonymous with modernity and progress.[5]

The optimistic program, declaring what seemed at that time like a promise to bring about a quasi-utopian advent of socialism within a matter of twenty years, envisioned a future Soviet society that would be sustained by a great literature and culture predicated on the Thaw period's motto—the demand from artists of absolute sincerity.[6] While in accordance with the new program, artists, as in the past, needed to conform to the party line, such fidelity was now defined in the broadest terms. Artists were now allowed greater freedom to demonstrate "individual creative initiative, a high degree of craftsmanship, and a variety of creative forms, styles, and genres."[7] The program focused on the farsighted revolutionary future instead of only factoring in Khrushchev's minor, tactical considerations. It reflected a genuine desire on his part to reenergize Soviet society and culture even at the price of compromising political stability in the short term, an approach that no other Soviet leader to succeed him would be willing to take.

If the elderly Soviet leader was young only in spirit, the other force that drove this change was also young in flesh: the group of newly arrived Soviet intellectuals who came to artistic maturity during the years 1956–1961—the *shestidesiatniki*—the Soviet

Union's "1960s generation."[8] The *shestidesiatniki* were a group of young people who were now in their late twenties and early thirties. They came of age during World War II and could vividly remember only the last years of Stalinism. Not experiencing the full cycle of the Stalinist terror, this new cohort of intellectuals was more adamant in their demand for freedom of expression when compared with their predecessors. These liberal values, coupled with a penchant for poetry, were meant to signify their contribution to the present as much as it harkened back to the previous century—to the Russian liberal intelligentsia of the 1860s, who also came to be known as the *shestidesiatniki*.[9]

In a young society, where only 10 percent of the population was over 60 years of age,[10] it was the members of this generation who took Khrushchev up on his willingness to loosen the screws of censorship and who gave Soviet culture of the early 1960s its new shape. While not radical and libertarian in comparison with their American peers, the *shestidesiatniki*—if we consider their dress code, language, literary taste, and civil courage—were perceived by the older generation in a manner similar to parallel developments in Western countries. These men and women were, clearly, a new, uneasy-to-digest force of youthful nature that exhibited reluctance to play by the rules of their predecessors, and they exhibited this reluctance rather overtly. The rebelliousness of the *shestidesiatniki* found expression not only in the new literary style of their representative writers but also in the way the latter were now venerated by their audiences. If in countries beyond the Iron Curtain the icons of the new mass culture of rebellious youth were rock-and-roll bands, a similar role was played in the Soviet Union by poets and bards, whose poetry recitation concerts drew thousands of keen poetry enthusiasts throughout the country. By way of renewing the Russian literary tradition of the Golden and Silver Ages, these rising young stars were now looked up to by their peers as the prophets of an entire generation. And while poets like Andrei Voznesensky and Bella Akhmadulina, or the bard Bulat Okudzhava, to name only a few, emerged as leading cultural figures of this new Soviet generation, no one came to epitomize and represent the *shestidesiatniki* more than Yevgeny Yevtushenko.[11]

Indeed, Yevtushenko self-identified as a *shestidesyatnik*, in addition to viewing himself as "a child of the Communist Party's Twentieth Congress."[12] Born in Siberia in 1932 in the small town of Zima located off the Trans-Siberian Railway, the poet spent his childhood in Moscow and was evacuated to his hometown when the war broke out. After the war ended, he moved back to the Soviet capital to attend a school for poets there and, later, between the years 1951 and 1954, the renowned Maxim Gorky Literature Institute.[13] Not unlike other members of his generation, he came to the forefront of the Russian literary scene right after Khrushchev's Secret Speech,[14] but it was only in the early 1960s, and more particularly with the publication of "Babi Yar" on September 19, 1961, in *Literaturnaya gazeta*, that his fame reached its zenith within and outside the Soviet Union. In fact, his fame at that time was unparalleled by any other Soviet cultural figure.[15]

Beyond any other reason, what made the poem "Babi Yar" so transformative, not only in the career of Yevtushenko but in Soviet literature in general, was the fact that for the first time since the death of Stalin a writer dared to touch upon a subject hitherto deemed nearly completely taboo. The poem's first readers found in it not only (as in the case of Nekrasov's article) a protest against the Soviet neglect of Babyn Yar, but also an accusation—implicit yet fairly clear even to the lay reader—that the absence of a monument at the site and the ongoing attempts to flood it were fraught with strong antisemitic underpinnings.[16] From the very first stanza of the poem, it was clear that for Yevtushenko Babyn Yar is a memory space standing for the tragedy of the Jewish people:

> *No monument stands over Babi Yar*
> *A drop sheer as a crude gravestone*
> *I am afraid.*
> *Today I am as old in years*
> *As all the Jewish people.*
> *Now I seem to be*
> *A Jew.*
> *Here I plod through ancient Egypt.*
> *Here I perish crucified, on the cross,*
> *And to this day, I bear the scars of nails.*[17]

As it transpired from the poem, it was antisemitism and nothing else that was the real cause of Babyn Yar's neglect, described now as a time-honored malice infecting many levels of Soviet society—a staple of the Stalinist past that Khrushchev's de-Stalinization campaign had either not succeeded in eradicating or had not attempted to abolish.

In his autobiography, published almost two years later in France without the permission of the Soviet censor, Yevtushenko went to great lengths to describe the vicissitudes that preceded the publication of his poem. He reports that soon after he came back to Moscow from his visit to Kyiv, he felt an urge to read the poem publicly. He managed to do it on September 16, 1961, when he recited the poem in front of a crowd of 12,000 students at the Moscow Polytechnic Institute.[18] As he finished the recitation, Yevtushenko recalls that the crowd turned from a deadly silence to frantic applause, a reaction that prompted the twenty-eight-year-old poet to rush to the *Literaturnaya gazeta* office and submit his poem for publication.[19] While approving of the sincerity and quest for justice reflected in the poem, the newspaper's editor in chief, Valery Kosolapov, warned the poet outright that he was crossing a line into new and dangerous territory.

Front page of the October 1961 issue of the *Literaturnaya gazeta*.
Yevtushenko's poem "Babi Yar" is at the bottom.

Kosolapov was right. The poem was perceived by its first readers, according to both Shimon Markish and Edith Clowes, as a literary bombshell.[20] After its appearance in *Literaturnaya gazeta*, it would not be reprinted in the Soviet Union in the many collections of his poetry published by Yevtushenko throughout his career up until 1983.[21] Its publication cost the editor in chief his position and, correspondingly, triggered a barrage of attacks by conservative critics that would reach a peak twice, in December 1962 and in March 1963, when the poem would be condemned by Khrushchev himself at two meetings with writers and artists.[22] Beyond the narrow realm of Soviet literature, the poem stirred a worldwide uproar. In historical perspective, no literary work was as pivotal as Yevtushenko's poem in turning the ravine into a focal point for the general Soviet as well as the particular Soviet Jewish nationalist dissident movements. In hindsight, there is no doubt that Yevtushenko's poem must receive full recognition for its role in leading to the construction of the official monuments for Babyn Yar's victims—the small obelisk in 1966 and the massive socialist-realist structure that was unveiled ten years later.[23]

There are differing accounts on what motivated Yevtushenko to take a particular interest in the tragedy of Babyn Yar and create for it a literary monument in the form of a poem. To begin with, it was not an event on the ground that provoked Yevtushenko to write "Babi Yar," but rather another poem carrying the same title and written by the Russian Jewish writer Lev Ozerov (Goldberg), a piece hailed by Maxim Shrayer as "the most profound treatment of the topic in Russian poetry."[24] Ozerov, who was also the author of the essay on Babyn Yar in *The Black Book*, wrote his "Babi Yar" in 1944–1945 in response to a request he had received from Ehrenburg to go back to his native Kyiv, visit Babyn Yar, and write a poem reflecting on the traces of carnage and destruction left in the wake of the German forces' retreat.[25] Ozerov's poem was published in the journal *Oktyabr'* (October) in April–May of 1946 and, as we shall see, shares with Yevtushenko's "Babi Yar" many intertextual similarities, as Yevtushenko elaborates on themes, metaphors, and the imperative call to action to never forget, following in Ozerov's footsteps.

According to another account, the origins of Yevtushenko's poem were not textual but physical—they were connected to his visit to Kyiv and Babyn Yar as a young man. Even for this visit, however, there is more than one origin story. In an interview with Yevtushenko, published six years before his passing, the poet recalled that the Russian writer and Kyiv resident Anatoly Kuznetsov was the one who traveled with him to Babyn Yar for the first time, so he could bear witness to the disparity between the sacred mass graves and the landfill it turned into. Yevtushenko relates the sense of shock as he stood in front a line of trucks driving in and out of the ravine and dumping trash into it. Others, like Rafael Nakhmanovich and Valentin Bondarovskoy, figures closely familiar with Viktor Nekrasov, suggested that it was not Kuznetsov but rather Nekrasov who told Yevtushenko first about Babyn Yar. Still others, like Vitaly Korotich, the editor of the journal *Ogonyok*, recall that it was during Yevtushenko's meeting with him and the Ukrainian literary critic Ivan Dziuba that he asked to see the site of Babyn Yar, not in connection with the massacre of Kyiv Jews almost twenty years earlier but due to a more recent calamity known as the *Kurenyovskaya tragedia* or the Kurenivka mudslide.[26]

On March, 13, 1961, a massive stream of mud poured into the Kurenivka district, which was in the vicinity of Babyn Yar, after the dam constructed nearby a year earlier had collapsed and led to the death of over 145 residents.[27] A rumor ran among Kyiv residents that those responsible for the mudslide were the dead victims of Babyn Yar, who exacted their ghostly revenge for the ravine's neglect on the people living in its vicinity. On a less metaphysical level, it was not hard to infer that Kurenivka's culprits were the local Kyiv authorities and all of those involved with the bid to flood the ravine, fill it with pulp, and construct a malfunctioning dam that could not hold this humongous pulp mix.

Regardless of any putative link between the Kurenivka tragedy and the Babyn Yar massacre, the former is not mentioned in Yevtushenko's "Babi Yar." His poem, as becomes apparent from its every verse, is only associated with the Nazi anti-Jewish massacre that took place there beginning in the fall of 1941. As we shall see, this fact represents one of the most salient features of Yevtushenko's artistic-political modus operandi. It would recur throughout his career: his quest for a constant balance between the urge to openly protest the crimes committed by the Soviet regime in the distant past, contrasted by the need to remain silent over the more recent wrongdoings of the Soviet authorities.

Without dismissing the audacity that Yevtushenko had to muster (and as we shall see, this is exactly what some of his critics did) in order to draw the world's attention to the neglect of Babyn Yar as a Holocaust site, the Kurenivka tragedy went totally missing in the poem. Furthermore, as Emanuel (Amik) Diamant, a figure we will return to later in this study, poignantly marked, Yevtushenko's visit to Babyn Yar took place at a time when no ravine in the vicinity of the infamous mass murder site could be found. Put another way, "Babi Yar" begins with a great inaccuracy—or, to be more precise, a falsehood. The ravine he writes about, the "sheer drop" unfolding before his eyes, existed in the fall of 1961 only in his literary imagination. As noted earlier, with the flooding of the area and the filling of Babyn Yar with pulp, Babyn Yar had long earlier turned into a ravine of memory. As we shall later see, this specter of the ravine that was no more is not the only point in "Babi Yar" when the poet takes license to shift from the realms of reality into that of fantasy and wishful thinking.[28]

## BROADENING THE BOUNDARIES OF PERMITTED DISSENT

It has already been noted that the most radical argument made by Yevtushenko in his poem was the accusation that the Soviet regime and large segments of Soviet society were deeply afflicted by antisemitic bias, something that found expression most conspicuously in the neglect of Babyn Yar. As in the case of Nekrasov's essay, what made the poem particularly explosive was the more latent charge embedded in it that Nikita Khrushchev, the present leader of the Soviet Union and the former head of the Ukrainian party apparatus, was deeply involved in this neglect, a vestige of the Stalinist past. Antisemitism, though, was not the only contentious issue conjured up in "Babi Yar." Another, quite sharp, deviation from Marxist-Leninist doctrine was the poem's characterization of the Jewish people. The poem begins with a statement that "no monument stands over Babi Yar," which is exclaimed as the poet's first reaction to the bleak vision he encountered at Babyn Yar. He then goes on to manifest absolute identification with the fate of the Jewish people and sets off on a historical journey through the milestones of Jewish martyrdom. Yevtushenko encompasses over 2,000 years of Jewish history, from the enslavement of the Hebrews in Egypt through the crucifixion of a Jewish man,[29] the Dreyfus affair, and the pogroms of the czarist era, up to the persecution of Jews by the Nazis during World War II as epitomized by the figure of Anne Frank.[30] From the point of view of a regime that insisted that Judaism was only a religion, a vestige of the old order that would sooner or later die out, and refused to acknowledge its ethnic, extraterritorial nature, this exposition of Jewish history as a thread running through different eras and lands was, in itself, irksome from the official Soviet standpoint. At a time when the Communist Party was soon to so proudly announce in its Communist Party program that "the greatest achievement of socialism is the resolution of the national question," or that "the economic and cultural inequality inherited from the old regime has been liquidated,"[31] Yevtushenko's acknowledgment of a historical and currently existing Jewish people, suffering then and now from antisemitism, dealt a blow to official attempts at representing the Jews as an ethnic minority that is well treated by the regime and that is equal to all other Soviet nationalities.

Yevtushenko's "Babi Yar" was thus a multifaceted attack leveled at both Soviet doctrine and the Soviet government, offering an explicit link between the ravine's memory and antisemitism and thereby constituting a break in the way this theme had been handled by Soviet writers up until then. Concomitantly, the poem was a turning point in the career of Yevtushenko himself. Even though in his earliest poems one could already recognize the voice of a rebellious, life-thirsty, and clamorous young man, "Babi Yar" was his first piece to seriously arouse the ire of the Soviet authorities and lead to a worldwide literary sensation. It was only after the appearance of "Babi Yar" that he became an icon of Soviet dissent in the West, a complete novelty for the Western public. It is not surprising that only in the aftermath of this poem's publication did his portrait appear on the cover of *Time* magazine, in April 1962; only after "Babi Yar" did he have 250 poetry reading performances a year that would attract thousands of young followers. Indeed, copies of his books were sold on an unprecedentedly large scale for a young contemporary poet.[32] Together with the upswing in his popularity as a poet, the appearance of "Babi Yar" also made Yevtushenko tower above any other intellectual of his generation as a political figure: he was a poet-dissident boldly ready to confront the Soviet regime by giving publicity to a wrongdoing it had been striving to silence for decades.

In the West, the arrival of a new, bold generation of Soviet poets was met with enthusiasm as evidenced in this *Time* magazine front page. (Image from TIME. © 1962 TIME USA LLC. All rights reserved. Used under license.) This figure appears in color online.

Without diminishing the role played by Yevtushenko in the struggle to commemorate the massacre of Kyiv Jews, his poem, if analyzed carefully, emerges as one endowed with a greater deal of ambiguity than almost any of its critics have acknowledged—that is, from both its liberal supporters and conservative detractors. As much as the poem threatened to split the right and left wings of the Soviet political spectrum when it first appeared, more than a few elements can be found in it that attest to the cautious manner in which the themes elaborated in the poem were selected by Yevtushenko. During the Cold War (and in the years that succeeded it, to a lesser extent)—and this should not come as a surprise—virtually all of the critics who dealt with "Babi Yar," while not oblivious to the fact that the poem appeared in a major Soviet publication, the organ of the Soviet Writers' Union, lauded what they saw as a lonely voice of dissent within the desert of Soviet autocracy. Such appraisals of "Babi Yar" were often made from a narrow angle that could neatly suit their authors' agendas, either regarding the struggle to commemorate Babyn Yar or the general struggle to sustain Jewish life under Soviet pressure. They were often made at the expense of a meticulous reading of the idiosyncratic way in which Yevtushenko chose to commemorate the Babyn Yar massacre.

This interpretation of Yevtushenko's poem through the prism of the Cold War goes back to the immediate years following its publication. Solomon Shvarts, for instance, in his broader discussion of antisemitism in the Soviet Union, contended that Yevtushenko's "Babi Yar" transformed the attitude of millions of Soviet readers toward Soviet Jews, "instilling within them an uncompromising attitude toward antisemitism."[33] As for Soviet Jews, he argued, the publication of "Babi Yar" was the most significant historic event since the Doctors' Plot was unmasked as an antisemitic sham in the weeks that followed the death of Stalin.[34] This is thus a view of "Babi Yar" as an utter condemnation of official and popular Soviet antisemitism. A few years later, William Korey offered another positive appraisal of "Babi Yar," arguing that the poem, together with the article by Nekrasov, was "brooding over the double tragedy of Babi Yar—first the Holocaust there and then suppression of any reference to it."[35] And lastly, at the turn of the twenty-first century Jeff Mankoff understood the poem as an emblem of the Jewish "counter-memory" of the World War II period, an alternative account of the tragedy that befell not only Kyiv Jews but Soviet Jews in other locations, who were all not merely victims of the Great Patriotic War, like other Soviet nationals (the "peace-loving Soviet citizens" we saw above), but rather victims of a well-planned and systematically implemented genocide.[36]

This positive appraisal of "Babi Yar," while having some textual evidence to support it, is by and large a product of the Cold War, although it continued to resonate in Western scholarship even beyond the Soviet era. Ingrained throughout the Cold War years, this stance toward "Babi Yar" amounts to a "wishful reading" of the poem, reflecting the hope that the voice of Yevtushenko was just a trickle of a larger current of dissent emanating from the Soviet Union, a current that could be utilized by Western readers as proof that the Soviet regime did not have the popular support it claimed to enjoy and that the antisemitic policies it espoused were about to cause a rift between the people and the regime.

Quite ironically, this positive perspective on Yevtushenko's poem, rather than relying entirely on the poem itself, was to a great degree influenced by the immediate reaction to "Babi Yar" of two of its most zealous detractors, Alexei Markov and Dmitry Starikov. Harshly attacking "Babi Yar," the former with a mock poem and the latter with an article, their pieces came out a few months after the publication of Yevtushenko's poem, appearing in the conservative journal *Literatura i zhizn'*.[37] In what seemed like an orchestrated attack against Yevtushenko from above,[38] Markov and Starikov accused the poet of a variety of transgressions: he distorted the historical memory of the Great Patriotic War by ignoring the death of millions of non-Jewish Soviet citizens; he displayed disloyalty to the Soviet state and the Russian nation; and he jeopardized the so-called *druzhba narodov* (friendship of peoples) by spreading enmity among Jews and non-Jews by arguing that Babyn Yar was a site of an exclusively Jewish tragedy.

For both those who reacted to the poem with outrage as well as those who did so with enthusiasm, "Babi Yar" was a poem of unparalleled radicalism, carrying unequivocal messages. In reality, however, Yevtushenko's poem had far more modest objectives. While Yevtushenko was attacked by Starikov for falsely arguing that the Babyn Yar massacre was a part of anti-Jewish genocide (Starikov further denied that such genocide had indeed happened), nowhere in the poem is found any conspicuous conception of the September 29–30 murder of Kyiv Jews in those terms. While Yevtushenko loosely connects the fate of Anne Frank with that of Kyiv Jews, nowhere in the poem does he explicitly present Babyn Yar as a symbol for the occurrence of the Holocaust on Soviet soil.

If recognition that the poem presents Babyn Yar as a Holocaust site per se was one conclusion that critics hastened to make, another one is the view that the poem constituted a demand made on the Soviet authorities to construct a monument at the ravine. In fact, such a demand is not really featured in "Babi Yar." Consider the poem's opening verse, asserting that "no monument stands over Babi Yar." It can be read as a statement about the gloomy reality that the poet encountered upon his visit to the ravine rather than as an attempt to interfere with the affairs of the local Ukrainian authorities by demanding that they undo this reality. In other words, the more literate reading of the text may suggest that this is a reflection on—a sober moment of confrontation with—the "presence of the absence" rather than an act of protest, the position so characteristic of Nekrasov's letter (and this is also a suggestion to read the essay and poem both intertextually and independent of each other). True, Yevtushenko's bewilderment and fury over the absence of a monument permeates every line in the poem. There is also little doubt that the poem played a pivotal role in bringing the Soviet government to concede and ultimately allow the construction of the first monument at Babyn Yar fifteen years later. Yet as politically charged as it may seem, this reading of "Babi Yar" in the narrowest sense, as a demand for a memorial for the Jewish victims of Babyn Yar, is often done in hindsight, projecting the monument laid at the site in the mid-1970s onto the past.

## YEVTUSHENKO'S CRITICS

The absence of a clear reference to the Holocaust or of a demand to lay a memorial at the site is not the only testimony to the poem's moderate tone. One may also examine the portrayal of antisemitism in the poem. Among those who have studied the commemoration of Babyn Yar in its Soviet context, it is only Richard Sheldon who pointed out the implicit guidelines to which Yevtushenko had to adhere in order to touch upon the sensitive issue of Soviet antisemitism without having his "Babi Yar" banned from publication. According to Sheldon, Yevtushenko was apparently more at ease with bringing up occasions of anti-Jewish persecution from either distant times or distant lands than with pointing to antisemitism in its Soviet context.[39] He did so only to imply that Soviet society and government were tainted with an antisemitic bias, rather than more bluntly castigating the two. After all, mentioning the enslavement of the Hebrews in Egypt and the harassment of Jews by the Nazis in Holland, the perpetrators of the Białystok pogrom during the late czarist era, and the chauvinistic Black Hundreds organization of the prerevolutionary era known as the Union of the Russian People was one thing (most conspicuously, in the case of the latter two examples it was not the Bolsheviks themselves but rather their enemies who were the antisemites). And blaming the Soviet regime for the more recent destruction of prominent Jewish cultural figures during the last years of Stalinism, for continuing the shutdown of all Jewish cultural activities in the country, and for turning a blind eye to more recent cases of popular antisemitic outbursts (concerns that were completely absent from Yevtushenko's poem) was, evidently, another.[40]

The ambiguous way in which the issue of antisemitism is handled in the poem does not close with the imaginary historical journey of Yevtushenko. It culminates when he exclaims:

> *In their callous rage, all anti-Semites*
> *must hate me now as a Jew*
> *For that reason*
> *I am a true Russian!*[41]

These lines bring the poem to a conclusion on a quite puzzling note: On the one hand, its chief subject is Babyn Yar that now becomes the epitome of Soviet antisemitism, at times rampant and at time subtle, yet always present. On the other hand, it portrays Soviet antisemitism as an elusive entity, admitted by the poet while, at the same time, never to be found in a "true Russian."[42] Hence one may infer from a statement like this that the hatred and persecution of Jews are alien to the Soviet system, rather than being a prejudice that has infected virtually all strata of Russian and Soviet society for generations.

One of the very few observers of this conundrum embedded in the poem—and by extension, of Yevtushenko's ideological ambiguity, which is evident in many of his other works and statements—was the Ukrainian Socialist leader, historian, publicist, and writer Panas Fedenko (1893–1981). In a harsh letter addressed to the poet sent on January 17, 1963—a letter that was intercepted by the Soviet censor and published recently in a voluminous collection of documents culled from the Communist Party's Central Committee archives—Fedenko bluntly demanded that Yevtushenko clarify his positions and dispel the cloud of ideological ambiguity shrouding them. Fedenko wondered how these oppositions—exhibiting opposition to the regime while being willing to represent it, fancying himself as a freedom fighter yet remaining silent on recent Soviet repressions in the empire's satellite states—could be harmonized.

Although he was wrong to dismiss the courage it took a prominent figure like Yevtushenko to embrace the cause of Babyn Yar, the questions raised in Fedenko's letter are noteworthy. Surprisingly, they were never asked by Yevtushenko's multitude of admirers in the West. Fedenko was perhaps too harsh, but he did hit the nail on the head when wondering how true the poet's self-characterization can be when he calls himself a "non-party-member communist" (*bespartiinym kommunistom*) and at the same time consistently gears his criticism of the Soviet regime's crimes and misdeeds toward the distant past, eschewing a frank look at the present situation. More than anything, Fedenko was disturbed by one of the leitmotifs in Yevtushenko's poetry: the frequent references to Russian patriotism, one of which is right in the concluding line of "Babi Yar." Not trying to sugarcoat how disturbing he finds Yevtushenko's nuanced role as a practitioner of "permitted dissent" (a coinage and conception he would probably dismiss), Fedenko wonders out loud:

> Reading your poems, I am particularly baffled by the emphasis on your Russian patriotism and the call to believe in the "prophetic greatness" of Russia. It sounds in your poetry like something old-fashioned, or [something] inspired by the Communist Party's propaganda, extolling "Big Brother." Independent-minded people, living in Russia prior to the 1917 Revolution, would call this kind of propaganda [extolling] the superiority of [the] dominant [Russian] nation "Kvas patriotism" [*kvasnym*

*patriotizmom*]. "Germany's greatness" was [indeed] one of the mottos of Hitler's propaganda. For me, and for many other readers of your work, your exaltation of Russia brings to mind very unfortunate associations.[43]

By linking Yevtushenko not with the camp of those pursuing postwar justice and the proper way to commemorate the Babyn Yar massacre, but rather with the Nazi camp, Fedenko seemed to be going too far. Yet, as it turned out, his was only the first voice of criticism against Yevtushenko as both an artistic and political figure (and to put into focus the delicate interplay between these two arenas). His letter briefly mentions "Babi Yar," though his critique can easily be projected onto the poem. The persistence of Soviet antisemitism in the Thaw period, the Soviet suppression of the Holocaust, and a demand to construct a memorial for Babyn Yar's Jewish victims—none of these are unequivocally stated in the poem.

In the ensuing decades, Fedenko was joined by other critics of Yevtushenko's, a group that remained in the minority, especially in English-language scholarship. They wished to call into question the credibility of Yevtushenko's image as a bold dissident, a person whose views and activities the Soviet regime saw as detrimental. For this small group of critics, Yevtushenko's ambivalent treatment of Soviet antisemitism demonstrated his willingness to accommodate Moscow, or, to go even further, they interpreted his ambiguous "Babi Yar" as the epitome of, in their view, Yevtushenko's opportunism. This characterization of Yevtushenko, bringing under scrutiny this complex figure and highlighting the more collaborative aspects of his oeuvre and activities, recurred throughout his career far beyond the specific context of "Babi Yar."

In 1987, for instance, upon Yevtushenko's induction as an honorary member of the American Academy and Institute of Arts and Letters, the poet and Nobel laureate Joseph Brodsky told a *New York Times* correspondent that Yevtushenko had never had any real confrontation with the Soviet regime and added that the latter chose to criticize the Stalinist terror and the regime's antisemitism only when it was safe to do so.[44] Two other Soviet literary critics also viewed Yevtushenko's oeuvre and activities in the same light. While praising the poet for his compelling and extremely sincere style, the scholar Deming Brown noted that "Yevtushenko surrounds his politically provocative poetry with reams of verse that is 'safe.' When he goes globe-trotting, he often writes friendly, appreciative verse about many features of the countries he visits but pays for his passport with politically orthodox commentary on other features."[45] The scholar David Lowe, for another, in his discussion of Moscow's new voices of the 1950s and 1960s, refers to Yevtushenko as "a court poet . . . a vivid example of the danger of imagining that one can meet the Soviet government only half-way."[46]

It is not hard to notice that, not unlike Jewish history scholars in the West for whom "Babi Yar" was a milestone in the development of Soviet Jewish national consciousness, those calling into question Yevtushenko's characterization as a dissident also viewed "Babi Yar" from a narrow and highly politicized standpoint. Driven by a need to draw a zero-sum distinction between only two types of Soviet writers, court poets versus bona fide dissidents, they suggested that Yevtushenko's portrayal of antisemitism in his "Babi Yar" could only benefit the regime that enabled the publication of such a piece. Here is how Ludmila Shtern in her book dedicated to her friend, fellow dissident Joseph Brodsky, characterizes Yevtushenko in the narrow context of "Babi Yar":

> Yevtushenko was not simply a prosperous Soviet poet who had no problem publishing in the Soviet press. He was one of "the cultural ambassadors," one of those artists sent abroad to testify that there was indeed freedom of speech and artistic freedom in the Soviet Union. And Yevtushenko would so testify. I remember visiting Edinburgh, Scotland [in 1962], during the theatre festival there and reading an interview with Yevtushenko who had published a poem about Babi Yar, the place near Kiev where the Nazis killed all Kiev Jews and where the Soviet government did not want to put a sign acknowledging the tragedy. "And you see," said Yevtushenko in the interview, "I was not punished." Words that were certain to make Brodsky's blood boil![47]

While Shtern does not offer a close reading of the poem and is oblivious to the sense of complete shock that the poem left on its first readers, her argument does rely on some substantiated evidence. Surprisingly, her claim that Yevtushenko used "Babi Yar" on his trips abroad to demonstrate the virtues of Soviet society rather than its flaws is corroborated by Yevtushenko himself. As he notes in his autobiography, some Western correspondents and critics misjudged the acerbic reactions that "Babi Yar" received in the Soviet press, viewing it wrongly as proof of the ubiquity of antisemitism in the Soviet Union. To these suggestions, Yevtushenko retorted that "some of these papers [the Western press] dishonestly distorted the meaning of my poem to suit their ends."[48] He went on to argue that, on the contrary, the overwhelmingly warm reaction of the Soviet audience to his poem illustrated how unpopular antisemitic sentiments were in his own country.[49] More than alluding to his role as a critic of his own society—which is how he has often been perceived—it happened that Yevtushenko was careful to dissociate himself from any of his Western admirers who might have been unambiguously hostile to the Soviet mainstream. Shtern is therefore correct in her assertion that once Yevtushenko realized that his criticism could be used not in order to improve the image of the Soviet regime but rather to unmask its flaws, he toned down his enthusiasm and self-assured criticism.

Shtern's critical account of Yevtushenko's work receives another affirmation when we explore "Babi Yar" in the context of the general development of the poet's career. When viewed from this perspective, it turns out that, rather than singling him out as a dangerous rebel, the poem actually helped bolster Yevtushenko's career in a country where poets—being, like all other workers, state employees—were often granted higher salaries and rare benefits that were reserved only for the Soviet *nomenklatura* and scientific as well as cultural elite.[50] Shtern alludes to one piece of evidence that the Soviet regime found Yevtushenko useful: Had it not been for the permission it gave Yevtushenko to travel abroad, she argues, he would not have been able to attend foreign poetry reading festivals in the first place. The permission he received, for instance, to visit Cuba and England soon after he wrote his "Babi Yar"[51] also shows that, while often wishing to restrain defiant intellectuals of Yevtushenko's type in the domestic arena, Moscow recognized the benefit it could gain by sending a young, open-minded intellectual like Yevtushenko abroad to act as a cultural ambassador. An artist like Yevtushenko, the Soviet authorities believed, could demonstrate to the Western public the new, far more liberal character of Soviet society and cultural life.

Doing so at a time when the Soviet Union was promoting its international policy of "peaceful coexistence" with the West could help Moscow win public support there, perhaps even more than cohorts of experienced, highly eloquent Soviet diplomats.[52] The appearance of another of his poems, "The Heirs of Stalin," in no less than the Communist Party organ *Pravda* provides another clue for Yevtushenko's ambivalence. Published in October 1962, soon before the campaign of de-Stalinization came to an end, this poem also helped consolidate the image of the poet who had written "Babi Yar" as one who could be ideologically agile enough to be a dissident and the regime's darling at the same time. Given his ability to acrobatically practice this walking the fine line of Soviet cultural diplomacy, it is not surprising that Yevtushenko managed to puzzle so many—and not only lay readers and literary critics, but also, as recently revealed, even FBI counterintelligence agents. The latter spent time and effort following his tracks during the 1960s and early 1970s on his different US tours, also monitoring the friends and colleagues with whom he would meet in America.

In an article published recently in *The New Republic* and dedicated to a 400-page file on Yevtushenko compiled by the FBI, Jacob Silverman muses about the distinct features of the bygone Cold War era, the time when a visit of a flamboyant foreign poet, wearing colored suits and rousing thousands of fans in poetry recitation concerts, could be the focal point of a great diplomatic event and, parallel to it, the grounds for an FBI investigation.[53] For our study, suffice it to say that the FBI agents' consideration of Yevtushenko as a potential recruit in their effort to undermine the Soviet regime, together with its Communist supporters at home (confronting them with the evidence of Soviet antisemitism embedded in "Babi Yar")—and vice versa, the agency's later suspicion that the poet may be just another loyal Soviet cultural diplomat—best illustrates how much ambiguity was associated with both Yevgeny Yevtushenko and his "Babi Yar."

All things considered, the variety of possible solutions to the Yevtushenko puzzle may lead the reader to a Socratic state of aporia, as we are left with a sense of puzzlement, wondering what Yevtushenko's real intent was when he wrote his "Babi Yar." Was it meant to, by way of touching upon the Jewish question in the USSR, condemn the Soviet regime and its leader Khrushchev (thus, constituting a break with the relatively moderate tone that had characterized the literature of the Thaw period that preceded it)? Or, rather, was it, in line with the campaign of de-Stalinization, a manifestation of support on the part of Yevtushenko for the Soviet way of life, one that had always resisted the antisemitic, reactionary elements within it?

Perhaps the best way to unravel the contradictory nature of "Babi Yar" is to see it as a product of the literature of permitted dissent and, more accurately, of permitted dissent stretched to the maximum: it is a poem harshly criticizing a dictatorial regime at a time when the regime was encouraging the appearance of such critical works. As noted above, this was a time when Soviet society was making preparations to launch its transformation from a "dictatorship of the proletariat" into a society reaching the utopian state of Communism, a future that would take place twenty years later, when class conflicts, state and society conflicts, the banning of freedom of speech, and the limiting of artistic freedom would all finally be overcome. It was this paradoxical historical background, this transitional stage between the repressive dictatorship and the future existence of artistic freedom, that may account for the interplay in "Babi Yar" between resistance to the Soviet regime and the concurrent enthusiastic support of it.

## THE POEM AS INTIMATE TESTIMONY

While the vagueness of Yevtushenko's "Babi Yar" from the political standpoint may be judged as either one of its greatest virtues or shortcomings, any appraisal of the poem would be fragmentary if it did not factor in another major aspect of "Babi Yar"—the poem as a personal account, the testimony of a traveler who bore witness to an arresting vision of horror that he felt compelled to share with his readers. Yevtushenko himself confessed in another autobiography published decades after "Babi Yar" that a profound sense of connection to the Jewish people compelled him to write his poem, not merely the desire to render a cold, rational analysis of the issue of antisemitism and its link to Babyn Yar. According to the poet, during the time of the Doctors' Plot, before he even turned twenty, he composed an antisemitic poem condemning the Jewish physicians, which he eventually decided not to publish.[54] His "Babi Yar" was, for this reason, a poem of atonement. The exploration of antisemitism in it, while at times criticized for being superficial, was not merely a political statement. It was rather based on Yevtushenko's own experience as someone who knew how easily one may fall prey to this kind of virulent spread of ethnic hatred.

Indeed, a desire to write personal poems exposing the life and thoughts of the writer in the most intimate fashion was a major feature of Yevtushenko's poetics. As Peter Vail and Alexander Genis point out in their work on the Soviet culture of the 1960s, Yevtushenko and the bard Bulat Okudzhava were the first Soviet poets to elaborate lyrical and intimate poetry after decades of the complete absence of this genre from the horizon of Soviet literature.⁵⁵ Their contributions may be seen as another phase in a trajectory that began with Vladimir Pomerantsev and Ilya Ehrenburg, who, as we have noted, called in the immediate aftermath of Stalin's death for sincerity in literature and for doing away with the mechanized language and clichés of socialist realism that left no room for the voice of the individual.⁵⁶ Yevtushenko's "Babi Yar," as a part of the general theme of his oeuvre, was a personal poem no less than it was a political statement. More accurately, its most profound political message lay in the personal, intimate perspective embedded in it, in the sincere voice of the individual poet atoning for his sins and calling on his fellow Russians to remove the obstacle of antisemitism, a Stalinist vestige blocking the Soviet state's path to a brighter future.

As it turns out, the personal aspect of the poem is no less intricate and fraught with ambiguity than the other aspects we have examined. As Vail and Genis contend, Yevtushenko's lyricism and sense of intimacy were always balanced by a contrasting tendency, which was his rare ability, apparent since the dawn of his poetic career (in early 1949, when he had his debut with a set of anti-American poems in *Sovetskii sport*), to render the Kremlin's ever-changing and often hard to understand political programs into a language accessible to his peers.⁵⁷ In a fashion reminiscent of his primary influence, the Russian futurist poet of the prerevolutionary avant-garde, Vladimir Mayakovsky, Yevtushenko's poetry is an interplay between the collective and the individual voice, where the boundaries demarcating lyricism and propaganda are often highly blurred.⁵⁸ The desire to harmonize these two contrasting tendencies, to be both a political agitator and a lyricist, becomes evident when we consider the medium through which Yevtushenko commonly addressed his readers—namely, that of poetry declamation events that took place in squares, university auditoriums, concert halls, and even stadiums, places where a single speaker could expose his inner world to a mass audience.

According to Patricia Blake, coeditor of *Half-Way to the Moon: New Writing from Russia*, who visited the Soviet Union during the early 1960s, "Babi Yar" rapidly became Yevtushenko's most popular piece in these poetry recitation concerts. At times, it seemed as though Yevtushenko could not satiate his crowd's demand to hear it recited more and more, which is perhaps the best testimony to the poem's suitability for the medium of declamation.⁵⁹ Both the structure and themes of his "Babi Yar" betray its designation as a performance piece. The poem's loosely organized iambic structure;⁶⁰ the excessive employment in it of a number of literary devices such as the anaphora (the recurrence of *nad Bab'im Yarom, ya kazhdyi*), alliteration (*damochki s bryussel'skimi oborkami*), oxymoron ("Here all things scream silently"); and the elaboration of unusual, surprising rhymes are all meant to endow the poem with a forceful dramatic effect that fully comes to light when one listens to a recording of Yevtushenko himself reading the poem.[61]

As we bear in mind that the poem was designed for public recitation, more and more of its intricacies start to surface. On the one hand, it is a complex poem full of historical allusions that were meant to engage the educated Russian reader initiated into the time-honored history of the Jewish people as well as Russian antisemitism. On the other hand, its theme is highly accessible, and its often bombastic and extravagant style—features for which Yevtushenko has often been criticized—shows that its message was meant to reach many readers and listeners, as it successfully did. One may perhaps go even further and suggest that the declamatory nature of Yevtushenko's poetic style amounted to one of the reasons he found the theme of Babyn Yar so appealing in the first place. Quite an odd choice for someone who was doubly foreign to Babyn Yar—who was neither Jewish nor a resident of Kyiv—the poem's theme was perfectly suitable for public recitation. For in this particular genre, the more astounding, controversial, and unpredictable a poem's subject matter was, the better it engaged the young enthusiasts that swarmed to hear it recited by the poet. "Babi Yar," in this respect, joined many other poems in Yevtushenko's repertoire (such as his "A Meeting in Copenhagen," reporting on the rendezvous he had in Copenhagen with Ernest Hemingway, or "A Beatnik Girl," telling of a meeting he had with young beatniks in New York, to mention only a few examples)[62] that included the impressions of his many trips that he, the dissident-traveler, wished to share with his audience.

While "Babi Yar" begins with a detailed (and, as we have already noted, ambiguous, and, some would say, superficial) survey of Jewish martyrdom and persecution, it is here, when Yevtushenko reflects on the daunting experience of visiting a World War II mass murder site, that the poem reaches its apogee. At this point, Yevtushenko's words echo those of Ilya Selvinsky, who in his poem "I Saw It" became the first Soviet writer to offer a poetic testimony to an *Aktion,* in his case to the murder of 7,000 Jews at the Bagerovo anti-tank ditch located outside the Crimean city of Kerch, shortly after the massacre had taken place.[63] For Selvinsky, the specter of standing by the recently dug anti-tank ditch and staring at the pile of corpses whose faces were still recognizable was a reality. For Yevtushenko, however, the act of seeing—both the ravine, that now no longer existed, and the Jewish victims—belonged only in the realm of his poetic imagination.

Now, standing on the brink of the ravine, he realizes the extreme contrast between the serene landscape covered with rustling grasses and surrounded by trees and the memory of the atrocities that the same place had witnessed a few decades earlier. This is also the point when Yevtushenko reaches complete identification with the Jewish victims of Babyn Yar, as he, the victims, and the site itself become one, as the distinction between victims and imaginary witness collapses:

*The wild grasses rustle over Babyn Yar.*
*The trees look ominous,*
*like judges.*
*Here all things scream silently,*
*and, baring my head,*
*slowly I feel myself*
*turning gray.*
*And I myself*
*am one massive, soundless scream*
*above the thousand thousand buried here.*
*I am*
*each old man*
*here shot dead.*
*I am*
*each child*
*here shot dead.*
*Nothing in me*
*shall ever forget!*[64]

While defying translation into English, it is here where Yevtushenko's poem reaches not only its dramatic but also its artistic peak, both thematically and musically. Employing both perfect and slanted rhymes, he blends the following elements into one: the serene landscape, the memory of the victims, the dismembered and incinerated bodies lying underneath, and, finally, the poet himself who turns into one scream. When one follows the rhyming scheme in this part of the poem, the amalgamation of all these elements becomes apparent: *shelest dikih trav . . . i shapku sniav* (the grasses rustle . . . and taking off my hat), *derevya smotrayat po-sudeiskii . . . ya chustvuyu kak medleno sedeyu* (the trees look like judges . . . I feel myself turning gray), *i sam ya, kak sploshnoi bezzvuchnii krik . . . ya kazhdii zdes' rasstrelyannyi starik* (I myself am one massive soundless scream . . . I am each old man here shot dead), *tisyach pogrebyonniyh . . . rasstrelyannyi rebyonok* (the thousand thousand buried here . . . shot-dead child). While some of these rhymes are more apparent than others in the printed version of the poem, it is far easier to grasp them and appreciate their musicality when listening to the poem's declamation. It is here where Yevtushenko's awareness of the need to suit the poem's message to its medium is most conspicuous. From these lines, it becomes clear that while the political drama of the absent monument at Babyn Yar appears at the poem's start, it is here, with the personal experience of identification with the victims, where the heart of Yevtushenko's poem lies.

Yevtushenko's poem thus weaves together two modes of thinking and expression that are normally hard to bring together: a panoramic, distanced reflection on history's *longue durée*, employing the scholastic, prosaic mode; and the testimony of the person who was there, both physically and metaphysically, both in the Babyn Yar of 1961 and 1941. This is precisely the moment when the lyrical mode bursts out, expressing pain, trauma, and the collapse of the prosaic one; this is the "deep memory," to use author Lawrence Langer's terminology—memory of trauma that is always experienced in the present, that "tries to recall the Auschwitz self as it was then."[65] It is the point where a survivor's endeavor to coldly and rationally tell their story of survival, to speak from the vantage point of their pre- or post-Holocaust self, is shattered into pieces. Or to employ another theoretical framework, this is the point when Yevtushenko's memory (of visiting Babyn Yar) turns into what author Marianne Hirsch terms "postmemory,"[66] the evocation of traumatic experiences and memories by the second generation, who now, recalling the stories of murder and survival of the first generation, reacts so severely up to complete identification, almost confusion, of the former with the latter, turning their secondhand experiences into firsthand ones. In other words, those who never witnessed these atrocities in the first place start conjuring up traumatic personal memories.

Hirsch's theoretical framework is very useful here. On the one hand, it is concerned mainly with the analysis of photographs and images and the recollection of traumatic events by children of Holocaust survivors. The bulk of her work deals with what she calls "familial postmemory," the transferring of memory from the first to the second generation within the family. On the other hand, Hirsch does allow postmemory to expand and transcend the realms of the immediate family by making a distinction between familial postmemory, "an intergenerational vertical identification of child and parent occurring within the family," and what she calls "affiliative postmemory," the "intergenerational horizontal identification that makes that child's position more broadly available to other contemporaries."[67] Although in both projections, horizontal and vertical, Hirsch refers to a survivor parent and child relationship, it becomes clear later in her study that affiliative postmemory can apply not only to the children of Holocaust survivors, but also to anyone recalling these memories.

If any person, not necessarily a child of a survivor, can be a practitioner of postmemory evocation, then not only Yevtushenko but virtually all writers surveyed in our study who had visited the site may be viewed as practitioners of postmemory, as they worked to project the specter of the desolate Babyn Yar to their contemporaries. We have seen this confrontation with the bleak sight of postwar Babyn Yar in Ehrenburg's work before. More specifically, Yevtushenko's work is in direct dialogue with Ozerov's "Babi Yar," his more immediate poetic predecessor. Compare, for instance, Yevtushenko's metaphor of judging trees with Ozerov's depiction of the natural scenery in what used to be a recreational site lying on the outskirts of Kyiv:

> *I ask the maple trees: reply.*
> *You are witnesses—tell your story!*
> *But all is quiet,*
> *Only the wind—*
> *Soughing in the leaves.*
> *I implore the sky: speak your piece.*
> *But its indifference is painful....*
> *There was life, there will be life.*
> *But your face gives no guidance.*
> *Perhaps the rocks will have an answer.*
> *No...*

When read intertextually, it is easier to appreciate Yevtushenko's screaming silence, the sense of a man going mad, who is expecting the surrounding nature to bear witness and speak, and feeling as though he becomes "each old man here shot dead... each child here shot dead." Yevtushenko relies on an earlier visit to the site paid by Ozerov, who came to search for the grave of his own relatives, to converse with them, to understand how they could have died such a cruel death. But here is also where the similarities between the two poetic renditions of Babyn Yar end. For Yevtushenko's work, while excelling in its lyrical, intimate reflections and projections, concludes on a bona fide propagandistic note, as we shall see. Ozerov's ending, in which the word "Jew" is never to be found, is more than anything a purely individual account of suffering, identification with his dead relatives, and a promise never to forget. As he is about to dive into the ravine and join his relatives, they plead with him:

> *Stop!*
> *You have a future.*
> *You must live out your life—and ours.*
> *You don't hold grudges—start holding them.*
> *You're forgetful—don't dare forget!*
> *And a child said, "Don't forget."*
> *And a mother said, "Don't forgive."*
> *And the earthen breast swung shut.*
> *I was no longer at the Yar but on my way.*

> *It leads to vengeance—that way*
> *Along which I must travel.*
> *Don't forget...*
> *Don't forgive...*

Yevtushenko iterates a similar call never to forget. But with the categorical imperative never to forget—the personal, intimate, categorical imperative—is interwoven the propagandistic element in a fashion so characteristic of Yevgeny Yevtushenko's poetics:

> May *"Internationale"* thunder and ring
> When, for all time, is buried and forgotten
> The last of the antisemites on this earth.
>
> There is no Jewish blood that's blood of mine,
> But, hated with a passion that's corrosive.
> Am I by antisemites like a Jew.
> And that is why I call myself a Russian!

In summary, if we bear in mind both the poem's medium and message, it is easier to view Yevtushenko's "Babi Yar" as a work fraught with contradictions. The poem is based on a personal, intimate experience, yet it means to share this with as many readers as possible. The poem contains ideas representing Yevtushenko's views only, but at the same time it had a propagandistic goal, as it helped communicate to its audience the message that Soviet life and literature were in the process of a shift away from Stalinism. It was a poem of protest against a specific, unwritten Soviet policy, yet the language used to address this policy was couched with vagueness so as not to exceedingly arouse the ire of those in power. Its attractiveness to young and defiant audiences alluded to its radical nature, but its recitation at various large public venues spoke volumes about the official Soviet approval with which it had to be stamped.

While these contradictions account for what made "Babi Yar" extraordinarily popular as a poem, they were also a staple feature of the literature of the Second Thaw, a time when Russian writers exhibited two contrasting tendencies. On the one hand, they wished to support a regime that had manifested its commitment to de-Stalinization and a return to the Leninist path. On the other hand, the *shestidesiatniki* remonstrated with Moscow on what they saw as an incomplete and slow movement away from the Stalin era. Yevtushenko's "Babi Yar" was among the finest works of the Soviet 1960s generation, whose socialist, optimistic, and utopian works were poignantly coined by Vladislav Zubok as reflecting "socialist romanticism" in order to underline the break this generation of artists made with the Stalinist and Zhdanovite dogmas of socialist realism. The ethos of this group was best emblematized in the words of the poet Bella Akhmadulina, Yevgeny Yevtushenko's first wife, who in one of her poems exclaimed "the Revolution is sick" and therefore must be cured. If viewed through the lens of this motto, Yevtushenko's "Babi Yar" was a call to cure the Russian Revolution from within in a restorative and not a destructive fashion, and to cure it in particular from one illness: the malice of antisemitism, of anti-Jewish prejudice and violence that had infected Russian society for centuries and, according to Yevtushenko, had not yet been overcome in Khrushchev's era of true socialism.

# 4

# BABYN YAR SET TO MUSIC

WHILE OFTEN REGARDED DURING THE COLD WAR AS A STAPLE FEAture of Soviet dissent during the Thaw era, "Babi Yar" by Yevgeny Yevtushenko was a nuanced, multifaceted work, never really constituting an all-out attack against Moscow's official, unwritten Babyn Yar policy. After the first wave of attacks aimed at Yevtushenko in late 1961 started to ebb, the young poet's predominance on the Soviet literary scene remained for a time unshakable.[1] Nothing attested better to the benign level of tolerance toward Yevtushenko than his partaking in public recitations of "Babi Yar," both within and beyond the Iron Curtain, as a part of the so-called cultural diplomacy visits to foreign countries. While our study has so far limited itself to an examination of literary works dedicated to Babyn Yar, arguing that the main channel through which the site was commemorated was literary, we must briefly delve into the arena of music. This shift is necessary, since a big part of what became in collective memory, both in the USSR and the West, the "Babi Yar affair"—that is, the excitement and fury that "Babi Yar" provoked—was connected with the decision of Dmitri Shostakovich, the towering Soviet composer, to set his score to Yevtushenko's poem. Without allotting adequate consideration to what became known as Shostakovich's Thirteenth Symphony, subtitled "Babi Yar," it would be impossible to fully understand the role that Yevtushenko's poem played in the Soviet culture of the Thaw period and come to a final assessment of both its provocative and moderate elements, which coalesced into the aforementioned practice of permitted dissent.

## AN INTERGENERATIONAL COPRODUCTION: YEVTUSHENKO AND SHOSTAKOVICH

It all began with an unexpected phone call Yevtushenko received at the end of March 1962. To the amazement of both his wife Galina, who picked up the phone, and Yevtushenko himself, the person at the other end of the line was none other than the foremost Soviet composer, Dmitri Shostakovich (1906–1975). The anxious young poet was told by the older composer that he was deeply moved by his "Babi Yar" and wanted to set it to music. According to Yevtushenko, who recounted the story about this phone conversation in his memoir, after recovering from the momentary shock and realizing it was not a prank, he responded to the offer in the affirmative enthusiastically, only to learn that Shostakovich had already completed a rough draft and was ready to perform it for him.[2]

As for Shostakovich, who came of age during the first years of Communism, collaboration on a project, crossing different artistic fields and genres and doing so particularly with a *shestidesyatnik*, was a particularly intriguing endeavor. In the Shostakovich archive, now available online thanks to the efforts of Irina Shostakovich, the late composer's third wife, we find a letter in which Shostakovich reflects on his impressions of working with Yevtushenko, which was a positive experience that made him decide to turn a single symphonic poem into a full-blown symphony, his Thirteenth (op. 113). In a letter he wrote to his close friend Isaak Glikman on July 1, 1962, he explains:

> While in hospital I began composing my Thirteenth Symphony. To be more exact, it will probably be a vocal-symphonic suite in five parts. It is to be performed by a bass soloist, a bass choir and, of course, a symphony orchestra. For this composition I have used words by the poet Yevgeny Yevtushenko. After closer acquaintance with this poet, I realized that his is a considerable and, most important of all, a thinking talent. I have met him and I liked him very much. He is 29. It is very pleasing to see young people like this appear on the scene. The Symphony consists of five parts.... The first three parts are completed.[3]

This collaborative effort, bridging two generations of the liberal Soviet intelligentsia, led to Shostakovich's Thirteenth Symphony, subtitled *Babi Yar*. From a single symphonic poem for bass, a bass choir, and an orchestra written on March 23, 1962, Shostakovich managed, from his hospital bed, to swiftly complete the entire piece within less than four months. Together, both composer and poet selected for this five-movement symphony four other poems taken from Yevtushenko's oeuvre to be set to music in addition to "Babi Yar." At first sight, the poems were in a way only loosely connected, all falling into the category of exposures of the moral flaws of Soviet society. But upon a closer look, perhaps nothing can better elucidate the point made above—that Yevtushenko's "Babi Yar" should not be singled out as a piece of Holocaust literature but should rather be construed as a product of the Thaw era—than the weaving together of these works. From antisemitism ("Babi Yar"), through the absence of humor in Soviet life ("Humor"), the exploitation of Soviet womenfolk in the government-owned grocery store ("In the Shop"), the fear of informants ("Fears"), and up to the heroic triumph of humanity over conformism ("A Career"), the Thirteenth Symphony emerged as a musical rendition of Yevtushenko's poetic *and* ideological stances.

What led Shostakovich to put himself under the spotlight of Moscow's chiefs supervising the ideological "purity" of Soviet art and to collaborate with a young artist already suspected of sharply deviating from Soviet orthodoxy and of trespassing the boundaries of permitted dissent? Shostakovich, after all, was a seasoned veteran of pushing these boundaries of artistic freedom. He had done so at two points during the Stalin era. In 1936, he did it with his *Lady Macbeth of Mtsensk*, an opera, which music critics at home hailed first, only to find out later that Joseph Stalin did not share their appraisal.[4] And in 1948, as the anti-Cosmopolitan campaign was gathering momentum, together with Aram Khachaturian and Sergei Prokofiev, he was accused of formalism, of creating art for art's sake—a sacrilegious practice for a bona fide Soviet composer expected to serve the building of socialism and compose music suitable for the edification of the working class.

A glimpse into the biography and earlier repertoire of Shostakovich only confirms that his motives in joining Yevtushenko were both profound and sincere. By that time, he already knew all too well what the cost of artistic freedom could be: harassments, which he had experienced, imprisonment, or death. It was clearly Yevtushenko's choice to uphold the banner of combating the bitter legacy of Russian as well as Soviet antisemitism—an open, intransigent battle fraught with risk—that made such a deep impression on Shostakovich. To the rise of this new generation, endowing socialism with a renewed spirit of innocence, he could not remain indifferent. By early 1962, Shostakovich had already established his reputation as a non-Jewish Russian artist and primary member of the Soviet intelligentsia who shared a strong affinity with Jewish culture, music, and folklore.

As Francis Maes argues in his work surveying the history of Russian and Soviet music, Shostakovich manifested his fondness for the Jews and their musical heritage through works written far earlier in his career, among them the Second Piano Trio[5] (op. 67, a piece written in 1944 and dedicated to the victims of Majdanek, the Jewish motifs of which are also echoed in the String Quartet No. 8), the First Violin Concerto, and his cycle *From Jewish Folk Poetry*.[6] The view of Shostakovich as a Judeophile composer gained currency among Western scholars, who tended to correlate what they deemed as a gifted, independent-minded artist with Shostakovich's heterodox and favorable view of Jews and Jewish culture. Appraised as a bold and innovative composer, Shostakovich came to be known posthumously in the West as a dissident, one who dared to challenge socialist realism as the official Soviet musical style.

Yet, as Maes cogently argues, our characterization of Yevtushenko as an artist willing to walk the fine line demarcating the boundaries between the permissible and the taboo in Soviet discourse would suit Dmitri Shostakovich as well. While the elaboration of Jewish themes for a non-Jewish Soviet composer was something undeniably laden with a great deal of nonconformism in a country where popular antisemitism had time-honored roots, the Soviet composer's affinity with Jewish culture should be taken with a grain of salt. To label this artistic predilection on the part of Shostakovich as an expression of dissent, Maes contends, would be untrue because of the virtual nonexistence of the concept in Soviet art past Stalin's cultural revolution of 1928–1929, and especially ever since the "meat grinder" of the Great Terror had been started up.[7] Accordingly, Shostakovich's elaboration of Jewish folk themes was something in concert with the current trends in Soviet music toward the building of a proletarian music predicated on the foundations of folk music. This explains why, after his works incorporating Jewish folk music themes were premiered, they were hailed as "a proof that music based on folk themes could triumph over the bad influence of modernism."[8]

## AN INTERGENERATIONAL DIALOGUE: YEVTUSHENKO AND KHRUSHCHEV

While contextualizing Shostakovich's affinity with Jewish music in order to dispel the notion broadly accepted during the Cold War of Shostakovich as a full-blown dissident (insofar as the term denotes complete deviation from the ideological posture of the regime) does not necessarily clear the fog surrounding his attitude toward the Soviet regime, other moves he took during the Thaw era in this direction were more transparent. The early 1960s was a time of increasing fluctuation between cooperation and dissent. During the years 1960–1961, to the puzzlement of many of his admirers, Shostakovich was admitted into the Communist Party, first on a provisional basis and, later on, as a full member.[9] Shostakovich's induction into the party reaffirmed his status as a loyal son of the Soviet regime.[10] Despite the clear age gap, both Shostakovich and Yevtushenko shared the conception of the artist's role as the regime's critic "from within." Their joint battle against antisemitism was predicated on similar ideological grounds and underpinned by the same restorative motivation: the aspiration to restore Communism to its pristine ideals of the Lenin era. Their shared views, however, did not mean that Shostakovich's joining in the campaign to turn Babyn Yar from a "memory black hole" to a

Dmitri Shostakovich and Yevgeny Yevtushenko celebrate after the premiere of the Thirteenth Symphony at the Great Hall of the Moscow Conservatory. 18 December 1962. (Photo by Bryan Rowell, *DSCH Journal*.)

memory space was hardly meaningful. On the contrary, there was a great deal of synergy in this joint project, insofar as it constituted a real turning point in the careers of Shostakovich and Yevtushenko. If before the symphony's premiere, which took place on December 18, 1962, Yevtushenko read his poem at a large number of poetry recitation concerts, evoking excessively enthusiastic reactions on the part of his audiences, it was exactly on the eve of the symphony's premiere that the poem came under the harshest attack from the Soviet premier Nikita Khrushchev himself and from Leonid Ilichev, the party secretary presiding over ideology.

The attack against Yevtushenko, implicating the Soviet composer as well, came from the very top of the Soviet hierarchy and was part of a broader ideological shift in Moscow's attitude toward artistic freedom. About two weeks before the symphony's premiere, on December 1, 1962, Nikita Khrushchev, surrounded by his entourage, showed up at the State Exhibition Hall in the Manege to view an exhibition of innovative abstract art. Khrushchev's reaction to the works displayed to him was brutal and appallingly vulgar: calling the artists "faggots" and their art "dog shit," the premiere threatened to send the artists to Siberia or expel them from the Soviet Union.[11] As Vladislav Zubok portrays the atmosphere following Khrushchev's visit to the Manege Exhibition Hall, there was a feeling in the air that a new campaign of terror against artists was about to be set in motion. Indeed, Khrushchev did order a "purge" of the media, art institutes, and the guild of graphic artists and book illustrators, and did mandate much closer scrutiny of all universities and colleges.[12] Ultimately, arrests did not follow these threats but were meaningful enough: they sent the Soviet liberal intelligentsia a clear signal that the path of art for art's sake did not belong in the Soviet state and that the role of art was instead to mobilize the masses to support the Soviet regime and the Communist Party of the Soviet Union by wholly subscribing to the tenets of socialist realism.

Following the Manege incident, on December 17, 1962, only one day before the premiere of the Thirteenth Symphony, Khrushchev, followed by other party leaders, convened what seemed like an informal meeting of about 400 artists and writers in the reception hall at Lenin Hills to discuss the state of Soviet art. It is likely that the proximity between the meeting and the premiere of the Thirteenth Symphony was a matter of chance.[13] Regardless, during the meeting both Yevtushenko and Shostakovich were singled out and came under attack by Ilichev and Khrushchev. According to Vladislav Zubok's account, Khrushchev made Yevtushenko a scapegoat almost by chance. When the Soviet premier wanted to sting the Soviet sculptor Ernst Neizvestny, remarking that "if a person is born ugly, only the grave will correct him," it was Yevtushenko who had the audacity to retort that "we live in a time when mistakes are corrected not by graves, but by live, honest, and truthful Bolshevik words."[14]

The exchange of words between the poet and the Soviet leader could be construed in more than one way. According to Zubok, the root of the matter was the legitimacy of artistic freedom and the opposition to a relapse to the days of Stalinist terror and his taming of Soviet artists. Other accounts, however, link the exchange of words directly to "Babi Yar." According to William Korey's version, what lay at the core of Khrushchev's animus toward Yevtushenko was not the latter's defense of abstract art or anything of that sort, but that through his "Babi Yar" he had "let the genie of antisemitism out the Soviet bottle." Apparently, as long as Yevtushenko acted alone, the Soviet leadership treated him with a great deal of ambiguity. But now, only one day before the premiere of the Thirteenth Symphony, something in the mood of the Soviet premier changed. At their meeting on December 17, according to Korey, the following exchange took place:

> The poem became a key issue. When Yevtushenko recited the last two lines of his poem to the audience, Khrushchev interjected: "Comrade Yevtushenko, this poem has no place here." At this point the poet commented that he had selected Babi Yar because "the problem of antisemitism" continues to have "a negative consequence" which has not yet been resolved. Khrushchev forcefully rejected the argument. "Antisemitism is not a problem," he declared. The young writer would not be silenced. He responded: "It is a problem, Nikita Sergeyevich. It cannot be denied, and it cannot be suppressed. It is necessary to come to grips with it time and again."[15]

Whether or not the timing of Khrushchev's attack was deliberately synchronized with the upcoming premiere of the Thirteenth Symphony, the signal from above that the Second Thaw's days were numbered had a detrimental impact on the Moscow performance. In an interview, Irina Shostakovich related the troubles and angst that her husband had had to go through, something that she could never imagine would be a prelude to the coming to light of a new musical piece:

> I was very struck by the first premiere which I attended—the premiere of the Thirteenth Symphony. I was struck by it all, because I had thought that once a composer has finished a work what comes afterwards would be pure pleasure—rehearsals would start, premieres, interviews, success, congratulations and so on. It turned out to be very different. That premiere was a very difficult and stressful one. The famous meeting between Khrushchev and the intelligentsia after his visit to an exhibition in the Manezh had taken place on the eve of the premiere. Shostakovich had returned home from that meeting very late and very agitated. The next morning, when the dress rehearsal was supposed to have taken place, the singer who was meant to sing the solo part was suddenly summoned to the Bolshoi. The choir and the orchestra turned up but there was no soloist. Another soloist was sent for, whom the Philharmonia [sic] supplied as a stand-in. They waited two hours for him. Then he arrived and sang, but at the rehearsal there were people from the Central Committee department present and during the break they told Shostakovich that he was expected at the Central Committee. Although he was told there that the premiere would take place, Shostakovich got very worked up. Strangely enough, when the next performance of the Symphony took place in Minsk, a similar meeting in Byelorussia was convened on the eve of the concert and there was the same agitation. The whole situation was very tense.
>
> The lead-up to this premiere was as follows: in the first place, Shostakovich had proposed that Mravinsky should conduct, but he didn't say Yes or No and set off on tour. This made it clear that he would not be conducting it. The soloist part was offered to Gmyrya, who with serious doubts took the score and went to seek advice from the Ukrainian Central Committee. There he was told that he could, of course, sing, but that this symphony would not be performed in the Ukraine. Then it was offered to Vedernikov, who also turned it down. All in all, it was a very nerve-wracking story.[16]

What transpired from the last preparations for the performance of the Thirteenth Symphony was the trepidation and fear that some of those involved with the production felt through associating themselves with the theme of Babyn Yar at the beginning of what seemed like a new crackdown on art and artistic freedom. Permitted dissent, thus,

Dmitri Shostakovich and Yevgeny Yevtushenko exiting the stage after the premiere of the Thirteenth Symphony. (Photo by Bryan Rowell, *DSCH Journal*.)

although nurtured by a dialogue with the regime, like the one Yevtushenko had with Shostakovich, was not tantamount to timidity and complicity: it took a lot of nerve.

Another conference of writers and artists held at the Kremlin on March 7–8, 1963, consolidated the impression that at the very heart of this new campaign against the liberal intelligentsia stood the poem, and now the symphony, "Babi Yar." At this meeting, Khrushchev once more directly attacked the thematic triangle of Jews, Babyn Yar, and antisemitism that lay at the heart of Yevtushenko's work. The premier fulminated against Yevtushenko for raising a made-up issue, for what he saw as "ignorance of the historical facts."[17] From Khrushchev's point of view, the October Revolution brought equality for Russia's Jewish citizens and consigned antisemitism to the dustbin of history. "The 'Jewish Question' does not exist here," he insisted.[18] As Olga Gershenson summarizes this spring meeting with the Soviet premier, "This was the closest the Soviets ever came to stating an official policy regarding the Holocaust."[19]

Crucially, the two meetings between Khrushchev and the Soviet artists, the one held in December 1962 and the one in March of the following year, followed very closely the evolution of Shostakovich's Thirteenth Symphony. The first meeting, as we recall, was a prelude to the symphony's premiere, a performance that was applauded by the audience, yet was attended by no Communist Party official and was followed by no official review by the Soviet press. The second meeting was followed by the decision "from above" to call off all performances of the symphony in the Soviet Union. Henceforth, although an official prohibition of the work in the USSR was never announced, the performing of it in the country resumed only on September 20, 1965, following the ouster of Khrushchev and the changing of the guard at the Kremlin.[20] The score of the symphony was not printed in the Soviet Union until 1971.[21]

One may conclude from all of the above that the setting of the poem to music by Shostakovich is what made Khrushchev lose his temper. More than the text of "Babi Yar" per se, it was the reinforcement the young Yevtushenko received from a well-established, internationally acclaimed composer like Shostakovich that constituted for Khrushchev and other Communist Party officials a serious crossing of a line. Evidently, in the age of permitted dissent, what could be written about the massacres that had taken place at the ravine on the outskirts of Kyiv, even in such a leading literary magazine as *Literaturnaya gazeta*, and what could be recited by a young "rebellious" poet at a mass gathering of Soviet youth, was not the same as including the text in a work by the most notable living Soviet composer. Furthermore, in view of the centrality of the symphony as a genre in Shostakovich's repertoire, joining a long series of other works dedicated, inter alia, to May Day, the Russian Revolution of 1905, the October Revolution, and the Siege of Leningrad, there was something almost sacrilegious in placing Babyn Yar as the latest latest link in this awe-inspiring musical chain.[22]

## "HERE RUSSIANS LIE, AND UKRAINIANS"

The examination of *Babi Yar* the symphony in conjunction with "Babi Yar" the poem underscores that it was not the poem itself that pitted Yevtushenko against those standing at the very top of the Soviet political and ideological pyramid but rather its amplification by Shostakovich's orchestral accompaniment. Yet, as befitted the practitioners of permitted dissent, the joint effort of the poet and the composer to commemorate Babyn Yar did not only make them more combative, but also forced them to display a great deal of prudence and, it would be fair to say, compliance as well: they had to make changes to the text. That this was done under pressure is indisputable, though who was the one to take the initiative here still remains unclear. According to one account, Yevtushenko insisted that these textual modifications were made at his own initiative. This account relies on an interview he gave in Paris in which the poet insisted that "he is not a man to take orders." Rather than capitulate to any political pressure, Yevtushenko insisted that these additions were his genuine reaction to a letter he had received from one of his readers describing a Russian woman's rescue of a Jewish child who was about to be murdered by the SS.[23] A contrasting account has it that Shostakovich was the one who pressured an initially reluctant Yevtushenko to introduce substantial changes to the original work. Shostakovich had in mind a clear goal: to facilitate the performance of his symphonies in concert halls across the Soviet Union and to give the conversation about antisemitism and the neglect of Babyn Yar within the country some outlet under the new circumstances, albeit a very limited one.[24] While initially resisting and objecting to the idea that the poem by which he was so inspired needed any modifications, Shostakovich finally relented since he was looking ahead to the forthcoming performances of the symphony scheduled for February 11 and 12, 1963.[25] One steadfast fact remained unchangeable and clear: if the two artists wished to see their collaborative creation continuing to be performed in the USSR, Yevtushenko and Shostakovich had to follow instructions to introduce several crucial textual changes to the poem.

In the next performance of the Thirteenth Symphony, prior to the complete banning of the piece, the two revised what was seen in the eyes of Moscow officials as the two most provocative stanzas. In place of the stanza beginning with the poet's alter ego identifying himself as a Jew and reading Jewish suffering all the way back to the enslavement of the Hebrews and then moving on to antiquity and to the death of a Jewish man on the cross came a new stanza that, at first blush, seems completely at odds with the *longue durée* of Jewish suffering:

> *Here I stand as if at the fountainhead*
> *That gives me faith in our brotherhood.*
> *Here Russians lie, and Ukrainians*
> *Lie together with Jews in the same ground.*[26]

Toward the end of the poem, another stanza, the one in which the poet's alter ego once again identifies with the Jewish victims of Babyn Yar (with an old man and a child—a clear reference to the Jews murdered at Babyn Yar), supplements the Soviet patriotism of the poem's conclusion with Russian nationalist sentiments:

> *I think of Russia's heroic deed*
> *In blocking the way to fascism.*
> *To the infinitesimal dewdrop she is close*
> *To me with her very being and her fate.*
> *Nothing in me will ever forget this.*[27]

The extent to which the substance of the imperative "never to forget" has changed from the first version to the second speaks for itself. There is no doubt that without outside pressure, neither of these two Judeophile Soviet artists would have supplanted the memory of the Jews murdered at Babyn Yar with the great exploits of the Red Army in its battle against fascism. Yet, when viewed as a part of a trajectory, as one of the phases in the evolution of "Babi Yar," the setting of the poem to a score affected the text in two contradictory ways. On the one hand, it pitted Yevtushenko against none other than Khrushchev himself, something that in future years would greatly enhance the reputation of Yevtushenko as one of the few Russian intellectuals who dared to protest Moscow's official stance toward Babyn Yar. On the other hand, the inclusion of the two stanzas, while never incorporated into the piece's manuscript,[28] turned "Babi Yar" in its alternative version into a piece dedicated not to the Holocaust but rather to the Great Patriotic War.

Thus, while the censored Viktor Nekrasov eschewed any clear references to the Holocaust or the Great Patriotic War, and the uncensored one saw both as interconnected, Yevtushenko and Shostakovich in the modified text established an unequivocal linkage between the two in the most explicit way. No personal harm would have befallen Yevtushenko and Shostakovich had they insisted on leaving the poem as is. Their joint project would just never have seen the light of day. Their decision to align Babyn Yar with the Great Patriotic War rather than the Holocaust does not signal the betrayal of the ideals that brought them together in the first place. By substituting two of the most controversial stanzas, they reveal something crucial about Babyn Yar itself: as a battle ground of two different historical narratives, Babyn Yar is extremely difficult to disentangle. The case of Anatoly Kuznetsov, who, as opposed to them, grew up in Kyiv and resided in the city during the German occupation, is no less layered and fraught with multiple meanings.

# 5

# DOCUMENTARY IN CONTENT, FICTIONAL IN FORM: ANATOLY KUZNETSOV

No LESS THAN YEVTUSHENKO'S "BABI YAR," THE DOCUMENTARY NOVEL (*roman-dokument*) by Anatoly Kuznetsov carrying the same title was a quintessential product of the Thaw era. The novel *Babi Yar* has often been discussed in connection with Yevtushenko's poem due to their obvious thematic similarity. Their close relationship also rests upon one account of the origin of the poem "Babi Yar." It was, we may recall (at least according to one account), the young Kuznetsov who told Yevtushenko, his classmate at the Maxim Gorky Literature Institute in Moscow, about the Babyn Yar massacre and brought him there for the first time.[1] However, the two works should be read in tandem for another reason. As a fellow *shestidesyatnik*, Kuznetsov, like Yevtushenko, was a young Russian writer who made his debut in the late 1950s with works that, despite some slight deviation, had followed the dictates of socialist realism. If Yevtushenko's rite of passage as a Soviet dissident was the poem "Babi Yar," Kuznetsov's inaugural novel as a Soviet Thaw era dissident—that is, as a practitioner of permitted dissent—was, with no doubt, *Babi Yar*. Whether it was because of his premature death at the age of fifty, the artistic muteness to which his life in his London exile had consigned him, or some other reason, *Babi Yar* has become Anatoly Kuznetsov's greatest work.

## NOTHING BUT THE TRUTH

The novel *Babi Yar*, published for the first time in the summer and fall issues of the literary periodical *Iunost'* (Youth),[2] owed its appearance to the same politico-cultural climate that facilitated the publication of Yevtushenko's "Babi Yar." It was published thanks to its approval by the new editor of the literary periodical, the Stalin Prize winner Boris Polevoi, who had won his fame as a World War II correspondent and as a writer of fictional works related to that era. Not unlike Valery Kosolapov, the editor in chief of *Literaturnaya gazeta*, Polevoi, who extended the circulation of *Iunost'* from 640,000 to 2,000,000 copies, also wished to attract the young and emerging writers of the 1960s generation and convince them to take an active part in writing for his periodical.[3]

The novel came only two years after a major power shift in the Soviet hierarchy took place with the ouster of Nikita Khrushchev on October 15, 1964, carried out by the collective leadership that replaced him, which was headed by Leonid Brezhnev and Alexei Kosygin. As much as the new leadership was critical of Khrushchev on many issues, including his mercurial attitude toward artistic freedom, the new Presidium led by Brezhnev and Kosygin wished to maintain for a while the modus vivendi of cooperation between the regime and the intelligentsia. As a matter of fact, not only did this relative relaxation in the literary arena persist, but it was also extended, especially in the specific context of our study. On the whole, the first years of the Kremlin power change saw less discrimination against Jews in the Soviet Union and greater tolerance of Jewish culture. These two years witnessed a surge in the number of books published containing Jewish themes, including the Holocaust. Among the most conspicuous signs that the new Soviet heads of state wished to display more laxity toward their Jewish subjects was the appearance of the novel *Babi Yar* by Kuznetsov.

When juxtaposing the two works, Yevtushenko's poem and Kuznetsov's novel, they seem strikingly similar and equally disparate as far as the impetus that led to their composition is concerned. On the one hand, both texts rest upon a similar moral premise: the demand of the younger generation of Soviet writers to tell their audience the truth and only the truth as a sine qua non for a better, purer, and more moral life that would be properly guided by the original principles of Marx and Lenin. Like in the case of the poem "Babi Yar," the publication of the novel *Babi Yar* was an auspicious moment for Soviet Jews, another sign—albeit a false one, as we shall see—that the silence permeating Babyn Yar as a Holocaust site was about to be broken. Naya Lekht recounts the reaction of Semen Gluzman, a former Soviet dissident, as a young boy to the publication of Kuznetsov's novel:

> There was an explosion—Anatoly Kuznetsov's novel. My parents discussed with great emotion some details of the text that were incomprehensible to me; their friends would visit us and also discuss nothing but this book. For a few weeks, the house lived on this alone.[4]

On the other hand, if for Yevtushenko what obstructed this truth from governing Soviet life was antisemitism—both its existence and the categorical refusal to admit it—Kuznetsov conceived of the term "truth" in a more literal sense. For him, what posed the greatest threat to a life guided by the truth was not mendacity but rather ignorance. In its originally published version, Kuznetsov does not fashion his work as an attack against the cover-up of the truth by old-guard Stalinist antisemites. The chief enemy of truth for Kuznetsov's young designated readers was not the mendacious Soviet censor but rather sheer ignorance of historical facts, the product of lack of interest by young adults in those dark and long bygone days of the Great Patriotic War experienced by their parents. Kuznetsov, whose novel begins with the sentence "This book contains nothing but the truth,"[5] addresses his young audience with the following exhortations:

> If you have already taken up this book and have had the patience to read this far, I congratulate you, and I would beg you in that case, please do not drop it, but read it to the end.
> You see, what I am offering you is, after all, not an ordinary novel. It is a document, an exact picture of what happened. Just imagine that had you been born just one historical moment sooner, this might have been your life and not just something to pick up and read.... You could have been me; you could have been born in Kiev, in Kurenyovka, and I could have been you, reading this page.[6]

For Kuznetsov, this battle against ignorance was two-edged: the moral imperative to uproot ignorance was a demand he made first and foremost of himself. His *Babi Yar* may be best understood as the product of this lifelong battle, the complexity of which may be realized only when one carefully reads his novel in its evolutionary process.

Indeed, this battle with the indifference toward the atrocities that had been committed on Soviet soil during World War II is reflected not only in the novel itself but in the intricate process that accompanied its composition. This process has already been amply described by Richard Sheldon and Leona Toker but is worth reiterating briefly. The story begins with Kuznetsov's first published work, the novella *Sequel to a Legend* (1958), which saw the light of day only after it was heavily censored, much to the chagrin of its author.[7] Embittered by this experience, Kuznetsov was appalled when he learned that his new work, *Babi Yar*, would be subject to more than 300 editorial changes. He was required to cut out "offending sections, amounting to a quarter of the novel, to only find out that in its published form, the censor took the liberty to cut out an additional quarter."[8] According to Sheldon, who bases his account on Kuznetsov's own testimonies, when Kuznetsov learned that his work would be printed only in this truncated form he demanded the manuscript back from the *Iunost'* editor in chief, Boris Polevoi. When he was refused, Kuznetsov grabbed the manuscript and later tore it to pieces. As it transpired, however, the editors of *Iunost'* had another copy, and by

August 13, 1969. Anatoly Kuznetsov getting ready for a television interview by the BBC soon after his defection to England. (Photo from Keystone Press / Alamy Stock Photo.)

Kuznetsov's own testimony it was only due to his dire financial straits that he gave his consent to its publication.[9]

After the Soviet invasion of Czechoslovakia in the Prague Spring of 1968, Kuznetsov understood that his work would never see the light of day in its unabridged form in the Soviet Union. This bitter realization drove him to plan his escape from the USSR. In order to win the trust of the authorities, he began collaborating with the KGB by composing secret denunciations of major Soviet artists, including his former classmate Yevgeny Yevtushenko.[10] This treacherous practice turned out to be Kuznetsov's ticket to freedom: in July of 1969, he was allowed to travel to London, presumably in order to do biographical research on Lenin's life as a Russian émigré in the British capital.[11] Upon Kuznetsov's arrival in London, he eluded the person who was supposed to track his whereabouts and managed to find asylum in the United Kingdom. He brought in his belongings the allegedly original, uncensored version of the novel stored on microfilm (he buried his manuscripts in a forest, outside Tula, his city of residence back then)[12] and managed to republish the book accompanied by additional comments that he incorporated into the text while in exile.

Wishing to dissociate himself from his past, Kuznetsov invented a new literary persona, A. Anatoli, and under this alias the novel *Babi Yar: A Document in the Form of a Novel* was published in its complete form in 1970, appearing both in Russian (in

Frankfurt) and English (in New York). As Masha Gessen notes, the most recent, uncensored edition of the novel became a masterpiece by virtue of both its author's life circumstances and desire to tell the truth:

> Kuznetsov devised a simple system of notations—italics and brackets in the first edition, boldface and brackets in subsequent editions—to denote, respectively, words and phrases that the Soviet censor had cut and material that Kuznetsov himself had added after the original publication of *Babi Yar*. He created layered text that told several stories: the story of the Babyn Yar massacre, the German occupation of Kyiv, and subsequent Soviet efforts to suppress this history; a story in heavier type, about the ways in which censorship shaped Soviet literature; and the stories, in brackets, of what the writer thought he couldn't say.[13]

Gessen's recommendation for the reader is to read the novel twice—"the first time as the (document in the form of a) novel that it is, ... and the second time as a document that tells a story about censorship."[14] Though the new text seems like an expanded version of the one published in the USSR, upon closer inspection the versions seem to contradict each other. As we read the 1970 version of the novel, it is astounding to realize how the censored parts, together with the later additions introduced by Kuznetsov from his London exile, do not complement the *Iunost'* edition but rather undo it. The peculiar coexistence of these two versions has repercussions that stretch far beyond our concern with the Babyn Yar massacre. The novel may very well function as a case in point of the role played by the censor as writer that any student of Soviet literature during the Thaw period should consider.

# A TESTIMONY OF THE WRITER AS A YOUNG MAN

Before we turn to a deeper analysis of these two ideological points of view and consider the intricate way in which they coexist and yet conflict with each other, it is necessary to observe one of the features of the novel that underlies both versions: the particular genre in which Kuznetsov decided to write his work—the documentary novel. In contrast to the choice of Yevtushenko to invoke the memory of Babyn Yar via the poetic mode in order to strike a chord in his readers, to rouse their emotions, and to awaken their conscience, the main drive of Kuznetsov's novel was to establish the facts about Babyn Yar. As the literary critic Emil Staiger asserts, it is in the lyrical mode, the one adopted by Yevtushenko, where there is no distance between subject and object, where "the 'I' swims along in the transience of things."[15] By contrast, a work of prose—and especially if the work in question makes a claim to veracity—maintains a clearer demarcation line between the self and reality and is thus less concerned with subjective feelings and more geared toward establishing the novel's fictional reality.

Because of Kuznetsov's almost obsessive desire to render the facts about Babyn Yar's history mainly during the German occupation, from September 1941 to November 1943, a wide audience of Soviet readers learned for the first time the full details about the carnage at the ravine, about events that the autobiographical protagonist, young Tolia, witnessed while growing up during the war years in Kurenivka, the suburb of Kyiv adjacent to Babyn Yar (which was flooded in the tragic event, discussed in chapter 3, in the spring of 1961). Only for brief intervals does the novel depart from this chronological time frame. One of these chronological shifts occurs when Kuznetsov turns to a discussion of the Ukrainian famine of 1932–1933, the historical event known as the Holodomor. Another shift occurs when dealing with the attempts to destroy Babyn Yar during the Khrushchev era. While these two deviations from the novel's chronological sweep are significant, it should be noted that they occur only in its uncensored version.[16]

For the most part, the main intent of the novel is to provide concrete details about life under German occupation in Kyiv in general, including the two dreadful days in the fall of 1941 when the Babyn Yar massacre wore on. This pursuit of factuality is the main reason that prompted Kuznetsov to make a very specific generic choice when designing his work. This is why he ultimately chose to give it the shape of a documentary novel. On numerous occasions, Kuznetsov incorporated into the novel authentic documents pertaining to the German occupation, which were mainly in the form of excerpts from the local newspapers *Ukrains'ke Slovo* and *Nove Ukrains'ke Slovo*, which were at his disposal while working on it.

Significantly, this specific generic choice made the novel a suitable candidate to be included in two different twentieth-century literary canons: Holocaust documentary fiction and gulag literature. Both these subgenres of the documentary novel share a basic common denominator: they are underlain by the author's desire to endow their work with a strong sense of authenticity, to win the attention of the reader not only by bringing forth materials hitherto unknown but also by utilizing their rhetorical faculties. At the highest moral level, the effect on the reader that the author wishes to achieve is to present themselves as the rare human being "who has been there" and managed to come back. While this is not always the case in documentary novels, in Kuznetsov's novel this pursuit of the reader's attention is stretched to the extreme: the author narrates the plot in the first-person singular; the main character himself is presented as a youngster; and, lastly, the narrator relentlessly repeats his opening statement in the novel that "it all really happened."

In his book *Writing and Rewriting the Holocaust*, James Young dwells on the documentary novel as a common genre used by Holocaust writers to endow their work with the greatest degree of credibility. These writers, of course, face a challenge greater than that of diarists and memoirists, whose credibility, while never guaranteed, is far less often called into question.[17] Young notes, though, that the narrator's impulse in Holocaust fiction to insist on a documentary link between the text and its inspiring events has not been limited to diarists and memoirists: it applies just as much to many novelists and playwrights who feature the Holocaust in their works. Kuznetsov's case in this respect is unique, as it is an account of documentary fiction only in its final form. As Kuznetsov relates in the novel itself, its nucleus initially took shape as a diary the young Kuznetsov started keeping as early as 1943.[18] He relates in the novel that after the war, as the antisemitic atmosphere of the late Stalin years intensified, he realized the danger of keeping such a personal, incriminating account and decided to get rid of it. In this respect, Kuznetsov makes the utmost endeavor in the novel to make the case that his work is nothing more than a sheer record of past events, which is not rendered in the form of a diary only due to some sorry circumstances.

Young recognizes a pattern: some writers of documentary fiction on the Holocaust—and Kuznetsov's *roman-dokument* is a good case in point for that—espouse this writing strategy "out of fear that the rhetoricity of their literary medium inadvertently confers fictiveness onto events themselves."[19] Elie Wiesel also echoes the same concern about the limitation of Holocaust literature as a genre, recognizing the fine line dividing fiction from fictiveness. The Holocaust writer thus finds himself in a bind: while silence would best convey the survivor's experience, it would amount to a betrayal of those who did not survive. And conversely, while telling their stories would sustain their experiences in collective memory, the act of narration itself would innately detract from their truthfulness. As Wiesel puts it: "A novel about Majdanek is either not a novel or not about Majdanek."[20]

The employment of the documentary mode is not done by Kuznetsov for only aesthetic or dramatic purposes. Admittedly, in the case of *Babi Yar* the narrator's insistence that he is telling nothing but the truth is one of the artistic merits of the work. This constant insistence that has the effect of "pounding on the reader's head" is one of the central artistic devices utilized by Kuznetsov in a work where one of the chief goals is to confront its young reader with human nature's unlimited capacity for brutality (and the reader's limited capacity to conceive of it). As Nina Tumarkin puts it, the adjective that would most suitably describe the novel is "relentless."[21] Kuznetsov consciously chooses narration in the first person and incessantly reiterates his claim to authenticity in order to provide a seamless account of cruelty and suffering that he is deliberately unwilling to relieve by offering any momentary humoristic anecdotes.

Kuznetsov is cognizant of the aesthetic merit of endowing his novel with a sense of urgency. But his main goal here is not to achieve any artistic heights but rather the rendition of a sound, coherent, and highly credible story about Kyiv under German occupation: to describe events to which—Kuznetsov was right to assume—many readers in the Soviet Union at the time remained oblivious. The Russian novelist makes it very clear from the outset that his novel has nothing to do with aesthetic aspirations. He strives to highlight the fact that the hyphenated *roman-dokument* is a genre in its own right, distinct not only from the Soviet socialist-realist novel (which he considers phony and deceiving as the portrayal of an ideal world that could not be more remote from what he saw as the dystopian Soviet reality), but from the tradition of European realism as well. The school of realism, we should bear in mind, never called into question the need to conjure up a fictional world that would reflect, like a mirror, the real one. Even in its most radical form, as emblematized, for instance, in the works of the nineteenth-century French masters of realism such as Balzac or Zola, who insisted that the human experience may be understood only by the rendition of the protagonists' full cultural and socioeconomic background (their assets, income, place of residence, attire, social status, social circle), there was never a real denial of a demarcation line dividing reality from fiction. Yet this is exactly what Kuznetsov claims to be doing in his novel:

> I am writing this book now without bothering about any literary rules [or any political systems, frontiers, censors, or national prejudices].
> I am writing it as though I were giving evidence under oath in the very highest court and I am ready to answer for every single word. This book records only the truth—AS IT REALLY HAPPENED.[22]

One of Kuznetsov's main strategies is precisely the blurring of these lines between fiction and reality. The novel implies that its readers should not waste their time reading the typical Soviet fictional accounts about the war years, which provide their readers with a grossly distorted image of historical reality. Yet, despite these ambitious goals, *Babi Yar* is not the pure transmission of facts that Kuznetsov presents it to be. The author's confidence that his is an unmediated account of the war given with the utmost veracity does not stand up to careful scrutiny. First, the novel contains numerous dialogues conducted within the narrator's domestic sphere, conversations that were clearly not transcribed verbatim. Second, the testimony of Dina Pronicheva, the Kyiv Puppet Theater actress who was among the Babyn Yar massacre's only survivors (a document lying at the core of Kuznetsov's discussion of the massacre), is only a secondhand account based on an interview that Kuznetsov had conducted with her. Apparently, this artistic choice betrays the author's realization that in absentia from the scene of the murder itself he did not have the moral right or sufficient experience to submit his own fictional account of the massacre.[23] Third, as the author confides to his readers, he was too young to remember the unfolding events under the German occupation and was not sufficiently mature to grasp their significance. It was his mother who helped him reconstruct the novel's supposedly unembellished reality.

In light of the gap between Kuznetsov's claim to total veracity and the variegated sources and voices from which he drew, the puzzling question remains why he saw himself suitable to be the author of a Holocaust testimony rendered in the format of a documentary novel. Young provides an answer by categorizing the novel within the realm of the specific genre of Holocaust documentary fiction. By correlating *Babi Yar* with *Treblinka* by Jean-François Steiner, *The White Hotel* by D. M. Thomas, or Gerald Green's *Holocaust*, Young contends, it is possible to make the claim that Kuznetsov was searching here for an appropriate genre that would befit his topic, which was the Holocaust as it unfolded in the Ukrainian capital. And like other Holocaust fiction writers, so the argument goes, Kuznetsov purports to enhance the veracity of the events described in the novel by way of supporting them with purely historical documents and sources, a practice that would minimize the fictiveness of his plot and endow the novel with "the rhetoric of fact."[24]

While this reading of Kuznetsov's work through the lens of Holocaust documentary fiction undoubtedly helps illuminate the distinctiveness of *Babi Yar*, it faces one major difficulty. No doubt, the novel carries the name of the ravine and was indeed the groundbreaking work that exposed the Soviet public to the atrocities in Babyn Yar for the first time. But the claim that this novel grapples with the question How should a Holocaust narrative, or novel, be told? overlooks one crucial fact: that neither in the *Iunost'* version nor in the one published in exile in 1970 does Kuznetsov frame his *Babi Yar* in the context of the Holocaust, the unique tragedy that befell the Jewish people. This fact should be not only highlighted but also more closely explored by anyone wishing not only to better understand the work's main message and ideological underpinnings but also to understand it as a staple feature of the specific historical conditions that spawned its creation.

## A COUNTERARGUMENT TO YEVTUSHENKO

Thus far, we have mentioned the classification of *Babyn Yar* as a part of the larger corpus of Holocaust literature and pondered the difficulty it poses in view of the fact that the concept of the Holocaust itself was quite foreign to Kuznetsov, as it was for many other Soviet writers. Rather than view the novel as a species of Holocaust documentary fiction, Leona Toker prefers to place it within the contours of the literature of testimony, a far broader genre, which gives voice to a very diverse set of texts dealing with human ordeals. While the Holocaust surely looms large among them, it is not the only experience that drove writers to blend documentation and fictionalization. Another body of literature in which the same kind of negotiation is carried out is gulag literature, and it is to this subgenre that Toker dedicates much of her essay "Toward a Poetics of

Documentary Prose."²⁵ This reading of Kuznetsov's novel from the angle of testimony literature helps Toker, inter alia, to explain the existence of the work in multiple versions as well as its printing in a "messy" edition like the one prepared in 1970, in which the text's creation process is embodied in the two different typefaces and the comments put into square brackets. Toker notes that while this hard-to-follow structure would be perceived in realistic prose as a shortcoming, in documentary prose it turns into a virtue, for it indicates the author's "uncompromising pursuit of factual and moral truth."²⁶

Beyond this curious point, the inclusion of *Babi Yar* within the framework of gulag literature, as we shall see, does more historical justice to Kuznetsov's novel. Likewise, this classifying choice helps flesh out the moral foundations upon which it rests. For it was not through the lens of the Holocaust only that Kuznetsov looked at the Babyn Yar massacre, but also through that of a parallel genre, as he zeroed in on the victims of another totalitarian system. It was thus not *The Diary of a Young Girl* that prompted him to render his testimony, but rather Alexander Solzhenitsyn's *One Day in the Life of Ivan Denisovich*, a novel that profoundly impacted Kuznetsov.²⁷ The question then becomes: To what story of survival did Kuznetsov dedicate this intimate, confessional novel? One possible answer would be that this is a story of survival under German occupation. If this is the case, then it should be emphasized that Kuznetsov's object of exploration is the general Soviet population, including Kuznetsov himself.

In the novel, he takes pains to mention the extent to which his life was hanging by a thread by listing twenty different transgressions that he had committed during the war, each potentially punishable by death.²⁸ So too, on numerous occasions throughout the novel—in both the original and the later version—Kuznetsov underlines the multinational nature of Babyn Yar. While the novel recounts Pronicheva's testimony in its first half, it gradually transpires that the novel includes in the list of Babyn Yar's victims multiple groups that vary from labor camp inmates and POWs to Roma, the Dynamo Kyiv football team players,²⁹ and even those who "met their deaths later in Babyn Yar because of the ban on keeping pigeons."³⁰

While the credibility of Kuznetsov's main argument need not be called into question, his conception of the ravine as a Soviet site bearing no distinctive meaning to the suffering of the Jewish people is a fact that must not be overlooked. In one of the earliest scenes in the novel, Kuznetsov, upon his encounter with an old man, sets the ideological tone of the novel, which would later go as far as positing that Babyn Yar was not just an ordinary mass grave where the bodies of humans of different ethnicities lie but was, rather, a symbol for the common fate shared on Soviet soil by different ethnic groups during World War II:

"Please, mister," I asked, "was it here they shot the Jews, or farther on?"

The old man stopped, looked me up and down and said:

"And what about all the Russians who were killed here? And the Ukrainians and other kinds of people?"[31]

Soon afterward, the narrator reaches a stream in which he recognizes pieces of the victims' bones being washed, a specter that helped him locate "the place where the Jews, Russians, Ukrainians and people of other nationalities had been shot." He recounts: "I picked up one of the pieces weighing four or five pounds and took it with me to keep. It contains the ashes of many people, all mixed up together—a sort of international mixture."[32]

Kuznetsov's conception of Babyn Yar as an international slaughter site is a fact that cannot be downplayed, and it would be wrong to argue that it holds true only with regard to the version of the novel originally published in the USSR. Clearly, with regard to the original version, this "internationalist" stance helped Kuznetsov see his work published in the USSR. There is nothing necessarily remarkable about this "internationalist" outlook in view of the fact that it was submitted by a young man who was half-Russian, half-Ukrainian.[33] It is equally important to note that these "internationalist," or rather universalist, comments made by Kuznetsov throughout the novel do not and should not earn him the epithet of an antisemite or Holocaust denier. Kuznetsov tried to establish the facts, and the facts indeed reveal that not only Jews were killed at Babyn Yar.

On the whole, Kuznetsov submits a fairly balanced account of the events that took place at Babyn Yar. Clearly, his account of the Babyn Yar massacre itself, provided in full detail and without concealing the fact that its targets were Jews, qualifies the novel as a groundbreaking work in the history of Babyn Yar's commemoration. Yet, if one wonders why a regime that stifled any attempt to correlate Babyn Yar with Jewish victimhood not only did not frown upon this new novel but rather allowed its publication and even its translation into English with hardly any editorial changes made to Pronicheva's account, the answer lies in the minor space that the tragedy of the Jews occupies in the novel. Interestingly, it is not the claim that members of other nationalities were killed in Babyn Yar that took from *Babyn Yar*, as far as Soviet officialdom was concerned, its ideological sting. Rather, the recurrence of this "internationalist" argument and the attempt to put in the spotlight the suffering of the entire Soviet population trapped in the German-occupied zone is what diminishes from the distinctiveness of Babyn Yar and the massacre that took place in the ravine as one of the Holocaust's defining places and moments, where on September 29, 1941, Kyiv became the first European capital to be *Judenrein*.

More than anything else, it is the minor room that the Babyn Yar massacre of Kyiv Jews occupies in the novel that not only allowed the publication of the original version of the novel but even justified it. Boris Polevoi, who carefully scrutinized the novel before its publication and could have easily thwarted it, made the quite puzzling claim that Kuznetsov's novel would counterbalance what he saw as Yevtushenko's overemphasis on Babyn Yar's Jewish context.[34] While apparently puzzling on first sight, this argument is validated if one considers the minor place that Jews occupy in the novel among other victims and, more importantly, Kuznetsov's failure to conceive of the Jews' murder as a part of a grander scheme to carry out genocide. On a few occasions throughout the novel, for example, Kuznetsov raises the hypothesis that the Babyn Yar massacre was carried out as a vengeful, impulsive act on the part of the Nazis as retribution for the blowing up of buildings on Khreshchatik Street in downtown Kyiv.[35] While Kuznetsov draws a true historical correlation between the explosions on Khreshchatik Street and the pretext for the perpetration of the massacre, the placing of the massacre in the midst of a whirlwind of savagery and destruction is exactly what impressed the one who gave the novel his approbation. Polevoi could not have missed realizing the potential of the novel to constitute an account of the war rendered by a non-Jew, who, rather than exclaim that "he is a Jew" as did Yevtushenko, preferred to honor all of those who died in Babyn Yar, irrespective of their national origins.

Lastly, to the reasons for the novel's approval we must add another. While Kuznetsov insisted time and again that his work was a document only couched in the form of a novel, those who approved it did not fail to realize its lack of historical credibility. While the official historiography of the Great Patriotic War would continue to downplay the Jewish identity of those among Babyn Yar's victims, *Babi Yar* would be judged for what it was: a work of fiction based on the recollections of a young and naïve individual who was only twelve years old when the Nazis entered the city of Kyiv, a youngster who throughout the novel is easily influenced by the adults that surround him and has a hard time making sense of the events unfolding before his eyes.

## ONE NOVEL, TWO PATHS: PERMITTED DISSENT AND DEFECTION

The expanded version of the novel printed in 1970—while, like the original version, is far from a credible historiographical work—is a far less naïve account. It was submitted by a mature writer who had by then been fully sobered by life under both Nazi and Soviet rule; he was a writer who was now far more prepared to make sense of the wartime events. We have already noted that the complete version of Kuznetsov's novel was radically different from the one published in *Iunost'*. While the two versions, for the most part, follow the same plotline in the grand scheme of things, it is their "ideological facet of focalization" (the abstract array of values that are embedded in every literary work)[36] that sets them apart from each other. In effect, the two versions offer an account of Tolia's life in the occupied zone so different from each other that when reading the 1970 edition of the novel where the two are juxtaposed, one is almost compelled to believe that two different authors were responsible for their composition.

To put it another way, Kuznetsov's *Babi Yar* is a good example of a novel where the censor becomes not merely a participant in the literary process but rather an almost independent player in it. In contrast to the final version of the novel that constitutes an indictment of the Soviet system as a totalitarian one, a system by no means better or less inhuman than Nazi Germany, the reader cannot find even a trace of this train of thought in the 1966 *Iunost'* version. The Ukrainian famine of 1932–1933, the blowing up of the old Kyiv-Pechersk monastery by the Soviets, and the flooding of Babyn Yar during the early Khrushchev years, resulting in the Kurenivka tragedy: these and many other events are all missing from the novel that came out through official Soviet publication channels.

When considering the final version of the novel only, it becomes clear that for Kuznetsov, who wished to fashion his novel along the lines of the genre of testimony literature, what lies at the core of this novel was not only the survival of the German occupation but also the far broader survival of life under both the Soviets and Nazis, two equally evil and destructive totalitarian systems. There is little doubt that when Kuznetsov read the *Iunost'* version of his novel and realized to what degree his semiautobiographical account had been distorted, he was anything but pleased. At the same time, though, we should bear in mind that in a dictatorial system where high levels of vigilance were in effect in the arena of literature, Kuznetsov could also see his novel as an achievement. As opposed to Vasily Grossman, who was told by Mikhail Suslov that his *Life and Fate*—a work that drew the same link between Nazism and Communism—could not see the light of day in the Soviet Union for the next 300 years, Kuznetsov saw his novel not only get published but also become a bestseller, bestowing upon the author both honor and honoraria.

If we borrow two terms from Leona Toker that illuminate the uniqueness of the literary process in the USSR, the term "target audience," as a reference to the designated readers of a work, and the term "hurdle audience," as a reference to the censor of the text, the reader whose job is "to obstruct its accessibility to the target audience,"[37] it is easier to describe Kuznetsov's *Babi Yar* as a work that passed the hurdle audience only to a limited extent. While the general contours of Kuznetsov's testimony were kept, the novel failed to pass the hurdle audience at the ideological level. What the target audience received was not a humanist, perhaps not even pacifist, work renouncing any kind of "ism," any sort of political oppression, but rather a Soviet-style antiwar novel that suited both the socialist tenet of *druzhba narodov* (the friendship of peoples) and Moscow's attempt to fancy itself as the international community's peacekeeper during the early Brezhnev years. In one of his conversations on Radio Liberty that took place during the early 1970s from his London exile, Kuznetsov recalled the revulsion he felt when he realized that his novel was a pawn played by those above him in the Soviet literary hierarchy, who tried to publicize him as a Soviet "antiwar" writer. Thereupon, this bitter realization completely disillusioned Kuznetsov with the practice of permitted dissent. When faced with the choice of whether to win minor battles with the Soviet censor or to see his entire work printed in exile, Kuznetsov ultimately chose to pursue the latter course of action.

Still, when considering the intricate connection between the representation of Babyn Yar in Soviet Russian literature and the specific historical conditions of the Thaw period, we must bear in mind that the story of the Babyn Yar massacre did not constitute a real hurdle on Kuznetsov's road to freedom. To a certain extent, Edith Clowes is correct when she asserts that many of the novel's reviews deemphasized Babyn Yar's Jewish context because the abridged version of the novel "allowed the readers to see a more generalized picture of suffering."[38] No doubt, the reading of the full version that contains materials on the anti-Cosmopolitan campaign and the post-Stalin-era attempts to eradicate Babyn Yar altogether helps bring the massacre of September 29–30 to the fore. Nonetheless, when carefully comparing the two versions, one cannot avoid the impression that the expanded version, while taking issue with so many of the statements made by Kuznetsov in the *Iunost'* edition, leaves the story about the massacre for the most part intact.

As Kuznetsov's chief target in the expanded version is the Soviet regime rather than the Nazis, the room that the Babyn Yar massacre occupies in it, on the whole, is only further diminished in the unabridged version. Concomitantly, his failure to grasp the Babyn Yar massacre as a part of a grander genocidal scheme applies to the unabridged version as much as to the original one. One way to make sense of Kuznetsov's failure to set Babyn Yar within the broader framework of what Lucy Dawidowicz called "Hitler's war against the Jews" would be to insist that, in order to endow the novel with a sense of immediacy and render it as an autobiographical novel presented from the very narrow angle of one young individual, Kuznetsov had to focus on the Babyn Yar massacre only and detach it from the wider context of the Final Solution. This explanation, however, is very precarious: the reading of the unabridged version of the novel plainly shows that when it comes to atrocities perpetrated by the Soviets, Kuznetsov never fails to conceive of them in the broadest terms, without considering them to be contingent upon any specific circumstances, such as the correlation he draws between the explosions on Khreshchatik Street and the Babyn Yar massacre.

Take, for example, Kuznetsov's discussion of the Holodomor, the human-made famine that was carried out by Stalin's henchmen in rural Ukraine in the early 1930s. For Kuznetsov, it was the far fresher memories of Soviet terror, among which the Holodomor loomed large, that prompted the writing of the novel and far less the recollections of life under the Nazis. This would sound strange to most readers of the novel today, given its title and focus on the years of the German occupation. Admittedly, this argument might have sounded preposterous to the original "target audience" of the novel, to the readers of the *Iunost'* version who could not have realized its anti-Soviet undertones, which were, of course, purged by the novel's hurdle audience. Yet in its full form, it is the attack leveled at the Soviet system—and the story of the man who had survived life under it—that constitutes a poignant and bitter part of Kuznetsov's criticism of totalitarianism and his defense of freedom.

To consolidate this reading of *Babyn Yar* in its final version as an anti-Soviet novel written by a Russian dissident living in exile, we should revisit Kuznetsov's participation in the program aired on Radio Liberty under the heading "A Writer at the Microphone." If one wishes to argue that while still in the Soviet Union it was a lack of vocabulary that prevented Kuznetsov from grasping the deeper meaning of the Holocaust, in his radio conversation no. 25, titled "Famine," he borrows the Western term "genocide," coined by Raphael Lemkin, in a discussion of the Holodomor. For Kuznetsov the writer, as it turns out, it was the Holodomor, and not the Holocaust, that deserved the world's attention as the greatest crime against humanity perpetrated during the twentieth century:

> I do not know whether certain documents dealing with the famine of 1932–33 in the Ukraine and Kuban have been preserved in the Soviet secret archives. Organized in the Ukraine a decade before Babi Yar ... that genocide was yet far greater than Hitler's: a number of researchers estimated the number of dead out of the famine to reach seven million. ... in such a short time, and even more so—and this should be emphasized—in an absolutely peaceful time, without any war—this was, in my opinion, the largest genocidal act in the history of humanity.[39]

For Kuznetsov, the Holodomor was not only the most horrifying event of the twentieth century, it was also a far less known and documented one, an event that was still shrouded in mystery and could not be disclosed to the Soviet public in his documentary novel. What Kuznetsov does here, and without necessarily meaning to engage in a futile dispute on "who had suffered more," is to relegate the Holocaust to a secondary place below the Holodomor. The former, he argues, killed a smaller number of people and therefore came only after the latter. While the data provided here by Kuznetsov will certainly continue to engage historians who will grapple with the question of whether or not the Holodomor was consciously perpetrated as a genocidal operation and the question of its exact number of victims, we may still be able to derive an important conclusion from the above passage. Kuznetsov's words teach us about the close link drawn in his mind—before his defection and after—not between Babyn Yar and the Holocaust (a link that is not highlighted in the original, abridged version either), but rather between Babyn Yar and the tragedy that befell Ukrainian peasants. It was the Holodomor—not the Holocaust—that haunted Kuznetsov in particular as half-Ukrainian and the son of a man who took part in Stalin's murderous collectivization of the Ukrainian countryside.

This correlation between the two events does not diminish the value of Kuznetsov's work in the particular context of Babyn Yar when appraised in hindsight: Kuznetsov was the first to provide the Soviet public with a full-blown report on the killings at the ravine; he did not refrain from indicating that its prime victims were Jews. When read through the lens of the Thaw period, this piece emerges, like that of Yevtushenko, as one step among many in both the gradual and convoluted negotiation that took place between writers and censors about the limits of the permissible regarding writing on Babyn Yar. As in the case of Yevtushenko, when set in the right historical context, *Babi Yar* also emerges as a characteristic feature of permitted dissent. In its originally published form, the work does little to challenge the general party line on the Holocaust and Babyn Yar other than providing Dina Pronicheva's full testimony about the massacre.

Although the novel has often been catalogued as a part of the genre of Holocaust literature, our study shows that the Holocaust occupies a rather minor place in the novel. As Efraim Sicher puts it, the 1970 version of the novel published abroad "fails to take into account antisemitism as the primary motive for the genocide of the Jews, because Kuznetsov is more interested in showing that the so-called progress of civilization is a sham, however many sputniks and televisions have been produced, and that the barbarity of totalitarianism was common to both Germany and the USSR."[40] As the unabridged version illustrates, the reason Kuznetsov did not put the Babyn Yar massacre of Kyiv Jews in the spotlight of his work might have had little to do with the constraints of censorship. Thus, Kuznetsov provides the reader with one novel with two versions and two differing interpretive paths: a documentary novel rendering either a curtailed version of the war's chronology, identifying the German Nazis' victims as Jews, but not in a way that would severely offend the Soviet censor's sensibilities, and the view of these victims as integral sacrifices of the Great Patriotic War; or an expanded version of the war's chronology, containing the equation between the Soviet and the German Nazi crimes that also leads to the dilution of the Holocaust's uniqueness.

Bearing in mind that the dilution of the Holocaust can be done in more than one way and is not endemic to the Soviet regime only, it remains unclear whether this was a deliberate or rather a more unintended goal on the part of Kuznetsov. In any event, when passing a final judgment on Kuznetsov's work by reading and comparing both versions, it is important to bear in mind the stated purpose of *Babi Yar*: the genuine choice of a young, non-Jewish Soviet writer to render an account not of Holocaust survival but rather of his *own* survival of the twentieth century's two major totalitarian systems. This choice betrays the unique case of a "traveling dissident" who found himself in exile and never came back, of a man who demonstrated in his work that between the two poles—the one where Babyn Yar's Jewish connection is completely denied and the one where the massacre is construed as a part of the Holocaust of European Jewry—lie other possibilities.

# 6

# "THEIR MEMORY IS ALIVE": BABYN YAR ON THE SOVIET YIDDISH LITERARY SCENE

Unlike the evolution of Babyn Yar in the Soviet Russian sphere, where it served as a magnet for practitioners of permitted dissent to pressure Moscow to broaden the realms of the permissible, the Soviet Yiddish writers who wished to leave a literary monument to those who lay buried at Babyn Yar had far more modest goals in mind. For them, Babyn Yar was not the terrifying name of a far-flung, forgotten ravine somewhere outside Kyiv. It was the graveyard of their loved ones—husbands and wives, relatives, friends, and neighbors. Without taking anything away from the solemnity with which the artistic works by Nekrasov, Yevtushenko, Shostakovich, and Kuznetsov were endowed, the process through which the representation of Babyn Yar in the Soviet Yiddish sphere had crystallized was far more personal, and for many of these authors far more tragic. The Soviet Yiddish writers were, after all, a group of Jews for whom the identification with the victims was an inevitable truth, not the product of a poetical odyssey in time like the one Yevgeny Yevtushenko, fancying himself a biblical Hebrew or an ancient Jew, had embarked upon. To put it another way, for these people the Holocaust was still a memory, not a postmemory. In contrast to Yevtushenko, these were not writers who had to meet Anatoly Kuznetsov at the Maxim Gorky Literature Institute in Moscow to learn about the tragedy that had taken place at Babyn Yar. Their first encounter with the name Babyn Yar, and for some of them their first visits to the site, took place as early as 1944. It happened in the immediate aftermath of Kyiv's liberation, once the evacuated Kyiv Jews who had survived the war started to return to the city bereaved, homeless, and, for the most part, unwelcomed by a Ukrainian population that had in many instances expropriated their apartments and belongings and, in some cases, had even taken active part in the murder of their brethren.

## KYIV: A SOVIET YIDDISH CULTURAL METROPOLIS

With very few exceptions, the Yiddish writers who engaged the theme of Babyn Yar in their works were all members of the Kyiv circle of Yiddish writers. Yiddish cultural activity in the city took a variety of forms from the time of its emergence as a center of Jewish nationalism and socialism as well as a hub for Yiddish modernism following the Revolution of 1905 up until the post-Stalin era, a time when Yiddish culture in the Soviet Union was severely curtailed.[1] Prior to the outbreak of the Russian Civil War and the pogroms that came on its heels, Kyiv was a magnet for Yiddish writers who wished to experiment with modernist trends. It was home to the Kultur Lige (Culture League), the largest network of Yiddish publishing houses, writers, and cultural centers that was established in 1918 and resumed its operations as an official Soviet organization after the hiatus caused by the civil war and the pogroms that followed.[2]

While Kyiv was, prior to the October Revolution, the most important center for Yiddish modernism, home to some of the best Jewish writers of the early twentieth century such as Peretz Markish, Dovid Bergelson, Dovid Hofshteyn, Der Nister, and Leyb Kvitko, its preeminence would be contested later on by the new Yiddish cultural centers that started to mushroom after the Russian Civil War: Moscow, Kharkiv, and Minsk.[3] Nonetheless, despite its many transformations, the most notable of which was the shift from a plethora of independent cultural organizations to a uniform body funded and supervised by the government and connected to the Soviet Writers' Union (which it had been since the early 1930s), the Kyiv circle of Yiddish writers remained dominant so long as Yiddish cultural activities were allowed to exist in the USSR.

In 1944, in the wake of Kyiv's liberation, the remaining writers and cultural activists who had survived the turbulent events of the war and the Holocaust started to come back to the city. They now came back to what used to be a hub for the state-sponsored Soviet cultural apparatus. At its zenith, it included day schools, theaters, daily newspapers and literary journals, publishing houses, cultural clubs, libraries, and research institutions all running their activities in the Yiddish language.[4] Emblematizing the promise of the first "dictatorship of the proletariat" to help the Jewish people build its own national culture predicated on what the new regime saw as just, socialist foundations, these institutions all operated during much of the interwar period in Yiddish.

The majority of the writers whose works will be explored in this chapter and the next were part of this new Soviet Yiddish literary apparatus that existed in interwar Kyiv. Despite the size of Kyiv as a major Jewish metropolis, this was a tight-knit group of writers who were on intimate terms with each other, who often published in the same Yiddish literary journals and magazines, attended literary events in local factories, and attended the lectures delivered by both Meir Viner and Max Erik, the primary literary critics and historians who taught at Kyiv's primary Jewish research center, the Institute of Jewish Proletarian Culture.[5] Although Kyiv's local Yiddish intelligentsia was cliquish by nature, due to the very centralized and vigilant nature of the cultural and political system of which it was a part, the ideological makeup of its Yiddish writers was not as uniform as one might think. Among them were young writers who were nurtured by the Soviet system, together with older ones whose views and artistic styles were shaped prior to the October Revolution. One may also find in this group party members and writers leaning toward the "fellow traveler" position.

All these cultural gaps never shook the intimate shape of the Kyiv Yiddish intelligentsia. In the wake of the destruction wrought by World War II, many of its members could reunite around a new locus: the common grave on the outskirts of town, in which many of their friends and relatives found their deaths—Babyn Yar. Having lived through a series of calamities—the Great Terror of the mid-1930s, the havoc wrought by World War II, and the antisemitic campaigns of the last years of Stalinism—many of these writers and cultural activists found themselves writing and publishing again in the Ukrainian capital in the Yiddish language. In comparison with their secure position in prewar Soviet culture and society, the new literary activities of the Kyiv Yiddish writers, who were fortunate enough to return from the gulag and resume their literary activities in the early 1960s, were mere fragments of what used to be a rich and solid Jewish cultural edifice.

Yet for all of their intimate relations and commonality of experience, the bitter truth is this: rare was a Jewish writer who, in the new climate of the post-Stalin era, would openly allude to Babyn Yar and, how much more so, to its Jewish victims. Why was this so, given, as we have seen, that no such absolute taboo existed in the sister sphere of Russian letters? To provide an explanation, we must review the fluctuations of Soviet policy vis-à-vis the state's Jewish subjects.

## SOCIALIST IN CONTENT, JEWISH IN FORM

The seeds of the challenge that Babyn Yar posed for Yiddish writers were sown, in fact, decades before the massacre itself in the years preceding the October Revolution. It was already then, when both Vladimir Lenin and his successor, Joseph Stalin, were searching for a proper Marxist definition of the Jewish people and a policy that could be accorded to them, that the general ideological contours of the still-embryonic Soviet Yiddish culture were given form. As Benjamin Pinkus notes, it was Lenin who, following the line of his teacher Karl Marx, argued from the outset of his career that the Jews were "not a nation but a historical remnant that owes its existence to the persistence of antisemitism."[6] For Lenin—as for his successor, Stalin—a nation could only be defined as a group possessing both a common territory and a common language. Hence world Jewry constituted merely a sect, not a nation.[7] This negative attitude, however, toward the Jews as an ethnic group "whose future," to quote Stalin, "is denied and whose very existence is yet to be proved"[8] precluded neither Lenin nor Stalin from enabling the establishment of a semi-autonomous Jewish administrative and cultural apparatus conducted in Yiddish.

Later on, however, recognizing the viability of the Jewish minority in their country, it was Stalin who wished to remedy the limbo state in which Soviet Jews were situated by assigning them a territory, the sine qua non of true nationhood. This plan, conceived in 1928 to establish a Jewish national "federative entity" in the Far East territory of Birobidzhan,[9] signaled for a while a turnaround in the Soviet negative attitude toward the sustenance of Soviet Jews as a distinct national minority. But as it became clear that Birobidzhan was too far and too underdeveloped to attract what had emerged as a highly urban and educated Jewish population, Soviet Jews realized that a simple territorial solution was not the panacea to their precarious position among other Soviet national minority groups.

Although the Birobidzhan enterprise was an overall failure, during the 1920s the highly variegated Soviet Yiddish culture, fully funded by the state, was the envy of many Jews abroad. Some of the Yiddish literary world's key writers, among them Dovid Bergelson, Peretz Markish, Dovid Hofshteyn, and Moyshe Kulbak, flocked to the Soviet Union during those years, believing that a true, viable home for the Yiddish language had been found only in the USSR. That the Soviet state signaled in the cultural arena the wave of the future was evidenced, not only by its central Jewish institutions, like the Jewish section of the Communist Party (the Evsektsia). As mentioned, a plethora of cultural and educational institutions conducted by Jews, in a Jewish language, were set up by the still-newborn Soviet regime: numerous newspapers and literary periodicals, professional and amateur theaters, research institutions, museums, a network of daily schools, and even local administrative institutions such as courts and police stations all functioned from the early 1920s in the Yiddish language.[10]

Later on, most of these institutions witnessed a gradual decline in the wake of Stalin's Cultural Revolution of the late 1920s, a grand policy that was designed, among other things, to turn the USSR from a fairly egalitarian union of its member nations into a country dominated by the Russian people, who had a "leading position ... among the equal nationalities of the Soviet Union."[11] In the 1930s, during the years of the Great Terror, Yiddish institutions and their members stood under the threat of constant attack due to Stalin's reversal of the egalitarian policies that he and Lenin had put in place earlier. But in the new atmosphere hostile to national particularism, Jews were not singled out. Rather, they had their "fair share" of the burden of Stalinist terror along with Ukrainian and Belorussian nationalists, and some would say they even had an easier share. It would take more than a decade for this hostile attitude toward non-Russian ethnicities to turn into an antisemitic campaign, which was launched in November 1948. A witch hunt was directed against hundreds of Jewish intellectuals, so-called rootless Cosmopolitans; this campaign, orchestrated by the aging and increasingly paranoid Stalin, escalated into the arrest of hundreds of Soviet Yiddish cultural activists, the execution of some of the foremost Soviet Yiddish writers, among them Bergelson, Kvitko, Markish, and Hofshteyn, and the complete effacement of Yiddish literature from the Soviet cultural scene embodied in the "Night of the Murdered Poets" on August 12, 1952.[12]

In this cultural climate in which the rights of Soviet Jews as a national minority were resting on shaky ideological foundations, in this environment in which Jews had to constantly prove that their language, literature, and culture might still be able to subscribe to the Stalinist maxim of "socialist in content and national in form," it is easier to understand, when seen in hindsight, why elaborating on the theme of Babyn Yar in Yiddish literature was a challenge for Soviet Yiddish writers during this period. For a Jewish writer, using a Jewish language and having only Jews as designated readers, writing about the site that had become a symbol for the suffering of the Jewish people during World War II was not an easy task. When observing the variety of works written on Babyn Yar in the Soviet Union, it emerges with almost no exceptions that historical and linguistic contexts mattered. Each period in Soviet history carried its own blessings and misfortunes. Ironically, the war years and the immediate aftermath of the war, a time when Soviet Jewry faced the greatest *khurbn* (Yiddish for "destruction," a term derived from the Hebrew word *hurban* and referring to the destruction of the First and Second Temples of Jerusalem) in Jewish history, was a time that witnessed a momentary revival of Yiddish culture in the USSR, thus preparing the ground for the appearance of the first works on Babyn Yar in Yiddish.

## THE WAR AND LAST YEARS OF STALINISM

In the early 1930s, the first signs foreshadowing the future demise of Soviet Yiddish culture were already apparent: the closure of the Evsektsia, the Yiddish organ *Der Emes*, and the network of Yiddish schools, among other Yiddish institutions, signaled the imminent demise of the Soviet Yiddish cultural enterprise. It was only because of the outbreak of World War II on the Eastern Front on June 22, 1941, that this otherwise linear process came to a temporary halt. The German attack, and especially the disarray into which the Red Army and the civilian administration had been thrown on the western frontiers, prompted Stalin to mitigate the Russification trend of the preceding decade and supplant it with a policy characterized by a positive attitude toward national minority cultures in the country.

This new move stemmed from Stalin's recognition of national sentiments as vital for motivating the minorities under his control to join the war effort and help drive out the Nazi invaders.[13] Among them were Ukrainians and Belarussians who were now living under German occupation and whose loyalty to Moscow could no longer be taken for granted. In a parallel measure meant to achieve the same goal, Stalin sanctioned the revival of the hitherto repressed Russian Orthodox Church and other religious institutions throughout the country. For the first time, the first atheist state in the history of humanity recognized the vital role those religious institutions—and sentiments—could play in the lives of the Soviet population.[14] In order to both channel these sentiments in the desired direction and improve the image of the Soviet Union abroad, Stalin ordered the establishment of the Soviet for Russian Orthodox Affairs in September 1943 and the Soviet for Religious Affairs in May 1944. The latter body would oversee the activities of all the other religions practiced in the USSR, including Judaism.[15] And so, the propagandistic potential of religion had to now be fully exploited.

This twofold move toward greater religious and artistic freedom had a double impact on Soviet Jews: no sooner had these decisions been put into effect than a revival of both Jewish synagogues and cultural creativity was set in motion. At the heart of this revival stood the Jewish Anti-Fascist Committee (JAFC), which was formed in 1942 (see chapter 1), the primary goal of which was to garner the political and financial support of Jewish communities in the West for Russia's war effort.[16] The JAFC was the only official Jewish institution active during the war years, and while conceived as a vehicle for propaganda, it did not limit itself to political activities but aspired, during the darkest days in the history of the Jewish people, to revitalize Jewish literary and cultural activities in Yiddish and offer both material and cultural support to Yiddish writers.[17] Although Stalin had no special interest in overemphasizing the uniqueness of the tragedy that befell Soviet Jews during the war, one may find in the course of the JAFC's existence, before it was disbanded in 1948, a large number of Yiddish publications written under the impact of the greatest catastrophe that the Jewish people had known, including numerous reports on Nazi atrocities against Jews in the committee's organ, *Eynikayt* (Unity), which was geared toward a Yiddish readership both in the USSR and the West.

Unity, for the JAFC, was twofold. It was a reference to the integration of Soviet Jews into Soviet society, as victims and fighters, civilians, and Red Army soldiers and officers. At the beginning of our study, we portrayed the Holocaust of European Jewry as a circle overlapping with another one, namely that of the Great Patriotic War. As we have already noticed in our review of Ilya Ehrenburg's "Sanctified Land," the organ *Eynikayt*, more than any other Soviet publication, projected an image of these two circles as one, embodying the Soviet Union's colossal war against the evils of fascism and Nazism that was deemed, in accordance with Communist doctrine, as the most degenerate forms of capitalism. As David Shneer contends, while Jewish readers of the Russian-language press received a largely universalized, de-Judaized image of Nazi atrocities, those reading *Eynikayt* could exclusively learn from these wartime reports about Nazi atrocities aimed at Jews in particular.[18]

The rumors about the Babyn Yar massacre, not unlike other reports of multiple cases of mass murder of which Jews constituted the chief target, reached the Soviet Yiddish cultural elite while many of its members were serving their country miles away from the scene of the atrocities, either on the battlefield or in evacuation.[19] These Yiddish writers were now caught up in the sense of shock and agony over the fate of entire Jewish communities that had existed along the Soviet western frontiers for ages and were now wiped out instantaneously. If a staple feature of Soviet Yiddish literature prior to the Holocaust was the writers' departure from the Jewish past (we will consider the extent of this departure at a later point, the subject of a lively recent scholarly debate), they were now coming back to their roots. Equally important, they now received from Moscow the signal that such emotional rapprochement with their Jewish identity was possible under the new circumstances of the Nazi invasion.

What characterized this new chapter in Soviet Yiddish literature was the intensification of Jewish national sentiments among Soviet Yiddish artists and their identification with the fate of their people during the darkest days of their history. This development cannot be exaggerated: indeed, after years of getting used to viewing Yiddish literature as a mere vehicle for the dissemination of socialist propaganda, they now saw it as a bridge between the present and the prerevolutionary past, the time when Yiddish literature knew no schism between West and East.[20] Yet, this upswing of a Jewish national self-consciousness among Yiddish writers, while enduring for a few years, was ill-fated. As Khone Shmeruk illustrates, this Soviet Yiddish renaissance was merely a product of a tactical move on the part of Stalin. It was a rare moment when the national aspirations and pathos of Soviet Yiddish writers coalesced with the interests of the entire Jewish people within and beyond the USSR, and, most importantly, with the specific wartime interests of the Soviet government.[21] It therefore did not take too long after the end of the war for Stalin to realize that the potential for exploiting Soviet Yiddish culture as an effective propaganda instrument had already been exhausted, a realization that prompted him, inter alia, to first shut down all Yiddish cultural institutions and, later, to order the purging of their key members.

While Shmeruk underlines the uniqueness of this period as a rare time when Yiddish writers could give vent to their national feelings, Harriet Murav views the same epoch through a different lens, dwelling at greater length on the irreconcilability between the two key features of works that appeared during the war and its aftermath by Yiddish writers. Some of these works reflected the need for mobilization, for a literature of war and hatred that would drive the Jewish multitudes to the Red Army.[22] Others were works of a very different nature, reflecting the need for a literature that would turn its gaze to loss and mourning, to brood the enormous toll that the Nazi attack took on European Jews, and the Soviet Jews among them. According to Murav, during the war itself both Russian Jewish writers and Yiddish writers could still embody in their lives and embed in their works the "Soviet" and the "Jew" as two categories that overlap "not seamlessly but closely enough."[23] In its aftermath, once the dimensions of the destruction became clearer, the Soviet Yiddish writers, grieving over the annihilation of an ancient Jewish civilization that many of them had earlier derided, began to realize how unsuitable the language of hatred and revenge was to deal with the reality of mass shootings and industrial killing.

In the particular context of Babyn Yar's handling in the Soviet Yiddish sphere, wartime reports on the massacres that had taken place at the ravine are, indeed, not typical of what we would usually find in works published in the West that could be labeled Holocaust literature. Before we turn to a discussion of the references to Babyn Yar themselves, it should be noted that these were very few: both in the reports by Yiddish correspondents in *Eynikayt* about the massacres at the ravine and in belletristic works. In contrast to the large number of works and reportage on the Warsaw Ghetto, for instance, or on the death factories of Auschwitz and Treblinka—that is, on Holocaust sites situated outside the Soviet Union and hence safe to write about—the number of references to Babyn Yar in the immediate years after the carnage there were quite few. This fact by itself is immensely important, as it shows us that even in the heyday of the freedom that Soviet Yiddish writers were given to express their national sentiments, writing about Babyn Yar was something extraordinary. As we observe the two major literary works in Yiddish on Babyn Yar of this period, "The Mother Rachel" by Aaron Kushnirov and *War* by Peretz Markish, we must bear in mind that these works were something unusual, even for a period that witnessed some degree of relaxed censorship.

The very few references to Babyn Yar, though, do not suggest that the *Eynikayt* editors meant to relegate Babyn Yar to a lower priority. Suffice it to note that in its October 5, 1944, issue, in a front page article carrying the title "Eynikayt in nekome" (Unity in revenge), Solomon Mikhoels, the head of the JAFC, listed the war sites that "will never be erased from our memory" in the following order: Babyn Yar, Traktorni (in Kharkiv), Majdanek, Treblinka, Trostinets (in Minsk), followed by "the Warsaw, Vilna, and Minsk Ghettos, the millions murdered in Bessarabia, Poland, Latvia, and Lithuania."[24] This contextualization of Babyn Yar with a list of Holocaust sites, coupled by the assertion that "together with the Red Army, together with all Soviet peoples, we [that is, Soviet Jews] draw closer to the day of anti-fascist victory,"[25] implies that Babyn Yar was construed by Mikhoels as a site pertaining to the destruction of European Jews.

A few months later, however, this current was reversed with an article titled "Zeyer ondenk lebt" (Their memory is alive), which was published on September 29, 1945, ostensibly to commemorate the fourth anniversary of the massacre. The subject of the article, however, is not the Jews of Kyiv but rather the male prisoners of the Syrets labor camp (among them Jews and non-Jews, Soviet POWs and civilians) near Babyn Yar, whose uprising shall forever be engraved in the collective memory of the Yiddish organ's readers. The emphasis in the two articles on revenge and resistance help further obfuscate the magnitude of the rupture that the war had caused between the old Jewish way of life, which despite the tribulations of the early twentieth century had been preserved to some limited extent, and the new, bleak reality of total war and destruction.

Why did Mikhoels employ the title "Their Memory Is Alive" not to engrave on the minds of Soviet Jews the memory of those who had been killed in Babyn Yar, but to turn instead to the memory of the POWs and "de-Judaize" it? We have already seen that another major *Eynikayt* contributor, Ilya Ehrenburg, gave the first reference to Babyn Yar published in *Eynikayt* the title "Sanctified Land," also in order to mean something else: the battlefield. These two titles, in fact, foreshadow the way in which the theme of Babyn Yar would be handled by Soviet Yiddish writers in the next period, that of the Thaw, and, in many ways, during the Brezhnev years as well. Without being able to ascertain what went on in the mind of each writer, we are able to recognize two conflicting tendencies that mimic the two positions described by Murav: a call for mobilization, on the one hand, and confrontation with destruction, on the other. One is a tendency to refer to the experience of the Great Patriotic War explicitly and to view Jews as one group of victims among others. Another is the view of Babyn Yar as a distinctly Jewish slaughter site—expressed only implicitly—and as a metonymy for the Jewish people's destruction as a whole. If this roundabout way of dealing with the Jewish aspect of Babyn Yar is evident in *Eynikayt* and would later characterize some of the works appearing in the course of the post-Stalin era, during the war years and in their immediate aftermath we find two Yiddish works, both published in 1948, that boldly portray the murder of the Jews at Babyn Yar: *War* by Peretz Markish and "The Mother Rachel" by Aaron Kushnirov. Both writers had spent substantial time in interwar Kyiv but had become by then key players in the Moscow Yiddish literary scene. Both works also appeared for the first time in Moscow, the first in book form and the second in the Yiddish literary almanac *Heymland*. Their appearance endowed the theme of Babyn Yar with a national resonance that transcended any local boundaries.[26]

When placed on a broader historical continuum, the two works may be regarded as transitional. In them, we may find traces of the Soviet Yiddish response to the Nazi invasion: a call for revenge, preoccupation with graphic descriptions of Nazi violence, and an overly heroic and saintly depiction of the Red Army. However, the theme of loss and the glimpse into what had been lost outweighs in these postwar pieces the

Soviet Yiddish poet Aaron Kushnirov. (Photo from the Archives of the YIVO Institute for Jewish Research, New York.)

attention given to revenge and heroism. In Kushnirov's poem, the singing of the praises of the Red Army is conspicuous. His affection for it was not that of an observer: Kushnirov was a Red Army officer decorated with three medals for the part he played in the war.[27] Yet these sentiments, remarkably, appear toward the end of his long poem and seem rather artificially grafted onto a poem otherwise suffused with Jewish nationalist emotions and biblical imagery, a longing for the Jewish past, and reflections on the Jewish people's devastation.

The greatest virtue of the poem is its reflection on loss on two levels concurrently: the national and the personal. The Mother Rachel of the poem, as it turns out, is not only a mother but a grandmother and a great-grandmother as well. She is a lonely woman whose descendants have, fortunately, left the city. Rachel herself spent "over seventy of her eighty years" in her old house on Tshumacki Street, a place that used to feel like home, where she knew every house and floor, she thinks to herself, while wondering "why they all look now so foreign and secluded." The reference to her motherhood is meant to turn her personal plight into a national one, as the old Rachel of Kyiv shares a similar fate with the biblical matriarch Rachel—a tragic, unexpected death on the road.

Kushnirov, in his work, thereby turns Babyn Yar into a Jewish space. His poem mentions a heroic struggle of a Soviet seaman with his Nazi captors, but for him, and he makes it most clear, Babyn Yar is the site whither Rachel is now ordered to go, "like all the other Jews." Moreover, the hero selected for the poem is another testimony to the great length to which Kushnirov was willing to go to endow his poem with Jewish national sentiment, which he did at the expense of the *druzhba narodov*, the so-called friendship of nations. If during the 1930s the young generation of Soviet Yiddish writers looked at the older generation as men of the old and decaying order, living relics of the bourgeois past, Mother Rachel, who had spent most of her life in Kyiv under czarism and now looks fondly at that past, most certainly falls short of being considered a proper Soviet hero.

Filled with many elements that would later become the staple features of Holocaust literature—such as the solemn, affectionate portrayal of the Jewish individual done in a restrained tone and underlining the moral superiority of the victim—the poem still contains the common literary tropes abundant in Yiddish literature of the war years. Even though by 1948 there was no longer a practical need to write a "literature of mobilization," in the poem's plot, right after reaching its climax when Rachel stretches her hands toward her German oppressors, thinking of her helplessness, she thinks to herself:

> *Kill me—it doesn't even hurt.*
> *What more could you do to cause me pain?*
> *Thank God that my children are in the Red Army.*
> *Thank God that I don't need to cry over them.*
> *My sons both serve in the Red Army.*
> *And I have grandchildren in the Red Army.*
> *Yes, she still lives, the Red Army.* [28]

The praise for the Red Army does suggest that the poem hinges on two different axes: that of Soviet Jewry's destruction—an ethnic group linked now to its age-old history—and that of the Great Patriotic War. The conclusion of the poem, with the killing by the Nazis of both Rachel and an injured Soviet seaman who had been carried to Babyn Yar, may be seen as proof that the poem sets the two master narratives in a state of equilibrium. This, however, is only partially correct. For no matter how many times the praises of the Red Army repeat themselves, no matter how long the hiatus of optimism these lines can bring, and no matter how brave the Soviet seaman is (who in his final moments tries to resist his aggressors), it does not eclipse the highly sentimental, reflective portrayal of Babyn Yar as a symbol of a Jewish national catastrophe carried out through the biblical archetype of Rachel the matriarch.

If the poem by Kushnirov is still situated at the crossroads between the literature of mobilization, hate, and revenge and that of mourning and commemoration, the four-volume epic poem *War* by Markish, a title from which the author deliberately omitted the conventional adjective "Great Patriotic," marks the crossing of a line toward the latter realm. Although, as Murav notes, the epic poem deals with the question of human suffering and does not focus on the tragedy of the Jews, its hero, Gur-Aryeh (a "young lion" in Hebrew, an image referring to the symbol of Israel in the Bible),[29] is struck by the destruction of his own kin to the point of no full recovery. If the archetype of the matriarch Rachel helps Kushnirov turn Babyn Yar into a Jewish national symbol of destruction, Markish does so through the figure of Gur-Aryeh, the Soviet Jewish man who had survived the shootings at Babyn Yar and managed to escape the ravine. If for Kushnirov Babyn Yar is a symbol of complete loss, for Markish it also marks the beginning of a new phase in Jewish history. Standing over Babyn Yar, Gur-Aryeh recalls the eschatological metaphor drawn from the Book of Ezekiel of the Valley of the Dry Bones (Ezek 37:1–14) soon to be resurrected.[30]

That for Markish Babyn Yar is not only a valley of death but of life as well does not diminish his awareness of the real dimensions of the loss. The prophetic language he resorts to is not meant to achieve an artificial effect of hope and consolation. On the contrary, the very fact that Gur-Aryeh had been killed and came back to life suggests that he will always belong to two worlds, that of the dead and that of the living, with no ability to ever bridge them. The soldier within him will continue with the war effort and defeat the Nazis. But the Jew will stay with his brethren in the ravine, destroyed and erased. If in his poem "To the Jewish Fighter," published in *Eynikayt* on August 31, 1943, around the time when the Soviet military started to march into lands populated by native Germans,[31] Markish's response to every slaughtered child and every defiled sister was taking revenge upon a German city, Gur-Aryeh becomes now fully aware of the futility of revenge as a means to compensate for loss. In *War*, Markish seems to have given up any hope of reconciling the "Soviet" and the "Jew,"[32] the grand project that he had embraced wholeheartedly earlier when he had left Poland and moved to the Soviet Union, aspiring thereby to find a remedy for the Jewish people by reforging it as an equal member in the Soviet multiethnic grand scheme.

Markish's work is remarkable for placing the Babyn Yar massacre at the core of a monumental work that traces the destruction of European Jews both within and beyond the boundaries of the Soviet Union. The epic poem itself testifies to the long way that Markish has gone from his earlier war works that came up with a far less complex reaction to the unfolding tragedy of the Jews: the call to mobilize the Soviet Jewish man into the Red Army, summoning him to first defend his motherland and then wreak vengeance upon its invaders. This change of mood in the oeuvre of Markish marks the transition from the wartime responses to the Holocaust, endowed with a sense of immediacy, to the more philosophical probing and theological responses emerging only after the smoke and dust of war had settled. Little could Peretz Markish have known that the Soviet Yiddish writers who would choose a few years later to represent the Babyn Yar massacre in their work would also emerge from the grave in which the blood of Markish and other Jewish writers flowed, leave the gulag, and come back to the land of the living.

## THE YEARS OF SILENCE

In 1948, the year that witnessed first the murder of the JAFC's head, Solomon Mikhoels, and later on the abolishment of the committee itself, Stalin launched his battle against Soviet Yiddish culture. Thereafter, its last vestiges were destroyed one after another: local Jewish sections of the Soviet Writers' Union were disbanded, virtually all Yiddish newspapers, periodicals, and books ceased to appear, and the main Yiddish theaters were closed down.[33] The condition of Jews and Jewish culture during this period reached its nadir in 1952 with the murder of the most towering Yiddish cultural figures: Peretz Markish, Dovid Bergelson, Itsik Fefer, Dovid Hofshteyn, Leib Kvitko, and others. It was followed by a witch hunt for Jewish physicians, "the murderers in white gowns," unleashed in January 1953 by the alarmingly more paranoid and Judeophobic Stalin, a new campaign that was thwarted only by his death two months later.

During the immediate years of the post-Stalin era, a tectonic shift could be felt in the Soviet Russian cultural domain. It was a time when the collective leadership that succeeded Stalin realized the grave need for a comprehensive overhaul of the stagnating Soviet state: its totalitarian economy, politics, and culture. The minor arena of Yiddish literature, however, remained, for the time being, somewhat impervious to these changes. That the Soviet Yiddish clock was frozen in the Stalin era was in many ways true, but some apparent changes did take place. Stalin's legacy of antisemitic terror was, to a certain extent, undone. So too, Yiddish culture started to gradually emerge from a static condition of complete nonexistence. The first, extremely modest, harbinger of a rehabilitation of Yiddish letters was the publication of a small book by Sholem Aleichem in Russian translation in 1954.[34] Then, the release from the gulag of dozens of Yiddish writers and cultural activists was set in motion,[35] coupled with the posthumous rehabilitation of Peretz Markish, the first Soviet Yiddish writer whose murder was disclosed by Moscow.[36] The next step was the resumption, in 1959, of Yiddish publishing in the USSR after a decade of complete silence.[37] No matter how gradual or hesitant these changes were, they did send a signal to those who wished to revive Yiddish culture in the Soviet Union that Moscow was now willing to veer away from the legacy of Stalinism and to allow Soviet Jews in general and Soviet Jewish intellectuals and artists in particular a benign degree of personal security.

These gradual changes suggested that Khrushchev's attitude toward Jewish culture would be a far cry from the brutal repression of the late Stalin years. But the refusal to revive Soviet Yiddish culture and elevate it back to its interwar status remained unchanged. In his groundbreaking Secret Speech at the Twentieth Party Congress, Khrushchev made no reference to Stalin's recent antisemitic repression.[38] This ambivalence toward Jews and Jewish culture was manifested in the fact that, on the one hand, antisemitic terrorism came to a halt while, on the other hand, those responsible for it remained in power.[39] This state of limbo made Soviet Jews only more insecure and fearful that anti-Jewish persecutions, still freshly stored in their memory, might resume.[40]

Furthermore, the new regime's negative stance toward the restoration of Soviet Yiddish culture ran parallel to other restrictions imposed on Soviet Jews that were meant to curb the very limited religious freedoms that they had been allowed at the outbreak of the German–Russian War. While these measures were taken as part of a comprehensive ideological attack against religion in general conducted from 1957 to 1964, it was hard not to notice the mendacious antisemitic character of the campaign against the Jewish religion in which Judaism was presented as a reactionary and unscientific entity, inciting enmity between Jews and non-Jews.[41] The direct outcome of this campaign was a surge in antisemitic sentiments among rank-and-file Soviet citizens, who were now exposed to antisemitic propaganda of the most virulent kind.[42]

To the propagandistic elements of this new attack against Judaism, promulgated in the midst of an era popularly remembered as a time of greater openness to diverse opinions and relaxation of state terror, were added other measures. These were all intended to further alienate Jews from mainstream Soviet society, from each other, and from their tradition: the closure of synagogues and the harassment of Jews attending those that remained open; the ban on baking matzah; the ban on establishing contacts with foreign Jews;[43] and, lastly, the more subtly antisemitic character of the economic trials that involved a large number of Jewish defendants charged with "speculation."[44]

In this environment, so hostile to accommodating any Jewish national and religious aspirations, it goes without saying that the restoration of Yiddish culture was not on the mind of Nikita Khrushchev, who after the Secret Speech of 1956 and the anti-party coup turned into the unassailable leader of the Soviet Union. Khrushchev's unwritten doctrine of maintaining a deep-seated prejudice toward the Jews (discussed with respect to the Russian literary sphere in chapter 4), which can be traced back to his Russian peasant background, while bringing state-sanctioned violence toward them to a halt had an indelible impact on Yiddish literature's response to the Holocaust in general and the Babyn Yar massacre in particular. While Soviet Yiddish literature was always a minor literature, the little sister of the Soviet Russian one, the attack against Jews and the extremely limited amount of Yiddish works whose publication was approved turned Soviet Yiddish literature of the Thaw period into a vestige. True, due to the lack of a common Jewish territory the practitioners of Yiddish culture always felt that their world was precarious, hanging by a thread. But now, with a minute number of works allowed to appear every year, and with only one Yiddish periodical, *Sovetish heymland*, which began to appear in 1961, Soviet Yiddish writers could easily take their cue and realize on their own how limited and how careful they would have to be when invoking the memory of a sensitive issue like Babyn Yar in their works. While the very few works on Babyn Yar that did appear on the pages of *Sovetish heymland* are the focus of the following chapter, these are all exceptions: rare moments and works in which the ravine of Babyn Yar is mentioned in the most oblique way.

That Soviet Yiddish literature of the Thaw period did not nurture anyone like Yevtushenko, who would not only touch upon the memory of the ravine but also openly protest its neglect, is not at all hard to understand. The three conditions that helped produce a *shestidesyatnik* the likes of Yevtushenko were not met in the case of the Soviet Yiddish writers who made their debut during the late Thaw and, for the most part, on the pages of *Sovetish heymland*. First, unlike an emerging talent such as Yevtushenko, who could choose between the left-leaning or the right-leaning Soviet intelligentsia, who were affiliated with such periodicals as *Novy mir* and *Oktyabr'*, respectively,

Soviet Yiddish writers had but a single, ideologically homogenous periodical that, due to its precarious existence, had to assume a very conservative character.[45] Second, unlike young Russian writers of the Thaw period, the Soviet Yiddish writers had firsthand experience of the Stalinist terror. As Abraham Brumberg points out, more than half of them spent time in prison until the mass releases of gulag inmates began in the mid-1950s.[46] Needless to say, the very few of them who had lived through the anti-Cosmopolitan campaign untouched lived in constant fear of arrest, exile, or execution. Many of them were broken men and women, who, based on their own life experience, lacked any enthusiasm for dangerous political adventures. Third, and no less importantly, the majority of the Soviet Yiddish writers who contributed to *Sovetish heymland* were now men and women in their fifties. In other words, twenty important years that would typically make one more sober separated them from figures like Yevgeny Yevtushenko, Anatoly Kuznetsov, and Andrei Voznesensky.

Finally, it should be recalled that the very appearance of a new, handsomely produced literary journal in the Yiddish language was itself the product of outside pressure on Moscow by the regime's Soviet sympathizers in the West, among them many Jews. Emerging from a state of nonexistence in the late 1950s into a more stable one in August of 1961, Soviet Yiddish literature was by no means ready to deal with the controversial subject of Babyn Yar. The stopgap solution, therefore, was to find an alternative platform for literary works and journalistic reports on Babyn Yar in the Polish Soviet satellite publication. Here, at last, was a safe path to publishing works of questionable ideological nature, both within the Soviet Bloc and beyond.

## NEIGHBORS: BABYN YAR IN COMMUNIST POLAND

Parallel to the shutdown of Soviet Yiddish institutions and the arrest of writers and artists in the Soviet Union, a process that brought Soviet Yiddish cultural activity to a complete standstill, the Polish government enjoyed, at that time, some degree of flexibility to form its own policy vis-à-vis Yiddish culture. Indeed, as opposed to the Soviet decision to withdraw from the earlier acceptance of the Jews as a legitimate national minority possessing its own language and even its own territory, the Polish authorities enabled the Holocaust survivors who remained in Poland and the refugees who started to come back to Poland to set up an officially sanctioned and government-funded Jewish community organization known as the Central Committee of Jews in Poland. This body oversaw a variety of cultural activities: Polish radio programs in Yiddish, schools, a publishing house, a theater, and a Yiddish press.[47] Short-lived and able to exist as a Jewish communal umbrella organization only so long as it served the immediate interests of the Polish government (who sought, at that time, support from Jewish philanthropic organizations),[48] this body, renamed in 1950 the Social and Cultural Association of Jews in Poland, survived, even though the extent of its autonomy and the range of its activities were curbed.

The facilitation of Yiddish cultural life in the postwar Republic of Poland (from 1952 to 1989 it would be called the People's Republic of Poland), while conceived as a Polish project, also played an instrumental role in fostering Yiddish culture on Soviet territory. Some Soviet writers—the most salient example being Itsik Kipnis with his "On khokhmes, on kheshboynes" (Without thinking, without calculation), a work suffused with Jewish patriotism, which we will turn to later on—dared to send their work to Poland even after it had been rejected for publication in the USSR, or when they realized that the work should be sent to the former as it had no chance of being published in the latter.[49] In light of the complete shutdown of the Yiddish press (except for the parochial and remote *Birobidzhaner shtern*) and Yiddish book publishing between the years 1948 and 1959, Communist Poland became the main channel through which some of the Soviet Yiddish writers who had survived the arrests and purges could continue to write and connect to their readers. This connection to Soviet Yiddish readers was possible, since many issues of Polish Yiddish books as well as press publications, such as *Dos naye lebn*, *Folks-shtime*, and *Yidishe shriftn*, were sent to audiences abroad, including to readers in the USSR.

In this last respect, the Communist Yiddish Polish press here played a peculiar role: it provided Soviet Jews with a properly socialist, extraterritorial cultural platform that prevented the complete demise of Soviet Yiddish literature. As Mordechai Altshuler explains, this contradictory practice, one that was certainly not encouraged by Moscow, was nonetheless tolerated. Indirectly, this condition helped Moscow to have information about Jewish activities in the USSR, to reach out beyond the Iron Curtain, and to also set a "safety valve" by way of which pressure coming from Soviet Yiddish writers could be securely released.[50] In a sense, the Polish Yiddish press amounted to a middle ground between two modes of publication: the illegal *tamizdat* mode—that is, the sending of a work for publication abroad, typically in a Western country—and the legal practice of permitted dissent explored in the first part of our study. It was, in other words, a form of permitted *tamizdat*.

It is noteworthy that while active during the years when Yiddish publications in the Soviet Union were nonexistent, the Polish Yiddish press continued to provide a safety valve even in the ensuing decade after the debut of *Sovetish heymland* in the summer of 1961, edited by Aron Vergelis, about whom much more will be said in the pages to come. It was in the Polish Yiddish newspaper *Folks-shtime* and the literary periodical *Yidishe shriftn* that one could find references during the Thaw period to two topics that never loomed large in *Sovetish heymland*: the murder of the Soviet Yiddish writers (epitomized in the milestone article "Our Pain and Consolation" by the editors of *Folks-shtime* that affirmed, for the first time, the rumors circulating about the murders to Western audiences) and the Holocaust.[51]

With regard to the latter topic, a glimpse into the works published in the Polish Yiddish press illuminates its ability to construct the Holocaust as a Jewish event in a fashion very similar to *War* by Markish and "The Mother Rachel" by Kushnirov, which were published in the USSR prior to the Stalinist antisemitic campaigns. It was, for instance, about a year before the appearance of *Sovetish heymland* that the Soviet Yiddish poet Moyshe Teyf published a poem in the Polish *Folks-shtime* with the title "Six Million" and used this as a mnemonic for the Jewish people's tragedy.[52] Remarkably, the greater openness to commemorating the Holocaust was not only the result of the general political mood prevailing in postwar Eastern Europe, it was also a result of internal conflicts among Yiddish literati on both sides of the Soviet–Polish border. As Hersh Smolyar, the editor in chief of *Folks-shtime*, reminisced, during a stay in Poland in 1965 Aron Vergelis "demanded that the editors of the Polish Yiddish press will publish works written by Soviet writers only after consulting him. He was supported by Avrom Gontar, his loyal assistant, who argued that the terms 'Yiddish, Jews and Judaism' are too prominent in *Folks-shtime*."[53] This ideological gap, which created a rift between the main Soviet Yiddish literary venue and its Polish equivalent, was also apparent in the narrower context of Babyn Yar's commemoration.

In the course of the Thaw period, *Folks-shtime* displayed a high level of openness toward literary works on Babyn Yar that highlighted its Jewish context, publishing them with no major delay. Admittedly, towering above all these works was "Babi Yar" by Yevgeny Yevtushenko, which appeared in *Folks-shtime* in Yiddish translation on October 3, 1961, only a few days after its debut in *Literaturnaya gazeta*. The response of *Sovetish heymland* to the earthquake that "Babi Yar" had triggered paled in comparison with this; the farthest that Vergelis was willing to go was to publish another poem by Yevtushenko, one titled "The Queen Beauty," that did not contain any diversions from Soviet dogma.[54] It thus transpired that, in contrast with its Polish equivalent, *Sovetish heymland* could only obliquely pay honor to a Soviet non-Jewish writer who dared to link Babyn Yar with the tragedy of the Jews.

While the dull and highly filtered-out way in which this process of the ravine's commemoration in *Sovetish heymland* played itself out, orchestrated by its editor Aron Vergelis, is the focus of chapter 9, for now it is sufficient to draw a couple of comparisons between the Polish newspaper and the Soviet periodical. Whereas *Sovetish heymland* only laconically noted in its "Notes on the Calendar: Writers and Works" section that Dmitri Shostakovich's Thirteenth Symphony set to music five of Yevgeny Yevtushenko's poems,[55] *Folks-shtime*, in its Jewish News column, dedicated an entire front page entry to the "Symphony to the Poem 'Babi Yar' Performed in Moscow."[56] Here, the author notes that Babyn Yar is the "mass grave of 80,000 Kiev Jews, murdered by the Hitlerites" and adds that the symphony is dedicated to the Jewish victims of fascism. Also, whereas *Sovetish heymland* chose to categorically ignore the contest opened in January 1966 at the Kyiv-based Architect's House designed to introduce to the public different sketches for the proposed official Babyn Yar monument and to select the winning project, *Folks-shtime* followed this development quite closely. As early as the summer of 1965, it communicated to its readers about the decision made by the Soviet Ukrainian authorities to erect a memorial at Babyn Yar.[57] When appreciating the Soviet system as a whole, including the satellite states that formed the Soviet Bloc, it becomes apparent that the memory of Babyn Yar had to be suppressed and marginalized, but it was never to completely fade away. In Communist Poland, on the edge of the Soviet cultural system, it could still find an outlet for expression.

# BETWEEN DE-STALINIZATION AND RE-STALINIZATION?

Upon surveying the evolution of Babyn Yar's literary commemoration during the war, during the last years of Stalinism, and in the course of the Thaw years, both in the USSR and in Poland, it is time to turn to the last era included in the chronological time frame of our study, the one in which the largest number of works on Babyn Yar appeared in the Soviet Yiddish literary arena. As we have noted in the first part of our study, the term "Thaw" in the general context of Soviet history is associated with the policies espoused by Nikita Khrushchev and altered by the more conservative rule of Leonid Brezhnev. While the latter's revisionist policies won him the unflattering title of "neo-Stalinist," insofar as Babyn Yar was concerned the term "Thaw" accurately describes what happened in the Soviet Yiddish literary sphere during the Brezhnev era.

The transition between these two modes of leadership occurred suddenly, on October 15, 1964, when, in an unprecedented step, a Soviet leader did not die while in office but, rather, was forced into retirement.[58] The ousting of Khrushchev by his Presidium members would usher in a new and prolonged era in Soviet history that would be recognized only in retrospect as Zastoi or the Era of Stagnation. The new regime was led, initially, by the duumvirate of Brezhnev and Alexei Kosygin. Toward the beginning of the 1970s, while the decision-making process was still primarily based on the consent of the Presidium members, Leonid Brezhnev would gradually emerge as primus inter pares in the Kremlin's hierarchy.[59] Those who had worked behind the scenes to oust Khrushchev were now weary of the contradictory nature of his policies. They saw them as an unviable form of moderate dictatorship that was partially susceptible to criticism by its subjects. To those who succeeded Khrushchev, it was clear that the

Soviet regime would not be able to sustain its revolutionary vibrancy and, at the same time, keep the existing political and social order intact.

Nonetheless, the Brezhnev regime that replaced Khrushchev's suffered from inner contradictions that were no less severe. To begin with, the Brezhnev era was the first time when relative economic prosperity was felt throughout the country. This new material comfort turned out to be very deceptive. In hindsight, the attainment of economic stability has been seen by many historians as one of the chief factors that set in motion the financial collapse of the Soviet system.[60] This was also a time when the Soviet leadership insisted, as opposed to Khrushchev's proclivity toward utopianism,[61] that Soviet citizens already lived in a state of "developed socialism"—that is, the main objectives of the October Revolution had already been realized. At the same time, at no prior point in Soviet history was the Soviet elite, including Brezhnev himself, so heavily afflicted by corruption, including, but not limited to, the reign of nepotism and the enjoyment of extravagant lifestyles. Another internal contradiction was the feeling of the Soviet populace (as well as the international community) that the Soviet regime was so stable that it would last for generations, a feeling that was contrasted by the growing alienation of this public from the ideals and tenets of Marxism–Leninism. By now, these were perceived by a growing number of Soviet citizens as nothing more than a hodgepodge of empty slogans and bankrupt dreams.[62]

Moreover, another contradictory feature of the Brezhnev regime that is especially relevant to our discussion has to do with its position on freedom of speech in the social sciences, an aggregate of disciplines that in the Soviet Union also embraced literature, philosophy, and history.[63] The Brezhnev era was characterized by two conflicting tendencies. During this period, there was a great leap back to the pre-Thaw period that saw the tightening of censorship and control on writers, artists, and intellectuals. In contrast to the liberal intelligentsia of the Khrushchev era that sought a strategy of cooperation with the Kremlin, in the Brezhnev period permitted dissent gave way to a new generation of dissidents who dared to challenge the entire moral foundation upon which the Soviet system rested and was not satisfied with the concrete, specific criticisms of the older generation of intellectuals. As early as 1965, dissent crystallized in the USSR in the form of a nationwide movement and turned *samizdat* into its primary vehicle of expression and outreach.[64] As both the regime and the dissidents grew apart from each other with respect to their ideologies, the pressure exerted on the latter became ever greater and came to include confinement to labor camps and mental asylums, and, in some cases, forced emigration (like in the case of Viktor Nekrasov, whose life and work was discussed at some length in chapter 4).

In clear contrast to the attack on dissidents, the banning of Solzhenitsyn's new works and the subsequent exiling of their author, and even the famous Sinyavsky–Daniel Trial, which marked the beginning of the Thaw's end, the Brezhnev regime displayed a certain degree of tolerance toward a variety of authors, both living and deceased, whose opinions often stood in direct conflict with the tenets of Marxism–Leninism.[65] It seems random, or perhaps even senseless, at first glance, but upon closer inspection this highly nuanced censorship did have its own inherent rationale: if Khrushchev, like his predecessor Stalin, showed a great deal of involvement in literary affairs, the apparatchik Brezhnev set the doctrine pretty straight: first-rate works of literature and art—even when imbued with emotional and intellectual depth that could potentially challenge the Soviet way of life—were permitted so long as the regime did not consider them to constitute an immediate threat to its own stability.[66] Remembering all too well the dark years of the Great Terror, both Brezhnev and his colleagues in the Presidium (later it changed its name to the Politburo) manifested in this policy a wish to find equilibrium in the shape of a regime that kept dissent in check for the sake of the regime's own survival, on the one hand, while ensuring that its crackdown would not spiral out of control into purges and mass terror, on the other. Thus, as the historian and political scientist Archie Brown puts it, the top leadership of the Communist Party of the Soviet Union and the government came to the sober realization that "de-Stalinization is potentially as dangerous for them as re-Stalinization."[67] A delicate balance between them had to be constantly negotiated and fine-tuned.

## ARE WE JEWISH NATIONALISTS?

The walking of this fine line between de- and re-Stalinization also played itself out in the commemoration of Babyn Yar. This happened in two different forms: in the arena of belles lettres and in commemorative activities at the ravine itself. As we shall see, Yiddish writers employed a great deal of caution when publishing works on Babyn Yar. All too often, any potentially provocative elements embedded in them were discernible only by a reader adept at carefully reading Soviet literature between the lines. By contrast, in the public sphere no room for ambiguity was allowed. Rather, the local Soviet authorities in Kyiv were ready to juxtapose their officially sanctioned commemorative narrative right next to the narratives of individual Jews, now forming as a collective, who spontaneously came to Babyn Yar to mark the anniversary of the massacre. While these commemorative practices for the most part exceed the boundaries of our study since they took place outside the realms of belles lettres, they help flesh out and place these literary works in their proper historical context. This comparison helps shed light on the boundaries of the permissible for Soviet Jews during the early years of the Stagnation era.

We have already mentioned the first public commemoration of the Babyn Yar massacre since the immediate postwar years, which was held on September 24, 1966, when a group of fifty to sixty people, both Jews and non-Jews, came to the old Jewish cemetery adjacent to the ravine in order to mark the twenty-fifth anniversary of the massacre. The rally or *meeting*, as it is called in Russian, was dispersed by KGB agents, a practice that would recur in the following years.

The Jewish nationalist activist Emmanuel (Amik) Diamant has left us a compelling portrayal of these Brezhnev-era manifestations of Jewish activism for the sake of keeping Babyn Yar's memory alive and of how through these experiences he and many of his peers, hitherto knowing close to nothing about Judaism and Jewish history, have become Zionists overnight through the 1966 meeting at the ravine. If what we have seen thus far is the underscoring of Babyn Yar's memory as a great patriotic site, carrying a universal message with or without any references to the ravine's Jewish context, the account rendered by Diamant is Jewish through and through, marked by the profound impact that the Holocaust of European Jews had had on young Jewish residents of Kyiv like Diamant and his peers.

As Diamant insists, his conception of Babyn Yar as a Jewish site preceded the universalistic one. As opposed to the common assumption that the Jewish nationalist movement in the USSR, seeking no longer to battle discrimination from within but rather to fight for the right to emigrate, sprang up in the summer of 1967, in the wake of the Six-Day War, the twenty-fifth anniversary of the Babyn Yar massacre illustrates the tremendous impact that the Holocaust had—and in particular the tremendous impact that Soviet official attitudes toward the Holocaust had—on the reawakening of Jewish nationalist sentiments among Soviet Jews. For Diamant and his Jewish peers,

The crowd at the first Babyn Yar commemoration since 1944—September 29, 1966. (Photo from the Central Archives for the History of the Jewish People; Emmanuel Diamant.)

the impetus for initiating the September 1966 meeting was different from that of the non-Jews who joined them.

According to Diamant, it all began with a poster, visible for passersby on the adjacent road and street that he and his peers had the audacity to put up near the site, that announced the imminent anniversary of the massacre in both Cyrillic and Hebrew characters: "Babyn Yar, September 1941–1966." Diamant relates that for Kyiv Jews who were born right after the war the memory black hole epitomized by Babyn Yar was like a magnet, sending him and his peers a chilling reminder that Jews in the USSR were far removed from the image of an assimilable and soon-to-disappear ethnic group experiencing no discrimination or antisemitism that Moscow was attempting to project. The first step in manifesting this sense of belonging to another nation was tending to Holocaust sites and ensuring that the mass murders that took place in those killing fields would be properly marked and remembered, a grassroots effort that emerged in different parts of the Soviet Union.[68]

The gravitation to Holocaust sites was not really the conscious choice of Jews fully aware of their national history and destiny. On the contrary, Diamant goes to great lengths to describe how thin and obscure his Jewish identity was to him and his peers—and how its sudden efflorescence was not the cause of his Holocaust commemoration activism but rather the result of it. The trigger was the accusation of "Jewish nationalism" leveled at them:

> If Nekrasov or Dziuba could somehow be called Ukrainian nationalists (the Russian writer, Viktor Nekrasov, go figure!), when it came to us, the term "Jewish nationalism" was a clearly unreasonable exaggeration. Are we Jewish nationalists? To be a nationalist, one needs to, at least, belong to a nation. Our national belonging truly came down to the fifth point (in the passport).[69] Additionally, this was a clear misunderstanding—after all, according to Stalin's definition of a nation, Jews, as a nation, simply did not exist! How can there be [Jewish] nationalists if they are devoid of the most elementary nationalistic character traits?
>
> About the existence of the notion of a Jewish nationalism—about the Bund or Zionism—we knew only from the [Soviet] propaganda and its harsh Marxist criticism of these false doctrines. Therefore, the main, fundamental aspect of our national self-consciousness (our future Jewish nationalism) was, obviously (and the only one left for us), the Jewish graves, scattered everywhere after the war, defiled, neglected, [and] doomed by the Soviet regime to decay and oblivion.[70]

Interestingly, Diamant and his peers *became* Zionists only after the local Soviet authorities in Kyiv accused them of being such. Prior to that, they had little clue about what Zionism even meant. Now they were able to grasp Zionism not only as

The improvised sign, hung by a group of young Jews on the occasion of the twenty-fifth anniversary of the Babyn Yar massacre. (Photo from the Central Archives for the History of the Jewish People; Emmanuel Diamant.)

anti-Communist doctrine but also as destiny, and realize that their future lay elsewhere—that is, in the Jewish state. Babyn Yar was a call to action leading them, young *shestidesiatniki* Jews, toward open dissent (known as dissidence) and emigration. But as we shall see, for other Jews, who were representative of an older generation, the commemoration of Babyn Yar was practiced differently.

## BREZHNEV'S MINI-THAW

In the wake of the arrests by KGB agents and the disruption of the first gathering at Babyn Yar in more than two decades (an event that would only attract greater numbers of participants in the coming years, who would meet fiercer and fiercer resistance by the authorities), the Soviet regime decided to stage its own, officially sanctioned memorial gatherings attended by workers and Communist Party officials and warmly welcoming, as a guest of honor, a loyal anti-Zionist World War II veteran of Jewish descent. Nowhere and never before did the contrast between Jewish nationalism and Soviet patriotism mirror the dichotomy between the memory of the Holocaust and the Great Patriotic War so vividly. In the aftermath of the Six-Day War, this nascent Jewish dissident emigration movement started to gather momentum. It captured the attention of the world with the Leningrad trial of December 1970, when a group of Jewish activists were arrested for plotting to hijack an airplane and to force its crew to land in Israel. In reaction to the arrest of the group's members, the Soviet authorities increased their vigilance when it came to monitoring Zionist activists and began launching anti-Israel campaigns.[71] Zionism, an ideology that had always been regarded by Moscow as bourgeois and anathema to socialism, had to be stamped out as long as the price to pay for this on the international arena was not too high.

All in all, in the physical space of Babyn Yar the Soviet authorities in the Brezhnev era displayed an uncompromising stance toward any manifestations of Jewish nationalism, including, of course, any attempts to link Babyn Yar with the Holocaust. These deviations from the party line had to be countered by repression and by the creation of a bona fide anti-Zionist rally superseding the unsanctioned one. As we go back to the arena of Soviet Yiddish literature published during the early Brezhnev years, we see that the commemoration of Babyn Yar, as carried out through literary memorials, assumed a different, much more passive, prudent, and low-key character. The reason for this was quite obvious: The very minor Soviet Yiddish cultural establishment of these years was categorized differently by Moscow. It was primarily seen as an ideological and cultural entity constituting no threat to the regime's stability and to the social order. The publishing of mainly middlebrow literature with a limited circulation and in a language becoming increasingly obscure amounted to hardly any discernible risk to Soviet censorship. As the statistical data shows, the number of Yiddish speakers in the USSR was constantly declining at this time (as Diamant relates, he and his contemporaries had already lost command of any tangible connection to it with their highly Russified, post-vernacular upbringing). Yiddish culture no longer constituted a feasible alternative to the assimilatory trends among Soviet Jews, who were, overall, being drawn further and further away from the orbit of a distinct Jewish culture made in the Soviet Union.

The decline of Yiddish language and literature was accompanied by developments in the Middle East that also impacted the position of Soviet Yiddish literature. In the midst of a renewed campaign against Zionism, Yiddish literature could now be maximally exploited by Moscow to counterbalance what it considered the pernicious and alarmingly growing influence of Zionism on the minds of Soviet Jews. Hence, the irrelevance of Soviet Yiddish literature as a mode of dissent and its potential expediency as a propaganda tool in the battle against Zionism may explain the Soviet regime's dual attitude toward Yiddish culture in the post-Khrushchev era. Together, they helped create a peculiar situation in which a general trend of neo-Stalinism was heavily felt in the country, affecting Jewish dissidents among other anti-government groups, while the narrow sphere of Soviet Yiddish literature enjoyed something of a mini-Thaw.[72]

One important area in which this easing of pressure found expression was the publication of Yiddish books in the USSR. While no single Yiddish book was published between 1961 and 1963, the first three years of the collective regime led by Brezhnev and Kosygin saw the publication of sixteen works in Yiddish.[73] Parallel to this, beginning in January 1965, *Sovetish heymland* turned from a bimonthly into a monthly publication and its scope was enlarged as well. According to a survey carried out by Joseph Brumberg and Abraham Brumberg of the material that appeared in *Sovetish heymland* around this time, the growth in the quantity of Yiddish works was accompanied by an improvement in their quality.[74] In many of these works, it seems as though the journal's contributors and editor dispensed with purely propagandistic literature in favor of works that discussed contemporary Jewish life in the USSR, the Jewish prerevolutionary past, and the Holocaust. This increase in both quality and quantity also left some apparent marks on the treatment of Babyn Yar in Soviet Yiddish literature.

It is finally possible to find, along with the occasional works on Babyn Yar that seem more like editorial accidents, a group of works that elaborate on the theme. While the relative security that Yiddish writers experienced at that time encouraged some of them to conjure up some of their long-suppressed memories of the Holocaust, the emergence of a Great Patriotic War cult, reaching its apogee between 1964 and 1980, also helped release the safety valve that for years precluded many publications on the war in general and Babyn Yar in particular from occupying center stage.[75] As Nina Tumarkin notes, the coming to the fore of World War II memories, a process that was in its embryonic phase under Khrushchev, led to the construction of Soviet memorials throughout the country during the Brezhnev years. Among them were the Volgograd Memorial (unveiled in 1967), the Brest Hero-Fortress memorial ensemble (completed in 1971), the Tomb of the Unknown Soldier memorial, and also the two monuments erected in Babyn Yar, the aforementioned small obelisk of 1966 and the massive statue by Mikhaylo Lysenko unveiled a decade later.

Parallel to these changes on the ground, we find for the first time a serious growth of Yiddish publications on Babyn Yar appearing not only in *Sovetish heymland* but in book form as well. Among them are works that had been waiting for more than two decades to be published in the Soviet Union. Two of them—an essay-story by Itsik Kipnis and a poem by Shike Driz, both carrying the title "Babi Yar"—are works of great value. They may be regarded as the classics of Babyn Yar's representation in the Yiddish sphere and deserve room in the canon of modern Yiddish literature. The rest, poems by Dore Khaykine, Motl Talalayevsky, and Shloyme Cherniavsky, approach the massacre less directly and often situate the ravine on the brink between the Holocaust and the Great Patriotic War, leaving the tension between the two master narratives suspended. While the literary value of the latter Yiddish works on Babyn Yar varies, they are interesting more as artistic tropes reflecting the cultural climate and the boundaries of the permissible allowed for Yiddish writers during the post-Stalin years.

# 7
# "LET US GO THERE BY FOOT": ITSIK KIPNIS

IN THE PREVIOUS CHAPTER, WE SURVEYED THE THREE STAGES IN THE EVOlution of Babyn Yar's literary representation in the Soviet Union. Our division into three periods—late Stalinism, the Thaw, and Stagnation—revealed that it was precisely in the course of the Thaw era that the suppression of Babyn Yar in Yiddish literature was in full effect, a time when anyone who wanted to obtain information about the massacre and its commemoration, or read in Yiddish translation the major works on Babyn Yar written in Russian and Ukrainian, had to get a hold of these works and articles through the mediation of the Polish media and literary apparatus.

The piece that most poignantly demonstrates the evolution of this three-phase process is the essay-story by Itsik Kipnis titled "Babi Yar." The chronological trajectory described in the last chapter suits the long process of this piece's fruition, spanning a quarter of a century. A work that challenged Soviet dogma on so many levels, its process of evolution, from conception to publication, exactly mimics the three stages. It was written during the last months of the war, when Jewish national sentiments found the fullest expression in Yiddish literary works but could not see the light of day at that time. Strikingly, it is the only work surveyed in our entire study whose title was changed to "Babi Yar," arguably so as to tone down the Jewish nationalist sentiment permeating almost every paragraph in it. Its original title, "Tsvishn yidn" (Among Jews),[1] indicated the desire of Jews like Kipnis to pursue the unfathomable: to fix their gaze on the killing fields that were now dotting the Soviet landscape, conceptualize them as Jewish realms of memory, and, daring to go even further, derive inspiration from them as the wellsprings from which Jewish life would then be reborn on Soviet soil. As we shall see, the legacy of Kipnis—one that he dearly paid for with exile and imprisonment in a gulag from 1949 till the end of 1956—stood out as a literary memorial, imagining the

Holocaust and the Great Patriotic War as two separate, monumental memory realms. Best emblematizing this conception was Kipnis's story "On hokhmes, on khesh-boynes" (Without thinking, without calculation), briefly mentioned in the previous chapter in our discussion of Babyn Yar in Soviet literature appearing in Poland.

## THE SOVIET STAR AND THE JEWISH STAR: COEXISTING MEMORIES

Published in Lodz in *Dos naye lebn*, the organ of the Central Committee of Jews in Poland, on May 19, 1947,[2] "Without Thinking, Without Calculation" triggered a well-orchestrated smear campaign against Kipnis, both in *Eynikayt* and in the Russian and Ukrainian press. It targeted what Kipnis's critics saw as a dangerous expression of Jewish chauvinism, contradicting the Soviet doctrine of the "friendship of peoples." In the story, Kipnis encapsulated the Jewish experience in those years as the juxtaposition of two memory realms, two non-concentric circles distinct from and on par one with another. He expresses the hope that the Jewish Red Army soldiers, now roaming about the streets of occupied Berlin, would proudly wear on their chest two badges of honor: the Soviet star (and medals) and the Jewish Star of David. As Mordechai Altshuler notes, to send to Poland this kind of heterodoxic piece only a few months after the start of the Zhdanovshchina was something that "required unusual courage" on the part of Kipnis.[3] The response to his open manifestation of Jewish nationalism did not take long to form and gather momentum. Here is only one sample of the deluge of criticism poured on Kipnis:

Soviet Yiddish writer Itsik Kipnis. (Photo from the Archives of the YIVO Institute for Jewish Research, New York.)

> Kipnis would like to place the Shield of David—that nationalist emblem—next to the Soviet emblem, the symbol of the nations' brotherhood and friendship. It did not bother Kipnis to know that the five-pointed Soviet Star has long ago overshadowed the six-pointed Star of David and the Trident Emblem of Petliura's followers, and all sorts of eagle [symbols] and nationalistic emblems.[4]

During the Thaw period, all Kipnis had been able to do, a year before Yevgeny Yevtushenko turned Babyn Yar into an international issue, was publish his "Babi Yar" abroad through a Communist-leaning Yiddish publication channel (the American Yiddish publication house Ikuf).[5] Evidently, the virtual silence of the Yiddish literary sources published within the USSR during this period, coupled with the signal sent by Nikita Khrushchev following the Twentieth Congress of the Communist Party of the Soviet Union that the years of purges and mass terror were over, encouraged Kipnis to send the work to New York. In 1969, at long last, by the time that there was a large number of works in both Russian and Yiddish relating in detail what had happened in Babyn Yar and by the time a modest monument could already be found at the ravine, Kipnis was finally able to publish this remarkable work in his collection of stories *Tsum lebn* (To life) via the publishing house Sovetskii Pisatel' (The Soviet Writer).[6]

Born in the shtetl of Sloveschne in 1896 and embarking on his literary career in 1922 in Soviet Kyiv, Itsik Kipnis had already won, by the time he engaged in the commemoration of Babyn Yar, international acclaim from major Yiddish literary critics and writers, among them Shmuel Niger, Zalmen Reyzen, and Dovid Bergelson. While Kipnis had no "tainted" literary past—that is, he belonged to the group of young Yiddish writers who started publishing their works following the October Revolution—his style singled him out as a writer who maintained a precarious balance between the prerevolutionary world of the past and the Soviet path of the future. Among his works written prior to the outbreak of the war, the one that brought him to the forefront of the young generation of Yiddish writers was *Khadoshim un teg: a khronik* (Months and days: A chronicle). It was published in 1926 and rendered a nostalgic picture of the shtetl in which he grew up, offering a loving portrayal of its religious and semireligious tradesmen. Considered by the literary critics as the cornerstone of the new Soviet Yiddish literature, as a piece in which an affectionate portrayal, à la Sholem Aleichem, of the shtetl is offered, and where the postrevolutionary reality of civil war and pogroms are interwoven, *Months and Days* brought Kipnis into his first clash with the Soviet literary establishment. As Yiddish educator and journalist Esther Rosenthal-Shneiderman notes, this was, after all, the same shtetl that the new regime, assisted by the Jewish section of the Communist Party, the Evsektsia, was fighting ferociously to transform, defining its inhabitants as *lishentsy*, as superfluous, nonproductive parasites devoid of the basic civil rights granted to Soviet citizens at that time.[7] As Mordechai Altshuler notes, equally controversial was the depiction of the Russian Civil War of 1918–1920, in the course of which gangs of Ukrainians in the vicinity of Sloveschne raided the town and brutally attacked the Jews. Furthermore, Kipnis took things a step further when daring to give voice to the feelings of revenge shared by his townsmen, sentiments that he clearly shared.[8] Kipnis soon turned into a "white crow" among black ones, a reference to the old Russian image of the individual who cannot fit into the collective.[9]

Almost two decades after *Months and Days* came out, history forced Kipnis to revisit the topic and again offer a portrayal of a Jewish community, now that of post–World War I Kyiv, engulfed by the same two desires: the first, to cling to each other and recover from a new cycle of anti-Jewish violence and to do so as members of a distinct ethnic group, sharing age-old historical ties and living in complete alienation from the surrounding nations; and the second, to recover from the ruins of the bygone world through an act of revenge toward their new oppressors—the German people. Although it was written while the Red Army was still marching westward, heading to Berlin, Harriet Murav cogently classifies "Babi Yar," written only five months after Kipnis returned to the city, as a work primarily concerned with postwar reconstruction.[10]

Written almost a year after Kyiv's liberation on November 6, 1943, the essay-story deals with the third anniversary of the Babyn Yar massacre. At that time, the Jewish returnees who came back to Kyiv and other Ukrainian cities and towns encountered a particularly hostile environment. According to Mikhail Mitsel, there was a "segment of the Ukrainian population [who] perceived the return of Jews from evacuation as something unnatural" that was now upsetting the new order, arousing the fear among Ukrainians that Jewish belongings and assets may now return to their original owners.[11] If that was not enough, the occurrence of pogroms across Ukraine, while the Red Army was still fighting the Germans, including one in Kyiv that took the lives of sixteen Jews, may explain the reigning moods of despair among Kyiv's Jews on the massacre's third anniversary, and the first one since the city's Soviet overtake. The local party apparatus's refusal to allow Jews to hold an official commemoration at the ravine only further exacerbated the already sour relations between Jews and non-Jews in the city.[12]

In the face of the Soviet attempt to suppress the memory of Babyn Yar, Kipnis, like other nationalistically oriented Jews, did his best to remain unfazed. He begins the story by reminding his readers that "today" is September 29. Perhaps the younger generation of his readers, who were already schooled in the first atheist state in history, needed this kind of reminder about the fact that for Jews the anniversary of the deceased is called *yortsayt*, a time when Jews attend the grave(s) of the deceased, light candles, and listen to the immediate relatives of the dead reciting the Aramaic prayer known as the Kaddish. From the generic point of view, this introductory section of "Babi Yar" comes in the form of a newspaper's editorial: it refers to events that are about to take place on that day, and this sense of immediacy is underscored by Kipnis's direct address to his readers.[13]

Immediately after these introductory comments, Kipnis changes his tone abruptly. He makes it very clear that this is no lesson in Jewish ethnography, for

> the great hall or the gigantic temple has not yet been built that could house so many flames, so many candles.... But here another thought comes to the fore that whispers: you fool; fires are burning now over vast reaches, into far-off distances!... The decorated cities of the foe are now blazing and flaming! Bear it in mind!... Take account of it on the holy mighty *yortsayt*.[14]

For Kipnis, the memory of the massacre at Babyn Yar attains its true, profound meaning only when reconfigured into a Jewish rite of remembering. Whereas the ritual is meant to be perpetuated from now until the end of time, Kipnis's gaze is fixed on the present moment. For the only way to commemorate the unprecedented genocide that had taken place at the site is through the act of revenge exacted at this very moment by the Red Army upon the civilian German population.

In his work *Against the Apocalypse*, which surveys the Jewish response to destruction from biblical times through the modern age, David Roskies demonstrates how Jewish writers in different epochs responded to anti-Jewish persecution by invoking archetypes drawn from Jewish tradition. He argues that, throughout the ages, of all Jewish traditions it is the response to catastrophe that is the "most viable, coherent and covenantal."[15] In lieu of the recording of factual data about each tragedy that befell them throughout their time-honored history, Jews have preferred, according to Roskies, to present the deep meaning of their suffering by conjuring up timeless archetypes.[16] The imagery invoked by Kipnis seamlessly joins the literary works surveyed by Roskies. The resorting to Jewish archetypes does not end with the lighting of candles on the *yortsayt*, a ritual that for Kipnis embodies in that given moment Jewish collective memory carried out through the vehicle of the Red Army's revenge. Later on in the story, Kipnis makes use of another Jewish archetype, that of the Jewish ritual wine glass, to link the third anniversary of the massacre to the Jewish people's ancient tradition:

> Our hearts have converged around a large overgrown place, which looks like a square goblet. A glass, on whose rim no drops of wine remain, but rather blood that has lost its color from the rain and snow.[17]

If one Jewish ritual embodies the dimensions of the revenge taking place in the fall of 1944, the other one, that of the benediction over a glass of wine, stands for Babyn Yar itself, the ravine that turned into the ghostly abode of what used to be the prewar Jewish community of Kyiv.

## ATONEMENT AND VENGEANCE

When offering a close reading of Kipnis's "Babi Yar," we are fortunate to have at our disposal all three versions: the typewritten manuscript, submitted to *Eynikayt* soon after the story was written (1945), the one appearing in New York (1960), and the one published in Moscow (1969). In addition to the change in title, noted above, the New York version comes very close to fully matching the original with two notable discrepancies: the high holidays and vengeance. Only in the original does Kipnis make the Jewish symbolism of both the Babyn Yar massacre and its annual commemoration most apparent. He reminds his readers of a common Nazi practice observed in other parts of Europe and at other stages of the Holocaust, which was to select notable dates from the Jewish calendar on which to carry out their heinous crimes:

> They came from Podol, Demyevke, from Kurenyovke Shuliavke. [The courtyards] of Big and Little Vasilkover had treacherously driven [from their courtyards] entire and half families. [Precisely on Yom Kippur, but not into a synagogue.] Young and old, little children and old people... On Lvov Street they poured together like small creeks into a river of death and annihilation.
>
> We went there deceived and as if possessed, close together, clinging to one another, terrifying those who caught sight of us, although some of us were dressed in the best clothes they had.[18]

Kipnis describes the multitudes of mourners who came to the ravine to attend the unofficially sanctioned, spontaneous commemoration held at the ravine in the fall of 1944. To Kipnis, they seemed like a flood, "those showing up earlier, seen from afar as if they dispersed, readying themselves for *tashlikh* [the Jewish atonement ritual, normally performed on Rosh Hashanah, in which Jews symbolically throw their sins into the water]." Like in a mourner's home, "here nobody greets another with '*gut yontev*' (happy holiday). And if one welcomes an acquaintance with a 'hello' by accident, he does not receive an answer."[19] These references to the Jewish High Holidays and mourning practices, the reminder of Babyn Yar as being embedded in the Jewish calendar, and the reminder of the massacre's third anniversary as a substitute for the traditional Jewish funeral that had never taken place all underscore the trajectory of the story's evolution: the more official and the later the version, the less Jewish the text becomes. And while we may never know with certainty why the references to Yom Kippur or the custom of *tashlikh* remained unpublished, it stands to reason that a conception of the Babyn Yar massacre as an act of atonement for a divine verdict (in recognition of individual or collective sins), and as an act of hope for future redemption, could not so peacefully coexist with the Soviet victimhood trope of innocent Soviet civilians who are devoid of any ethnic singularity.

Second, the theme of revenge, represented at the beginning of "Babi Yar" by the image of the *yortsayt* candles, resurfaces throughout Kipnis's brief essay-story and is another marker of the inconsistencies among the text's different versions. Of all the references to revenge, the image of the burning cities of Germany is the only one that saw the light of day, to be included in both versions and published both domestically and overseas. All other references to vengeance appear only in the New York version. In this respect, too, "Babi Yar" joins a large number of Soviet Yiddish works published both within and beyond the borders of the Soviet Union and containing textual discrepancies between the work meant for "domestic consumption" and the one published abroad.[20] We will leave for now the question of why the issue of revenge was curtailed in the Soviet version. For the time being, let us note that in the New York version of "Babi Yar" Kipnis turns revenge into the work's framework. It begins with the blazing cities of Germany and with Kipnis sharing with his readers his innermost thoughts. All he wishes is that some woman in Germany named Greta, waiting for her beloved one Hans to come back from the front, would not die in the Allied air raids but, instead, stay crippled, "howling with her broken back, looking at her trampled and choked little snakes."[21] At the end of the essay-story, Kipnis returns to the theme of revenge when he describes the Jews returning from Babyn Yar and passing by a camp for Nazi POWs. This rendezvous between the relatives and acquaintances of the victims with their now-wretched former oppressors is for Kipnis a sign that the balance between the two groups has been altered for good:

> Three years ago, Babi Yar was the abyss where "none who go thither ever return" [Proverbs 2:19]. Those who left for that place never returned. The enemy rejoiced: Babi Yar, the last abode of the Jewish people, the last speck of Jewish existence. Babi Yar—the word with which the history of a people comes to an end. That's what the foe decided three years ago. And now, one may see in front of Babi Yar a camp for captive German soldiers rubbing their shoes in their wounds, eating the lice of their own bodies. We look at them with disgust, as if on rotting garbage, their eyes bulge with envy—they see before them human beings.[22]

It comes as quite a shock to the twenty-first-century reader to see this expanded ending of Kipnis's "Babi Yar," which speaks about the recovery of Jewish dignity through an act of revenge, through the dehumanization of those who had only a while ago considered the Jews to be subhuman. When read in its historical context as a work written before the conclusion of World War II, however, it becomes clear that Kipnis, like his colleagues Aron Kushnirov and Peretz Markish, can make sense of the Holocaust and the Soviet victory only as two complementary events: the crime and the punishment, the victimization and the revenge. The theme of revenge is in line with the periodization of Holocaust memory set forth by David Roskies. So long as Holocaust memory still resided within the confines of each individual community, "the plain style, which is thought of today as the gold standard of Holocaust writing, was never a foregone conclusion."[23] Thus, long before Holocaust writers would dwell on the most profound philosophical repercussions of the Holocaust, wonder whether it is not categorically barbaric to write poetry after Auschwitz, as the cultural critic Theodor Adorno put it, "Babi Yar" by Kipnis echoes the voice of an incipient Holocaust literature that not only is unwilling to forgive and forget but also gives vent to the most instinctive and base sentiments of retribution.

"Relentless" was the adjective used by Nina Tumarkin to describe the style of Anatoly Kuznetsov's novel *Babi Yar*. If this is true of a work written two decades after the German occupation of Kyiv, how much more so is it true of Kipnis's "Babi Yar," which was written under the immediate impact of the German occupation in a city whose center was destroyed, which saw its residents stricken by hunger and poverty, and where the spectacle of starved Nazi POWs could still be seen. As much as Kipnis's imagery is driven by the desire to render an unembellished portrayal of the horrific condition of the mass grave, complemented by a no less brutal description of the German civilian population and military now under attack, relentlessness also characterizes its structure.

We noted earlier that Kipnis opens "Babi Yar" by adopting the voice of the reporter. Later on, while he maintains this voice, informing his readers who are not present at the ravine about the mass procession heading there, Kipnis pauses to tell his readers that "from the beginning" (that is, from the moment he came back to Kyiv) he had one request from the Jews like him who were starting to return to Kyiv after its liberation lying "deep in his heart":

> My friends! Let us not take the tram there. Let us go by foot, let us go on that road, on those streets which are full to overflowing with the living bodies of our brothers. They came from Podol, Demyevke, from Kurenyovke, Big and Little Vasilkover had treacherously let go of whole and half families from their courtyards, young and old, little children and old people ... they poured together like a river of death and annihilation. They went there deceived and as if possessed, close together, clinging to one another, terrifying those who caught sight of them, although some of them were dressed in the best clothes they had.[24]

Right afterward, Kipnis asks his readers whether they knew the sisters Dolin, the two old inhabitants of Kyiv. He moves swiftly from addressing his readers in the second person to a different point of focalization: that of the omniscient writer, who now begins to tell the story of the sisters Emma and Eva, narrating their inner thoughts of fear, doubt, and disbelief as they had to leave their apartment and set out on the march to Babyn Yar, reassuring themselves that such an enormous crowd could not be going to their deaths. By delving into the minds of the victims, Kipnis enhances the feeling of terror and disbelief that was shared by the Jews who were ordered to make their last way to Babyn Yar three years before.

The act of going to Babyn Yar by foot that for Kipnis becomes a moral dictum is grounded not only in the need to pay tribute to the victims through this act of pilgrimage. Kipnis gives voice here—obliquely yet fairly intelligibly—to the fear that if he chose not to reach the ravine by foot he might encounter on the Kyiv public tram "a foreign look [that] may unwittingly coarsely abrade my look."[25] The identity of that foreign look is not fully disclosed. But Kipnis's intent is clear: in a concise phrase, he delivers the psychological pressure that the Jewish survivors who had returned to Kyiv after it was reoccupied by the Red Army in November 1943 had to now endure as they were met with the hostility of a large segment of the local population. In one concise sentence, Kipnis boldly evinces a great awareness (and of course, a great deal of courage expressing this awareness in print) of this new condition. In the new reality of postwar Kyiv, he fears that as much as Babyn Yar functioned as a centripetal force that brought Soviet Jews back together, it also operated as a centrifugal one, further alienating them from the rest of the Soviet population.

In her brief article dedicated to "Babi Yar," Rosenthal-Shneiderman credits Kipnis for being the one who dared to open the wound of Babyn Yar's neglect years before Yevgeny Yevtushenko and Anatoly Kuznetsov did so.[26] When surveying Yiddish works dedicated to Babyn Yar published during the war, we have noted that initially, before Soviet Yiddish writers started to allow themselves more liberty to express their national sentiments, the tragedy that befell the Jewish people was read through the lens of the Great Patriotic War. *To the People and the Fatherland* is the title of Peretz Markish's work, referring to the general fight joined by Soviet Jews and members of other Soviet ethnicities to defend the motherland and drive out the Nazi invader.[27] Kipnis, by contrast, does not offer the point of view of the Soviet Jewish fighter, who could more easily share—despite the antisemitism endemic to the Red Army—a feeling of solidarity with his non-Jewish brothers-in-arms. Instead, his is a look at Babyn Yar from the standpoint of the returning evacuee. The author, who came to Kyiv with a collection of radio personnel in April 1944, was among the group of Yiddish writers and cultural activists, including his close friend, the celebrated poet Dovid Hofshteyn, who joined together in organizing the mass gathering on the third anniversary of the massacre. For these returning evacuees, by September 1944 the so-called friendship of peoples had turned into a completely empty slogan. Instead of friendship, Kipnis and his fellow evacuees encountered a hostile population that had in many instances taken over Jewish property and "welcomed" the retuning Jews without concealing feelings of enmity and bitterness about the appearance of the Jewish returnees.

In this atmosphere, highly negative to the prospects of Jewish cultural and communal rehabilitation, Kipnis realizes how slim the chance is that the Soviet authorities would undertake the restoration of Babyn Yar and bring the annual gathering at the site under its auspices. According to Rosenthal-Shneiderman, Kipnis's hope that someone would break the silence at Babyn Yar, that "someone might come and address the people with a word,"[28] is a carefully disguised reference exactly to those who most noticeably did not show up at Babyn Yar on that day:

Who is that "someone" on whose words of consolation the Jews are waiting, mourning at the ravine for their 70,000 tormented brothers and sisters?

That "someone" means—the Bolshevik leaders of the Ukrainian people, of our "folks" whose sons and daughters helped the German murderers, with an easy hand, to exterminate those who lie here buried without a gravestone. *But no one comes.*[29]

Those "folks" (*di eygene*) mentioned by Rosenthal-Shneiderman refer to the thoughts that hover on the mind of Kipnis as he encounters other Jews and joins them on the way toward Babyn Yar: "Somewhere deep in one's mind leaps a thought... what is at stake here are certain grievances against one's folks that need to be resolved with no noise, as befitting things that need to remain among folks."

Rosenthal-Shneiderman further clarifies the identity of that "someone" (*emetser*) whose absence from the memorial service was painfully and silently noticed by Kipnis: the members of the Ukrainian Central Committee, who according to her could not rise to the occasion "because it was busy with far more important things—with making the decision to allow back to the Ukraine as few as possible of its past Jewish residents[—]sending a representative to Babyn Yar would have been contradictory to the whole line of the Soviet rulers."[30] The terms "someone" and "one's folks" are examples of doublespeak, the euphemistic speech that flourishes under totalitarian regimes. Nothing stands in greater contrast to these terms than the blunt, direct way in which Kipnis describes the grievances his kin have toward the German people. Thus, the two allusive terms *emetser* and *di eygene* mark the boundaries of the permissible of "Babi Yar": what could be said about the atrocities committed by the Nazis could be only vaguely hinted at with regard to their collaborators and the Soviet authorities, who now seemed to be backing the latter at the expense of Kyiv's returning Jews.

In the absence of the authorities' representatives at the ravine, Kipnis imagines that he is the one to fill that void. He wants to whisper in the ear of each of his fellows who attended the third anniversary of the Babyn Yar massacre. In his address, with which the version of the story that saw the light of day in the Soviet Union ends, the journalist and narrator of the work's beginning turns now into a biblical prophet:

> Dear brothers, let us rise from the earth, let us shake the ashes from us and flare up with all the light stored in each of us.... As the body of a man, whose foot, hand or even one finger has been amputated becomes incomplete, smaller than what it used to be. But a people, a people. When it befalls a disaster, like the one we endured; a people—when you divide it by half, or into three thirds, is like a drip of water, like a round drop of quicksilver. You pluck half of it out, but the second half rounds off, is filled in and turns back to being full.
>
> Let us rise from the earth, let us stand up strong.[31]

These stirring words echo the famous prophecy of the Valley of the Dry Bones from the Book of Ezekiel (Ezek 37:1–14). In Kipnis's cyclical conception of Jewish history, the biblical prophet's words of solace offered to the people of Judea in the wake of the destruction of the First Temple in 586 BCE gain relevancy again in the fall of 1944. But in their first iteration, as we recall, these verses of prophetic solace were not the last word. Kipnis reserved the last word for the encounter between the Jews coming back from Babyn Yar with the Nazi POWs. The version published in New York ended with the sweet smell of revenge.

Other conspicuous differences exist between the American and Soviet versions that demand an explanation. Indeed, in the version of "Babi Yar" published in Moscow, the author refers neither to the fact that ravine's prime victims were Jews nor to the ethnic identity of those who came to Babyn Yar on the occasion of the massacre's third anniversary. In the version published abroad, by contrast, Kipnis does not begin his imagined prophetic speech with the words "dear brothers," but rather with the words "Jews, dear brothers." In this version, Kipnis describes his encounter with "a young Jew," a stranger. The man approaches him on the way home back from Babyn Yar:

> There are enough Jews—he says—who go to Babi Yar.
> And Jews—I answer—come back from Babi Yar in one piece, thank God.[32]

Inasmuch as Babyn Yar used to be the hub of the Jewish people's death, it will now become the wellspring of the Jewish people's renewal.

All told, there are two significant omissions from the Soviet version: the detailed description of wretched German civilians and POWs mentioned earlier and the clear reference to Jews as both Babyn Yar's victims and the people who were in the crowds that gathered at the site three years later. The omission of the suffering Germans from the later Soviet version might be explained as reflecting a tendency to update the text in accordance with the spirit of the times. It may well be that these sections were excised from the work in its Soviet version in order to highlight the victimization of the Jews and present their suffering as a crime too enormous to be avenged. But as for the absence of the word "Jews" in the text, here we come across an omission typical of Babyn Yar's representation in the Soviet Yiddish sphere. As we shall see in the following chapters, Kipnis was not the only Soviet Yiddish writer who omitted the term "Jews" from the portrayal of Babyn Yar, blurring thereby the site's linkage to the Holocaust of European Jewry.

Apparently, recognizing that drawing an explicit link between the ravine and Jews would hurt his chance to see his essay-story published in the USSR, Kipnis must have felt that many other components of the text made the subject matter of his text—for example, Babyn Yar's Jewish victims—clear enough. The mass shootings that took place at Babyn Yar, we recall, spanned a time period far longer than two days. By focusing his attention on the anniversary of the massacre that took place on September 29–30, Kipnis left no room for ambiguity about who the primary victims that concerned him were. The Jewish subtext of the work was only further augmented as he drew upon Jewish archetypes and customs in his portrayal of this occasion of the anniversary. When reading the works of Soviet Yiddish writers of the next generation—those younger than Kipnis (and Shike Driz, the focus of our next chapter) yet older than the Russian *shestidesiatniki*—the connection between Babyn Yar and the Holocaust will only be further blurred. These writers, more at ease accommodating to the new Soviet way of life, further clouded Babyn Yar's linkage to the Holocaust, tending to portray it, rather, as a Great Patriotic War site. But before we turn from one generation to the other, let us explore the second masterpiece in the Yiddish corpus of literary memorials for Babyn Yar and the complex figure of the sad clown who wrote it.

# 8

# A LULLABY TO BABYN YAR: SHIKE DRIZ

I F "BABI YAR" BY ITSIK KIPNIS IS A WORK THAT STILL AWAITS RECOGNITION as a masterpiece of Holocaust literature, the poem "Babi Yar" by Shike (Ovsei) Driz (1908–1971) is the one work of Soviet Yiddish literature that has achieved recognition from audiences and readers far and wide. This has much to do with the fact that the poem is a song in the guise of a lullaby. In an interesting parallel with the declamatory mode of Yevgeny Yevtushenko's "Babi Yar," the generic character of Driz's work is what made it so appealing as a performance piece. The poem became a staple in the repertoire of the Yiddish folk singer Nehama Lifshitz, whose career as a Soviet Yiddish singer between the years 1955 and 1969 turned her, in the words of Yaacov Ro'i, into "the center of the Jewish national movement and made her in many ways its focus, its symbol, and its heroine."[1] During these years, Lifshitz toured Jewish communities throughout the entire Soviet Union and offered her audiences a rare thread that could connect Soviet Jews, both young and old, to the treasure trove of Yiddish and Hebrew literature and folklore. By virtue of the inclusion of Driz's song in her repertoire, set to a score by Riva Boyarsky, the poem gained great popularity on both sides of the Iron Curtain when it was included, three decades after it was written, in the collection of "songs of the Holocaust" titled *We Are Here*.[2]

In addition to the poem's remarkable career as the only work of Yiddish literature surveyed here that does not need to be rescued from oblivion, it is also noteworthy for another reason: this is a Holocaust poem that depicts Babyn Yar ever so graphically and yet does so in the form of a children's song or cradle song whose main function ostensibly is to soothe and lull a child to sleep. As we shall see, the fashioning of Babyn Yar as a lullaby encapsulates not only the poem's overt meaning, but through its "generic DNA"

Soviet Yiddish writer Shike (Ovsei) Driz, Moscow, 1965. (Photo courtesy of the United States Holocaust Memorial Museum, from the Centropa Collection.)

Driz, like Kipnis, appropriates the ravine as an unequivocal Jewish memory site. The choice of a lullaby for a work about the Babyn Yar massacre might seem to a contemporary reader somewhat strange. For its author, however, who was another member of the Kyiv circle of Yiddish writers, to invoke the memory of Babyn Yar through a literary mode designated for children was a natural choice. Driz, after all, was one of the foremost Yiddish children's songwriters in the Soviet Union. Born in the Ukrainian shtetl of Krasne, Driz left for Kyiv on his own when he was fourteen and enrolled in the Kyiv Art Institute, dreaming of becoming a sculptor. He came from a very humble background, "from a family of artisans who have never lost their love for humor, for a witty proverb and a merry song," writes Chaim Beider in his *Lexicon of Soviet Yiddish Writers*.[3] The cheerful atmosphere in which Driz grew up left an indelible mark on the career of a man who composed numerous playful and humorous poems intended for the youngest age group of Yiddish readers.

The frivolity of his character, while perfectly suiting a Yiddish children's poet, was also a perfect disguise for a man who was a heavy drinker and was well aware from the outset of his career of the artistic constraints of the literary system to which he was a contributor. In many of his poems, the frivolity, as a matter of fact, serves as a cover for works endowed with Jewish nationalist sentiments.[4] While the decline of Driz's career had already begun in the 1930s when he lost his readers, an outcome of the liquidation of the state-run Yiddish schools and Yiddish publishing houses specializing in children's books,[5] matters for Driz got far worse when he was arrested and sentenced to a labor camp during the height of Stalin's antisemitic campaign. It was only in the Thaw period, through the venue of *Sovetish heymland*, that Driz's career as a Yiddish children's poet resumed.

## THE BABYN YAR LULLABY

Like the essay-story by Kipnis, Driz's poem overlaps with more than one period in the history of Soviet Yiddish literature: while written in 1953, during the very early Thaw, the poem was published in the Soviet Union for the first time in 1969. Included in Driz's collection *Di ferte strune* (The fourth string), it appeared in the same year that Kipnis's work came out.[6] Together, the publication of these two works testifies to the conditions of relative freedom of expression for Yiddish writers during a period that we have already labeled as the mini-Thaw of the Brezhnev years.

Due to the work's significance and brevity, let us cite it in full and then turn to an analysis of its thematic and generic components:

> *I would hang the cradle on a beam,*
> *And rock, and rock my little boy, my Yankl.*
> *But the home has vanished in a flame of fire,*
> *So how can I rock my little boy, my dear one?*
> *With thorns and nettles*
> *Are the footpaths covered,*
> *The quiet white doves*
> *Become cinders...*
>
> *I would hang the cradle on a little tree,*
> *And rock, and rock my little boy, my Shleyml.*
> *But I have been left without a thread of bed cover,*
> *But I have been left without a shoelace.*
>
> *No little branch, no little leaf...*
> *From the oak, the hollow one,*
> *Has remained a little hill*
> *of glowing coals...*
>
> *I would shear my braids, my long ones,*
> *And hang on them the cradle, the cradle,*

*But I do not know where to look for the little bones now,*
*The dear little bones of both my children.*

*Help me, mothers, help me,*
*To wail to the end my melody.*
*Help me, mothers, help me.*
*To lull Babi Yar to sleep.*[7]

From the very first reading of the poem, the incongruence between form and content instantly leaps to mind. Here is a poem dealing with a mother lulling her children to sleep. And at the same time, its subject is the carnage at Babyn Yar. While in the later canonized versions of the poem it would be called "The Babi Yar Cradle Song," in Driz's printed version this generic designation is missing. As someone steeped in the folk traditions of the world, however, Driz understood that the lullabies of many nations share a predilection for the frightening and sincere that is due, in all likelihood, to the parental fears of the speaker.[8] Still, a lullaby whose subject is mass murder would seem to stretch the genre to its limit. What is more, the fact that in "Babi Yar" the narrator is a mother who has already lost her two children, Yankl and Shleyml, to the Nazi slaughter, a woman trying to soothe dead children, rather than half-asleep, living children, further underscores the incongruence in Driz's poem between content and form.

The poem is included in a section of *The Fourth String* given the Hebrew title "Po nikbar" (Here lie buried). As the use of Hebrew and the thematic scope of this section suggest, Driz intended to place his "Babi Yar" in the context of other songs related to the Holocaust. As a prelude to the song, Driz included another poem titled "Luftbalonen" (Balloons), recounting the story of a man who brings a balloon to his dead grandson, who is buried at Babyn Yar. Like "Luftbalonen," written in 1945, "Babi Yar" concerns an imaginary relationship between a living adult and a dead child. In both poems, the adult displays concern for the child by attempting to provide the latter with something material: a balloon in one and a cradle in the other, a cradle that the mother wishes to hang on an inanimate beam, a tree, and finally, her own braids. In both poems, the adult's action can be construed in two conflicting ways: as a testimony to the adult's feelings of affection toward the child and, equally, as the adult's inability to cope with the loss and make sense of its repercussions. The juxtaposition of the two poems only sharpens the interplay of love and madness. For a woman to be searching for the bones of her two children, Yankl and Shleyml, to no avail, is already a testament to the positioning of the poem's heroine on the brink of sanity. The fashioning of the poem as a lullaby only helps throw into high relief this dismal condition of the mother. While the content of the poem suggests her acceptance of her children's death, the creation of the poem as a lullaby suggests the very opposite: it was an attempt to connect to them and to all the dead children whose bodies were lying at Babyn Yar.[9]

# THE MEDIUM IS THE MESSAGE

Why a lullaby? As Dov Noy illustrates in his structural analysis of Yiddish lullabies, which cites a version of Driz's poem, he positions the lullaby or *viglid* (cradle song) at the heart of the Yiddish folk song repertoire.[10] According to Noy, every authentic Yiddish lullaby must display the following six features: (a) an infant directly addressed by the singer; (b) a mention of the function of lulling; (c) a three-part structure, often modeled on the pattern of *gradatio*; (d) an absent father; (e) the future greatness of the infant; and (f) extraordinary events (either supernatural or uncanny). By analyzing "Babi Yar" according to these six standard features of the *viglid*, Noy reaches a surprising conclusion: although Driz's poem partakes of the genre of the wailing song, featuring a Job-like heroine, it cannot be considered a true Yiddish lullaby. That is because only four of the standard elements of the *viglid* are in evidence: (a) the three-part structure (the transition from the beam in the first stanza to a tree in the second and the mother's braids in the third); (b) the *gradatio* (the repetition of *volt ikh* . . . ); (c) the absent father; and (d) the unrealistic element (an attempt to lull to sleep dead children in Babyn Yar).

If Driz's work falls short of constituting a bona fide Yiddish cradle song, what, then, made him draw upon lullaby motifs, if only partially? First, the model of the Yiddish lullaby allowed Driz to underscore the bleakness that pervades both Babyn Yar and his literary memorial dedicated to it; second, it is through the genre of the *viglid* that Driz alludes to the cultural DNA of the people described in it. Put another way, the distinct Jewish medium of the *viglid* is for Driz a vehicle (not the only one though) through which he can allude to the fact that the victims of Babyn Yar he is concerned with were Jewish, and so is the mourning mother-speaker, something that is not explicitly indicated in the body of the poem.

Upon closer inspection, it may be argued that "Babi Yar" does not contain all the standard features of the Yiddish lullaby because it is, in fact, an anti-*viglid*, a poem in which the main premise of the genre has been turned on its head. If in the lullaby the mother-singer acts as an intermediary between the real child lying in her bed and the realm of the fantastic or uncanny, then in "Babi Yar" the opposite happens. Here, it is the children Yankl and Shleyml and the act of singing them to sleep that are unreal. Conversely, what is expected to belong to the fantastic or uncanny is now real: a ravine filled with the charred, unrecognizable, and yet partially exposed bodies of thousands of children. In short, Driz is exploiting the genre of the *viglid* only partially in order to heighten the enormity of the tragedy that took place at Babyn Yar as well as the mother's misery. The speaker in this poem is either unwilling or unable to accept her new condition as a bereaved mother.

By encrypting the poem with the markers of a lullaby, Driz signals that this is a poem dealing with the massacre of Jews in Babyn Yar and not the members of other national groups. What Kipnis does by concentrating on September 29 and by elaborating in his essay-story on Jewish customs, archetypes, and rhetoric, Driz does most powerfully through the elaboration of *viglid* motifs in his poem. No doubt, the model of the *viglid*, only partially adopted, is not the only clue at the reader's disposal that Driz's view of Babyn Yar gravitates toward the master narrative of the Holocaust. The names of the two boys and, most conspicuously, the choice of the Yiddish language as Driz's vehicle of expression give the reader a similar indication about the identity of the victims. Nonetheless, for a poem written and published in a cultural and political system that had for decades expunged from Yiddish culture anyone and anything that could smack of the Jewish religion, literature, and culture, the choice of language did not seem adequate for Driz for a poem dealing with the symbol of Jewish victimhood during World War II as it unfolded on Soviet soil.

What could not be said in the poem's content was therefore said through its genre. In a way, for Driz the form of the *viglid* had a twofold function. It served as a key and a lock, both revealing the deeper, latent subject matter and, at the same time, encrypting it. It was a key, insofar as the initiated reader could identify its intertextual connection with the larger corpus of Yiddish lullabies. It acted as a lock because no generic choice was more impervious, obfuscated, and misleading for a poem subverting Moscow's view of Babyn Yar than a folksy children's song written by a writer whose regular contributions to *Sovetish heymland* were always published under the rubric *Far kleyn un groys* (for young and old), songs that for the most part were characterized by merry wordplays written in trochaic meter, a staple of children's poetry, and by topics that were characteristically lighthearted, even silly. Indeed, if one is to look for an explanation for the appearance of such a Jewish national poem in the Soviet Union, there could be perhaps no better way to mask its heterodox message than by the fashioning of Shike Driz as no more than a poet for the "young and old." Most certainly, what was allowed in the Soviet Russian sphere at the beginning of the 1960s—that is, the publishing of a poem on Babyn Yar and its Jewish victims in the declamatory, revolutionary style of Yevtushenko—was out of the question in the Soviet Yiddish cultural system. Driz, who was very well aware of this, offered his own memorial to Babyn Yar that was modest and cryptic, one that was fraught with neither the ambition nor the mass appeal that characterized Yevtushenko's poem.

The fate of "Babi Yar" by Driz would have been similar to that of many other products of Soviet Yiddish literature during the post-Stalin era had it not been for its inclusion in the repertoire of the Yiddish folk singer Nehama Lifshitz. The poem, slightly modified to fit the mode of singing and set to music by Riva Boyarsky, was one of the highlights of Lifshitz's repertoire, which included translations of songs to Yiddish from Russian, old Yiddish folk songs, and the works of contemporary Soviet Yiddish writers. When analyzing Driz's poem along the six-point structure of the *viglid*, Noy notes that the poem did not go through a substantial process of folklorization—that is, the process that "alters the literary (written or printed) item into an ethno-political (oral) one"—and that he therefore prefers to regard it as an art song rather than a folk song.¹¹ Noy, however, overlooks the fact that it was through the performance of the poem by Lifshitz that "Babi Yar" was transformed from a marginal work, published in one Yiddish book with a very modest circulation, into a classical piece. More than anywhere else, this transformation is evidenced in the poem's title provided by Noy, "The Babi Yar Cradle Song," an addition missing from the poem's original, written publication. While Noy may be right that the song did not gain universal currency, it was through the performing of the poem by Lifshitz that it came to be regarded by her Soviet Jewish audience as a lullaby, a change that speaks volumes about the process of folklorization that Driz's original "Babi Yar" had undergone.

Thus, it was through the performances of Nehama Lifshitz that this otherwise forgotten poem turned into an expression of Jewish national self-assertion in the Soviet Union, a work that turned Driz's implicit, personal view of Babyn Yar into something both explicit and widespread. One can only imagine the amount of courage it required on the part of Lifshitz to perform this song in the first concert she gave in Kyiv, in December 1959, a city where not only the memory of Babyn Yar but also other repressive measures directed at the local Jewish community were in effect, and where public concerts carrying any Jewish content were a rarity.¹² As Victoria Khiterer notes:

> Anti-Semitism in Kyiv was always stronger than in other places of the Russian Empire. Kyiv had a long history of pogroms, Jewish expulsions, religious anti-Semitism and chauvinistic Black Hundred organizations, which organized the Beilis Affair in Kyiv in 1911–1913. So the Nazis anticipated correctly that much of the local gentile population hated Jews and would not resist their extermination.¹³

In her interviews conducted after her immigration to Israel, Lifshitz noted that she would usually sing Driz's song last. But

> to sing about Babyn Yar in Kyiv was not like singing about it elsewhere. Here no one applauded. The hall seemed to be electrified. The entire audience rose to its feet like one man and stood in absolute silence, in the atmosphere of fear that characterized the Jews of Kyiv.... "This was a curtain of tears." As she left the hall people stood outside, still silently weeping, in order to touch her hand or sleeve as though she was a holy person.¹⁴

Perhaps of all the cultural artifacts in the Yiddish literary sphere surveyed thus far, the December 1959 performance of "Babi Yar" by Nehama Lifshitz in the city of Kyiv is the closest manifestation of Dina Spechler's term "permitted dissent." To what extent this performance was something the local authorities in Kyiv really permitted is attested by the fact that Lifshitz was reprimanded for including in her repertoire too much Jewish content and too little praise for the Soviet conquest of space, and that her next concerts in the city were called off.[15] As we shall see in our next chapter, the ambitions that cultural figures like Itsik Kipnis, Shike Driz, and Nehama Lifshitz had in the post-Stalin years, their daring to imagine Soviet Yiddish literature as an outlet for a future Jewish cultural renaissance in the USSR, were dashed by a Soviet Yiddish literary establishment that regarded faithfulness to the Soviet regime and the party line on every crucial ideological matter a sine qua non of its own survival.

# 9

# BETWEEN MARRANOS AND CONVERSOS: THE NEXT GENERATION OF KYIV YIDDISH WRITERS

IN THE JUNE 1975 ISSUE OF *SOVETISH HEYMLAND*, THE SINGLE YIDDISH PERIodical published in the Soviet Union during the Cold War era, a curious article with no prelude titled "The Memorial at Babi Yar Will Stand Forever" could not have been missed by its committed readers.[1] Though buried at the end of the issue, it seemed for a moment that the almost complete silence about the Babyn Yar massacre strictly observed by the journal thus far was broken. The author of this six-page article was none other than Aron Vergelis, the poet who had been the journal's editor in chief for the past fourteen years and still enjoyed the status of being a towering authority in Soviet Yiddish cultural affairs.

Born in 1918, Vergelis was a product of the Soviet grand project of human engineering that intended, among other things, to alter the geographical, socioeconomic, and cultural face of Soviet Jewry. When he was twelve, his family moved from Volhynia to the Jewish Autonomous Region in Birobidzhan in the Far East, where the young Vergelis, a salt of the earth Jewish cow herder, published his first poems.[2] No sooner had Vergelis settled in the Soviet capital following the conclusion of World War II than his rise to eminence began. He became the youngest member of the Moscow Yiddish literary elite as the head of the Moscow Yiddish radio program, a secretary of the Writers' Union Yiddish section, and a member on the editorial board of the Moscow-based Yiddish periodical *Heymland*.[3]

## BABYN YAR: FULLY DE-JUDAIZED IN YIDDISH

In spite of this impressive record for an emerging Soviet literato, Aron Vergelis became known beyond the realms of the Soviet Union only during the Thaw period. This happened when, after more than a decade of a complete halt in the publishing of Yiddish literary works in the USSR, the Soviet regime decided to revive Yiddish culture—ever so partially—and appointed Vergelis as the editor in chief of its flagship publication. Vergelis won this stature not only by virtue of his Birobidzhan past, his ability to claim and fancy himself to be the favorite Jewish son of the Soviet fatherland, but first and foremost by his slavish loyalty to the Soviet dogma for which he was repaid with the trust of his bosses. His silence over the Babyn Yar massacre, observed thus far, did not surprise any of his readers who followed his poetry, articles, and editorial comments that had appeared on the pages of *Sovetish heymland*, the periodical that was conceived as a bimonthly publication in the summer of 1961 and that turned, four years later, into a monthly one. But now—more than three decades after the massacre of Kyiv Jews at the ravine had taken place—it was apparently time to give the primary Holocaust site found in the USSR adequate attention. The occasion on which the article appeared was not incidental: Vergelis offered here a reportage of his recent visit to Gosstroy, the special section of the Ukrainian Construction Department, where the last preparations to erect the official, fifteen-meter-tall monument dedicated to the Soviet citizens and POWs who had been shot at Babyn Yar were going full speed ahead.

While the theme of Babyn Yar would surface every now and then in the pages of *Sovetish heymland*, mostly the work of the members of the Kyiv circle of Yiddish writers, who had resided in interwar Kyiv and whose relatives and friends were among the massacre's victims, it was hard to miss the screaming absence of Babyn Yar among the plethora of poems, short stories, serialized novels, scholarly articles, and news reports in the primary platform for Yiddish literary works during the post-Stalin era. Now, nearly twenty-four years after the September 29–30, 1941, massacre of Kyiv Jews, the journal's editor finally found the moment auspicious to offer a sentimental depiction of Babyn Yar, expressed in the most hyperbolic terms:

> The ravine on the outskirts of Kyiv, that old ravine drenched with inexhaustible sorrow, endowed with its own melancholy climate,[4] with the silence of its air, with the secrecy of its skies, with, so to speak, a unique body and soul.... This piece of land, almost transparent from above and endlessly labyrinthine from deep under; soaked with blood and tears, completely empty and, at the same time, densely populated—with what and with whom God only knows—on the banks of the gray Dnieper, at the foot of the mother of the Russian cities—it was always Babi Yar, not another ravine [*yar*].[5]

Confirming the stature of Babyn Yar as a site of symbolic proportions and going as far as making the peculiar assertion that the ravine has been a locus of horror and doom since time immemorial, Aron Vergelis found no reason to justify to his readers the practice of silence that had been hitherto so meticulously observed in *Sovetish heymland*. For him, in spite of this silence, his readers needed no introductory explanation for the article's timely appearance. Nearly ten years after the Thaw came to an end, the Ukrainian Soviet Socialist Republic was about to reverse its decades-long policy of silence with regard to Babyn Yar. The minor granite plaque heralding the future construction of a monument at Babyn Yar, laid at the site as early as 1966, was about to be superseded by a compelling, megalithic structure featuring ill-fated victims on one side and brave Soviet POWs on the other. It was a sign that a major change on the part of the Soviet regime toward Babyn Yar was about to take place, a sign that Vergelis, the man who could always skillfully follow the zigzags of Soviet policy, could not miss.

Babyn Yar was finally about to turn from a memory black hole into a public, legitimate focal point for the commemoration of one of the most horrific events in the history of World War II on Soviet soil. But did these preparations for the erection of an official monument at the site constitute a dramatic change in the Soviet authorities' attitude toward Babyn Yar's memory? The answer would be yes, only so long as Babyn Yar was deemed an exclusively Great Patriotic War site. More than anything, the remarkably long article by Vergelis was only a confirmation that *Sovetish heymland* would continue to do what it had done since its inception: faithfully follow Soviet officialdom. Recognizing that the Soviet authorities were about to extract Babyn Yar from its previous state of nearly complete oblivion and were now turning it into a memory locus, a place where "in 1941–1943 the German Fascist Invaders executed more than 100,000 citizens of the city of Kyiv,"[6] as the bronze tablet of the new monument would suggest, Vergelis aligned himself with this new position.

Remarkably, of all the Yiddish literati, no one went to such lengths as Vergelis to *explicitly* state that Babyn Yar's memory was one-directional, belonging exclusively within the orbit of the Great Patriotic War. In this respect, Vergelis shares with his Western critics a similar failure to link the memory of Babyn Yar to more than one memory orbit. One of them, William Korey, when attempting to tackle one of the most difficult challenges posed by Babyn Yar, its uniqueness as a mass grave not only for both Jews and non-Jews, but also for both civilians and soldiers, pointed out that the Soviet POWs shot at Babyn Yar were often targeted for being Jewish.[7] Korey, no doubt, was referring here to a well-documented Nazi practice. Vergelis, quite strikingly, corroborated in his article the exact same historical data: he was also referring to the murder of both civilians and military personnel who were Jewish. Yet, he did so in order to make the diametrically opposite argument. Recollecting a conversation that he had had at the *Sovetish heymland* office with a group of Jewish tourists from California who wanted

The Soviet monument marking the murder of "peaceful Soviet citizens" and POWs at Babyn Yar, designed by Mikhaylo Lysenko and erected in 1976. One may find no mentioning of Jews in the monument's inscription, not even in the Yiddish plaque added to it in the early 1980s. (Photo 1275/4, Yad Vashem Photo Archive.)

to find out how the memory of the 70,000 Jews killed at Babyn Yar would be remembered, Vergelis found it necessary to educate them. His words merit full citation:

> In Babi Yar lie 70,000 dead, shot because they were Jews, 40,000—because they were Red Army soldiers, 10,000—because they belonged to the Communist party or the Communist Youth Movement. These distinctions were made by the fascists: but who does not understand that both within the Jewish population and among the soldiers and commanders of the Red Army there were thousands and thousands of Communists and Communist Youth members. On the other hand, were there few Jews among the Red Army soldiers and the underground fighters?
>
> For all of those murdered, no matter whether they were women or men, children or elderly, Jews or non-Jews—for all those martyrs, the blood that had been spilled out of their veins had one color.[8]

More than anything else, by invoking the conversation with his American guests, Vergelis wished to validate as well as justify the rationale that had underlain the Soviet official handling of Babyn Yar for decades. It was only the fascists, so Vergelis's argument went, and implicitly, their imperialist Western successors, who would apply the Nazi racial dogma in order to arbitrarily distinguish Jews from non-Jews. As for himself, Vergelis made it clear that, for a Jew fully assimilated into Soviet society, and no less important for the victims of the Babyn Yar tragedy themselves, these kinds of racial or ethnic distinctions were superfluous, obsolete, and groundless. The *kdoyshim*, a Yiddish word derived from Biblical Hebrew denoting Jewish martyrs, the victims of anti-Jewish persecutions, now meant something new in Vergelis's lexicon: it was a reference to Communists, to those who had been killed at Babyn Yar for their loyalty to their Soviet motherland irrespective of their ethnic background.[9]

Here Vergelis simply offers a de-Judaized version of Babyn Yar, completely emptying it of any distinct Jewish significance and insisting that any ethnic distinctions drawn between the victims buried there range between irrelevance and tastelessness.[10] Here is the only case of someone who most explicitly associated Babyn Yar with the Great Patriotic War refusing to lend any legitimacy to the view of the ravine as a key Holocaust site. Vergelis's, to be sure, was the most extreme articulation of this one-directional memory, but under his stewardship there existed a broad spectrum of obfuscation and doublespeak.

## BABYN YAR IN *SOVETISH HEYMLAND*

In 1959, after a hiatus of more than a decade, a time when Yiddish letters almost completely disappeared from the Soviet cultural scene, the printing of Yiddish works resumed in the USSR with the appearance of a few books of mainly Yiddish classics.

Thereupon, new works started to appear in August of 1961 with the launching of *Sovetish heymland* under the auspices of the Soviet Writers' Union.[11] When it first appeared, the Soviet minister of culture made it very clear that it was conceived in order to appease some Soviet sympathizers in the West after much "pleading and sobbing" on their part.[12] In the first two years of its existence, the journal focused primarily on the Soviet reality and assumed an unmistakably propagandistic tone, a trend that persisted but that was somewhat mitigated a few years later when greater attention began to be given to Jewish themes.

Among the occasional references made in *Sovetish heymland* to inherently Jewish subjects, the Holocaust occupied quite a central place, especially since the middle of the 1960s. When one peruses the stories, reports, and poems elaborating on the Holocaust in *Sovetish heymland*, it is hard to overlook the great disparity between the room allotted to Babyn Yar—a site that assumed such a symbolic role among Soviet Jews—and the far greater space assigned to other Holocaust sites and events. Despite the very conservative character of the periodical, the tragedy of European Jewry during the war was by no means a topic that the editor in chief felt compelled to categorically ignore. Evidently, as long as the works of prose or poetry or the documentary materials connected with the memory of the Holocaust did not blatantly violate the official Soviet narrative of a Great Patriotic War—a narrative according to which both the living and the dead were all Soviet brothers and sisters, irrespective of their ethnic roots—their writers could, with little difficulty, receive the consent of the periodical's editorial board.

A case in point for the double standard held by the periodical's editorial board, which drew a clear distinction between Babyn Yar and other Holocaust sites, is the comprehensive coverage given to the Warsaw Ghetto Uprising in an issue appearing in April 1963 on the occasion of its twentieth anniversary. No doubt, the coverage of the topic, impressive as it was, was fraught with Soviet clichés and factual errors, which were most evident in the leading historical article in the issue, titled "The Great Battle between the Ghetto Walls" and written by the editor in chief of the Polish *Folks-shtime* periodical, Hersh Smolyar.[13] At the same time that this central chapter of the Holocaust was given considerable attention, the readers of *Sovetish heymland* had to dig really deep to find any mention of Babyn Yar.

During the first half of the 1960s, such excavations would yield very little. This changed after the ouster of Nikita Khrushchev in the fall of 1964 and as the Thaw period approached its last two years. Now the trickle of references to Babyn Yar, while never turning into a torrent, did grow considerably, both in the journal itself and in works appearing in book form. In the very first years of *Sovetish heymland*'s existence, though, the silence over Babyn Yar was almost complete. We have already mentioned the appearance of Yevgeny Yevtushenko's "Babi Yar" only in the Polish periodical

*At Babi Yar* by Russian painter Boris Prorokov. From the series Never Again, 1958–1959. (From https://lechaim.ru/events/babiy-yar-v-zhivopisi-i-skulypture-ot-vasiliya-ovchinnikova-do-vadima-sidura-2/.)

*Folks-shtime*. If the main point that Yevtushenko wanted to bring home was to bring Babyn Yar closer to the orbit of the Holocaust, *Sovetish heymland* would invoke the name of Babyn Yar by way of linking it to the general war experience.

A good example of this view of Babyn Yar as a Great Patriotic War site is the ink and watercolor drawing from the series Never Again (*eto ne dolzhno povtoryt'sya*) appearing in the very first issue of *Sovetish heymland*.[14] Made by the Russian graphic artist and painter Boris Prorokov (1911–1972), it featured three women who came to Babyn Yar to mourn and honor their dead.[15] The illustration's title *At Babi Yar* and the biographical comments describing Prorokov's work made no reference to the Jewish identity of either the mourners or those who had been victimized at the ravine.

Prorokov's illustration appearing here, in this celebratory issue of the journal that promised to revitalize Soviet Yiddish literature, foreshadowed the future treatment of Babyn Yar in *Sovetish heymland*. In line with Vergelis's attempt to gloss over the relevance of Babyn Yar as a Jewish site, what the illustration by Prorokov did was to delineate from the outset the contours of Jewish national sentiments that the journal had set for itself. While Holocaust-related atrocities would be mentioned and even elaborately portrayed in *Sovetish heymland*, sometimes with reference to the victims of one atrocity as Jews, Babyn Yar would continue to constitute a black hole in the Soviet memory of the Holocaust, being preserved, paradoxically, in a journal written in a Jewish language and designated almost entirely for a Jewish audience.

## A BLACK CROW: MOTL TALALAYEVSKY

That the illustration by Prorokov was a prelude to a trend is evidenced in the works published in *Sovetish heymland* in its ensuing issues. The next Yiddish writer who obliquely touched upon the massacre of Kyiv Jews at Babyn Yar was the Yiddish poet and writer Motl (Matvei) Talalayevsky (1908–1978). Born in the small village of Makhnatshke in the Zhitomir region of Ukraine, Talalayevsky belonged to the generation of Soviet Yiddish writers whose literary career commenced after the October Revolution. Talalayevsky, who spent his boyhood and adolescence in Kyiv, where he studied at the Yiddish branch of the Department of Literature at the University of Kyiv, was a Jewish *Homo sovieticus*. In the postrevolutionary reality, this was a new type of Jewish man, one who was born and nurtured in the Soviet motherland and who had fully internalized the Communist dogma without being "contaminated" by any relation to the prerevolutionary past or by any exposure to Western culture.[16] As a graduate of the Soviet youth movements the Young Pioneers and the Young Communist League (Komsomol), Talalayevsky, more than being the visionary of the Soviet Yiddish literary enterprise, was one of its products.

While the adaptation to the new reality of a multiethnic empire in which minority cultures were fostered in an anti-religious, socialist environment did not come easy to writers who had been reared in and shaped by the traditional Jewish milieu, it was far easier for Talalayevsky and his cohort to undergo this adjustment. Although Talalayevsky made his Yiddish debut in 1926, only a few years after Itsik Kipnis, they deserve to be viewed as representatives of two different generations. The contrast was reflected not only in the ideology underlying their respective oeuvres but in their personal lives as well. Clearly demonstrating this fact were the grudges that Kipnis held toward Talalayevsky. As a Communist Party member and the one in charge of the ideological purity of the Yiddish almanac *Der shtern* (The star), which appeared in Kyiv in the late 1940s, the latter turned out to be one of the many detractors of the former, berating Kipnis's expression of Jewish national sentiments in his works.[17]

When considering the outlook of the two men, it is hard, in fact, to imagine a starker contrast: on the one hand, there was Kipnis, the "white crow," nostalgic, homesick for the shtetl, a man longing for the bygone Jewish ways of life, who, from his early career, faced harsh criticism for his ideological ineptitude. And on the other, there was Talalayevsky, the ideologically "clean" writer who embodied the birth of the new Jewish man that the Soviet Union aspired to create. This was not only a contrast between two different outlooks of Jewish writers onto the legacy of their own people but was also a watershed dividing the czarist past from the Soviet present. After all, it was the minor writer Talalayevsky, and not the internationally acclaimed Kipnis, who emblematized in his work the Soviet image of the future. A poet who used the Yiddish language in order to promote socialism and further the internationalist cause, who saw the existence of a multiethnic culture as only a transitional stage toward the dissolving of all national particularities in the future dictatorship of the proletariat—this kind of writer was a far better candidate for stardom in postrevolutionary Russia than the one who was psychologically unable to sever his ties to the past.

The imminent evaporation of all ethnic distinctions was already evident in the literary career of the young Talalayevsky, the poet, novelist, playwright, and translator who published in Yiddish, Ukrainian, and Russian, demonstrating thereby the ability to transcend the narrow confines of the Jewish world.[18] This linguistic precocity, though, came at the expense of familiarity with the roots of Yiddish literature as well as with the age-old Jewish literary legacy. The Soviet Yiddish literary critic and historian Maks Erik, a man who aspired to preserve this legacy within the framework of Soviet culture, was abhorred when he realized how unfamiliar Talalayevsky was in matters that concerned traditional Jewish culture. Erik condescendingly called him a "Yiddish poet"—*a yidisher poet*—that is, a poet whose only identity mark as a Jew was his use of the Yiddish language as a vehicle of expression. No doubt, Talalayevsky was in this regard not the only one to possess such a description. Esther Rosenthal-Shneiderman reminisces that, of another writer of his cohort, Erik bitterly once remarked that "for this young man the Jewish people has not even existed prior to the October Revolution."[19] Nonetheless, it was precisely this obliviousness to the Jewish past that ensured the rise of Talalayevsky to primacy, and it was also precisely what saved him from the purges of the late 1930s that took the life of Erik, among many other Yiddish cultural activists who came to the Soviet Union from capitalist Poland and whose political purity was contested during the years of the Great Terror.

If Motl Talalayevsky was a Soviet writer whose language of expression merely happened to be Yiddish, a writer who embodied in his work and career a multinational stance and opposition to national particularism,[20] one experience did shake his hitherto firm belief in the Soviet brotherhood of all peoples. In the wake of the war, after joining the Red Army and serving at the front as an officer and journalist (his reports would appear in the organ of the Jewish Anti-Fascist Committee, *Eynikayt*), Talalayevsky started searching for his Jewish roots. In a poem titled "My Second Beginning," he even expressed torment and self-doubt about his earlier careless attitude toward his people's legacy and wished to do penance for it.[21] In 1951, after the poem had been discovered in his notes during the midst of the Stalinist antisemitic campaign against Yiddish writers and culture-doers, Talalayevsky was arrested while on a poetry reading tour in the southern Ukrainian city of Mykolaiv. Like Kipnis before him, and many other Yiddish writers, he was arrested and sent to a labor camp in Central Asia. Unlike Kipnis, who even after his release from the gulag remained for a while a pariah and was forbidden from living in Kyiv, Talalayevsky was released fairly early (in 1954), re-inducted into the Communist Party,[22] and started to publish both original works and translations in Russian and Ukrainian. As early as 1961, he became a frequent contributor to *Sovetish heymland*.[23]

Perhaps it was the bitter memories of the gulag, or maybe the renewed membership in the Communist Party (which carried both privileges and the fear one day of losing them), that made the works of Talalayevsky published in *Sovetish heymland* or in book form during the post-Stalin era highly conservative in character. It requires some effort to find any allusions to the Holocaust lurking beneath the properly socialist-realist and exceedingly optimistic façade of his poetry. It may well be that for Talalayevsky the commitment to the Jewish language, the number of speakers of which were constantly dwindling in the Soviet Union like anywhere else, was enough of a statement of his Jewish roots. But if one is to search for parallel expressions of commitment to his Jewish identity during this period in the poet's message, rather than in his medium, the task becomes much more difficult.

Curiously, in the rare moments during which Talalayevsky does choose to manifest this kind of a bond with the fate of his people and to do so in the most personal fashion—that is, by reminiscing on the tragedy of his own family members—he connects to his Jewish roots by invoking, though in a very allusive and elusive way, the memories of the Babyn Yar massacre. The circumlocutory manner in which he mentions the massacre of Kyiv Jews is evidenced in the following poem, which is titled "At Those Ditches":

> *No, it wasn't curiosity that led my heart,*
> *Here, to these green, deep ditches....*
> *Twenty years have passed since that fall,*
> *When I had to sit shiva here,*
> *At that time, I was far away*
> *And only heard of the countless murders...*
> *It is quiet here, but it seems to me, that he screams—*
> *My brother cries out from these deep ditches.*[24]

Talalayevsky portrays a typical Soviet postwar landscape of a serene, unmarked, and seemingly forgotten pit, where the dead bodies of dozens of thousands of the Nazis' victims lie. As much as the ideological outlook of Talalayevsky is so much removed from that of Kipnis, he emulates the latter when he refers to the mass grave by invoking a Jewish mourner's ritual. If Kipnis spoke in his "Babi Yar" about the *yortsayt*, Talalayevsky conjures up the shiva (*shive* in Yiddish), the observation of seven days of mourning of a first-degree relative. The comparison between the two writers is, again, very telling. For if Kipnis, eschewing in the Soviet version of his "Babi Yar" a clear reference to Jewish

Soviet Yiddish poet Motl Talalayevsky. (Photo from the Archives of the YIVO Institute for Jewish Research, New York.)

victims, Talalayevsky leaves the identity of the ditches unidentified and alludes to its Jewish victims only by mentioning the practice of the seven days of mourning.

It turns out only at the very last line of the poem that the poet is not afflicted by feelings of remorse for failing to mourn the victims at the nameless ditches as a Jewish collective. Rather, it is the death of his own brother that concerns him. The reference to his brother is what gives the reader familiar with Talalayevsky's oeuvre a clue that the locus concerned in the poem is none other than Babyn Yar. The key to unlock the secret of the location of the ditches may be found in an earlier and longer poem by Talalayevsky that carries the title "Kiev." In this fairly conservative poem abounding with hyperbolic Soviet self-praise, a poem that hails the postwar capital of the Ukrainian Soviet Socialist Republic as the green, the forever young city where "on Shevchenko's bright boulevard stands Lenin's monument crowned with bright glory,"[25] Talalayevsky refers directly to Babyn Yar and identifies it as his brother's burial ground:

> *Not far from Podol lies Babi Yar.*
> *The cedars around it are blooming and clean,*
> *But a different song the trees there sing....*
> *I stand there for a moment, not talking, in silence,*
> *I look at the tree with a naked branch—*
> *It's my eternal witness... years ago*
> *a German rope was hanging from it.*
> *The German rope, the accursed rope,*
> *that in cold sweat strangled my brother there.*[26]

Only by juxtaposing these few lines "hiding" in the middle of a poem stretching over four pages with the concise "At Those Ditches" is it possible to ascertain that the massacre portrayed in the poem took place at Babyn Yar.

Notably, neither "Kiev" nor "At Those Ditches" approaches the Babyn Yar massacre in a way that would pay honor to its Jewish dead as victims of genocide. While in "Kiev" Talalayevsky, for some reason, does not refrain from explicitly spelling out the name Babyn Yar; his depiction of the Soviet Jewish experience during World War II is compromised in a different respect. The poem "Kiev," overall, other than including the two words "Babi Yar," is a bona fide Soviet poem of the Cold War. The poem concludes with the call of an older veteran to his son, now a young soldier, to protect the Soviet motherland "wherever you are and whenever the ominous hour (*beyze sho*) will find you." Babyn Yar and the haunting memories of the war are approached by Talalayevsky only within the narrow, officially sanctioned constraints of the "brotherhood of the (Soviet) nations." "Kiev," it turns out, is a eulogy of two of Talalayevsky's brothers-in-arms: the Jewish Zyame Kornblum and the Ukrainian Vadim Brotshenko, whose heroism the poet extolls:

> *The number of Kyiv's devoted sons is great,*
> *those who carried their flame all the way to Berlin . . .*
> *For Kyiv has paid back for the blood on its stones,*
> *for fathers, mothers and the children the little,*
> *For all those murdered and for all of our martyrs,*
> *For my friends who died here,*
> *For Zyame Kornblum and Vadim Brotshenko.* [27]

In these words, Talalayevsky, who was a decorated Red Army major and also took part in the march to Berlin,[28] aligns himself in this stanza with Vergelis's contextualization of Babyn Yar as a Great Patriotic War site. Babyn Yar here is a topic that cuts across all ethnic boundaries without attributing any significance to its Jewish facet. So, too, it is only the two brothers-in-arms, the Jewish and Ukrainian, that deserve the title *kdoyshim* and deserve their full name to be mentioned. The other victims of war, the mass of fathers, mothers, and small children who died in the ditches, remain anonymous. For this reason, not unlike "At Those Ditches," "Kiev" is a poem that dares not to deviate from Moscow's official narrative of World War II.

In summary, it is by the most cryptic means that Motl Talalayevsky refers to Babyn Yar in his two poems published in the early years of *Sovetish heymland*'s existence. Furthermore, if the Yiddish writers discussed thus far tended to correlate Babyn Yar with the master narrative of the genocide of European Jews, for Talalayevsky the site remained tightly connected with the memories of the Great Patriotic War. If, as noted in chapter 7, the angle from which Itsik Kipnis looked at Babyn Yar was that of the evacuee who encountered a hostile environment, then the angle from which the Red Army major who had returned from battle could not let the ideal image of a Soviet brotherhood be dashed by a more complex reality, one in which antisemitic moods were endemic to the Soviet military no less than to the civilian populace. Yet, this inclination to view Babyn Yar as a Great Patriotic War site should not be explained only in terms of Talalayevsky's wartime experience. For a writer who, from the early years of his career, understood that prominence on the Soviet literary scene was predicated on ideological purity, it seems that there was no other choice than to refer to Babyn Yar in the most oblique manner—that is, in a way that was politically proper. That Talalayevsky was not the only one to pursue this course is evidenced in the work of another Yiddish poet, Dore Khaykine, who, like him, occupied a primary place in the poetry section of *Sovetish heymland*—a result not of her rare literary gift but rather of her staunch political loyalty.

## BACK TO THAT SAME ROAD: DORE KHAYKINE

Like Istik Kipnis, Shike Driz, and Motl Talalayevsky, the Soviet Yiddish poet Dore Khaykine (1913–2006) was a member of the Yiddish circle of writers during the interwar period. A native of Chernihiv, she resettled in the Ukrainian capital in the aftermath of the war. Like many other Yiddish writers of her cohort, Khaykine came from a humble background and moved to Kyiv not to pursue a splendid literary career but in order to find employment as a weaver in one of the city's textile factories.[29] She, too, belonged to the new generation of proletarian writers whose record was a "blank slate," not contaminated by prerevolutionary "politically incorrect" literary works or non-Communist political affiliations. The fate of a weaver-turned-poet reflected a larger trend in the Soviet literature of the mid-1930s following the establishment of the Soviet Writers' Union in 1932, the disbandment of all literary groups active in the country, and the increase in Communist Party of the Soviet Union (CPSU) control over literary activity.

Soviet Yiddish Poet Dore Khaykine. (Photo from Dore Khaykine, *Fun ale mayne vegn* [Sovetskii Pisatel', 1975].)

Khaykine made her debut just before this grand transition from Soviet culture as a revolutionary entity capable of embracing a whole range of modernist trends in art to a vehicle of Stalin's totalitarian cultural revolution that envisioned writers as "engineers of the human soul"—namely, as useful tools in the Soviet propaganda machine. Khaykine's first poem appeared in the Yiddish journal *Prolit*, a periodical that already signaled Soviet literature's future path. As David Shneer notes, the appearance in early 1928 of *Prolit* (i.e., proletarian literature) coincided with the beginning of the cultural revolution and the rise to eminence of literature that was not only created for the proletariat but also forged by it. In the same vein, the scholar Evgeny Dobrenko, turning his attention to the mainstream of Soviet literature rather than concentrating on rare talents like Boris Pasternak, Osip Mandelstam, or Anna Akhmatova, also stresses that literary creativity in the Soviet Union of the Stalin era was a mass phenomenon. In many cases, he argues, those who filled the ranks of the new cohort of Soviet writers were workers—sometimes even semiliterate—who had been ushered into the literary world through creative writing workshops and amateur literary groups.[30]

To say that Khaykine deserves to be classified as a worker who only by accident was included in the group of the most prolific Soviet Yiddish poets of the post-Stalin era may be somewhat of an exaggeration. Yet, like the case of her fellow Yiddish poet Talalayevsky, what accounted for Khaykine's rise to prominence was not poetic innovativeness nor a particular message of her own, but a willingness to pay lip service to those who controlled the literary means of production in the Soviet state. Before the war, Khaykine was a minor figure on the scene of Soviet Yiddish culture: in the early 1930s, we find her working as an assistant bibliographer at the Institute of Jewish Proletarian Culture, having published only one collection of poems as late as 1938.[31] After the decade-long hiatus of Yiddish publication in the USSR in the wake of the Stalinist antisemitic campaigns, Khaykine had the privilege to publish a poem in the first issue of *Sovetish heymland* and to become one of its contributors. Similar to other members of the Kyiv circle of Yiddish writers, Khaykine also engaged the theme of Babyn Yar in two of her poems. In the first, "Der zelber veg" (That same road), Babyn Yar lies at the very heart of the poem's narrative, yet the ravine's name is never mentioned. The second poem, "Ikh bin dort oykh geven" (I too was there), though it mentions Babyn Yar only in passing, is a work that places it in the broader context of World War II and is hence pertinent to our discussion. Despite her frequent contributions to Soviet Yiddish literature's flagship journal, it was not here but in the anthology of the new generation of Soviet Yiddish poetry titled *Horizontn* (Horizons) that appeared in 1965 in a press run of 5,000 copies that "That Same Road" was first published.[32]

The poem bears some resemblance to a work we have discussed: "Babi Yar" by Itsik Kipnis. Both were written in the same year, 1944, in the immediate aftermath of Kyiv's liberation, but their publication was delayed until the Brezhnev era. Also, both were works that reflected the experience of the returning evacuee. Khaykine, who spent the war in the Kazakh Soviet Socialist Republic, in its northeastern city of Kustanay, describes what seems like a first encounter with Babyn Yar:

> *That same road. The same white sands,*
> *The same green trees by the dirt road.*
> *A heart can rip from pain,*
> *And a human heart can endure a lot.*
> *I take the road now*
> *That they, the many, have taken before—*
> *My sisters with their mothers and their children*
> *From Demyevke, Vasilkov Minor, and Podol.*[33]

Having returned to Kyiv, the speaker wishes to march through the same streets that led her kin to their death, to turn the road to Babyn Yar into a Holocaust via dolorosa that could help those who were not there to relive the two days of terror experienced by their loved ones. It was a time when "a young woman exactly like me cuddled her child so close to her heart." Khaykine, it is clear, defines the massacre that took place at Babyn Yar as a Jewish event. Her focus on the death of women and children and on a massive march toward the ravine is indicative of the subject of the poem, as well as of the objects of Nazi terror depicted in it. If these hints seem too oblique, by providing the names Demyevke, Kleyn Vasilkov, and Podol—districts that were heavily populated by Jews in interwar Kyiv—Khaykine makes the Jewish identity of the victims clear.

It is clear, provided the reader is intimately familiar with the geography and demography of Kyiv. For nowhere in the poem can one find any mention of Babyn Yar. "That Same Road" is a striking example of how Holocaust literature took shape in a Soviet context during the time that David Roskies calls one of "communal memory." On the one hand, the poem is endowed with a sense of immediacy: like virtually all other Soviet Yiddish works on Babyn Yar, it does not recognize the Holocaust as a separate category, nor does it stop to dwell on its far-reaching ethical or philosophical implications. This is a poem written at a time when the memory of Nazi atrocities was still fresh and raw, and highly malleable. The designated readers of the poem did not comprise the broadest readership one can imagine but, rather, the small community of Yiddish readers who knew something about Jewish Kyiv of the interwar years.

On the other hand, the absence of an explicit reference to Babyn Yar does not only stem from the designation of this poem as part of a local, communal memory. The political end that it served should not be overlooked. For not unlike the ditches depicted by Talalayevsky, the omission of the ravine's name makes the poem almost invisible, hardly a candidate for a canonical poem on the massacre of Kyiv Jews if it dares not mention the dreadful name of the ravine out loud. The absence of the ravine's name, while superfluous for the Kyiv Yiddish reader, was necessary in order to endow the poem with the proper underlying political direction.

In "I Too Was There," Khaykine places Babyn Yar in a historical context that would only further enhance its political aptness. If the first poem centered on the feelings of guilt of the one who escaped the Nazi beast, in the second, recalling her evacuation eastward on the path to Siberia boarding a troop train, Khaykine remembers to thank her rescuer:

> *My land has saved me from the fire—*
> *From a horrible death in Babi Yar.*
> *The small children, myself,*
> *My mom my beloved,*
> *It moved us from peril, no matter how far.* [34]

The slanted rhyme most central in the poem—*Babi Yar, gefar* (peril)—only helps to highlight the gratitude Khaykine expresses toward the Soviet authorities, who, as she contends in the poem, recognized the urgent need to evacuate Soviet Jews like her from the scene of atrocities. In what is essentially an ode to the Soviet motherland that rescued thousands of Jews by allowing them to board the trains designated for the withdrawing Red Army and essential industries, Khaykine is much more at ease referring to Babyn Yar without the need to camouflage the identity of the site. In order to achieve this heightened sense of political correctness, there is nothing better than to make mention of Lenin:

> *The day has spread out for me the Siberian expanse,*
> *At night the sky was bright from the stars.*
> *The whole time I thought to myself:*
> *Here's the flame of the pyre,*
> *The one that kept Lenin from the cold.*[35]

When compared with two other members of the Kyiv circle discussed above, it is possible to place Dore Khaykine's view of Babyn Yar somewhere in between that of Kipnis and that of Talalayevsky. With the former, she shares the experience of the returning evacuee who is confronted for the first time by the destruction of their community, a calamity that the writer was fortunate to evade. Khaykine, like Kipnis, construes Babyn Yar as a Jewish locus, focusing on "her sisters," on the Jewish women accompanied by their children on their last road, which leads to Babyn Yar. Khaykine also aligns herself with a member of her cohort, the bona fide Yiddish poet Talalayevsky. Refraining from a direct reference to the ravine on the outskirts of Kyiv or doing so only in order to contrast Nazi cruelty with Soviet nobility, Khaykine, like Talalayevsky, blurs the boundaries between the official Soviet narrative of the Babyn Yar massacre and its conceptualization as a site marking an exclusively Jewish tragedy.

As few and far between as are the references to Babyn Yar in the works of Khaykine and Talalayevsky, in the case of our next Kyiv-based Yiddish poet, Shloyme Cherniavsky (1909–1974), the reader needs to cross linguistic territories before finding such a poem in a posthumously published work, as it appears in a Russian translation.

## METONYMS OF MASS MURDER: SHLOYME CHERNIAVSKY

Last is by no means least, though it is certainly ironic that one of the most moving Yiddish poems on Babyn Yar was written by an almost unknown poet and never saw the light of day in its original language. It is even more ironic that this remarkable poem appeared in Russian in a dramatically modified form—twice shorter, more somber, and more haunting than the Yiddish original—more than thirty years after the original had been composed. A poem that deserves to be compared substantively and stylistically with "Babi Yar" by Yevtushenko, it best demonstrates the limitations of the minor, Yiddish literary sphere when compared with her far bigger and dominant Russian counterpart. The poem was written by Shloyme Cherniavsky (1909–1974), another member of the Kyiv circle of Yiddish writers, about whose life and career little is known.

This remarkable poem is a modified rendition of an older one, which had been written in Yiddish in July 1944 upon the poet's first visit to Babyn Yar and submitted to the *Eynikayt* editorial board, a version that was never published. In its later form—abridged, modified, untitled, undated, and written in Russian—the poem appeared in a tiny, esoteric book. It is phrased as a far later memory of that first encounter. Nevertheless, between the Yiddish and the Russian versions some content bears enough resemblance to suggest that these are two versions of the same poem, rather than two distinct pieces. It is this last work in our survey that says so little but, at the same time, says it all: how the agony, and the desire to give voice to the agony over the murder of Kyiv Jews, knew no limits; and, conversely, how the ability to do so, in a Jewish language, by Jews, knew so many limitations. If, for a Russian writer the likes of Yevtushenko, the expectation was to keep quiet, for his Yiddish peer the unwritten decree was silence.

From the very few biographical details available about him, we know that Shloyme Cherniavsky was disabled from birth and was raised in an orphanage after the murder of his parents in a pogrom. Cherniavsky was one of the very few Yiddish writers who avoided the anti-Jewish repressions of the late Stalin era. He was a prolific writer but managed during his lifetime to have only two poetry collections of his published, both prior to the outbreak of the Great Patriotic War.[36] In 1975, about a year after his death, his finest poems were translated into Russian and appeared in an anthology carrying the title *Po moskovskomu vremeni* (On Moscow time). Even though his work occasionally appeared in *Sovetish heymland*, it was here, and only in Russian translation, that his chilling poem on Babyn Yar appeared.

Soviet Yiddish Poet Shloyme Cherniavsky. (Photo from Shloyme Cherniavsky, *Po moskovskomu vremeni: lirika raznykh let* [Moscow: Sovetskii Pisatel'], 1975.)

In light of the striking difference between the Russian version and the Yiddish original, let us turn our focus first to the published piece, which appeared posthumously over thirty years after the poem's encounter with the bleakness and neglect at the ravine. As noted above, Cherniavsky's approach to Babyn Yar bears a striking resemblance to that of Yevtushenko: both works reflect on a visit to the site before the first official monument was laid there. Both poems contemplate the oxymoronic character of Babyn Yar as a site blending natural scenery with images of horror; both contrast the dedication of the speaker to the victims' memory with the site's neglect, with the careless manner in which Soviet officialdom treated the memory of the dead. While Yevtushenko, the non-Jewish poet, traveled to Babyn Yar from Moscow to see this neglect for himself, the Kyivan Cherniavsky seemed almost forced, impelled to be there. "A horrible disaster swept through," he exclaims, before pausing to think about this sense of compulsion:

> *In what desperate hope,*
> *Am I coming here, like before?*
> *Why am I coming here?*

While the poem in its published version is undated, it is clear that the speaker's recent visit to the site is projected onto an earlier one, which took place in 1944. This was a pivotal year in the history of Babyn Yar's representation that, as we have already seen, marks the watershed between the immediate war experience and postwar reconstruction:

> *That bygone year of forty-four*
> *The soul has turned blind from sorrow.*
> *Once again the wind will carry clouds of ash*
> *Over Babi Yar...*
>
> *A little child's shoe lies on the grass*
> *It's half-rotten... but where's the child?*
> *The mother's hands, she's half-awake,*
> *They wander over the child's head...*
>
> *They touch upon his gentle cheeks...*
> *They slide—not hands—but shadows...*
> *A child's shoe rots here on the grass,*
> *But whose?*
> *And who will put it on?*
>
> *Over Babi Yar—the wind's whistle.*
> *What was in vain, and what was not?*
> *The leaves are flying over Babi Yar.*
> *A leaf descends on a shoe.*[37]

In the Russian poem, the Jewish identity of the victims is pointed out only metonymically, via the child's slipper and the image/shadow of his mother's hands, a clear allusion to the murder of children and women at Babyn Yar, which happened mainly on September 29–30, 1941. While not drawing on any symbol, metaphor, or archetype from the Jewish tradition, Cherniavsky should have been aware by then of the shoe as a trope, as a living, present metonym signifying the absent, dead humans to whom they belonged. He is making use of a powerful metonym used by Avrom Sutzkever, the dean of Yiddish poetry and, at that point, in the immediate postwar years, a bona fide Soviet poet and a veteran partisan, who in his "A Wagon of Shoes," written in the Vilna Ghetto in January 1943, conjured up an image that would forever be associated with the destruction of European Jewry:

> *I must not ask you whose,*
> *My heart, it skips a beat:*
> *Tell me the truth, oh, shoes,*
> *Where disappeared the feet?*
>
> *The feet of pumps so shoddy,*
> *With buttondrops like dew—*
> *Where is the little body?*
> *Where is the woman too?*
>
> *All children's shoes—but where*
> *Are all the children's feet?*
> *Why does the bride not wear*
> *Her shoes so bright and neat?*[38]

Apart from this linkage between Jews and shoes, there is nothing remarkably Jewish about Cherniavsky's "Babi Yar," nothing to disqualify it as a fine Great Patriotic War poem underlining the theme of universal suffering. It is only the focus on the civilian population that was murdered at Babyn Yar, coupled with the graphic descriptions of the site's condition, that situates it firmly within the corpus of Holocaust poetry.

By contrast, the unpublished version of the poem leaves no doubt as to the identity of the victims:

> *From one generation to another they'll follow*
> *Like, a shrine, not like a stone.*
> *Reminding grandchildren of horror valleys*
> *Where lying defiled the Jewish bones.*[39]

In the original Yiddish version, presenting a scene that is far more complex and gruesome, Cherniavsky's victims are explicitly Jewish. Their victimizers, in a text suffused with uncontrolled desire for revenge, are also called by their name: the Germans, the descendants of the Teutonic Knights. As we saw in chapter 7, these frequent calls for retribution were characteristic of Holocaust literature of the immediate postwar period—that is, in the communal memory phase:

> *They'll be reminded a thousand times*
> *From Germans be on guard they must*
> *For in the blood of the Teuton's grandchildren*
> *Lurks the Satanic spirit of humanity's devourers!*[40]

In Russian, these two identity markers simply fade away. In summary, the poem by Cherniavsky here is simply another case of a poem slightly deviating from Moscow's line appearing at the very end of a work published in translation only after its author was already dead. To those who might suggest that a Yiddish poem in Russian translation was likely to receive more exposure and that it was a testimony perhaps to the permissibility of the topics concerned in the poem, we may respond by referring to the limited circulation of the work. There were only a few thousand copies published, which is a standard number for Yiddish poetry books. If we take into account the quantity of books sent to private readers and libraries overseas, then the number of copies available in the Soviet Union was even smaller. While this confessional poem by Cherniavsky may be on par with Yevtushenko's work—both confessional, declamatory pieces centering on the confrontation of the living witness/visitor with the dead corpses at Babyn Yar, corpses of innocent civilians—its poor circulation ensured that no Yevgeny Yevtushenko would ever emerge in the Soviet Yiddish literary sphere.

## THE MEANINGS OF DISSENT

The discussion of the works by Kipnis, Driz, Talalayevsky, Khaykine, and Cherniavsky, all of which appeared in the Soviet Union during the periods lying at the core of our discussion—the Thaw and the decade that followed it—helps establish the patterns that underlay the representation of Babyn Yar in Soviet Yiddish literature: it has helped us put disparate pieces of the literary puzzle together. It is now easier to discern a tendency on the part of *Sovetish heymland* and other Soviet Yiddish publications to let other events pertaining to the Holocaust overshadow the Babyn Yar massacre; to circulate the works that do refer to Babyn Yar among only a small audience; and to only publish the latter if they reference Babyn Yar in allusive, carefully measured ways. Most crucially, we have observed that the Kyiv Yiddish writers carefully avoided any consistent correlation between the Babyn Yar massacre and the Holocaust of European Jewry.

In other words, when carefully investigating all of these texts and paying equal attention to their publication dates and places, and the specific historical contexts in which they appeared, it is difficult not to notice both the cultural suppression and, vice versa, the resistance to it underpinning them all, albeit to differing degrees. One thing remains clear: what could be said in the mainstream literary platforms in Russian—even though this might have irritated the Communist Party bosses presiding over literary matters—had to be marginalized and almost ignored in Yiddish. This was a twofold suppressive process, for if we draw internal comparisons among the Yiddish works, it emerges that those informed by the view of Babyn Yar as a Great Patriotic War site—the most conspicuous among them being "Kiev" by Talalayevsky—appeared at the forefront of the Soviet sphere's flagship publication *Sovetish heymland*, whereas "Babi Yar" by Kipnis appeared at the very end of his collection of stories, published twenty-five years after it had been composed and in a book with a small circulation.[41] To put it another way, it was our task as readers to juxtapose literature and politics, thereby gauging both the degree of freedom enjoyed by the Soviet Yiddish writers and the ideological and creative freedom they each wished to pursue.

Diverse as this group of writers may have been, when looking at the postwar Kyiv circle of writers as a group, as the members of the Soviet Yiddish intelligentsia who survived the Stalinist purges and chose to partake in the difficult and very partial recovery that Soviet Yiddish culture witnessed during the Post-Stalin era, one wonders what made them erect such a modest literary memorial to the Jewish victims of Babyn Yar. Why did these writers not choose or manage to place Babyn Yar more firmly and conspicuously within the inner circle of the Holocaust?

When all is said and done, it bears remembering that for the Kyiv Yiddish writers there was good reason to align oneself with the CPSU's stance toward Babyn Yar. In the Soviet Yiddish literary apparatus, which generally assumed a conservative character and had only one functioning periodical in the whole country, what mattered beyond anything else was one's ability to write works that manifested loyalty to the owners of the means of literary production—namely, the Soviet regime. While the demand to write paeans to the Soviet regime was not as draconian as during the 1930s and was not a matter of life or death, paying lip service to Communist ideology, not poetic gift or originality, was the decisive factor that distinguished an obscure writer from a prolific one. As some of the Kyiv Yiddish writers had fresh, firsthand memories of Soviet persecution from the late Stalin years and had known, in the flesh, what might happen to those giving vent to their Jewish national sentiment, it may well be that these works on Babyn Yar reflect a wish to "stay on track," avoid mentioning Babyn Yar as a Holocaust site, and make sure not to manifest any heterodox thoughts. As these writers may have known well, such deviationist expressions of Jewish national sentiment always had the potential to catch up to them later, which did indeed happen to many Yiddish writers during the black years of Soviet Jewry at the peak of Stalin's antisemitic campaign.

As a reminder that the Kyiv Yiddish writers were exposed to political pressure even during an epoch in Soviet history often nostalgically remembered as a time of artistic vibrancy and political relaxation, we may mention the fact that in Ukraine in general and Kyiv in particular the suppression of Jewish culture and religion was felt more strongly than in other parts of the USSR—a republic and a city that became, as early as 1971, a hub for the dissident movement of Jews who had "betrayed" their Soviet motherland by demanding the right to leave it. In the specific context of Babyn Yar, we have already mentioned Emmanuel (Amik) Diamant and his peers, members of the budding dissident movement that was responsible for the mass gatherings, both legally and illegally conducted, that took place at Babyn Yar from the mid-1960s onward. This political pressure, however, spawning the backlash in the shape of the Jewish dissident movement, also reveals the other face of the Soviet Jewish elite, the far more conservative side, willing to cater to or even harness themselves to Soviet dogma. While there were Jews who chose to risk their personal security for the sake of "never forget," a Communist Party member like Aron Vergelis the editor or Motl Talalayevsky the poet—perhaps the most extreme examples of members of the Soviet Jewish intelligentsia who construed Babyn Yar mainly as a Great Patriotic War site—preferred to align themselves with Moscow on this matter and play it safe. Compare these two men with Boris Kochubievsky, a Jewish factory worker of the younger generation, who was arrested for his Zionist activities following an illegal ceremony that took place at Babyn Yar in 1968. His only crime was the proclamation he made there: "Here lies a part of the Jewish people."[42] Kochubievsky was arrested for doing exactly what his Soviet Yiddish coreligionists refused to do: to assert that Babyn Yar is a Holocaust site and a Jewish site and to do so by way of squarely confronting Moscow on its decade of neglect and silence.

Kochubievsky's stance toward Babyn Yar, so different from the one taken by the Soviet Yiddish cultural establishment, may be accounted for as a mark of a generational gap. On one side stood the cohort of aging Yiddish writers, veterans of the battlefields and gulags who had by the late 1960s come to see the Soviet Union as their "Soviet homeland," for better or worse, despite the limited opportunities it gave them to develop a sustainable Jewish culture. On the other side stood the first generation of Jewish dissidents who, in the wake of the Thaw, became completely disillusioned with ever being able to reconcile the Soviet and the Jewish, and wished instead to pursue a new Jewish life elsewhere, beyond the Iron Curtain. Yet the young versus the old, the idealistic versus the practical-minded and sober, is only one paradigm that may account for these differences. A finer lens would suggest a more nuanced reading of the Babyn Yar literary memorials by Khaykine, Talalayevsky, Driz, Kipnis, and Cherniavsky as works that required not only a great deal of loyalty to Moscow's stance but also the courage to quietly deviate from it, doing so in a way intelligible to the astute reader, the one living in the USSR or beyond the Iron Curtain, the one capable of reading between the lines and decoding the Soviet Yiddish doublespeak.

True, virtually all of the works touching upon the theme of Babyn Yar in Yiddish literature tended to tone down the connection between Babyn Yar and the Jews. Some of them even correlated the death of the Jews at Babyn Yar with that of other nationalities or concealed from the reader the exact identity of the ravine. Nonetheless, one must remember that it was by virtue of these writers that some—albeit very few—poignant works on Babyn Yar did find their way into the officially sanctioned Soviet Yiddish literature. As Rudolph Tőkés reminds us, while dissent may be narrowly defined as an act of protest against an oppressive dictatorial regime, as a head-on confrontation of a single citizen or members of a group with the state, the term may also be construed in a broader sense as an existential experience, a spiritual act of defiance that may not necessarily be followed by any external manifestations.[43] The commemoration of Babyn Yar in the Soviet Yiddish sphere may fall, indeed, into this categorization of dissent.

It is quite easy to discern the underlying subversive drive in the writing of Kipnis, who other than the omission of the term "Jews" did use every tool at his disposal to orient Babyn Yar toward the circle of the Holocaust in the story that he managed to publish in the USSR. Kipnis's case is fairly obvious. But even when considering the more ambivalent writers, or those who used more oblique methods, one is compelled to appreciate the fair amount of courage it took for this group of writers to put Babyn Yar on the map of Soviet Yiddish belles lettres. The personal tone of Talalayevsky, the burden of memories haunting the poem of Khaykine, the grief of a crazed Jewish mother who had lost her two sons portrayed by Driz, or the bleak vision of the neglected, ghostly ravine visited by Cherniavsky—these all underscore the portrayal of a site that for Soviet officialdom remained a complete memory black hole up until the mid-1960s. Being fully aware that the agony, theirs as much as that of their people, had hardly any room in Soviet officialdom's memory of World War II, we must acknowledge the fact that none of these writers fully capitulated to the psychological pressure exerted on Soviet Jews and still found *a* way—perhaps not *the* way (a choice reserved for the more privileged Russian writers)—to rescue Babyn Yar from oblivion and place it on Yiddish literature's real, geographical map.

The evaluation of the underlying motivations of the Soviet Yiddish writers may thus be made in more than one way. It is therefore possible to see the Kyiv Yiddish writers as a group who consciously chose to subscribe to the marginalization of Babyn Yar by Moscow and, vice versa, to recognize the effort they made to sustain the site in the collective memory of their readers. But a more complete assessment of the crystallizing of Babyn Yar's memory in Soviet Yiddish belles lettres is possible only if we come full circle and examine the contribution to this literary process by another player, a Moscow Yiddish poet, Aron Vergelis, whose unabashed support for the party line vis-à-vis Babyn Yar has already been illustrated.

## "WHAT MAKES YIDDISH LITERATURE VIBRANT"?

Aron Vergelis, the editor of *Sovetish heymland* and the most powerful man in the sphere of Soviet Yiddish belles lettres, provides us with the perfect case in point for how difficult, perhaps impossible, it is to unequivocally draw any clear political (and by extension, literary) conclusions from the analysis of literary works published by an official publishing channel in a dictatorship that placed a very strong emphasis on the role of literature as a propagandistic tool. The Stalinist dictatorship demanded that writers rise to the level of "engineers of the soul." Admittedly, in such a political system no editor in whatever language of a publication appearing in the Soviet Union was omnipotent, having full discretion over matters of ideology. Nonetheless, while having limited powers, these editors in the more decentralized post-Stalin era were still given a great degree of "wiggle room" to give literary works their final shape.[44] This relatively significant power of editors to act independently without getting the central censorship apparatus Glavlit involved, while practiced across the board,[45] was greatly magnified in the case of Aron Vergelis, for he was given even more liberty with *Sovetish heymland* because he wore two different hats: that of editor and that of censor.[46]

*Sovetish heymland* was not the only literary platform in Yiddish available in the USSR. And although its editorial board was not an ideologically homogeneous entity—rivalries among its members, in fact, were not so rare—the power of Vergelis over the supervision of literary works in Yiddish published within the USSR was never matched. Some of these rivalries assumed a more personal nature. Yet, beyond these unavoidable small conflicts endemic to any literary republic, Soviet Yiddish writers often found themselves split over fundamental questions. And one of them touched the very heart of our study: the space that the Holocaust (and by extension its symbol, Babyn Yar) had to occupy in a proper Soviet Yiddish journal. During a meeting held on November 29, 1962, to address the demand of a group of Yiddish writers to replace Vergelis (they considered him, for various reasons, unsuitable for the position of the journal's editor), the Yiddish poet Yosef Kerler, who later immigrated to Israel and became an anti-Communist activist, lashed out at Vergelis:

> It must be noted that the journal deliberately enforces the policy of silencing, not only with regard to the Stalin era of the cult of personality, but to Hitler's brutality against the [civilian] population during the years of the Great Patriotic War. As an

The impresario of Soviet Yiddish letters during the Cold War, Aron Vergelis (seated, with glasses) with a group of Soviet Yiddish writers. (Photo from *Forward*, https://forward.com/yiddish/473127/lectures-and-memoirs-of-the-last-soviet-yiddish-magazine/.)

exception to this rule, one may mention the recently published notes from the Riga Ghetto that have been lying around in the editorial board's office from the journal's inception. It is well known that our Polish comrades have sent back all the copies of issue no. 4 of *Sovetish heymland*. They did it as an act of protest of the fact that the journal failed to mention in this issue the nineteenth anniversary of the heroic uprising in the Warsaw Ghetto. [This was done] while the progressive press across the world went to great lengths to mark this date, endeavoring to inform public opinion against neo-Fascism, Revanchism and about the dangers of a nuclear war.[47]

Earlier that year, the manuscript of the autobiographical story *Ikh muz dertseyln* (I have to tell) by Masha Rolnikaite, the diary of a Lithuanian Jewish girl relating her hardships growing up in the Vilna Ghetto, was also rejected by Vergelis. This did not thwart, however, the publication of the work: it appeared later on in both Lithuanian and Russian and, in 1965, even in Yiddish through the channels of the Polish Yiddish cultural apparatus.[48] The words of Kerler and the case of Rolnikaite provide yet another clue about the general absence of Babyn Yar from the mainstream of Soviet Yiddish literature. Without ignoring the fact that the ideology inherent in a given literary text always reflects the view of its author, there is enough evidence to suggest that an "invisible hand" was operating here to a certain degree, allowing Cherniavsky's poem to appear only in Russian translation, Khaykine's and Driz's works to appear only in poetry collections meant for a small circle of readers, and only an insignificant poem by Yevtushenko to appear in translation from Russian to Yiddish in that tumultuous fall of 1961.

That this "invisible hand" toning down the memory of Babyn Yar as a Jewish site in Yiddish literature belonged, indeed, to Vergelis, the editor-censor, cannot be proven with the data at our disposal. But as much as future archival work may shed light on this question, what lies at the crux of this issue is the general ideological makeup of Soviet Yiddish literature as one that did not completely refrain from touching upon the Holocaust but always did so in a way that would not result in a blunt clash with Moscow's ideological line. Furthermore, it did so by blurring the difference between one master narrative of the twentieth century and another. No doubt, what was prescribed for the treatment of the Holocaust as a general rule was even more apparent with regard to Babyn Yar, its most controversial site in the USSR. When exploring the Weltanschauung of Aron Vergelis, when defining his view of the character of Soviet Yiddish literature and the role it had to play in the larger framework of Soviet culture, it is easier to construe the works surveyed above on Babyn Yar, published in the post-Stalin era, as more than random works in which the memory of Babyn Yar was to be somehow mentioned in a circumlocutory fashion. The image of what Soviet Yiddish literature had to be helps establish, in other words, the suppression of Babyn Yar as a part of a general pattern.

The paradoxical world of Vergelis is a subject that has already been amply discussed. It has already drawn sufficient attention on the part of Soviet Jewish history scholars who have pointed to the editor's adoption of Mikhail Suslov's stance toward Yiddish culture as a dead culture, on the one hand, while, on the other hand, justifying the need to sustain it so long as lovers of the Yiddish word could yet be found in the USSR.[49] The quotation from Vergelis's article written before the inauguration of the official monument at Babyn Yar with which we opened our discussion of Babyn Yar in the Soviet Yiddish sphere makes it very clear that for Vergelis this site could play a prominent role in Soviet Jewish memory only if the compound term "Soviet Jewish" signified an amalgamated, rather than a hyphenated, identity. According to Vergelis, only one who counts the Jewish and the non-Jewish victims as one indistinguishable group of Communists can grasp the true historical meaning of Babyn Yar. Vergelis's debate, mentioned in the article, with his American Jewish guests gives the impression that the question at stake concerned who could more accurately place Babyn Yar in its historical context. But a closer look at the legacy of Vergelis may reveal that his words with respect to Babyn Yar were only one facet of a full-fledged literary theory that defined the role that Soviet Yiddish literature of the postwar period was destined to play.

In his article "Mit vos iz lebedik di yidishe literatur" (What makes Yiddish literature vibrant),[50] a piece in which he attempts to define the tasks of Soviet Yiddish literature, Vergelis takes issue with non-Communist Yiddish intellectuals living in America who envisioned Yiddish literature's role as the preserver of the essence of Eastern European Jewish civilization in the wake of its demise. For Vergelis, this drive for preservation was a sign of the decay and irrelevancy endemic to American Yiddish cultural figures such as Isaac Bashevis Singer, his brother Israel Joshua, and the literary critic Shmuel Niger. If Yiddish literature had any place in the world of the twentieth-century Jew, it was only if it was capable of portraying the unique condition of the Jew living in "the atomic and space era, in the era of social and anti-colonial revolutions, of giant industrial revolutions."[51] In contrast to what he viewed as an anachronistic contemplation of the bygone Jewish past, of the shtetl reality as perpetuated by the three masters of Yiddish literature—Sholem Abramovitsh, Sholem Aleichem, and I. L. Peretz—Vergelis took pride in the fact that postwar Soviet Yiddish literature evinced interest in the shtetl of the present, in the place where now, in the Communist motherland, Jews continued to live happily as fully integrated members of Soviet society freed from the suffocating constraints of the ghetto mentality that their American bourgeois brethren insisted, for some reason, on maintaining.

Toward the end of his discussion, Vergelis explains the relevance of this cutting-edge Soviet Yiddish literature to our subject. He draws a link between the break that Soviet Yiddish literature had with the ghetto mentality (with what he dubs as "Jewish affairs," or *yidishe asokim*) and the proper way that the Holocaust had to be portrayed in Soviet Yiddish literature. For Vergelis, the atrocities that took place on Soviet soil during the German occupation ought not to be read through the lens of the Holocaust of European Jewry. This was by no means an act of betrayal. On the contrary, it was an attempt to endow Yiddish literature with some relevancy to the world surrounding it. Moreover, this was the only way, Vergelis argues, to keep Yiddish literature alive. To read these events in a different way was, according to Vergelis, something tantamount to an anachronistic, "back to the ghetto" mentality, where the Jews and non-Jews live and die in two totally different spaces:

> How would a bourgeois writer portray the war against Hitler, for example? When one reads his work, it may seem as though this was a war of Germans against Jews. The Soviet Yiddish war novels (by P. Markish, Y. Falikman) construct the [true] picture of the World War with its mighty coalitions and in its [entire] strategic scope. The plot's focus in the works of these writers is their own ethnic environment—touching upon issues of battle as well as the martyrology and heroism of the Jewish people.[52]

From Vergelis's words it follows that, unlike the excessively nationalistic character that Soviet Yiddish literature assumed during the war and the immediate postwar years, the time was now auspicious to leap back to the Soviet Yiddish literature of Stalin's late 1920s and early 1930s, which was predominated by the socialist element far more than the nationalist one. If Vergelis's contention can be taken here at face value, then the very minor role that Babyn Yar played in the Soviet literary sphere was not the outcome of external coercion but, on the contrary, a reflection of the wish of Yiddish cultural activists with the stature of Vergelis to *fully* internalize Soviet dogma. Thus, the downplaying of Babyn Yar in the Soviet Yiddish sphere emerges, not as a chain of mere literary "accidents," but rather as a central element in the Soviet Yiddish literary edifice. Evidently, for a "perfect Jewish *Homo Sovieticus*," as Gennady Estraikh describes Vergelis,[53] presenting Babyn Yar as merely a Great Patriotic War site is exactly what, according to Vergelis, "made Yiddish literature vibrant."

## THE SOVIET JEWISH EXPERIENCE: FOUR PATTERNS

As our discussion of Babyn Yar in Soviet Yiddish literature comes to an end, we have to ask: does it chart out the multidirectionality of the ravine's memory or, rather, does it hit a dead end? Was Babyn Yar the symbol of Jewish nationalism that was destined for repression and consigned to oblivion? Perhaps nothing could be less true, if we are to believe and subscribe to the ideological posture of Aron Vergelis and view Babyn Yar as a multinational site and its Jewish victims as peaceful Soviet civilians. But are we to believe Vergelis? Was he an ideologue, or an opportunist? Did he truly believe in what he said? In recent years, Soviet Jewish historiography has seen an explosion of new books and articles providing a panoramic exploration of the life and activities of the Soviet Jewish *Homo sovieticus*, attempting to find an answer to a difficult question: How Jewish—and also how Soviet—were Soviet Jews? What does the hyphenated Soviet Jewish identity truly mean? Dealing with the Soviet Jewish experience in different eras and locations, under Lenin, Stalin, Khrushchev, and Brezhnev, we may discern four different patterns portraying the life of the Soviet Jew.

The first, emerging from *Becoming Soviet Jews* by Elissa Bemporad, places the Jewish and the Soviet on a continuum: the Soviet path was certainly the path of the future, yet old, traditional Jewish customs died hard. Members of the Soviet Jewish elite experienced a break with Judaism, yet they often made the not so obvious choice of circumcising their male children, as one example among many ideologically detrimental and obsolete Jewish customs that remained widely practiced to the chagrin of Moscow and the local Jewish authorities in Minsk.[54] Anna Shternshis has proposed another pattern in a book carrying the provocative title *Soviet and Kosher*,[55] which illustrates how the old, traditional Jewish world was vigorously opposed and negated, giving way to a new, somewhat syncretistic Soviet Jewish culture, one in which pork became kosher and in which Jewish holidays and customs were completely transformed, gaining a totally new, bona fide meaning (in Soviet terms, of course).

One may glean a third pattern, emerging from the work of Mordechai Altshuler, Benjamin Pinkus, and Zvi Gitelman, of a people living behind the Iron Curtain in a reality toward which they had no choice but to adapt. They had to adapt, then, to a system that displayed ambivalence toward its Jewish subjects, who were both its beneficiaries and its targets. Practitioners of a "thin culture,"[56] a national minority facing discrimination and cultural repression, they did what they could to uphold and preserve what was left of Judaism and their sluggishly waning Jewish identity or fight for their right to emigrate (perhaps something was lost in translation when Mordechai Altshuler's book *Judaism in the Soviet Vise* assumed the more neutral title *Religion and Jewish Identity in the Soviet Union*).[57] And finally a fourth pattern—a more peaceful coexistence between the two ends of this hyphenated identity—was espoused by Harriet Murav in *Music from a Speeding Train*[58] and Arkadi Zeltser in *Unwelcome Memory*, which suggest a pattern of a vibrant Jewish life filled with meaningful Jewish literary and Holocaust commemoration activities, respectively, taking place sometimes parallel to and sometimes in spite of, and at still other times under the influence of, Soviet officialdom.

Our study of Babyn Yar's representation in Soviet Russian and Yiddish literature does not stand in contradistinction to these four trends. If anything, it validates each of them. But when delving all the way to the rock bottom of the Soviet Jewish identity, down to the depths of the ravine—where the dead are buried, victims of genocide and other war crimes and whose ghosts continue to haunt the living—the Soviet Jewish experience appears a great deal less rosy. When the memory of Babyn Yar is used as the measuring rod of this experience; when the extreme of mass murder during the Holocaust is used to assess the duller, day-to-day moments, Jewish existence on Soviet soil starts to resemble more and more the life of the Marranos—of those who, like their Spanish and Portuguese coreligionists from centuries ago, could practice their faith, celebrate their identity, and give its most profound dimensions only in a cryptic fashion.[59]

Further complicating matters is the question of where the line drawn was—between what may seem at first as oblique references to Babyn Yar in encrypted language (as we saw with Dore Khaykine's references to Kyiv neighborhoods, or with Cherniavsky's child-size shoe), as befits modern Marranos, and the sincere effort made by Soviet Jewish writers to de-Judaize Babyn Yar, as exemplified by Aron Vergelis. To put it another way, while reading these coded works of the Soviet Jewish writers, where Vergelis is perhaps the most salient example, we may still wonder: Is there a cautious, yet faithful, Jewish Marrano in front of us, or perhaps the most loyal Jewish apparatchik that Soviet Jewish history has ever produced, a quintessential Soviet Jewish Converso? Inasmuch as we will never find out what the exact proportion of the total number of persons brutally killed at the ravine on the northwestern outskirts of Kyiv were Jews, slight is the chance that we will ever know whether the heroes of Soviet Yiddish literature, representative figures of which included Aron Vergelis, were celebrating what made their beloved Yiddish language and literature vibrant or rather bemoaning the obstacles that brought it closer and closer to its demise.

# EPILOGUE

IN SEPTEMBER 1987, AT A COMMEMORATIVE EVENT DEDICATED TO THE JEWish victims of Babyn Yar held at the Jewish section of a Moscow cemetery, Samuil Zivs, the third speaker on this evening, came to address the crowd. Zivs, the deputy chairman of the Anti-Zionist Committee of the Soviet Public, an official propaganda body hosting key Jewish cultural and political figures that had been set up in 1983, came to reiterate Moscow's long-standing stance toward Babyn Yar. He reminded his audience that Babyn Yar was indeed the mass graveyard of Jews. Yet, he continued, these victims were defending their motherland: they died as Soviet citizens for the sake of a country that now a growing number of Soviet citizens of Jewish origin were asking to leave, betraying, in the eyes of Zivs, the Soviet martyrs of Babyn Yar.[1]

As a holder of a key position in an official Soviet organization, Zivs was apparently instructed to deliver the decades-old Soviet stance toward Babyn Yar: that the ravine was the emblem not of the destruction of European Jewry but rather of the effort made by Soviet citizens crossing all ethnic boundaries to drive away and defeat the fascist invader. But now, with Glasnost in full swing, he was not met by the silent consent of his audience but rather by booing. The signal finally came about that Zivs, like Aaron Vergelis, another member of the committee, were figures of the past. In addition to the booing, the permission given to a number of local Jewish groups to convene the ceremony, among which the Jewish refuseniks were predominant, signaled for the first time that the Soviet government, ever since it decided to turn Babyn Yar into a memory black hole in the mid-1940s, was now willing to openly acknowledge or even encourage a new public discourse about Babyn Yar.

The beginning of a real change in the official Soviet view of Babyn Yar that this commemorative event marked was a part of a grander tectonic shift in Soviet culture, which was heralded by the coming to power of Mikhail Gorbachev and the launching of Glasnost. The new program, marking a real cultural revolution in Soviet politics, encouraged, inter alia, the filling in of the "blank spots" of Soviet history.[2] The regime's willingness to revisit and revise the memory of Babyn Yar was therefore not an incidental, isolated gesture, nor a testimony to the capitulation of the Soviet government to pressure both domestic and diplomatic. It reflected a profound recognition of those in power in the Kremlin as well as those in power in Kyiv that the safety valve screwed so tightly during the Cold War, allowing only a limited amount of literary works on Babyn Yar to surface, was about to finally be loosened altogether.

This is indeed what happened in the following years: what started as an event held in Moscow and attended by both Zionist activists and vigilant KGB agents turned fairly rapidly into a full-blown wave of activities revolving around Babyn Yar, now in Kyiv rather than the Russian capital. These were all geared toward the complete undoing of Babyn Yar as a memory black hole. In a way, the process that began in 1966 with the laying at the ravine of a plaque announcing the arrival of an imminent, permanent monument at the site (a monument that in reality took about a decade to lay at the site) was about to now reach completion. If the megalithic structure erected in Babyn Yar in July 1976 featured the Soviet POWs and civilians whose ethnic identity was glossed over, in September of 1991, soon before the dissolution of the Soviet Union, another monument would be placed nearby it: a monument standing for the Jewish victims of Babyn Yar exclusively. Initiated by historian, pedagogue, and journalist Ilya Levitas, funded by the Joint Distribution Committee and the Jewish Agency and designed by the artist Yuri Paskevich, a structure featuring a menorah was unveiled in September 1991 as a part of the week of ceremonies—now, these commemorative programs were not only permitted, but rather officially sanctioned and partaken by the newly independent Ukrainian government—to mark the fiftieth anniversary of the massacre.[3]

Only less than two months earlier, in a gesture indicating that Babyn Yar was no longer a divisive issue on the Cold War front, President George H. W. Bush, as a part of an official trip to the Ukrainian capital, came to Babyn Yar and became the first head of state to visit the ravine.[4] Significantly, President Bush chose in his speech not only to openly discuss the murder of Jews at the ravine while mentioning alongside them other victims of the "Nazi madman"—Romani, Communists, and Christians—he also wished to conclude his address with a citation of Yevgeny Yevtushenko's "Babi Yar" that now, thirty years after it first appeared, became a poetic symbol of the victory of freedom and truthfulness against bigotry or prejudice.[5]

The events of the summer and fall of 1991 suggested that Babyn Yar would alter its face forever, turning from a Soviet site, expunged of any ethnic distinctiveness, into a

# EPILOGUE

The post–Cold War menorah monument at Babyn Yar. (Photo by Amos Ben Gershom / GPO.) This figure appears in color online.

Jewish site. This was an impression easy to receive if one considered the fact that all government–dissident tensions of the past were now dissolved. Commemorating Babyn Yar as a Jewish site seemed now to be a goal shared by both the former dissident Jewish groups and the government of the newly independent state of Ukraine. Whereas, for the former, the battle to allow the free emigration of Soviet Jews was now decisively won, the latter lent its support to the commemorative effort. A time-honored opponent of Soviet Russification policies and the suppression of national minorities, the Ukrainian government wished to align itself now with the view of Babyn Yar as a Jewish memory space.

While the visit of President Bush heralded this new development (and he would be followed by President Clinton in 1995 and Pope John Paul II in 2001),[6] his comments about the death of Jews, Romani, Communists, and Christians foreshadowed the failure of Babyn Yar to turn into the exclusive domain of the now-rejuvenated Jewish community of Kyiv, the new, post-Soviet Ukrainian capital. Half a century of authoritarian rule that had targeted a highly diverse group of Soviet victims left, evidently, an indelible mark on Babyn Yar. As the post-Soviet era wore on, it turned out that the Jewish memory associated with Babyn Yar was not the only one to be repressed. The erection in 2000 of a cross in the precincts of Babyn Yar only thirty to forty meters away from the menorah by a group of Orthodox Christians to mark the murder of two monks there in 1941 and the erection of another one commemorating the death of Organization of Ukrainian Nationalists members (which, prior to its victimization by the Nazis, played an active role in the slaughtering of Jews)—these actions sent a clear signal to the Kyiv Jewish community. They made it clear that the battle of histories endemic to Babyn Yar would continue, now to be waged in the open and to assume perhaps an even more disturbing nature in comparison with the epoch of Soviet totalitarianism and post-Stalinist authoritarianism.[7] As Victoria Khiterer shows, the years of Soviet suppression were now giving way to a "monument jungle," a commemorative explosion that came to compensate for decades of silence in the newly founded Ukrainian democracy.[8]

Ukrainian Jews were, for the most part, appalled by the attempts of Organization of Ukrainian Nationalists veterans and supporters to take possession of Babyn Yar, depriving the Jews one more time of what they deemed as their rightful demand to turn Babyn Yar into a sacred Holocaust site rather than merely a broad platform containing a plethora of conflicting memories.[9] It seemed as though both sides of the debate, the local Jewish community of Kyiv and the Ukrainian activists, were unprepared to meet the new challenge of the post-Soviet era: the transformation of Babyn Yar from a site standing for a uniform Soviet narrative, towering above and suppressing any alternative memory not aligned with it, into a site now placed in an entirely new arena—that of a democratic, multicultural, and increasingly open society where collective memories often conflict with each other, offering very little prospects or hope for reconciliation.[10]

Indeed, the battle to once and for all get the history (and memory) of Babyn Yar set straight, pitting now the descendants of the Holocaust's Jewish victims and the descendants of their oppressors, is far from being over. The emergence of *holokost*, now a Russian term more and more in common use in post-Soviet Russia and Ukraine denoting the annihilation of European Jewry during World War II on Soviet territories and beyond them, and the resurfacing of *holodomor* is a good indication to the two sides that the task of reconciling the two victimhood narratives, the Jewish and the Ukrainian ones, respectively, is far from being complete. This pessimistic note concluding our study notwithstanding, some room for optimism is warranted. With the rise of a twenty-first-century pro-Western and democratic Ukraine, now fighting for its life as I write these words, there is and there must be some hope. In my personal conversations with fellow Ukrainians, both peers and colleagues, there was something I could not remain indifferent to: as Babyn Yar brought young Ukrainians in front of a mirror, reflecting before them a collective history not only of valor but also of complicity in mass atrocities, there were those who chose to turn the mirror into a flashlight, redirecting the image of victimizers elsewhere (the Communists, the Jewish Bolsheviks, world Jewry, etc.). But there were also those—and there is a growing number of them now—who courageously chose to remain in front of the mirror, recognizing the imperative of a young nation to mature by reflecting on both its bright and dark histories and, yes, to muster the courage to face even their nation's heart of darkness. It is this group of young Ukrainians—seekers of freedom, justice, and truth—that the future of Holocaust education in Eastern Europe and, by extension, the future of education, humanism, and humanity rest on.

# NOTES

### PREFACE

1. Wendy Lower, *The Ravine: A Family, a Photograph, a Holocaust Massacre Revealed* (Houghton Mifflin Harcourt, 2021).
2. For the most recent presentation of Babyn Yar in Ukrainian literature, see both the introduction and poems in Ostap Kin, ed., *Babyn Yar: Ukrainian Poets Respond*, trans. John Hennessy and Ostap Kin (Ukrainian Research Institute, 2022). See Also Iryna Zakharchuk, "Babyn Yar in Belles-Lettres," in *Babyn Yar: History and Memory*, ed. Vladyslav Hrynevych and Paul R. Magocsi (Dukh I Litera, 2016), 205–38.
3. Michael Berenbaum, "The Impact of the Holocaust on Contemporary Ethics," in *Ethics in the Shadow of the Holocaust: Christian and Jewish Perspectives*, ed. Judith H. Banki and John T. Pawlikowski (Sheed & Ward, 2001), 235–60, here 235.

### INTRODUCTION

1. Zvi Gitelman, *A Century of Ambivalence: The Jews of Russia and the Soviet Union, 1881 to the Present*, 2nd, expanded ed. (Indiana University Press, 2001), 123.
2. Karel C. Berkhoff, *Harvest of Despair: Life and Death in Ukraine Under Nazi Rule* (Harvard University Press, 2004), 65.
3. Lucy Dawidowicz, "Babi Yar's Legacy," *New York Times Magazine*, September 27, 1981, http://www.nytimes.com/1981/09/27/magazine/Babyn-yar-s-legacy.html.
4. Semion Viguchin, "Babi Yar – uroki tragedii," in *Pamyat' Babyego Yara*, ed. Ilya Levitas (Evreyskii Sovet Ukrainy, 2001), 237.
5. According to the Holocaust history scholar Yehuda Bauer, the order to embark upon the systematic annihilation of European Jewry was transmitted to Heinrich Himmler by Adolf Hitler in March of 1941 as a part of Nazi Germany's preparation for the imminent invasion of the Soviet Union. See Yehuda Bauer, *Teguvot be'et haShoah: nisyonot amida, hitnagdut, hatsala* (Israel Ministry of Defense Press, 1983), 78.
6. Dawidowicz, "Babi Yar's Legacy." It is noteworthy that the initial reports appearing in November 1941 in the two leading Soviet newspapers, *Pravda* and *Izvestiia*, referred to a higher figure: 52,000 Jews. See Arkady Zeltser, "Tema 'Evrei v Bab'yem Yaru' v Sovetskom Soyuze v 1941–1945,'" in *Babyn Yar: masove ubistvo i pamiat' pro noho*. (Ukr. Ukr. tsentr vyvchennia istorii Holokostu, 2017), 84.
7. See Karel Berkhoff et al., *Basic Historical Narrative of the Babyn Yar Holocaust Memorial Center*, Charity Fund Babyn Yar Holocaust Memorial, Kyiv, October 2018, https://

bit.ly/3fkHqU6. These figures come close to estimates made by former prisoners of the Syrets concentration camp, who took part in the incineration of the corpses at the ravine in August–September 1943 and established the death toll at 45,000 Jews and 25,000 non-Jews.

8. In recent years, at least two scholars presented a human tally at Babyn Yar that is much higher. The Ukrainian Jewish journalist Liubov Khazan, in a lecture delivered on the occasion of the Babyn Yar massacre's eightieth anniversary, called the German figures into question. Khazan argued that the Nazis had a number of reasons to underreport the number of civilian casualties, not the least of which was the practice of excluding young children from their tally, many of whom had been beaten to death at the Jewish cemetery adjacent to Babyn Yar, rather than being shot at the ravine. She concurs with the figure of 95,000–97,000 corroborated by Ilya Levitas, the former vice president of the Jewish Confederation of Ukraine and founder of the Memory of the Babyn Yar Foundation. See "Рыцари Бабьего Яра. 80-летию трагедии киевских евреев посвящается" (Knights of Babi Yar: Dedicated to the 80th anniversary of the tragedy of the Kyiv Jews) at https://www.youtube.com/watch?v=mrsiXR1t4lo (accessed January 1, 2022). Victoria Khiterer also rejects the prevalent reliance by historians on the Nazi figure of 33,771 Jewish victims and refers to a higher figure: "Over a few days, more than 100,000 Jews were killed." See Victoria Khiterer, "Babi Yar, the Tragedy of Kyiv's Jews," *Brandeis Graduate Journal* 2 (2004): 1–16, here 2.

9. Yitzhak Arad, *The Holocaust in the Soviet Union*, trans. Ora Cummings (University of Nebraska Press; Yad Vashem, 2009).

10. Patrick Desbois (also known as Father Desbois), *The Holocaust by Bullets: A Priest's Journey to Uncover the Truth Behind the Murder of 1.5 Million Jews* (Palgrave Macmillan, 2008).

11. Timothy Snyder, "The Holocaust: The Ignored Reality," *New York Review*, July 16, 2009. https://www.nybooks.com/articles/2009/07/16/holocaust-the-ignored-reality/; Snyder, *Bloodlands: Europe Between Hitler and Stalin* (Basic Books, 2016).

12. Hannah Arendt, *The Origins of Totalitarianism* (Harcourt Brace Jovanovich, 1973).

13. The linkage between the Holocaust and the Great Patriotic War took more time to materialize. Whereas Arad's monograph on the Holocaust in the USSR squarely deals with the Final Solution, the trend of blurring the difference between the Great Patriotic War and the Holocaust is a salient feature of David Shneer's work on Soviet Jewish World War II and Holocaust photography. See Arad, *The Holocaust in the Soviet Union*; and David Shneer, *Through Soviet Jewish Eyes: Photography, War, and the Holocaust* (Rutgers University Press, 2011).

14. Boris Pasternak, *In the Interlude: Poems 1945–1960*, trans. Henry Kamen (Oxford University Press, 1962), 213.

15. Perhaps no better evidence of this trend is the popularity that Father Desbois's *The*

*Holocaust by Bullets* gained in the second decade of the twenty-first century, appearing also as a traveling exhibit. This high degree of public attention culminated in the appearance of Father Desbois on CBS's news magazine *60 Minutes* in the summer of 2016, marking the subject as consequential not only for a limited circle of historians but also for the public at large. For a brief summary of the book and its media coverage, see Rick Sallinger, "'Holocaust by Bullets' Uncovers Mass Graves, 1.6+ Million Victims," *CBS News Colorado*, November 6, 2017, https://www.cbsnews.com/colorado/news/holocaust-mass-graves/.

16. R. E. Finnin, "Timothy Snyder: 'Holocaust: The Ignored Reality,'" *Memory at War: Blog*, June 21, 2009, http://cambridgeculturalmemory.blogspot.com/2009/06/masha-lipman-russia-again-evading.html. See also Mark Mazower, *Dark Continent: Europe's Twentieth Century* (Vintage, 2001).

17. Shneer, *Through Soviet Jewish Eyes*, 149. The symbolic statue of Babyn Yar is also echoed in Mordechai Altshuler's study of Jewish religion and culture during the war, the late Stalin years, and the Thaw era. See Mordechai Altshuler, *Yahadut bamakhbesh haSovieti: bein dat lezehut yehudit biVrit haMo'atsot, 1941–1964* (Zalman Shazar Center, 2008), 136.

18. Jan Assmann, "Collective Memory and Cultural Identity," *New German Critique* 65 (Spring–Summer 1995): 126–29.

19. Jeffrey K. Olick, "Collective Memory: The Two Cultures," in *The Collective Memory Reader*, ed. Jeffrey K. Olick, Vered Vinitzky-Serousi, and Daniel Levy (Oxford University Press, 2008), 225–28. In an attempt to draw two disciplines—psychology and sociology—closer to each other, Olick argues that "it is not just that we remember as members of groups, but that we constitute those groups and their members simultaneously in the act (thus re-member-ing)" (228). See also Olick's 2012 lecture "What Is Memory Studies?" at https://www.youtube.com/watch?v=FdU_hYosb40 (accessed January 1, 2014).

20. See Pierre Nora, "Between Memory and History: Les Lieux de Mémoire," *Representations* 26 (Spring 1989): 12.

21. Nora, "Between Memory and History," 8.

22. James Young, *The Texture of Memory: Holocaust Memorials and Meaning* (Yale University Press, 1993), 5.

23. Young, *The Texture of Memory*, 2.

24. Zvi Gitelman, "Politics and the Historiography of the Holocaust in the Soviet Union," in *Bitter Legacy: Confronting the Holocaust in the USSR*, ed. Zvi Gitelman (Indiana University Press, 1997), 20.

25. William Korey is the author who has written about the suppression of Babyn Yar's memory most extensively. See William Korey, "Babi Yar Remembered," *Midstream* 15, no. 3 (1969): 24–32; Korey, "In History's 'Memory Hole': The Soviet Treatment

of the Holocaust," in *Contemporary Views on the Holocaust*, ed. Randolph L. Braham (Kluwer-Nijhoff, 1983), 145–56, here 154; Korey, "Forty Years Ago at Babi Yar: Reliving the Crime," *Present Tense* 9, no. 1 (1981): 27–31; and Korey, "A Monument over Babi Yar?," in *The Holocaust in the Soviet Union: Studies and Sources on the Destruction of the Jews in the Nazi-Occupied Territories of the USSR, 1941–1945*, ed. Lucjan Dobroszycki and Jeffrey S. Gurock (M.E. Sharpe, 1993), 61–74. As for the contribution by the scholar Lucy Dawidowicz and the novelist Elie Wiesel, see Dawidowicz, "Babi Yar's Legacy"; Elie Wiesel, *The Jews of Silence: A Personal Report on Soviet Jewry* (Schocken Books, 1987), 25–32; and Wiesel, "Bezokhrenu et Babi Yar: Ka'avor arba'im shanah," *Masua* 10 (1982): 28–31.

26. Richard Sheldon, "The Transformation of Babi Yar," in *Soviet Society and Culture: Essays in Honor of Vera S. Dunham*, ed. Terry L. Thompson and Richard Sheldon (Westview Press, 1988), 124–61, here 145. This unofficial anniversary ceremony would continue to take place annually during the ensuing years. According to Ludmilla Alexeyeva, in 1968 only fifty to seventy people attended the annual ceremony at the site. These figures kept increasing together with the growth of the Soviet Jewish immigration dissident movement. In 1971, for instance, the year when the Soviet gates opened up for the first wave of the mass emigration of Jews, about a thousand participants came to lay wreaths at the ravine. See Ludmilla Alexeyeva, *Soviet Dissent: Contemporary Movements for National, Religious, and Human Rights* (Wesleyan University Press, 1987), 175.

27. Edith Clowes, "Constructing the Memory of the Holocaust: The Ambiguous Treatment of Babi Yar in Soviet Literature," *Partial Answers* 3, no. 2 (2005): 154–82, here 156; Jeff Mankoff, "Babi Yar and the Struggle for Memory, 1944–2004," *Ab Imperio* 2 (2004): 393–415, here 393–94, 398–400.

28. Berkhoff, *Harvest of Despair*, 62.

29. Richard Overy, *Russia's War* (Penguin Books, 1997), 91–92; A. I. Balashov and G. P. Rudakov, *Istoriya velikoy otechestvennoi voiny* (Peter, 2005), 98.

30. Arad, *The Holocaust in the Soviet Union*, 541. In addition to the ravine in which the Jews of Kyiv died on September 29–30, 1941, the second-largest war crime site in the vicinity of Babyn Yar was the Syrets concentration camp, which was set up in 1942 and located on the northern outskirts of Kyiv. In this camp, "undesirable elements," including Jews, POWs, Communists, and captured partisans, were interned, tortured, and shot. According to the official Soviet records, over 25,000 people were victims of Syrets. Vitalii Nakhmanovich notes that these were buried both in Babyn Yar and other ditches surrounding the city of Kyiv. See Vitalii Nakhmanovich, "Rasstrely i zakhoroneniya v rayone Babyego Yara vo vremya nemetskoy okkupatsii g. Kieva 1941-1943 gg. Problemy khronologii i topografii," in *Babi Yar: chelovek, vlast', istoriya*, ed. Vitalii Nakhmanovich and Tatiana Evstafyeva (Vneshtorgizdat Ukrainy, 2004), 84–163, here 163. On the Syrets (= Sieretskii) camp, see Tatiana Evstafyeva, "Sieretskii kontsentratsionnyi lager',"

in *Babi Yar: chelovek, vlast', istoriya*, ed. Vitalii Nakhmanovich and Tatiana Evstafyeva (Vneshtorgizdat Ukrainy, 2004), 171–86; and Bohdan Martinenko, "Babi Yar vehashmadat ha'am hayehudi beUkraina 'al yedei haNatsim," *Mikhael* 13 (1993): 85–91, here 85.

31. Shmuel Spector, "Babi Yar," in *Encyclopedia of the Holocaust*, 4 vols., ed. Israel Gutman (Macmillan, 1989).
32. Feliks Levitas and Mark Shimanovskii, *Babii Yar: stranitsy tragedii* (Slid, 1991), 22.
33. Jeff Mankoff notes that toward the end of the twentieth century Babyn Yar became a magnet for Ukrainian nationalists, who would rally at the site every September 29 to commemorate the death of the Organization of Ukrainian Nationalists members. On Babyn Yar as a trigger for conflicts between Ukrainians and Jews in the post-Soviet period, see Mankoff, "Babi Yar and the Struggle for Memory, 1944–2004," 412–13.
34. Gitelman, "Politics and the Historiography of the Holocaust," 18–19.
35. For an extensive survey of Holocaust commemorative activities led by Soviet Jews, see Arkadi Zeltser, *Unwelcome Memory: Holocaust Monuments in the Soviet Union* (Yad Vashem, 2018). For the legal status of these activities as a "gray area," see Zeltser, *Unwelcome Memory*, 49. See also Altshuler, *Yahadut bamakhbesh haSovieti*, 345–47.
36. Karel C. Berkhoff, *Motherland in Danger: Soviet Propaganda During World War II* (Harvard University Press, 2012), 145–50.
37. According to Zvi Gitelman, a careful estimate of Jewish casualties during the war indicates that 2,711,000 Jews who were citizens of the Soviet Union in 1941 died in the course of the war (this number includes Jewish Red Army soldiers who died while in combat as well as Jewish POWs). Since over 26 million Soviet citizens died during the war, one may infer from this estimate that more than 10 percent of the Soviet victims of Nazism were Jewish, whereas Jews constituted only 2.5 percent of the Soviet population prior to the war. See Zvi Gitelman, "Internationalism, Patriotism, and Disillusion: Soviet Jewish Veterans Remember World War II and the Holocaust," in *The Holocaust in the Soviet Union: Symposium Presentations* (United States Holocaust Memorial Museum, 2005), http://www.ushmm.org/research/center/publications/occasional/2005-10/paper.pdf.
38. Alan Mintz, *Popular Culture and the Shaping of Holocaust Memory in America* (University of Washington Press, 2001), 39.
39. Wiesel, "Bezokhrenu et Babi Yar," 30–31.
40. Nakhmanovich, "Rasstrely i zakhoroneniya," 120, 162.
41. Nakhmanovich, "Rasstrely i zakhoroneniya," 88, 94–95.
42. David G. Roskies and Naomi Diamant, *Holocaust Literature: A History and Guide* (Brandeis University Press, 2013), 1–3.
43. Zeltser, *Unwelcome Memory*, 26–27, 37–38.
44. Nina Tumarkin, *The Living and the Dead: The Rise and Fall of the Cult of World War II in Russia* (Basic Books, 1994), 103.

45. Catherine Merridale, *Night of Stone: Death and Memory in Twentieth-Century Russia* (Basic Books, 2002), 213.
46. The term "thaw" (*ottepel'*) was coined after a novel by Ilya Ehrenburg. Published in 1954, a year after the death of Stalin, this novel was the first literary work to contain allusions to Stalin's despotic character. By and large, this term refers to the period of reforms and relaxation of censorship that was ushered in only in 1956, in the wake of Khrushchev's denunciation of Stalin in his Secret Speech at the 20th Congress of the Communist Party. This new trend of relative openness, however, was apparent as early as the immediate months following Stalin's death, and this explains my inclusion of the time period 1953–1956 within the chronological framework of the era known as the "Thaw" (= "Khrushchev's Thaw"). See Edward Brown, *Russian Literature Since the Revolution* (Collier Books, 1982), 238–57; and Dina Spechler, *Permitted Dissent: "Novy Mir" and the Soviet Regime* (Praeger 1982), 4.
47. Tumarkin, *The Living and the Dead*, 110, 132.
48. Gitelman, "Politics and the Historiography of the Holocaust," 28.
49. Nina Tumarkin presents her view of the Great Patriotic War as a predominantly manipulative, cynical cult that was blind to the real suffering of the Soviet people in her book *The Living and the Dead*. For Catherine Merridale's conception of the term in the same vein, see Merridale, *Night of Stone*, 235–40; and Merridale, *Ivan's War: Life and Death in the Red Army, 1939–1945* (Picador, 2006), 374–75.
50. Lisa Kirschenbaum, "Nothing Is Forgotten: Individual Memory and the Myth of the Great Patriotic War," in *History of the Aftermath: The Legacies of the Second World War in Europe*, ed. Frank Biess and Robert G. Moeller (Berghahn Books, 2010), 67–82, here 68–70.
51. Kirschenbaum, "Nothing Is Forgotten," 69, 72.

CHAPTER 1

1. Ilya Ehrenburg, "Babi Yar," trans. Alyssa Dinega Gillespie, in *An Anthology of Jewish-Russian Literature: Two Centuries of Dual Identity in Prose and Poetry*, Vol. 1, *1801–1953*, ed. Maxim D. Shrayer (M.E. Sharpe, 2007), 531.
2. Maxim D. Shrayer, "Jewish-Russian Holocaust Poetry in Official Soviet Venues: 1944–1946 (Ehrenburg, Antokolsky, Ozerov)," paper presented at the Annual Conference of the Association for Jewish Studies (AJS), Washington, DC, December 21, 2008.
3. Printed in 1946, *The Black Book* never saw the light of day in the USSR after the Communist Party's Propaganda Department decided that it contained "grave political errors." In 1948, following this decision, all existing copies of the work found in the USSR were destroyed, including the type that had been prepared for it. Only because several manuscript copies of the work were sent abroad did it survive: a Hebrew, English, Romanian, and Russian version of it appeared in the West. See Gitelman, "Politics and the

Historiography of the Holocaust," 19; Benjamin Pinkus, *The Soviet Government and the Jews 1948–1967: A Documented Study* (Cambridge University Press, 1984), 422–23. For the English version of *The Black Book*, see Ilya Ehrenburg and Vasily Grossman, *The Black Book* (Holocaust Library, 1981).

4. See Shneer, *Through Soviet Jewish Eyes*, 134–35, 225.
5. Joshua Rubenstein, *Tangled Loyalties: The Life and Times of Ilya Ehrenburg* (University of Alabama Press, 1999), 201.
6. As Ostap Kin notes, although the poem has been referenced by several scholars, the text has been largely undiscovered. Presumably, the poem was printed in one of the Soviet newspapers or journals. Later on, the author was condemned for portraying Ukrainians and Russians in "Avraham" as passive bystanders to the Babyn Yar massacre. See Kin, *Babyn Yar*, 233.
7. Berkhoff, *Motherland in Danger*, 119. NKVD refers to the Narodnyi komissariat vnutrennikh dyel, the People's Commissariat for Internal Affairs.
8. Berkhoff, *Motherland in Danger*, 119. See also Sheldon, "The Transformation of Babi Yar," 126. Most significantly, the note indicated that the Nazis' chief targets were "defenseless Jewish working people." The note also appeared in *Pravda*, January 7, 1942. From Molotov's reaction, it was clear that the Soviet government did not recognize any potential harm at first, even as they openly acknowledged the fact that an unprecedented event in European history, the turning of the first European city into a *Judenrein* zone, had happened in the then German-occupied Ukrainian capital. Sheldon suggests that Molotov felt prompted to inform the international community about the massacre, as his wife, Polina Zhemchuzhina, was of Jewish descent. See Sheldon, "The Transformation of Babi Yar," 154.
9. Shneer, *Through Soviet Jewish Eyes*, 171.
10. Berkhoff, *Motherland in Danger*, 139.
11. Berkhoff, *Motherland in Danger*, 145.
12. Ilya Ehrenburg, "Gebentshte erd," *Eynikayt*, October 1942, 2.
13. That these moods of all-Soviet solidarity and call to harness oneself in the colossal battle against Germany were shared across the board is perhaps most evident in the public recitation of a poem written soon before the first anniversary of the Babyn Yar massacre by one of the greatest Ukrainian poets of the twentieth century, Volodymyr Sosiura (1898–1965). See Kin, *Babyn Yar*, 200–203, 240–41. Reading his poem at an anti-fascist rally in the city of Ufa, Sosiura promised the murdered Jews that their blood will be avenged, and offered a conception of the Jewish people as an old, historic entity, one that would be repeated in Soviet literature again by another non-Jewish writer only nineteen years later in Yevgeny Yevtushenko's "Babi Yar":

*You walked all night in pain, persecuted through centuries.*
*Through the smoke of fires, the wild smoke of pogroms.*

> *Along cliffsides you looked for Canaan,*
> *In deserts, always walking a difficult path.*
> *You walked centuries through a long steel night,*
> *through tears and blood, and finally you reached the goal:*
> *in the country of the Soviets you found your homeland,*
> *among us, the free, you flourished.*
> *Together we built a bright home to live in,*
> *for the joy of generations.*
> *But the time arrived roaring with metal,*
> *and a menacing shadow cast from the West.*
> *And again howl, groan, and curse,*
> *the smoke of pogroms and the crosses of gallows.*
> *The nations go into battle in many columns, and with them you walk fearlessly.*
> *Together we weathered the whirlwind,*
> *merged into one, pouring blood for happiness,*
> *and your hatred, you rejuvenated people,*
> *is our hatred, as well as your love.*
> *We'll drive the beast together into the abyss,*
> *We'll scatter the black ashes of brownshirt hordes,*
> *because we love our native land beyond measure,*
> *because Stalin is leading us forward into battle.*
> *Our bright home will shine across the world,*
> *Rise even more visibly into the sky.*
> *Because the eyes of the Kremlin can't be closed,*
> *And no one can stop the beating heart of our nations.*

14. Zeltser, "Tema 'Evrei v Bab'yem Yaru,'" 100. Such a nationalistically oriented reference to Babyn Yar like the one we find in "Gebentshte erd," is quite rare. The celebrated Yiddish writer Dovid Bergelson, when describing Nazi atrocities in the Kyiv area, makes no mention of the ravine. Neither does the Yiddish poet Dovid Hofshteyn in his poem "Kiev." See Zeltser, "Tema 'Evrei v Bab'yem Yaru'" 87–88, 96.

15. Sheldon, "The Transformation of Babi Yar," 130. See also Arad, *The Holocaust in the Soviet Union*, 539.

16. Gitelman, "Politics and the Historiography of the Holocaust," 21.

17. Amir Weiner, *Making Sense of War: The Second World War and the Fate of the Bolshevik Revolution* (Princeton University Press, 2001), 212. On the takeover of Jewish property by the non-Jewish population of Ukraine after the war, see Mordechai Altshuler, "Antisemitism in Ukraine Toward the End of World War II," in *Bitter Legacy: Confronting the Holocaust in the USSR*, ed. Zvi Gitelman (Indiana University Press, 1997), 77–90, here 80–82.

18. The poem first appeared in a small collection by Ozerov entitled *Liven'* (Downpour) in 1947. It is cited and translated into English in Clowes, "Constructing the Memory of the Holocaust," 162. Ozerov tried to publish a sequel to the poem later in 1948, "Anew in Babyn Yar," but failed to do so and had to resort to propagating it illegally through the Soviet underground publication method known as *samizdat* (self-publication).
19. Klebanov's symphony came under attack and was described at a meeting of Kyiv composers as a Cosmopolitan work slandering the Russian and Ukrainian people. A report about the meeting was published in *Pravda Ukrainy* on March 19, 1949. See Pinkus, *The Soviet Government and the Jews 1948–1967*, 151, 174–75.
20. See Karel C. Berkhoff, "Babyn Yar in Cinema," in *Babyn Yar: History and Memory*, ed. Vladyslav Hrynevych and Paul Robert Magocsi, trans. Marta D. Olynyk (Dukh I Litera, 2016), 239–57, here 240–34. Donskoi was a staunch Communist whose career reached its zenith during the Stalin years and met its demise right afterward as he was reluctant to change his political outlook in accordance with the new cinematic values of the Thaw period. It is noteworthy that during the anti-Cosmopolitan campaign of the late 1940s, Donskoi openly denounced some of his Jewish colleagues. See Peter Rollberg, *Historical Dictionary of Russian and Soviet Cinema* (Scarecrow Press, 2009), 183.
21. Peter Kenez, *A History of the Soviet Union from the Beginning to the End*, 2nd ed. (Cambridge University Press, 2006), 177.
22. Gitelman, *A Century of Ambivalence*, 147–56.
23. Pinkus, *The Soviet Government and the Jews 1948–1967*, 390.
24. Pinkus, *The Soviet Government and the Jews 1948–1967*, 423.
25. Altshuler, *Yahadut bamakhbesh haSovieti*, 136.
26. Clowes, "Constructing the Memory of the Holocaust," 164–65.
27. For Clowes, this generational divide between the youth of the 1960s and their parents runs parallel to similar tensions that engulfed West German society in the postwar era. For another testimony on the tendency of scholars to distinguish between the commemoration of Babyn Yar during the Stalin and the Thaw eras, see Mankoff, "Babi Yar and the Struggle for Memory," 402. As Mankoff notes, while the death of Stalin hardly led to any change in the official Soviet reaction to Babyn Yar, it did lead to the appearance of new voices that increasingly challenged the official Soviet line on this issue.
28. Nissan Rosenthal, *Hahayim haYehudiyim biVrit-hamo'atsot 1935–1958* (Hakibbutz Hameuhad, 1993), 19; Viktor Nekrasov, "Zapiski zevaki," in *Kak ya stal shevalye: rasskazy, portrety, ocherki, povesti* (U-factoria, 2005), 388. For a description of Babyn Yar's vicinity as a Kyiv landfill, with trucks moving in and out dumping loads of waste at the site, see Emanuel Diamant, "Babi Yar, ili Pamyat' o tom, kak v narod prevrashchalos' stroptivoye plemya," n.d., https://www.academia.edu/43265556/Baby_Yar_or_a_story_of_how_a_wayward_tribe_has_strived_to_become_again_a_folk, p. 5.

29. Alexeyeva, *Soviet Dissent*, 175.
30. Kenez, *A History of the Soviet Union*, 188–89.

CHAPTER 2

1. Rubenstein, *Tangled Loyalties*, 280. For more details about the Thaw, see Brown, *Russian Literature Since the Revolution*, 247–54.
2. Vladislav Zubok, *Zhivago's Children: The Last Russian Intelligentsia* (Belknap Press, 2009), 52.
3. Brown, *Russian Literature Since the Revolution*, 247, 253.
4. Spechler, *Permitted Dissent*, 3–20.
5. Spechler, *Permitted Dissent*, 21–22; Zubok, *Zhivago's Children*, 54–55.
6. Nakhmanovich, "Rasstrely i zakhoroneniya," 191; Mankoff, "Babi Yar and the Struggle for Memory," 402.
7. Nakhmanovich, "Rasstrely i zakhoroneniya," 190, 196.
8. Sheldon, "The Transformation of Babi Yar," 133.
9. Sheldon, "The Transformation of Babi Yar," 133. See also Mankoff, "Babi Yar and the Struggle for Memory," 402.
10. Joshua Rubenstein notes that the Yiddish writers who were arrested during the anti-Cosmopolitan campaign were among the first to be released from Soviet prison camps. They were released as early as November 1955. See Rubenstein, *Tangled Loyalties*, 313.
11. R. G. Pikhoya, *Sovetskiy Soyuz: istoriya vlasti* (Sibirskiy khronograf, 2000), 90, 96.
12. Ironically, as Pikhoya contends, it was Beria, the man who later came to be seen, more than anyone else, as Stalin's hangman, who, with courage and a sense of urgency, took the first essential steps to turn the Soviet state from totalitarianism into a more benign form of dictatorship. See Pikhoya, *Sovetskiy Soyuz*, 94, 96–97.
13. Kenez, *A History of the Soviet Union*, 188.
14. Kenez, *A History of the Soviet Union*, 190.
15. For how this process played itself out with the attempt to portray Beria as the sole Presidium member responsible for Stalinist repression, see Pikhoya, *Sovetskiy Soyuz*, 99–102. No sooner had Khrushchev eliminated Beria as a potential contender to become Stalin's inheritor did he move on, espousing the language of de-Stalinization, to overcome the powerful Malenkov, who together with him had ruled the Soviet Union in a duumvirate between 1953 and 1955 (122). Later on, Khrushchev's confrontation with Malenkov, who was now supported by Molotov and Kaganovich, reached its climax in the so-called anti-party coup, when the three failed to oust the Soviet leader during the Presidium of June 1957. Four years later, at the Twenty-Second Party Congress, Khrushchev would openly denounce Stalin for the second time, doing so, again, by way of blackening the reputation of the Politburo members who had conspired against him earlier and presenting them as "old guard" Stalin loyalists. See Zubok, *Zhivago's Children*, 196.

16. Yaroslav Bilinsky, *The Second Soviet Republic: The Ukraine After World War II* (Rutgers University Press, 1964), 234–36.
17. Mankoff, "Babi Yar and the Struggle for Memory," 402.
18. Zubok, *Zhivago's Children*, 60.
19. Mankoff, "Babi Yar and the Struggle for Memory," 402.
20. Mankoff, "Babi Yar and the Struggle for Memory," 403; Sheldon, "The Transformation of Babi Yar," 135.
21. Victoria Khiterer, "Suppressed Memory: Memorialization of the Holocaust in Babi Yar (Kyiv)," paper presented at the Association for the Study of Nationalities World Convention, Columbia University, New York, April 23–25, 2015.
22. Cited in Gennady V. Kostyrchenko, *Tainaya politika Khrushcheva: vlast', intelligentsiya, evreiskii vopros* (Mezhdunarodnye Otnosheniya, 2012), 352–53.
23. Kiril Feferman prefers not to view Babyn Yar's neglect and the turning of the Holocaust into a stepchild of Soviet culture as chiefly the consequence of Stalin's and Khrushchev's antisemitism. From a review of the Soviet reporting on Nazi atrocities during the war and the coverage of the Eichmann trial, he infers that the quote above by Khrushchev may be taken at face value. As Feferman puts it, the Soviet regime recognized "the fact that the Jews constituted the majority of the people victimized, in accordance with Adolf Eichmann's orders. On the other hand, it denies that the Germans singled them out for extermination. Rather, fascism was declared to be an anti-human ideology which marked many nations and politically subversive groups for annihilation." See Kiril Feferman, *Soviet Jewish Stepchild: The Holocaust in the Soviet Mindset, 1941–1964* (VDM Verlag Dr. Müller, 2009), 60 (see also 5–7).
24. Mankoff, "Babi Yar and the Struggle for Memory," 404.
25. Denis Kozlov, *The Readers of Novyi Mir: Coming to Terms with the Stalinist Past* (Harvard University Press, 2013).
26. Spechler, *Permitted Dissent*, xv–xxiii. In his work on dissent in the Soviet Union, Rudolph Tőkés identifies the same phenomenon as "within-system opposition." See Rudolph Tőkés, "Varieties of Soviet Dissent: An Overview," in *Dissent in the USSR: Politics, Ideology, and People*, ed. Rudolph Tőkés (Johns Hopkins University Press, 1975), 1–34, here 22. On *Novy Mir*, see Kozlov, *The Readers of Novyi Mir*.
27. The Komitet Gosudarstvennoy Bezopasnosti (lit. the "Committee for State Security").
28. Viktor Nekrasov, *Arestovannye stranitsy: rasskazy, intervyu, pis'ma iz arkhivov KGB* (Laurus, 2014), 148.
29. Nekrasov, *Arestovannye stranitsy*, 178.
30. Brown, *Russian Literature Since the Revolution*, 266.
31. Brown, *Russian Literature Since the Revolution*, 267; Zubok, *Zhivago's Children*, 121.
32. Brown, *Russian Literature Since the Revolution*, 267.
33. Viktor Nekrasov, "Pochemu eto ne sdelano?" *Literaturnaya gazeta*, October 10, 1959, 4.
34. The first major Soviet writer to protest the Soviet handling of Babyn Yar was Ilya

Ehrenburg, who appealed right after the liberation of Kyiv, while the war was still wearing on, to the first secretary of the Communist Party, Nikita Khrushchev, and protested a plan to build a market over Babyn Yar. Khrushchev retorted to Ehrenburg's protest: "I advise you not to intervene in matters not your own. Better write good novels instead." As Ehrenburg communicated his protest to Khrushchev in a personal letter, the essay by Nekrasov was the first time when such claims were publicly made. See Rubenstein, *Tangled Loyalties*, 211. It is worth noting that Ehrenburg was among those who favorably responded to Nekrasov's demands in his "Why Has It Not Been Done?" See Rubenstein, *Tangled Loyalties*, 440.

35. For the essay's translation into English, see Pinkus, *The Soviet Government and the Jews 1948–1967*, 437–38.
36. Nekrasov, "Zapiski zevaki," 388.
37. The battle against amnesia and its view as disgraceful is one of the key tropes of the ravine literature. A similar sentiment was expressed more than a decade later by the Ukrainian Jewish poet Sava Holovanivsky in "Melnyk Street," written in 1975 and published in 1980:

> On the road that goes past Babyn Yar, they're laying asphalt.
> In the slow feverish whirl
> tar boils, and the workers,
> dirty and stubborn, spread it out.
> From now on, thanks to the efforts
> of this celebrated city's council,
> here will lie, without potholes or pits,
> a road, arrow-like and solemn.
> Because it's not a cart or ancient tarantass
> that cruises by with the haste of ants these days—
> in the age of rockets and interplanetary routes
> people and cars have to rush.
> Well, fine. Give thanks and praise
> to everyone for their grand attentive efforts
> to save from ruin the tires and shoes we lack,
> and in such a rushed and hurried fashion.
> Only it's a pity that those who were marched
> in muted crowds toward their death here
> had to wear down their own shoe-bottoms
> as they trod along the pockmarked road in despair.
> Maybe it would have been easier to endure
> the pain while taking those last steps
> if those potholes and pits couldn't breathe

> *their grave-like dreams in advance.*
> *O, it'd be better if the sparkling asphalt*
> *didn't cover the potholes and pits—*
> *didn't curb what's still aching*
> *and didn't heal wounds on this mournful street!*
> *Let the young people walk along here*
> *and sometimes trip over potholes*
> *lest they forget the terror of those times,*
> *those columns of the condemned and despairing!*

See Kin, *Babyn Yar*, 112–15, 233–34.

38. Pinkus, *The Soviet Government and the Jews 1948–1967*, 437.
39. For a comparative study of the gulag versus the Nazi concentration camp experience as reflected in literary works, among them survivor memoirs, see Leona Toker, *Gulag Literature and the Literature of Nazi Camps: An Intertextual Reading* (Indiana University Press, 2019). For Toker, the comparative reading between the two is a case in point for multidirectional memory and the possibility that the two experiences may reciprocally shed light on each other, rather than compete in a zero-sum game. Nonetheless, she notes a key distinction between the gulag and the extermination centers of the Nazis' Final Solution, the latter being where mass murder in and of itself was the ultimate goal.
40. Zakharchuk, "Babyn Yar in Belles-Lettres," 225.
41. Nekrasov, *Arestovannye stranitsy*, 188.
42. Nekrasov, *Arestovannye stranitsy*, 191–92.
43. See "Aktion 1005," Shoah Resource Center, accessed January 1, 2019, https://www.yadvashem.org/odot_pdf/Microsoft%20Word%20-%205721.pdf. As Victoria Khiterer notes, "Beginning in July 1943 SS personnel were given the task of eliminating all evidence of the massacre. To achieve this, the corpses were exhumed and burnt. The task of exhumation, moving and burning was forced on inmates of the Syrets concentration camp." SS colonel Paul Blobel, who oversaw the destruction of all evidence of Nazi war crimes in the East, testified: "During my visit in August (1943) I myself witnessed the burning of corpses in a mass grave near Kyiv. This grave was approximately 55 meters long, 3 meters wide and 2.5 meters deep." See Khiterer, "Babi Yar," 10.
44. Nekrasov, "Zapiski zevaki," 386 (author's translation).
45. Nekrasov, "Zapiski zevaki," 345; Michael Falchikov, introduction to *Postscripts* by Viktor Nekrasov (Quartet Books, 1991), ix–xvii, here xiv. Nekrasov was, in fact, ambivalent about his expulsion from the party. While he joined it in Stalingrad, at the peak of World War II, and wholeheartedly embraced its dogma, he never forgot how critical his aunt was about his becoming a party member, a move she saw as a sheer expression of careerism. The loss of party membership, Nekrasov admitted, only further loosened

his obligation to Soviet dogma and allowed him to both live and write more candidly. See Nekrasov, *Arestovannye stranitsy*, 81.
46. Pinkus, *The Soviet Government and the Jews 1948–1967*, 436.
47. Gitelman, *A Century of Ambivalence*, 161–67.
48. Pinkus, *The Soviet Government and the Jews 1948–1967*, 96. The Soviet authorities responded to the affair, first in complete denial. Three weeks later, they relented and made several arrests, sentencing the culprits to no longer than ten to twelve years in prison. Western lawyers who inquired about the affair could not obtain full details of the events in Malakhovka. See Bilinsky, *The Second Soviet Republic*, 406. Bilinsky, in his discussion of Ukrainian–Jewish relations, cites this case by way of showing that antisemitic bias was not something endemic only to Ukrainian society. On the Malakhovka affair, see also Ben Zion Goldberg, *The Jewish Problem in the Soviet Union: Analysis and Solution* (Greenwood Press, 1982), 282–86.
49. Mankoff, "Babi Yar and the Struggle for Memory," 403.
50. Pinkus, *The Soviet Government and the Jews 1948–1967*, 436.
51. Nekrasov, "Zapiski zevaki," 391.
52. *Samizdat* refers to self-published materials that were illegally printed and circulated, and *tamizdat* refers to works published abroad.
53. Nekrasov, *Arestovannye stranitsy*, 133.
54. Richard Sheldon noted that Nekrasov's essay was a "bold and passionate appeal to commemorate the [Jewish] victims [of Babyn Yar]." See Sheldon, "The Transformation of Babi Yar," 134; and Pinkus, *The Soviet Government and the Jews 1948–1967*, 97.
55. Clowes, "Constructing the Memory of the Holocaust," 166.
56. Nekrasov, "Zapiski zevaki," 385.
57. Nekrasov, "Zapiski zevaki," 390.
58. Nekrasov, *Arestovannye stranitsy*, 184.
59. Feferman, *Soviet Jewish Stepchild*, 7.
60. Michael Rothberg, *Multidirectional Memory: Remembering the Holocaust in the Age of Decolonization* (Stanford University Press, 2009), 3.
61. Rothberg, *Multidirectional Memory*, 11.

CHAPTER 3

1. Zubok, *Zhivago's Children*, 196. According to Zubok, the Second Thaw was ushered in only in October 1961 in the wake of the Twenty-Second Party Congress. Khrushchev's attack on abstract art upon his visit to the State Exhibition Hall in the Manege (the former czarist stables near the Kremlin) on December 1, 1962, was the first sign that this period of liberalization was about to end. The scholar Katerina Clark offers a different division of the Thaw era into three subperiods, with the first thaw occurring in 1954 (after the September 1953 Central Committee plenum), the second in 1956 following

Khrushchev's Secret Speech, and the third after the Twenty-Second Party Congress. See Katerina Clark, *The Soviet Novel: History as Ritual*, 3rd ed. (Indiana University Press, 2000), 211. Edward Brown proposes a similar division into three thaws in his book on Soviet literature. See Brown, *Russian Literature Since the Revolution*, 238–93. In my discussion of the Second Thaw, I adhere to Peter Rudy's periodical categorization, dating its beginning point to early to mid-1961 (prior to the Party Congress), when a number of works signaling a change of current in the Russian literary climate were published, among them the story "Kira Georgevna" by Viktor Nekrasov, the short story "By the Light of the Day" by E. Kazakevich, the novel *A Ticket to the Stars* by Vasilii Aksyonov, and the poem "Babi Yar" by Yevgeny Yevtushenko. See Peter Rudy, "The Soviet Russian Literary Scene in 1961: A Mild Permafrost Thaw," *Modern Language Journal* 46, no. 6 (1962): 245–54.

2. Zubok, *Zhivago's Children*, 194, 204.
3. Ehrenburg's memoirs began to be serialized in *Novy mir* as early as 1960, embodying the aspirations of its new editor, Alexander Tvardovsky, who in June 1958, after he had been dismissed from this position four years earlier, was reappointed as the periodical's editor. It was, however, only in 1961 that Ehrenburg's memoirs started to include anti-Stalinist materials of a more radical character, where vivid descriptions of the Great Terror and anti-Stalinist campaigns were rendered to the Soviet reader. See Spechler, *Permitted Dissent*, 144; Rubenstein, *Tangled Loyalties*, 344; and Patricia Blake, introduction to *Half-Way to the Moon: New Writing from Russia*, ed. Patricia Blake and Max Hayward (Encounter, 1964), 14.
4. Kenez, *A History of the Soviet Union*, 210–12.
5. Peter Vail and Alexander Genis, *Shestidesyatie: mir Sovetskogo cheloveka* (Ardis, 1989), 3.
6. Vail and Genis, *Shestidesyatie*, 7.
7. Rudy, "The Soviet Russian Literary Scene in 1961," 247.
8. As Vladislav Zubok notes, the term *shestidesiatniki*, translated as "[the generation] of the sixties," was coined as early as 1960. It referred to a young group of people who conceived of themselves as people who could think more independently and be able to better reflect on life's complexities than the generation of their parents, who had spent their formative years in the Stalinist terrorist state. See Zubok, *Zhivago's Children*, 162.
9. Gennady Estraikh, "Yevgeny Yevtushenko's 'Babi Yar': A Russian Poet's Page in Post-Holocaust History," in *Distrust, Animosity, and Solidarity: Jews and Non-Jews During the Holocaust in the USSR*, ed. Christoph Dieckmann and Arkdai Zeltser (Yad Vashem, 2021), 331–70, here 331.
10. Estraikh, "Yevgeny Yevtushenko's 'Babi Yar,'" 121.
11. M. F. P'yanyh, "Yevtushenko, Yevgenii Alexandrovich," in *Russkie pisateli: dvadtsatyy vek* (Prosveshchenie, 1987).
12. Estraikh, "Yevgeny Yevtushenko's 'Babi Yar,'" 334.

13. Estraikh, "Yevgeny Yevtushenko's 'Babi Yar,'" 334. See also E. Sidorov, *Yevgenii Yevtushenko: lichnost' i tvorchestvo* (Hudozesvennaya Literatura, 1987), 22.
14. Sidorov, *Yevgenii Yevtushenko*, 31.
15. B. Rubin, commenting on Yevtushenko's success less than two years after the publication of his "Babi Yar," goes even further to argue that the commercial success of Yevtushenko as a young poet who managed in a short period of time to sell more than 100,000 copies of his books was unparalleled in the history of poetry. See B. Rubin, "Uroki odnoi poeticheskoi biografii: zametki o lirike Yevgeniya Yevtushenko," *Voprosy literatury* 2 (1963): 17–45, here 17.
16. While never touching upon the theme of antisemitism as blatantly as he did in "Babi Yar," Yevtushenko was among the first Soviet writers to engage this theme, which he did as early as 1954. See Albert Todd, ed. *Yevgeny Yevtushenko: The Collected Poems, 1952–1990* (Henry Holt, 1991), xxi.
17. Yevgeny Yevtushenko, *Early Poems* (Marion Boyars, 1989), 145.
18. Feferman, *Soviet Jewish Stepchild*, 48.
19. Yevgeny Yevtushenko, *A Precocious Autobiography*, trans. Andrew R. MacAndrew (Dutton, 1963), 116.
20. Shimon Markish, "The Role of Officially Published Russian Literature in the Reawakening of Jewish National Consciousness (1953–1970)," in *Jewish Culture and Identity in the Soviet Union*, ed. Yaacov Ro'i and Avi Beker (New York University Press, 1991), 208–30, here 224; Clowes, "Constructing the Memory of the Holocaust," 168.
21. Todd, *Yevgeny Yevtushenko*, xix. Todd notes that it was only in 1983 when a three-volume edition of Yevtuhsenko's poetry came out that the ban on the reprinting of the poem was lifted. Even then, though, the poem was elucidated by a footnote explaining to the reader that not only Jews were among Babyn Yar's victims. Todd further adds that Yevtushenko was not allowed to take part in any poetry recitation event in the Soviet Republic of the Ukraine until perestroika.
22. Korey, "In History's 'Memory Hole,'" 154.
23. Sidorov, *Yevgenii Yevtushenko*, 70; Clowes, "Constructing the Memory of the Holocaust," 166.
24. The poem was translated into English by Richard Sheldon and appeared in the anthology edited by Maxim Shrayer, *Voices of Jewish-Russian Literature: An Anthology* (Academic Studies Press, 2018), 464–69.
25. Assia Kovrigina Kreidich, "Babyn Yar in Personal Accounts," in *Babyn Yar: History and Memory*, ed. Vladyslav Hrynevych and Paul Robert Magocsi (Dukh I Litera, 2016), 157–78, here 165, 167.
26. For the differing accounts of the reasons that led Yevtushenko to familiarize himself and take a keen interest in Babyn Yar, see Emanuel Diamant, "Babi Yar, o kotorom vy nichego (ili pochti nichego) ne znaete: neizvestnyie I maloizvestnyie materialy po

istorii Bab'ego Yara," accessed January 1, 2018, https://nekrasov-viktor.com/images/Papers/Diamant-Emanuel-Babiy-Yar-o-kotorom-vi-nichego-ili-pochti-nichego-ne-znaete.pdf.

27. Nakhmanovich, "Rasstrely i zakhoroneniya," 201. The unofficial figure of casualties of the Kurenivka mudslide was a great deal higher, reaching 1,500 persons.

28. Diamant, "Babi Yar, o kotorom vy nichego (ili pochti nichego) ne znaete." For Diamant, the mentioning of a ravine in the poem had a clear political underlying motive: "In August 1961, Yevgeny Yevtushenko was brought here, who then wrote his famous poem. But Yevtushenko, as always, was disingenuous—he wrote not about the destruction of Babi Yar, but that everything was in order, Babi Yar exists, only there is no monument.... This was exactly what the authorities needed to deflect attention from the destruction of Babyn Yar. Yevtushenko was slightly reprimanded for his poem and sent on a business trip abroad to convince people that everything was okay and nothing happened" (14).

29. In all likelihood, the crucified Jew featured in the poem is a reference to Jesus. It makes one wonder how relevant and tasteful the mentioning of the murder of Christ is—a crime for which Jews have been persecuted throughout the generations—in a poem dedicated to Jewish martyrdom. Richard Sheldon considers this one of the poem's most apparent flaws, as he argues that its "extravagant, presumptuous list of parallels [of the Hebrews in Egypt, Christ, the boy in Białystok, and Anne Frank] imparts to the poem a bombastic, egocentric quality that does not accord well with the subject matter." See Sheldon, "The Transformation of Babi Yar," 138. In Yevtushenko's defense, it may be argued that growing up in the first atheist state in history he might have simply been unaware of the crucifixion of Jesus seen from the historical perspective of the Jewish people. Wishing to conjure up an image of Jewish martyrdom drawn from ancient times, Yevtushenko found it in Christ, a symbol far more familiar to him. Interestingly, Sheldon's criticism of Yevtushenko for being egocentric and often overly pompous in his tone was echoed in the reaction of Soviet conservative critics, who from the time Yevtushenko made his debut leveled at him similar accusations for being loud, immodest, bombastic, and frivolous. See Rubin, "Uroki odnoi poeticheskoi biografii," 21.

30. On the publication of Anne Frank's diary in the USSR, together with the featuring of theatrical performances of plays based on it, see Gennady Estraikh, "Soviet Publications of Holocaust Diaries in the 1960s: Anne Frank and Masha Rolnikaite," *Holocaust and Genocide Studies* 36, no. 1 (Spring 2022): 60–73, https://doi.org/10.1093/hgs/dcac004.

31. Richard Sakwa, *The Rise and Fall of the Soviet Union, 1917–1991* (Routledge, 1999), 329–30.

32. Vail and Genis, *Shestidesyatie*, 25. As George Reavey notes, the years 1959–1962 saw the swift rise of Yevtushenko's editions from 20,000 to 100,000 copies. See George

Reavey, "Yevgeny Yevtushenko: Man and Poet," in Yevgeny Yevtushenko, *Early Poems*, trans. George Reavey (Marion Boyars, 1989), xxii.
33. Solomon Shvarts, *Evrei v Sovetskom Soyuze: s nachala Vtoroi mirovoi voiny 1939–1965* (Amerikanskogo Evreisokogo Rabochego Komiteta, 1966), 371.
34. Shvarts, *Evrei v Sovetskom Soyuze*, 371.
35. William Korey, *The Soviet Cage: Antisemitism in Russia* (Viking Press, 1973), 106.
36. Mankoff, "Babi Yar and the Struggle for Memory," 404. Mankoff offers an exploration of Soviet literary pieces dedicated to Babyn Yar from the Stalin era up until the collapse of the Soviet Union. The underlying argument of his discussion is that these works helped gradually galvanize the Soviet Jewish "counter-memory" of the events that took place at Babyn Yar. He notes that "Babi Yar" by Yevtushenko was pivotal in turning the ravine from the concern of a few families and Kyiv residents into an international issue.
37. A. Markov, "Moi otvet," *Literatura i zhizn'*, September 24, 1961; D. Starikov, "Ob odnom sithotvorenii," *Literatura i zhizn'*, September 27, 1961.
38. Shvarts, *Evrei v Sovetskom Soyuze*, 363–64.
39. Sheldon, "The Transformation of Babi Yar," 138. Sheldon argues that "like Ehrenburg, Yevtushenko has an almost uncanny ability to sense the limits to which he can go in challenging official positions, and this poem demonstrates this quality."
40. Sheldon, "The Transformation of Babi Yar," 138.
41. Yevtushenko, *Early Poems*, 149.
42. Sheldon, "The Transformation of Babi Yar," 138.
43. V. Y. Afian et al., eds. *Apparat Ts.K. K.P.S.S. I kul'tura 1958–1964: Dokumenty* (Rosspen, 2005), 543.
44. Edwin McDowell, "Brodsky Quits Arts Group over Yevtushenko Induction," *New York Times*, June 20, 1987, https://www.nytimes.com/1987/06/20/arts/brodsky-quits-arts-group-over-yevtushenko-induction.html.
45. Deming Brown, *Soviet Russian Literature Since Stalin* (Cambridge University Press, 1978), 114.
46. See David Lowe, *Russian Writing Since 1953: A Critical Survey* (Ungar, 1987), 135. For another critical account of Yevtushenko presented from a similar angle from a post-Soviet Russian critic, see Viktor Erofeev, *Muzhchiny* (Zebra E, 2004), 102.
47. Ludmila Shtern, *Brodsky: A Personal Memoir* (Baskerville Publishers, 2004), 286–87.
48. Yevtushenko, *A Precocious Autobiography*, 124.
49. Yevtushenko, *A Precocious Autobiography*, 124–25.
50. John Garrard and Carol Garrard, *Inside the Soviet Writers' Union* (Free Press, 1990), 114–36.
51. Reavey, "Yevgeny Yevtushenko," xxvii. On the proximity of the publication of "Babi Yar"

to Yevtushenko's trip to Cuba, see also Yevgeny Yevtushenko, *Shestidesyatnik: memuarnaya proza* (Zebra E, 2006), 218–20.
52. Zubok, *Zhivago's Children*, 73, 197.
53. Jacob Silverman, "Inside the FBI's File on Soviet Poet-Dissident Yevgeny Yevtushenko: What the Bureau's Decades-Long Surveillance of the International Celebrity Reveals About the U.S. Government's Cold War Pathologies," *New Republic*, September 21, 2020. https://newrepublic.com/article/159382/fbi-surveillance-russian-poet-yevgeny-yevtushenko-cold-war.
54. Yevgeny Yevtushenko, "Styd kak soavtor," in *Shestidesyatnik: memuarnaya proza* (Zebra E, 2006), 412–15. See also Alice Nakhimovsky, "Yevgenii Yevtushenko," in *Holocaust Literature: An Encyclopedia of Writers and Their Work*, ed. S. Lillian Kremer (Routledge, 2002).
55. Vail and Genis, *Shestidesyatie*, 22.
56. Svetlana Boym, *Common Places: Mythologies of Everyday Life in Russia* (Harvard University Press, 1994), 94–95; James H. Billington, *The Icon and the Axe: An Interpretive History of Russian Culture* (Knopf, 1966), 567.
57. Vail and Genis, *Shestidesyatie*, 21.
58. See Edward J. Brown, *Mayakovsky: A Poet in the Revolution* (Princeton University Press, 1973), 24.
59. Blake, introduction, 25.
60. Patricia Polock Brodsky, "'Babi Yar': Poem by Yevgenii Yevtushenko, 1961," in *Reference Guide to Holocaust Literature*, ed. Thomas Riggs (St. James Press, 2002).
61. The application of these literary devices by Yevtushenko so as to conjure up a poetic style suitable for public declamation is discussed in Brown, *Soviet Russian Literature Since Stalin*, 115.
62. Yevtushenko, *Early Poems*, 112–15, 120–23.
63. The Bagerovo ditch is the first major anti-Jewish Nazi mass murder site on Soviet soil to be retaken by the Red Army. In Selvinsky's case, the poetic response to the mass murder was immediate. Selvinsky visited the site on January 11, 1942, only a few weeks after the carnage. His poem "I Saw It" was published right afterward, on January 23, 1942. See Maxim D. Shrayer, *I Saw It: Ilya Selvinsky and the Legacy of Bearing Witness to the Shoah* (Academic Studies Press, 2013), 82–86.
64. Shrayer, *I Saw It*, 149.
65. Lawrence L. Langer, *Holocaust Testimonies: The Ruins of Memory* (Yale University Press, 1991), 6.
66. Marianne Hirsch, *The Generation of Postmemory: Writing and Visual Culture After the Holocaust* (Columbia University Press, 2012), 3.
67. Hirsch, *The Generation of Postmemory*, 36.

CHAPTER 4

1. Pinkus, *The Soviet Government and the Jews*, 98; Shvarts, *Evrei v Sovetskom Soyuze*, 366–68.
2. Yevtushenko, *Shestidesyatnik*, 417–19.
3. "1962," Dmitri Shostakovich, Life Chronicles, accessed January 1, 2019, http://shostakovich.ru/en/life/1962/.
4. On the attack launched against *Lady Macbeth*, see Roy Blokker and Robert Dearling, *The Music of Dmitri Shostakovich: The Symphonies* (Fairleigh Dickinson University Press, 1979), 24–27. See also Laurel E. Fay, *Shostakovich: A Life* (Oxford University Press, 2000), 87–105.
5. This trio was composed in 1944 and was dedicated to the victims of Majdanek, Jews and non-Jews alike. The Majdanek theme from it was also quoted in a later work by the composer, the celebrated String Quartet No. 8, which was composed in 1960. See Robert Stradling, "Shostakovich and the Soviet System, 1925–1975," in *Shostakovich: The Man and His Music*, ed. Christopher Norris (Marion Boyars, 1982), 189–218, here 211.
6. Francis Maes, *A History of Russian Music: From* Kamarinskaya *to* Babi Yar, trans. Arnold J. Pomerans and Erica Pomerans (University of California Press, 2006), 365.
7. Maes, *A History of Russian Music*, 353.
8. Maes, *A History of Russian Music*, 365.
9. Fay, *Shostakovich*, 218–19.
10. Fay, *Shostakovich*, 218–19.
11. Zubok, *Zhivago's Children*, 193.
12. Zubok, *Zhivago's Children*, 211.
13. Shvarts, *Evrei v Sovetskom Soyuze*, 368.
14. Zubok, *Zhivago's Children*, 212.
15. Korey, "Babyn Yar Remembered," 33. Korey's account is confirmed by Solomon Shvarts, who also linked the December 17 meeting between Khrushchev and the artists to the provocation that Yevtushenko's "Babi Yar" caused. See Shvarts, *Evrei v Sovetskom Soyuze*, 368.
16. From an interview given to O. Dvornichenko. See "1962," accessed January 1, 2019, http://shostakovich.ru/en/life/1962/.
17. Korey, "Babyn Yar Remembered," 34.
18. Cited in Olga Gershenson, *The Phantom Holocaust: Soviet Cinema and Jewish Catastrophe* (Rutgers University Press, 2013), 58.
19. Gershenson, *The Phantom Holocaust*, 58.
20. Fay, *Shostakovich*, 237; Shvarts, *Evrei v Sovetskom Soyuze*, 370.
21. "Symphony No 13. Op. 113. Score," Dmitri Shostakovich, New Collected Works, accessed January 1, 2019, http://shostakovich.ru/en/issue/13/.
22. Even further highlighting the boldness that Shostakovich displayed by writing a symphony dedicated to Babyn Yar is the suggestion that Shostakovich's "Babi Yar" is

seamlessly linked to his symphonic cycle. According to Hugh Ottaway, it is very telling that the opus numbers of the Twelfth Symphony, which dealt with the October Revolution and concluded with a final movement titled "The Dawn of Humanity," are consecutive with the opus numbers of the Thirteenth Symphony. Ottaway wonders aloud whether Shostakovich consciously chose to turn from what was seen in Soviet eyes as the pinnacle in the history of humankind to the first movement in his next symphony, focusing on one of its most barbarous moments. See Blokker and Dearling, *The Music of Dmitri Shostakovich*, 134.

23. See Korey, *The Soviet Cage*, 114; and Sheldon, "The Transformation of Babi Yar," 141.
24. Sheldon, "The Transformation of Babyn Yar," 140.
25. "Symphony No 13. Op. 113. Score," accessed January 1, 2019, http://shostakovich.ru /en/issue/13/.
26. Blokker and Dearling, *The Music of Dmitri Shostakovich*, 174.
27. Blokker and Dearling, *The Music of Dmitri Shostakovich*, 174.
28. Maes, *A History of Russian Music*, 368.

## CHAPTER 5

1. See chapter 4. See also P. A. Nikolaev, ed., *Russkie pisateli 20 veka: biograficheskii slovar'* (Randevu-AM, 2000), s.v. "Kuznetsov, Anatolii Vasil'evich." Among Kuznetsov's classmates who attended the institute from 1955 to 1960 were also the poet Bella Akhmadulina and the writer Anatoly Gladilin. See conversation no. 10 in the transcription of Kuznetsov's Radio Liberty conversation in Anatoly Kuznetsov, *Babi Yar: roman-dokument* (Astrel', 2010), 536.
2. Anatoly Kuznetsov, "Babi Yar," *Iunost'* 8–10 (1966).
3. Sheldon, "The Transformation of Babi Yar," 143.
4. Naya Lekht, "Narratives of Return: Babii Yar and Holocaust Literature in the Soviet Union," PhD diss., University of California, Los Angeles, 2013, 5.
5. Anatoly Kuznetsov, *Babi Yar: A Document in the Form of a Novel*, trans. David Floyd (Farrar, Straus and Giroux, 1970), 13. All of the citations from Kuznetsov's novel will be quoted from Floyd's translation. For the first full Russian version of the novel, see Anatoly Kuznetsov, *Babi Yar: roman-dokument* (Posev, 1970). Except for the *Iunost'* edition, the novel also appeared in the USSR in book form. See Anatoly Kuznetsov, *Babi Yar: roman-dokument* (Molodaya Gvardiya, 1967). The Floyd edition contains the expanded version of the novel that includes the parts excised by the Soviet censor as well as later additions introduced by Kuznetsov in exile. In order to highlight the distinctiveness of each part of the novel, the Floyd edition has the censored component printed in regular typeface, the uncensored in a bold one, and the additions introduced while in exile in brackets. The novel also appeared three years earlier in its first English edition under a different title: *Babi Yar: A Documentary Novel* (Dial, 1967).
6. Kuznetsov, *Babi Yar*, 65 (emphasis in the original).

7. This novella was among the pieces that inaugurated the genre of the semi-confessional "young prose" of the Thaw period, works that sought to revitalize Communists' values and rebel against what was perceived by their authors as an older, stagnating Stalin-era generation. See Leona Toker, "Anatolii Kuznetsov," in *Dictionary of Literary Biography*, Vol. 299, *Holocaust Novelists*, ed. Ephraim Sicher (Gale, 2004), 195–200.
8. Efraim Sicher, *The Holocaust Novel* (Routledge, 2005), 116.
9. Sheldon, "The Transformation of Babi Yar," 144.
10. Toker, "Anatolii Kuznetsov," 195–200; Sheldon, "The Transformation of Babi Yar," 145.
11. Kuznetsov's son Aleksei provides interesting background details about the trip. Prior to the trip, Kuznetsov declared that he would like to work on a new novel dealing with one of the early congresses of the Russian Social-Democratic Labour Party in London. Kuznetsov insisted that he would be allowed to travel to the city in order to "feel its atmosphere" and to be able to visit Karl Marx's grave and spend time in the British Museum's library, where Vladimir I. Lenin had worked. Aleksei Kuznetsov also notes that what helped his father get the consent of the authorities for this writing project was the imminent centennial of Lenin's birth. See Aleksei Kuznetsov, *Mezhdu Grinvichem i Kurenevkoy: pis'ma Anatoliya Kuznetsova materi iz emigratsii v Kiev* (Zaharov, 2002), 11.
12. Nikolaev, *Russkie pisateli 20 veka*, s.v. "Kuznetsov, Anatolii Vasil'evich."
13. Masha Gessen, introduction to *Babi Yar: A Document in the Form of a Novel; New, Complete, Uncensored Version*, by Anatoly Kuznetsov, trans. David Floyd (Picador, 2023), ix–xxiv, here xvii.
14. Gessen, introduction, xviii.
15. Emil Staiger, *Basic Concepts of Poetics*, ed. Marianne Burkhard and Luanne T. Frank, trans. Janette C. Hudson and Luanne T. Frank (Pennsylvania State University Press, 1991), 181.
16. For the section on the human-made famine that occurred because of Stalin's forced collectivization policy, a crime that, as Kuznetsov confesses in his novel, his staunch Stalinist father partook in, see Kuznetsov, *Babi Yar*, 120–22. On the attempts to flood Babyn Yar after the war with pulp, leading to its tragic flooding, and the first mass ceremony at the site conducted on the twenty-fifth anniversary of the massacre, see 471–75.
17. James Young, *Writing and Rewriting the Holocaust: Narrative and the Consequences of Interpretation* (Indiana University Press, 1988), 25.
18. Kuznetsov, *Babi Yar*, 13.
19. Young, *Writing and Rewriting the Holocaust*, 51.
20. Sicher, *The Holocaust Novel*, x.
21. Tumarkin, *The Living and the Dead*, 123.
22. Kuznetsov, *Babi Yar*, 14 (emphasis in the original).
23. Young, *Writing and Rewriting the Holocaust*, 55. While Kuznetsov insists in the prelude to Pronicheva's account that he submitted her account "from her own words, without

adding anything of my own," the historian Karel Berkhoff has called this proclamation into question. In his careful analysis of the twelve testimonies that Dina Pronicheva submitted from 1946 to 1968 dealing with her survival of the Babyn Yar massacre, Berkhoff further undermines Kuznetsov's claim for veracity in his novel. While his exploration of all these documents points to Pronicheva's consistency and reliability, he points to the fact that Kuznetsov's account includes greater detail. Berkhoff raises the suspicion that these additions were a result of the novelist's "notion that he had some artistic license." See Karel C. Berkhoff, "Dina Pronicheva's Story of Surviving the Babi Yar Massacre: German, Jewish, Soviet, Russian, and Ukrainian Records," in *The Shoah in the Ukraine: History, Testimony, Memorialization*, ed. Ray Brandon and Wendy Lower (Indiana University Press, 2008), 291–317, here 305.

24. Young, *Writing and Rewriting the Holocaust*, 62.
25. Leona Toker, "Toward a Poetic of Documentary Prose: From the Perspective of Gulag Testimonies," *Poetics Today* 18, no. 2 (1997): 187–222.
26. Toker, "Toward a Poetic of Documentary Prose," 196.
27. Nikolaev, *Russkie pisateli 20 veka*, s.v. "Kuznetsov, Anatolii Vasil'evich."
28. Kuznetsov, *Babi Yar*, 420.
29. Kuznetsov, *Babi Yar*, 292.
30. Kuznetsov, *Babi Yar*, 155.
31. Kuznetsov, *Babi Yar*, 16–17.
32. Kuznetsov, *Babi Yar*, 16–17.
33. Kuznetsov, *Babi Yar*, 67.
34. Clowes, "Constructing the Memory of the Holocaust," 171.
35. Kuznetsov, *Babi Yar*, 88, 152.
36. For a good summary of the different facets of focalization in a work of fiction, see Shlomith Rimmon-Kenan, *Narrative Fiction: Contemporary Poetics*, 2nd ed. (Routledge, 2002), 83.
37. Leona Toker, "Target Audience, Hurdle Audience, and the General Reader: Varlam Shalamov's Art of Testimony," *Poetics Today* 26, no. 2 (2005): 281–303.
38. Clowes, "Constructing the Memory of the Holocaust," 173.
39. Kuznetsov, *Babi Yar*, 565 (author's translation).
40. Sicher, *The Holocaust Novel*, 117.

## CHAPTER 6

1. David Shneer, *Yiddish and the Creation of Soviet Yiddish Culture, 1918–1930* (Cambridge University Press, 2004), 91.
2. Shneer, *Yiddish and the Creation of Soviet Yiddish Culture*, 103. For more on the Kultur Lige, see Gennady Estraikh, *In Harness, Yiddish Writer's Romance with Communism* (Syracuse University Press, 2005), 6–36.
3. Shneer, *Yiddish and the Creation of Soviet Yiddish Culture*, 123, 144.

4. For a detailed list of Yiddish cultural institutions operating in the Ukraine, see Esther Rosenthal-Shneiderman, *Oyf vegn un umvegn: zikhroynes, geshe'enishen, perzenlekhkeytn*, Vol. 2 (Farlag Y.L. Perets, 1978), 126–31.
5. This institute was founded in 1929 as the reorganization of the Department of Jewish Culture operating under the aegis of the Ukrainian Academy of Sciences. For a description of this institution beyond its depiction in the memoir by Rosenthal-Shneiderman, who was one of its staff members, see Vladimir Bilovitski, "Institute of Jewish Proletarian Culture," *The Yivo Encyclopedia of Jews in Eastern Europe*, accessed December 12, 2012, http://www.yivoencyclopedia.org/article.aspx/Institute_of_Jewish_Proletarian _Culture.
6. Pinkus, *The Soviet Government and the Jews 1948–1967*, 11.
7. This negative attitude was also reflected later on in the definition of the Jews as a "nationality" (*natsionalnost'*), the lowest category in the Soviet ranking of nations: below a nation, a people, or even a "minute people" (*narondnost'*) like the small ethnic groups living in Siberia and the Northern Caucasus. The term "nationality" was mainly political, as it had to be recorded on all passports from December 1932. This practice allowed the Soviet regime to treat the Jews as scattered individuals on the one hand and, at the same time, devise a system that would identify them and assist the Soviet state in introducing any discriminatory policies aimed at Soviet Jews, on the other. See Pinkus, *The Soviet Government and the Jews 1948–1967*, 14.
8. Pinkus, *The Soviet Government and the Jews 1948–1967*, 12.
9. Benjamin Pinkus, *The Jews of the Soviet Union: The History of a National Minority* (Cambridge University Press, 1988), 72.
10. Gitelman, *A Century of Ambivalence*, 89.
11. Hans Kohn, "Soviet Communism and Nationalism: Three Stages of Historical Development," in *Soviet Nationality Problems*, ed. Edward Allworth (Columbia University Press, 1971), 43–71, here 57. As Benjamin Pinkus notes, Stalin's turn from the internationalist stance of Lenin to "socialism in one country" also affected the closure of non-Russian nationalist institutions in general and the Yiddish ones in particular, as it freed the Soviet government from the need to care too much about its image abroad. See Pinkus, *The Jews of the Soviet Union*, 62.
12. Joshua Rubenstein and Vladimir P. Naumov, eds., *Stalin's Secret Pogrom: The Postwar Inquisition of the Jewish Anti-Fascist Committee*, trans. Laura Wolfson (Yale University Press, 2001), 2, 60.
13. Yehoshua Gilboa, *The Black Years of Soviet Jewry: 1939–1953* (Little, Brown, 1971), 104.
14. Altshuler, *Yahadut bamakhbesh haSovieti*, 13, 23.
15. Altshuler, *Yahadut bamakhbesh haSovieti*, 27, 30. Altshuler notes that on the eve of World War II only a handful of synagogues were still functioning in the Soviet Union; most of them remained empty. This situation was altered when, soon after the outbreak

of the war, Jews in the many Soviet cities thronged to new synagogues and old ones. Among those attending these synagogues were many Jewish refugees who fled the western frontiers and went to the Russian heartland. Later on, the Soviet for Religious Affairs started to supervise the legalization of Jewish community centers (*obshiny*, which in the Soviet sense, it should be noted, was a reference to synagogues) in many localities. By 1948, there were 161 such communities registered in the USSR (16, 24, 48).

16. Gitelman, *A Century of Ambivalence*, 145.
17. Gitelman, *A Century of Ambivalence*, 145.
18. Shneer, *Through Soviet Jewish Eyes*, 203.
19. During the Nazi invasion, over fifty Soviet Yiddish writers fell at the front. See S. L. Shneiderman, "Yiddish in the USSR," *New York Times Book Review*, November 25, 1970, 71.
20. While this renaissance of Jewish nationalism in Soviet Yiddish literature was characterized by the elaboration of themes that up until the outbreak of the war were either neglected or suppressed, it also had an important linguistic aspect. With the outbreak of the war and the news about the mass murders of Jews, one may discern in the language of many Soviet Yiddish writers a new predilection to include more Hebrew words and expressions, including terms and concepts drawn from Biblical Hebrew, a practice that was overwhelmingly banned during the 1930s. This development was another indication of the Soviet Yiddish writers' desire to view themselves as part of a long-standing Yiddish literary and linguistic continuum rooted in the medieval Ashkenazi past. See Khone Shmeruk, "Sifrut Yidish biVrit-hamo'atsot," *Behinot* 1 (1970): 5–26, here 24.
21. Shmeruk, "Sifrut Yidish biVrit-hamo'atsot," 23–24.
22. This unique feature of wartime Soviet Yiddish literature focusing on the theme of revenge was observed by the two great American Yiddish literature critics, Nahman Mayzel and Shmuel Niger, the former, a Soviet sympathizer (who moderated his support for Moscow in the wake of the anti-Cosmopolitan campaign) and the latter, a vehement critique of the course that Soviet Jewish literature had taken prior to the outbreak of World War II. Mayzel, aware of the absence of a specific Jewish reaction in Soviet Yiddish literary responses to the war and the abundance of works that viewed the Jews as no more than rank-and-file members of the larger Soviet nation (Markish's poem, echoing the slogan espoused by the Soviet regime during the war "For the People and the Fatherland," is representative of this trend), concentrated on the uniqueness of the Soviet Jewish response to the Nazis. He noted that in contrast to many Yiddish writers in other countries who wrote about the war from a distance, it was only the Soviet Yiddish writers who took active part in the military struggle against the Nazis. See Nahman Mayzel, *Dos yidishe shafn un der yidisher shrayber in sovetnfarband* (Ikuf, 1959), 82. Shmuel Niger, by contrast, was not impressed by what he saw as empty slogans, as the transmission of hackneyed Soviet war propaganda in a Jewish language, geared toward

a Jewish audience. Nonetheless, even Niger had to soften his tone and explain to his American readers that in the Soviet Union, in a country where "one is totally preoccupied, and one has to be preoccupied by one thing—getting rid of the dangerous and murderous foe"—Soviet Yiddish literature had to emphasize the themes of heroism and revenge. See Shmuel Niger, *Yidishe shrayber in Sovet-rusland* (Altveltlekhn Kultur Kongres, 1958), 254–55, 424.

23. Harriet Murav, *Music from a Speeding Train: Jewish Literature in Post-Revolution Russia* (Stanford University Press, 2011), 119.
24. Solomon Mikhoels, "Eynikayt in nekome," *Eynikayt*, October 5, 1944, 1.
25. Mikhoels, "Eynikayt in nekome," 1.
26. Aron Kushnirov, "Di muter Rokhl," *Heymland: literarish-kinstlerisher almanakh* 5 (1948): 36–40. I am indebted to Gennady Estraikh for publishing this poem in the Yiddish *Forverts*; Aron Kushnirov, "Di muter Rokhl," *Forverts*, September 30–October 6, 2011, 13. The poem tells the story of an eighty-year-old Kyiv Jewess whose fate was to march, "like all other Jews," to Babyn Yar.
27. Mayzel, *Dos yidishe shafn*, 120.
28. Kushnirov, "Di muter Rokhl," 39 (author's translation).
29. Murav, *Music from a Speeding Train*, 170.
30. Peretz Markish, *Milhome*, Vol. 1 (Ikuf, 1956), 129.
31. The poem was reprinted in Khone Shmeruk, ed., *A shpigl oyf a shteyn: antologye: poezye un proze fun tsvelf farshnitene yidishe shraybers in ratn-farband* (Magnes Press, 1988; photo-offset of the 1964 edition), 490–92.
32. Murav, *Music from a Speeding Train*, 169.
33. Altshuler, *Yahadut bamakhbesh haSovieti*, 102.
34. Mordechai Altshuler, *Yahadut Berit haMo'atsot beaspaklariyah shel itonut Yidish bePolin* (Hebrew University, 1975), xi.
35. The first Yiddish literati who had survived the Stalinist gulag started to come back from exile in 1954–1955. See Gennady Estraikh, *Yiddish in the Cold War* (Legenda, 2008), 48.
36. For the account of Markish's wife Esther, who was notified about the writer's death on November 27, 1955, see Esther Markish, *The Long Return* (Ballantine Books, 1978), 241. About a month later, the literary weekly *Literaturnaya gazeta* announced the foundation of a committee to preside over Markish's legacy. Yiddish cultural activists in the West could have learned from this communication that Markish was no longer alive (as many had suspected) and that his name and reputation had been fully recovered. For more, see p. 248; and Estraikh, *Yiddish in the Cold War*, 18.
37. Benjamin Pinkus points out that not only substantial but also technical obstacles accounted for the delay in the resumption of Yiddish publications in the USSR. See Pinkus, *The Soviet Government and the Jews*, 266. Pinkus, though, joins virtually all scholars who offered a critical analysis of Soviet Yiddish publications and contends

that the chief reason for the delay was the hope of Soviet officials that the demand for the revival of Soviet Yiddish culture would abate parallel to the decline in the number of Yiddish speakers in the Soviet Union. Most representative of this approach was Mikhail Suslov (then a Central Committee and Presidium member and later on the chief party ideologue during the Brezhnev years), who, in 1956, asserted that Yiddish culture was dead and was not worth the effort of rehabilitating. See Abraham Brumberg, "*Sovyetish Heymland* and the Dilemmas of Jewish Life in the USSR," *Soviet Jewish Affairs* 2, no. 1 (1972): 27–41, here 28.

38. Rosenthal, *Hahayim haYehudiyim biVrit-hamo'atsot 1935–1958*, 89.
39. Estraikh, *Yiddish in the Cold War*, 51.
40. Rosental, *Hahayim haYehudiyim biVrit-hamo'atsot 1935–1958*, 89.
41. Gitelman, *A Century of Ambivalence*, 164. In January 1959, Khrushchev ratified this anti-religious campaign, which he saw as an indispensable part of the "transition from socialism to communism." See Altshuler, *Yahadut bamakhbesh haSovieti*, 159.
42. As Zvi Gitelman notes, while the anti-religious campaigns of the early 1920s were carried out by the Evsektsia mainly in the Yiddish language, making, thus, the slandering of Judaism available exclusively for Jews, the Khrushchev campaign was executed in languages accessible to non-Jews. The outcome of this linguistic choice was a surge of antisemitic sentiments. Most malicious of the antisemitic propaganda works of the time was *Judaism Without Embellishment* by Vadim Kichko, which was published in Kyiv in 1963 by the Ukrainian Academy of Sciences. See Gitelman, *A Century of Ambivalence*, 165.
43. A vivid portrayal of Jewish life in the Soviet Union in the early 1960s was given by the writer Elie Wiesel in a book that brought the anti-Jewish repressions implemented by the Khrushchev regime to the attention of the public in the West. See Wiesel, *The Jews of Silence*.
44. Gitelman, *A Century of Ambivalence*, 159–68. Mordechai Altshuler notes that the battle against the "black economy," while ostensibly conducted irrespective of the campaign against Judaism, was, in reality, correlated with it as the Soviet authorities tried to blacken the image of the Jewish communal activists operating the few synagogues still functioning in the country as "charlatans who under the camouflage of religion engage in illegal acts." See Altshuler, *Yahadut bamakhbesh haSovieti*, 168.
45. Joseph Brumberg and Abraham Brumberg, *Sovyetish Heymland: An Analysis* (Anti-Defamation League of B'nai B'rith, 1966), 34.
46. A. Brumberg, "*Sovyetish Heymland* and the Dilemmas," 33.
47. Eleonora Bergman, "Yiddish in Poland After 1945," in *Yiddish and the Left: Papers of the Third Mendel Friedman International Conference on Yiddish*, ed. Mikhail Krutikov and Gennady Estraikh (Legenda, 2001), 167–77, here 169.
48. David Engel, "The Reconstruction of Jewish Communal Institutions in Postwar

Poland: The Origins of the Central Committee of Polish Jews, 1944–1945," *East European Politics and Societies* 10, no. 1 (1996): 85–107, here 87–88, 92, 101, https://doi.org/10.1177/0888325496010001004.
49. See Itsik Kipnis, "On khokhmes, on kheshboynes," *Dos naye lebn*, May 17, 1947, 4, 8.
50. Altshuler, *Yahadut Berit haMo'atsot beaspaklariyah*, xiv.
51. "Undzer veytik un undzer treyst," *Folks-shtime*, April 4, 1956. The article appeared in English in Pinkus, *The Soviet Government and the Jews*, 211. For a list of the publications related to the Holocaust appearing in the Soviet Yiddish press, see Altshuler, *Yahadut Berit haMo'atsot beaspaklariyah*, 39–48.
52. Moyshe Teyf, "Zeks milion," *Folks-shtime*, April 16, 1960, 5.
53. Altshuler, *Yahadut Berit haMo'atsot beaspaklariyah*, 21.
54. Yevgeny Yevtushenko, "Di malke sheynhayt," *Sovetish heymland* 3 (1961): 43.
55. "Notitsn for calendar," *Sovetish heymland* 9 (1966): 160.
56. *Folks-shtime*, October 2, 1965, 1.
57. Sh. Rabinovitsh, "In Babi-Yar vert geshtelt a denkmol," *Folks-shtime*, August 28, 1965, 1. See also a short blurb in the "Jewish News" column: "33 proyektn fun a denkmol in Babyn Yar," January 22, 1966, 1.
58. For a vivid description of the coup that forced Khrushchev out of office, see William Taubman, *Khrushchev: The Man and His Era* (W. W. Norton, 2003), 3–17.
59. Kenez, *A History of the Soviet Union*, 214–15.
60. Kenez, *A History of the Soviet Union*, 218; Robert Service, *A History of Twentieth-Century Russia* (Harvard University Press, 1998), 401–10.
61. Service, *A History of Twentieth-Century Russia*, 216, 218.
62. Service, *A History of Twentieth-Century Russia*, 222–23, 416, 418.
63. Service, *A History of Twentieth-Century Russia*, 419.
64. Tőkés, "Varieties of Soviet Dissent," 11.
65. The filmmaker Andrei Tarkovski, the theater director and performer Vladimir Vysotski, and many others belong to this group of living artists. Among the deceased, one may mention Osip Mandelstam, Fyodor M. Dostoevsky, and Franz Kafka, whose works started to be printed in the USSR either for the first time or after decades. See Martin Dewhirst, "Soviet Russian Literature and Literary Policy," in *The Soviet Union Since the Fall of Khrushchev*, ed. Archie Brown and Michael Kaser (Macmillan, 1978), 181–95, here 187; and Service, *A History of Twentieth-Century Russia*, 415.
66. Archie Brown, "Political Developments: Some Conclusions and an Interpretation," in *The Soviet Union Since the Fall of Khrushchev*, ed. Archie Brown and Michael Kaser (Macmillan, 1978), 218–75, here 231.
67. Brown, "Political Developments," 233.
68. For a monograph dedicated to the efforts to commemorate the murder of Riga Jews and offer their remains proper burial, see Shmuel Tseitlin, *Dokumental'naya istoriya evreev Rigi* (Jerusalem: n.p., 1989).

69. The indication of ethnicity in the fifth paragraph of the Soviet passport has been enforced since the early 1930s.
70. Diamant, "Babi Yar, ili Pamyat'," 20.
71. As Abraham Brumberg notes, in the wake of this renewed campaign against Zionism, the Soviet regime would now conjure up the theme of Birobidzhan by way of countering Israel's claim to be the national homeland of the Jewish people worldwide. Evidently, as a part of this anti-Zionist attack, *Sovetish heymland* became a useful vehicle for the state's propaganda. See A. Brumberg, "*Sovyetish Heymland* and the Dilemmas," 27–41.
72. As Benjamin Pinkus notes, it is possible to distinguish between two periods of strong antisemitism in postwar Soviet history—1948–1953 and 1959–1963—and two periods of greater tolerance—1953–1955 and 1965–1966. See Pinkus, *The Soviet Government and the Jews*, 101.
73. Pinkus, *The Soviet Government and the Jews*, 265.
74. Brumberg and Brumberg, *Sovyetish Heymland: An Analysis*, 31.
75. Tumarkin, *The Living and the Dead*, 134.

## CHAPTER 7

1. Itsik Kipnis, "Tsvishn yidn," USHMM Archives, RG-22.028M, Jewish Anti-Fascist Committee, Reel 177. The original records can be found at the State Archives of the Russian Federation (GARF, Fond 8114, Opis 1, Delo 297).
2. Mordechai Altshuler, "Itsik Kipnis: The 'White Crow' of Soviet Yiddish Literature," *Jews in Russia and Eastern Europe* 2 (2004): 68–167, here 77–78. The story was written in June 1945. A censored version of it appeared in *Eynikayt* a month later under the title "Frayntshaft" (Friendship).
3. Altshuler, "Itsik Kipnis," 78.
4. Cited in Pavel Polyan, *Glukhoye echo: poslesloviye k antologii* (Memorial Holokostu Babyn Yar, 2021), 108.
5. Itsik Kipnis, *Untervegns un andere dertseylungen* (Ikuf, 1960), 347–52.
6. Itsik Kipnis, *Tsum lebn: dertseylungen* (Sovetskii Pisatel', 1969), 205–10.
7. Esther Rosenthal-Shneiderman, "Itsik Kipnis, aza vi ikh ken im (tsu zany vern a ben shivim)," *Di Goldene Keyt* 61 (1967): 123–68, here 130–32.
8. Altshuler, "Itsik Kipnis," 69.
9. Rosenthal-Shneiderman, "Itsik Kipnis," 127.
10. Murav, *Music from a Speeding Train*, 245. When the Nazis invaded the Soviet Union, Kipnis, like many other Soviet writers, was allowed to be evacuated to the Soviet interior. Initially, his family stayed in a village in the Northern Caucasus, but once the Nazis reached the area he was allowed to be included among the railroad workers and moved to Saratov. See Altshuler, "Itsik Kipnis," 72–73.
11. Mikhail Mitsel, *Evrei Ukrainy v 1943–1953 gg: ocherki dokumentirovannoy istorii* (Dukh i litera, 2004), 27.

12. Mitsel, *Evrei ukrainy v 1943–1953 gg*, 26.
13. This journalistic character of the work accounts perhaps for the error committed by two scholars, Yehoshua Gilboa and Richard Sheldon, the former in the broader context of Soviet Yiddish culture during the war and the latter in an article dedicated to Babyn Yar, who remarked that it was first published on September 29, 1944, without giving clear reference to its provenance. See Gilboa, *The Black Years of Soviet Jewry*, 143; and Sheldon, "The Transformation of Babi Yar," 127.
14. Kipnis, *Tsum lebn*, 205 (author's translation for all citations from the story).
15. David G. Roskies, *Against the Apocalypse: Responses to Catastrophe in Modern Jewish Culture* (Syracuse University Press, 1999), 10.
16. Roskies, *Against the Apocalypse*, 35.
17. Kipnis, *Untervegns*, 350.
18. Kipnis, "Tvishn yidn," 118–19. See also the New York version, 347–48, and the Moscow one, 205–6.
19. Kipnis, "Tvishn yidn," 121.
20. The comparative study of Soviet Yiddish literary works as they appeared in their Soviet version with the one published abroad was initiated by Khone Shmeruk. The scholarly apparatus that accompanies *A shpigl oyf a shteyn*, his landmark anthology of the work of twelve Soviet writers murdered by Stalin's henchmen, contains a synoptic comparison of variant readings of the same work published in the USSR and abroad. See Shmeruk, *A shpigl oyf a shteyn*, 773–804.
21. Kipnis, *Untervegns*, 347.
22. Kipnis, *Untervegns*, 352.
23. Roskies and Diamant, *Holocaust Literature*, 113.
24. Kipnis, *Tsum lebn*, 205–6.
25. Kipnis, *Tsum lebn*, 207 (cited in Gilboa, *The Black Years of Soviet Jewry*, 143).
26. Esther Rosenthal-Shneiderman, "Itsik Kipnises 'Babi Yar,'" *Lebns-fragen* 347/348 (1981): 7.
27. Peretz Markish, *Far folk un heymland* (Emes, 1943).
28. Kipnis, *Untervegns*, 351.
29. Rosenthal-Shneiderman, "Itsik Kipnises 'Babi Yar,'" 7.
30. Rosenthal-Shneiderman, "Itsik Kipnises 'Babi Yar,'" 7.
31. Kipnis, *Tsum lebn*, 210.
32. Kipnis, *Untervegns*, 352.

## CHAPTER 8

1. Yaacov Ro'i, "Nehama Lifshitz: Symbol of the Jewish National Awakening," in Yaacov Ro'i and Avi Beker, ed., *Jewish Culture and Identity in the Soviet Union* (New York University Press, 1991), 168–88, here 169. Nehama Lifshitz belonged to a small group of actors and singers who were given very limited permission to appear in front of Jewish

audiences following the death of Stalin. During the two decades of her career as a singer (she initially sang in a variety of Soviet languages but not in Yiddish), Lifshitz was affiliated with the Lithuanian SSR Philharmonic Society. Three main reasons accounted for her ability to sustain her career for decades: the greater open-mindedness of Soviet officials in the Baltic states toward the nurturing of non-Russian ethnic cultures, Lifshitz's membership in the Communist Party, and the benefit Moscow could gain from Lifshitz's partaking in tours of "cultural diplomacy" to Western countries as a way of showcasing the vibrancy of Yiddish culture in the USSR.

2. The anthology contained over forty Yiddish songs written in the ghettos and Nazi labor camps. See Eleanor Mlotek and Malke Gottlieb, eds., *We Are Here: Songs of the Holocaust* (Workmen's Circle and Hippocrene Books, 1983), 60–61.

3. Chaim Beider, *Leksikon fun yidishe shrayber in ratn-farband* (Congress for Jewish Culture, 2011), 105.

4. Yosef Kerler, *Geklibene proze: Eseyen, zikhroynes, dertseylungen* (Yerushalaymer Almanakh, 1991), 159. See also Yosef Kerler, "Hayetsira hasifrutit haYehudit-Sovyetit batekufa hapost-Stalinistit," in *Tarbut Yehudit Bivrit-Hamo'atsot*, ed. Arye Tartakower (Jewish World Congress, 1972), 40–72. As Dov Ber Kerler notes, while some of Driz's children's songs were characterized by a serious tone, the ones he wrote for adults were often playful, something that made it further difficult to set clear boundaries between the two. See Dov Ber Kerler, "Shike Driz," *The Yivo Encyclopedia of Jews in Eastern Europe*, accessed December 12, 2012, http://www.yivoencyclopedia.org/article.aspx/Driz_Shike.

5. Beider, *Leksikon fun yidishe shrayber*, 106.

6. Shike Driz, *Di ferte strune* (Sovetskii Pisatel', 1969), 135–36.

7. Cited in Dov Noy, "The Model of the Yiddish Lullaby," *Studies in Yiddish Literature and Folklore* 7 (1986): 208–35, here 223.

8. Emer O'Sullivan, *Historical Dictionary of Children's Literature* (Scarecrow Press, 2010), 166.

9. In "At Babyn Yar" by the Jewish poet Leonid Pervomaisky (1908–1973), Ukrainian literature has also produced a classic Babyn Yar poem, engaging the theme of parental protection and its futility, when both parent and son stand at the edge of the ravine, waiting to be shot to death:

> Stand near me, stand close, my son,
> I will cover your eyes with my hand
> So you don't see your death, but only the blood on my fingers in the sun,
> That blood that became yours too
> And is about to spill on the ground.

See Kin, *Babyn Yar*, 178–79. For the murdered child as a signifier for the victim's Jewish identity, see the discussion of Shloyme Cherniavsky's untitled poem in chapter 9.

10. Noy's research shows that in a sample of 3,558 Yiddish folk songs there were 200

lullabies. Noy further adds that it is hard to find a modern Yiddish poet who has not written a lullaby or used motifs derived from this genre in his or her poetry. See Noy, "The Model of the Yiddish Lullaby," 209.
11. Noy, "The Model of the Yiddish Lullaby," 213, 225.
12. Ro'i, "Nehama Lifshitz," 179.
13. Victoria Khiterer, "Suppressed Memory: Memorialization of the Holocaust in Babi Yar (Kyiv)," paper presented at the Association for the Study of Nationalities World Convention, Columbia University, New York, April 23–25, 2015.
14. Khiterer, "Suppressed Memory."
15. Ro'i, "Nehama Lifshitz," 172.

### CHAPTER 9

1. Aron Vergelis, "Der denkmol in Babi Yar vet shteyn ledoyres," *Sovetish heymland* 6 (1975): 158–64.
2. Gennady Estraikh, "Aron Vergelis: The Perfect Jewish *Homo Sovieticus*," *East European Jewish Affairs* 27, no. 2 (1997): 3–20, here 3.
3. Estraikh, "Aron Vergelis," 4.
4. In the Yiddish original, the author refers to the month of Elul, the time when it was customary for Jews to visit the graves of their ancestors.
5. Vergelis, "Der denkmol," 158 (author's translation for all Yiddish poems and quotes in this chapter).
6. Dawidowicz, "Babi Yar's Legacy."
7. Korey, "Forty Years Ago at Babi Yar," 31.
8. Vergelis, "Der denkmol," 159 (orthography normalized).
9. For literary sources on the medieval concept of *kiddush hashem*, see David G. Roskies, ed., *The Literature of Destruction: Jewish Responses to Catastrophe* (Jewish Publication Society, 1989).
10. Gary Rosenshield, "Socialist Realism and the Holocaust: Jewish Life and Death in Anatoly Rybakov's Heavy Sand," *PMLA* 111, no. 2 (1996): 240–55, here 248. Rosenshield uses this term in his evaluation of one of the most important novels published in the Soviet Union dealing with the Holocaust in Ukraine: *Heavy Sand* by Anatoly Rybakov. Appearing in 1979, the novel depicts the life and death of a family of Jewish craftsmen who are positively portrayed as "salt-of-the-earth," savvy, and industrious workers. According to Rosenshield, this characterization, underpinned by the maxim of socialist realism, debunks many stereotypes about the wily and dishonest Jewish trader of the *shtetl*. Yet, in many other respects, it drains Rybakov's Jews of any distinctly Jewish cultural attributes.
11. More than anything else, it was this tactical move toward the appeasement of Communist-leaning activists in the West—among them many Jews—that lay behind

the willingness of Khrushchev's regime to deviate from its view of Yiddish culture as a relic of the past and to allow its partial recovery in the form of an officially sanctioned bimonthly Yiddish publication. When the journal first appeared, the Soviet Minister of Culture made no secret of the fact that it was only foreign pressure, and not any kind of reconsideration of the Soviet stance toward Yiddish, that accounted for the Yiddish journal's conception. See A. Brumberg, "*Sovyetish Heymland* and the Dilemmas," 28. Estraikh notes another reason for this Soviet concession: the wish to meet these foreign protesters on the dire straits of Soviet Yiddish culture halfway by allowing only the establishment of a journal and the limited renewal of Yiddish book printing, as opposed to the far more ambitious wishes of many Soviet sympathizers in the West to see the re-creation of Soviet Yiddish culture according to the Polish communal organization model. See Estraikh, *Yiddish in the Cold War*, 64–65.

12. Estraikh, *Yiddish in the Cold War*, 113. See also A. Brumberg, "*Sovyetish Heymland* and the Dilemmas," 28.
13. Hersh Smolyar, "Di groyse shlakht tsvishn di geto-vent," *Sovetish heymland* 2 (1963): 131–39. On the historical distortion in the article, see Brumberg and Brumberg, *Sovyetish Heymland: An Analysis*, 16. Smolyar credits the underground Polish Communist Party in leading the uprising, something that cannot be substantiated by historical data. While downplaying the contribution of the Zionists to the uprising, Smolyar does describe the uprising overall as a battle fought by Jews. The mentioning of Mordechai Anielewicz, the leader of the Zionist youth group Hashomer Hatsair and the head of the ZOB (the Jewish Fighting Organization) as one of the heroes of the Warsaw Ghetto Uprising is another sign that *Sovetish heymland* did not categorically deny the relevance of the uprising to the Holocaust.
14. For a discussion of Prorokov's work, together with a survey of close to two dozen visual representations of Babyn Yar from the late 1940s till the early 1990s, see Pavel Polyan, "Babi Yar v zhivopisi I skul'pture: ot Vasiliya Ovchinnikova do Vadima Sidura," August 31, 2022, https://lechaim.ru/events/babiy-yar-v-zhivopisi-i-skulypture-ot-vasiliya-ovchinnikova-do-vadima-sidura-2/.
15. See *Sovetish heymland* 1 (1961): 49.
16. Estraikh, "Aron Vergelis," 3.
17. Rosenthal-Shneiderman, "Itsik Kipnis," 155.
18. Beider, *Leksikon fun yidishe shrayber*, 159.
19. Rosenthal-Shneiderman, *Oyf vegn un umvegn*, 212.
20. Interestingly, Talalayevsky was consistent in his opposition to nationalist deviation and did not center his attack on Yiddish writers only. In September 1947, he expressed his multinational stance by partaking in the writing of a collective article, published in the Ukrainian literary magazine *Literaturnaya gazeta*, which fulminated against Itsik Kipnis's Jewish nationalist sentiments expressed only a few months earlier in his aforemen-

tioned story "Without Thinking, Without Calculation." See Rosenthal-Shneiderman, "Itsik Kipnis," 155. Similarly, Talalayevsky was no less hostile to Soviet Ukrainian writers whose works also deviated from the maxim of "national in form, socialist in content." As Mordechai Altshuler points out, when Talalayevsky appeared before the presidium of the Ukrainian Writers' Union in order to condemn Kipnis's controversial story, he devoted the lion's share of his speech to an attack against Ukrainian writers whose works were also "contaminated" by Ukrainian nationalist moods. See Altshuler, "Itsik Kipnis," 84–85.

21. Beider, *Leksikon fun yidishe shrayber*, 159.
22. Rosenthal-Shneiderman, *Oyf vegn un umvegn*, 355.
23. Bohdan Kozachenko, "'... Gde tvoya rodina, brat?' Matveii Talalayevskii: mezhdu kosmopolitizmom i kosmosom," *Zerkalo nedeli*, December 27, 2008, http://zn.ua /CULTURE/gde_tvoya_rodina,_brat_matvey_talalaevskiy_mezhdu_kosmo politizmom_i_kosmosom-55788.html.
24. Motl Talalayevsky, "Ba yene rivn," *Sovetish heymland* 6 (1963): 66 (orthography normalized).
25. Motl Talalayevsky, "Kiev," *Sovetish heymland* 4 (1962): 6.
26. Talalayevsky, "Kiev," 5 (orthography normalized).
27. Talalayevsky, "Kiev," 4 (orthography normalized).
28. On the heroic feats of Talalayevsky the "poet and fighter," see Y. Dobrushin, "A dikhter – a shlakhtman," *Eynikayt*, September 9, 1945, 3.
29. Beider, *Leksikon fun yidishe shrayber*, 191.
30. Dobrenko comments that at one point in the history of the Soviet Writers' Union its membership reached about 10,000 authors. See Evgeny Dobrenko, *The Making of the State Writer: Social and Aesthetic Origins of Soviet Literary Culture*, trans. Jesse M. Savage (Stanford University Press, 2002), xiv.
31. Beider, *Leksikon fun yidishe shrayber*, 191; Rosenthal-Shneiderman, *Oyf vegn un umvegn*, 217, 279–80.
32. See Dore Khaykine, "Der zelber veg," in Arn Vergelis, ed., *Horizontn: fun der hayntsaytiker sovetisher yidisher dikhtung* (Sovetskii Pisatel', 1965), 340–42. The poem was also published in one of Khaykine's later collections of poems. See Dore Khaykine, *Fun ale mayne vegn: lider* (Sovetskii Pisatel', 1975), 163–64.
33. Khaykine, "Der zelber veg," 340–42.
34. Dore Khaykine, "Ikh bin dort oykh geven," *Sovetish heymland* 10 (1968): 56–57.
35. Khaykine, "Ikh bin dort oykh geven," 56.
36. Beider, *Leksikon fun yidishe shrayber*, 169–70.
37. Shloyme Cherniavsky, *Po moskovskomu vremeni: lirika raznykh let* (Sovetskii Pisatel', 1975), 134.
38. Avrom Sutzkever, *Selected Poetry and Prose*, trans. Barbara and Benjamin Harshav (University of California Press, 1991), 151.

39. Shloyme Cherniavsky, "Babi Yar," USHMM Archives, RG-22.028M, Jewish Anti-Fascist Committee, Reel 146. The original records can be found at the State Archives of the Russian Federation (GARF, Fond 8114, Opis 1, Delo 396).
40. Cherniavsky, "Babi Yar."
41. Another example for work that positioned the Babyn Yar massacre front and center is the novel *Dos Shvartser Vint* (The black wind) by Yekhiel Falikman, serialized in *Sovetish Heymland* in 1968 and later published in Russian translation. See Ikhil Falikman, *Chernyi veter:roman* (Sovetskii Pisatel', 1974). Like with Talalayevsky's work, *The Black Wind* presents the same paradigm. On the one hand, there is an explicit and detailed reference to Babyn Yar—that is actually the title of the novel's second section. On the other, this openness is moderated by conceptualization of Babyn Yar as a Great Patriotic War site. As Naya Lekht puts it: "Written in Yiddish and appearing in the only Yiddish journal in the Soviet Union, Falikman's novel is obviously marked as a 'Jewish' text, but first and foremost, it is Soviet. Published only one year after the Six-Day War, Falikman was careful to avoid inciting Jewish nationalism." See Lekht, "Narratives of Return," 123.
42. Sheldon, "The Transformation of Babyn Yar," 146; Benjamin Pinkus, *Tehiyah utekumah leumit: hatsionut vehatenu'ah hatsionit biVrit-hamo'atsot, 1947–1987* (Ben-Gurion University of the Negev Press, 1993), 278.
43. Tőkés, "Varieties of Soviet Dissent," 31.
44. Katerina Clark comments that the main difference between Russian literature of the nineteenth century and the Soviet literature that succeeded it lies in the fact that the Soviet government "has not only censored the writers—has told them what they must *not* write; it has also told them what they *must* write." See Clark, *The Soviet Novel*, 253. Evgeny Dobrenko goes even one step further, arguing that in the Soviet Union the question of the censor's role cannot really exist, as the writer is the real bearer of the Soviet ideology: he is the one to create it and he is, conversely, the one who is being created by it. See Dobrenko, *The Making of the State Writer*, xviii.
45. See the interview with the man who had worked in Glavlit since 1961 and headed its fourth Department of Artistic and Political Literature in Steven Richmond, "'The Eye of the State': An Interview with Soviet Chief Censor Vladimir Solodin," *Russian Review* 56, no. 4 (1997): 581–90. As Solodin notes, working censors operated in each publishing house or newspaper. Only if problems arose with a certain work that seemed to have crossed ideological lines would the local Glavlit staff involve the central bureau in Moscow.
46. Estraikh, *Yiddish in the Cold War*, 82. The amalgamation of these two roles was nothing unusual during both the Khrushchev and Brezhnev years, during which literary freedom existed in a very limited form. Although the Soviet central censorship body, the Glavlit, remained in place, most literary works of that era were "filtered" through the intervention of the editor (a person the regime, obviously, deemed trustworthy)

or through the practice of so-called self-censorship. Gennady Estraikh illuminates this twofold role played by Vergelis when he contends that, despite Vergelis's position as the unchallenged authority in Soviet Yiddish cultural affairs of his era, the CPSU leader Brezhnev and other members of the Politburo were surprised to find out in 1973 that a Yiddish periodical even existed in the USSR "edited by a certain Aron Vergelis." This comment speaks volumes about the decentralized character that Soviet censorship assumed during the "Era of Stagnation." See Estraikh, "Aron Vergelis," 13.

47. Cited in Gennday Estraikh, "'Sovetish heymland': der zhurnal vos hot zikh bavizn mit 50 yor tsurik," *Forverts*, July 29, 2011, http://yiddish.forward.com/node/3811.
48. Estraikh, *Yiddish and the Cold War*, 89.
49. Brumberg and Brumberg, *Sovyetish Heymland: An Analysis*, 23.
50. Aron Vergelis, "Mit vos iz lebedik di yidishe literatur," *Sovetish heymland* 2 (1967): 124–35.
51. Vergelis, "Mit vos iz lebedik di yidishe literatur," 125.
52. Vergelis, "Mit vos iz lebedik di yidishe literatur," 134 (orthography normalized).
53. Estraikh, "Aron Vergelis," 3.
54. Elissa Bemporad, *Becoming Soviet Jews: The Bolshevik Experiment in Minsk* (Indiana University Press, 2013).
55. Anna Shternshis, *Soviet and Kosher: Jewish Popular Culture in the Soviet Union, 1923–1939* (Indiana University Press, 2006).
56. Zvi Gitelman, "Thinking About Being Jewish in Russia and Ukraine," in *Jewish Life After the USSR*, ed. Zvi Gitelman, Musya Glants, and Marshall I. Goldman (Indiana University Press, 2003), 49–59, here 49.
57. Mordechai Altshuler, *Religion and Jewish Identity in the Soviet Union, 1941–1964* (Brandeis University Press, 2012).
58. Murav, *Music from a Speeding Train*.
59. See Leon Shapiro, "Soviet Jewry Since the Death of Stalin: A Twenty-Five Year Perspective," *The American Jewish Year Book* 79 (1979): 77–103, here 81; Olga Litvak, "The New Marranos," in *A Club of Their Own: Jewish Humorists and the Contemporary World*, ed. Eli Lederhendler (Oxford University Press), 245–67. A good example of the conception of Soviet Jews as a modern transfiguration of the late medieval Spanish and Portuguese Marranos can be found in Mordechai Yushkovsky, "Ha-anusim shel hameah ha-esrim: hane-emanut haleumit etsel sofrim Yehudim Bivrit hamo'atsot," *Ma'amakim* 34 (2008), https://www.daat.ac.il/daat/ktav_et/maamar.asp?ktavet=1&id=955.

### EPILOGUE

1. Korey, "A Monument over Babi Yar?," 72.
2. Korey, "A Monument over Babi Yar?," 72.
3. Mankoff, "Babi Yar and the Struggle for Memory," 411. See also Pavel Polyan's introduc-

tion to his anthology of poems dedicated to Babyn Yar in Pavel Polyan, ed., *Stihi o Bab'em Yare: antologiya*, Vol. 1 (Babyn Yar Holocaust Memorial Center, 2021), 17–18.
4. Korey, "A Monument over Babi Yar?," 74.
5. For the president's speech at Babyn Yar, see "Remarks at the Babi Yar Memorial in Kiev, Soviet Union," https://www.presidency.ucsb.edu/node/265654.
6. Khiterer, "Babi Yar, the Tragedy of Kyiv's Jews," 13.
7. In a city divided between ethnic Russians and Ukrainians, in which Jews amounted to a small yet visible minority, a distinctly Jewish memorial such as the new menorah rose from the ashes of Soviet Ukraine fairly rapidly. In western Ukraine, where the population was far more homogenously Ukrainian and the Jewish community smaller, the latter were far less comfortable in asserting the Jewish nature of Nazi atrocities even after the fall of the Soviet Union. See Omer Bartov, *Erased: Vanishing Traces of Jewish Galicia in Present-Day Ukraine* (Princeton University Press, 2007), 31.
8. Khiterer, "Suppressed Memory."
9. Mankoff, "Babi Yar and the Struggle for Memory," 413.
10. A good example of an analogous "victimization contest," related to the Holocaust yet situated in an American context, can be found in Walter Benn Michaels, *The Trouble with Diversity: How We Learned to Love Identity and Ignore Inequality* (Metropolitan, 2006), 55–56.

# BIBLIOGRAPHY

"33 proyektn fun a denkmol in Babyn Yar." *Folks-shtime*, January 22, 1966, 1.
Afian, V. Y., et al., eds. *Apparat Ts.K. K.P.S.S. I kul'tura 1958–1964: Dokumenty*. Rosspen, 2005.
Alexeyeva, Ludmilla. *Soviet Dissent: Contemporary Movements for National, Religious, and Human Rights*. Wesleyan University Press, 1987.
Altshuler, Mordechai. "Antisemitism in Ukraine Toward the End of World War II." In *Bitter Legacy: Confronting the Holocaust in the USSR*, edited by Zvi Gitelman. Indiana University Press, 1997.
Altshuler, Mordechai. "Itsik Kipnis: The 'White Crow' of Soviet Yiddish Literature." *Jews in Russia and Eastern Europe* 2 (2004): 68–167.
Altshuler, Mordechai. *Religion and Jewish Identity in the Soviet Union, 1941–1964*. Brandeis University Press, 2012.
Altshuler, Mordechai. *Yahadut bamakhbesh haSovieti: bein dat lezehut yehudit biVrit haMo'atsot, 1941–1964*. Zalman Shazar Center, 2008.
Altshuler, Mordechai. *Yahadut Berit haMo'atsot beaspaklariyah shel itonut Yidish bePolin*. Hebrew University, 1975.
Arad, Yitzhak. *The Holocaust in the Soviet Union*. Translated by Ora Cummings. University of Nebraska Press, 2009.
Arendt, Hannah. *The Origins of Totalitarianism*. Harcourt Brace Jovanovich, 1973.
Assmann, Jan. "Collective Memory and Cultural Identity." *New German Critique* 65 (Spring–Summer 1995): 125–33.
Balashov, A. I., and G. P. Rudakov. *Istoriya velikoy otechestvennoi voiny*. Peter, 2005.
Bartov, Omer. *Erased: Vanishing Traces of Jewish Galicia in Present-Day Ukraine*. Princeton University Press, 2007.
Bauer, Yehuda. *Teguvot be'et haShoah: nisyonot amida, hitnagdut, hatsala*. Israel Ministry of Defense Press, 1983.
Beider, Chaim. *Leksikon fun yidishe shrayber in ratn-farband*. Congress for Jewish Culture, 2011.
Bemporad, Elissa. *Becoming Soviet Jews: The Bolshevik Experiment in Minsk*. Indiana University Press, 2013.
Berenbaum, Michael. "The Impact of the Holocaust on Contemporary Ethics." In *Ethics in the Shadow of the Holocaust: Christian and Jewish Perspectives*, edited by Judith H. Banki and John T. Pawlikowski. Sheed & Ward, 2001.
Bergman, Eleonora. "Yiddish in Poland After 1945." In *Yiddish and the Left: Papers of the*

*Third Mendel Friedman International Conference on Yiddish*, edited by Mikhail Krutikov and Gennady Estraikh. Legenda, 2001.

Berkhoff, Karel, et al. *Basic Historical Narrative of the Babyn Yar Holocaust Memorial Center*. Charity Fund Babyn Yar Holocaust Memorial. Kyiv. October 2018. https://bit.ly/3fkHqU6.

Berkhoff, Karel C. "Babyn Yar in Cinema." In *Babyn Yar: History and Memory*, edited by Vladyslav Hrynevych and Paul Robert Magocsi, translated by Marta D. Olynyk. Dukh I Litera, 2016.

Berkhoff, Karel C. "Dina Pronicheva's Story of Surviving the Babi Yar Massacre: German, Jewish, Soviet, Russian, and Ukrainian Records." In *The Shoah in the Ukraine: History, Testimony, Memorialization*, edited by Ray Brandon and Wendy Lower. Indiana University Press, 2008.

Berkhoff, Karel C. *Harvest of Despair: Life and Death in Ukraine Under Nazi Rule*. Harvard University Press, 2004.

Berkhoff, Karel C. *Motherland in Danger: Soviet Propaganda During World War II*. Harvard University Press, 2012.

Bilinsky, Yaroslav. *The Second Soviet Republic: The Ukraine After World War II*. Rutgers University Press, 1964.

Billington, James H. *The Icon and the Axe: An Interpretive History of Russian Culture*. Knopf, 1966.

Bilovitski, Vladimir. "Institute of Jewish Proletarian Culture." *The Yivo Encyclopedia of Jews in Eastern Europe*. Accessed December 12, 2012. http://www.yivoencyclopedia.org/article.aspx/Institute_of_Jewish_Proletarian_Culture.

Blake, Patricia. Introduction to *Half-Way to the Moon: New Writing from Russia*. Edited by Patricia Blake and Max Hayward. Encounter, 1964.

Blokker, Roy, and Robert Dearling. *The Music of Dmitri Shostakovich: The Symphonies*. Fairleigh Dickinson University Press, 1979.

Boym, Svetlana. *Common Places: Mythologies of Everyday Life in Russia*. Harvard University Press, 1994.

Brodsky, Patricia Pollock. "'Babi Yar': Poem by Yevgenii Yevtushenko, 1961." In *Reference Guide to Holocaust Literature*, edited by Thomas Riggs. St. James Press, 2002.

Brown, Archie. "Political Developments: Some Conclusions and an Interpretation." In *The Soviet Union Since the Fall of Khrushchev*, edited by Archie Brown and Michael Kaser. Macmillan, 1978.

Brown, Deming. *Soviet Russian Literature Since Stalin*. Cambridge University Press, 1978.

Brown, Edward J. *Mayakovsky: A Poet in the Revolution*. Princeton University Press, 1973.

Brown, Edward J. *Russian Literature Since the Revolution*. Collier Books, 1982.

Brumberg, Abraham. "*Sovyetish Heymland* and the Dilemmas of Jewish Life in the USSR." *Soviet Jewish Affairs* 2, no. 1 (1972): 27–41.

Brumberg, Joseph, and Abraham Brumberg. *Sovyetish Heymland: An Analysis.* Anti-Defamation League of B'nai B'rith, 1966.

Cherniavsky, Shloyme. *Po moskovskomu vremeni: lirika raznykh let.* Sovetskii Pisatel', 1975.

Clark, Katerina. *The Soviet Novel: History as Ritual.* 3rd ed. Indiana University Press, 2000.

Clowes, Edith. "Constructing the Memory of the Holocaust: The Ambiguous Treatment of Babi Yar in Soviet Literature." *Partial Answers* 3, no. 2 (2005): 154–82.

Dawidowicz, Lucy. "Babi Yar's Legacy." *New York Times Magazine*, September 27, 1981. Accessed December 12, 2012. http://www.nytimes.com/1981/09/27/magazine/Babyn-yar-s-legacy.html.

Desbois, Patrick. *The Holocaust by Bullets: A Priest's Journey to Uncover the Truth Behind the Murder of 1.5 Million Jews.* Palgrave Macmillan, 2008.

Dewhirst, Martin. "Soviet Russian Literature and Literary Policy." In *The Soviet Union Since the Fall of Khrushchev*, edited by Archie Brown and Michael Kaser. Macmillan, 1978.

Diamant, Emanuel. "Babi Yar, ili Pamyat' o tom, kak v narod prevrashchalos' stroptivoye plemya." Accessed September 9, 2024. https://www.academia.edu/43265556/Baby_Yar_or_a_story_of_how_a_wayward_tribe_has_strived_to_become_again_a_folk.

Diamant, Emanuel. "Babi Yar, o kotorom vy nichego (ili pochti nichego) ne znaete: neizvestnyie I maloizvestnyie materialy po istorii Bab'ego Yara." Accessed September 9, 2024. https://nekrasov-viktor.com/images/Papers/Diamant-Emanuel-Babiy-Yar-o-kotorom-vi-nichego-ili-pochti-nichego-ne-znaete.pdf.

Dieckmann, Christoph, and Arkadi Zeltser, eds. *Distrust, Animosity, and Solidarity: Jews and Non-Jews During the Holocaust in the USSR.* Yad Vashem, 2022.

Dobrenko, Evgeny. *The Making of the State Writer: Social and Aesthetic Origins of Soviet Literary Culture.* Translated by Jesse M. Savage. Stanford University Press, 2002.

Dobrushin, Y. "A dikhter – a shlakhtman." *Eynikayt*, September 9, 1945, 3.

Driz, Shike. *Di ferte strune.* Sovetskii Pisatel', 1969.

Ehrenburg, Ilya. "Babi Yar," translated by Alyssa Dinega Gillespie. In *An Anthology of Jewish-Russian Literature: Two Centuries of Dual Identity in Prose and Poetry.* Vol. 1, *1801–1953*, edited by Maxim D. Shrayer. M.E. Sharpe, 2007.

Ehrenburg, Ilya. "Gebentshte erd." *Eynikayt*, October 1942, 2.

Ehrenburg, Ilya, and Vasily Grossman. *The Black Book.* Holocaust Library, 1981.

Engel, David. "The Reconstruction of Jewish Communal Institutions in Postwar Poland: The Origins of the Central Committee of Polish Jews, 1944–1945." *East European Politics and Societies* 10, no. 1 (1995): 85–107. https://doi.org/10.1177/0888325496010001004.

Erofeev, Viktor. *Muzhchiny.* Zebra E, 2004.

Estraikh, Gennady. "Aron Vergelis: The Perfect Jewish *Homo Sovieticus*." *East European Jewish Affairs* 27, no. 2 (1997): 3–20. https://doi.org/10.1080/13501679708577856.

Estraikh, Gennady. *In Harness, Yiddish Writers' Romance with Communism.* Syracuse University Press, 2005.

Estraikh, Gennady. "'Sovetish heymland': der zhurnal vos hot zikh bavizn mit 50 yor tsurik." *Forverts*, July 29, 2011. Accessed December 12, 2012. http://yiddish.forward.com/node/3811.

Estraikh, Gennady. "Soviet Publications of Holocaust Diaries in the 1960s: Anne Frank and Masha Rolnikaite." *Holocaust and Genocide Studies* 36, no. 1 (Spring 2022): 1–14. https://doi.org/10.1093/hgs/dcac004.

Estraikh, Gennady. "Yevgeny Yevtushenko's 'Babi Yar': A Russian Poet's Page in Post-Holocaust History." In Dieckmann and Zeltser, *Distrust, Animosity, and Solidarity*.

Estraikh, Gennady. *Yiddish in the Cold War*. Legenda, 2008.

Evstafyeva, Tatiana. "Sieretskii kontsentratsionnyi lager'." In *Babi Yar: chelovek, vlast', istoriya*, edited by Vitalii Nakhmanovich and Tatiana Evstafyeva. Vneshtorgizdat Ukrainy, 2004.

Falchikov, Michael. Introduction to *Postscripts: Short Stories*, by Victor Nekrasov. Quartet Books, 1991.

Falikman, Ikhil. *Chernyi veter: roman*. Sovetskii Pisatel', 1974.

Fay, Laurel E. *Shostakovich: A Life*. Oxford University Press, 2000.

Feferman, Kiril. *Soviet Jewish Stepchild: The Holocaust in the Soviet Mindset, 1941–1964*. VDM Verlag Dr. Müller, 2009.

Finnin, R. E. "Timothy Snyder: 'Holocaust: The Ignored Reality.'" *Memory at War: Blog*, June 21, 2009. http://cambridgeculturalmemory.blogspot.com/2009/06/masha-lipman-russia-again-evading.html.

Garrard, John, and Carol Garrard. *Inside the Soviet Writers' Union*. Free Press, 1990.

Gershenson, Olga. *The Phantom Holocaust: Soviet Cinema and Jewish Catastrophe*. Rutgers University Press, 2013.

Gessen, Masha. Introduction to *Babi Yar: A Document in the Form of a Novel; New, Complete, Uncensored Version*, by Anatoly Kuznetsov. Translated by David Floyd. Picador, 2023.

Gilboa, Yehoshua. *The Black Years of Soviet Jewry: 1939–1953*. Little, Brown, 1971.

Gitelman, Zvi. *A Century of Ambivalence: The Jews of Russia and the Soviet Union, 1881 to the Present*. 2nd, expanded ed. Indiana University Press, 2001.

Gitelman, Zvi. "Internationalism, Patriotism, and Disillusion: Soviet Jewish Veterans Remember World War II and the Holocaust." In *The Holocaust in the Soviet Union: Symposium Presentations*. United States Holocaust Memorial Museum, 2005. Accessed December 12, 2012. https://www.ushmm.org/research/center/publications/occasional/2005-10/paper.pdf.

Gitelman, Zvi. "Politics and the Historiography of the Holocaust in the Soviet Union." In *Bitter Legacy: Confronting the Holocaust in the USSR*, edited by Zvi Gitelman. Indiana University Press, 1997.

Gitelman, Zvi. "Thinking About Being Jewish in Russia and Ukraine." In *Jewish Life After the USSR*, edited by Zvi Gitelman, Musya Glants, and Marshall I. Goldman. Indiana University Press, 2003.

Goldberg, Ben Zion. *The Jewish Problem in the Soviet Union: Analysis and Solution.* Greenwood Press, 1982.

Hirsch, Marianne. *The Generation of Postmemory: Writing and Visual Culture After the Holocaust.* Columbia University Press, 2012.

Kenez, Peter. *A History of the Soviet Union from the Beginning to the End.* 2nd ed. Cambridge University Press, 2006.

Kerler, Dov Ber. "Shike Driz." *The Yivo Encyclopedia of Jews in Eastern Europe.* Accessed December 12, 2012. http://www.yivoencyclopedia.org/article.aspx/Driz_Shike.

Kerler, Yosef. *Geklibene proze: Eseyen, zikhroynes, dertseylungen.* Yerushalaymer Almanakh, 1991.

Kerler, Yosef. "Hayetsira hasifrutit haYehudit-Sovyetit batekufa hapost-Stalinistit." In *Tarbut Yehudit Bivrit-Hamo'atsot*, edited by Arye Tartakower. Jewish World Congress, 1972.

Khaykine, Dore. "Der zelber veg." In Vergelis, *Horizontn*.

Khaykine, Dore. *Fun ale mayne vegn: lider.* Sovetskii Pisatel', 1975.

Khaykine, Dore. "Ikh bin dort oykh geven." *Sovetish heymland* 10 (1968): 56–57.

Khiterer, Victoria. "Babi Yar, the Tragedy of Kyiv's Jews." *Brandeis Graduate Journal* 2 (2004): 1–16.

Khiterer, Victoria. "Suppressed Memory: Memorialization of the Holocaust in Babi Yar (Kyiv)." Paper presented at the Association for the Study of Nationalities World Convention, Columbia University, New York, April 23–25, 2015.

Kin, Ostap, ed. *Babyn Yar: Ukrainian Poets Respond.* Translated by John Hennessy and Ostap Kin. Ukrainian Research Institute, 2022.

Kipnis, Itsik. "On khokhmes, on kheshboynes." *Dos naye lebn*, May 17, 1947, 4, 8.

Kipnis, Itsik. *Tsum lebn: dertseylungen.* Sovetskii Pisatel', 1969.

Kipnis, Itsik. *Untervegns un andere dertseylungen.* Ikuf, 1960.

Kirschenbaum, Lisa. "Nothing Is Forgotten: Individual Memory and the Myth of the Great Patriotic War." In *History of the Aftermath: The Legacies of the Second World War in Europe*, edited by Frank Biess and Robert G. Moeller. Berghahn Books, 2010.

Kohn, Hans. "Soviet Communism and Nationalism: Three Stages of Historical Development." In *Soviet Nationality Problems*, edited by Edward Allworth. Columbia University Press, 1971.

Korey, William. "Babi Yar Remembered." *Midstream* 15, no. 3 (1969): 24–39.

Korey, William. "Forty Years Ago at Babi Yar: Reliving the Crime." *Present Tense* 9, no. 1 (1981): 27–31.

Korey, William. "In History's 'Memory Hole': The Soviet Treatment of the Holocaust." In *Contemporary Views on the Holocaust*, edited by Randolph L. Braham. Kluwer-Nijhoff, 1983.

Korey, William. "A Monument over Babi Yar?" In *The Holocaust in the Soviet Union: Studies and Sources on the Destruction of the Jews in the Nazi-Occupied Territories of the USSR, 1941–1945*, edited by Lucjan Dobroszycki and Jeffrey S. Gurock. M.E. Sharpe, 1993.

Korey, William. *The Soviet Cage: Antisemitism in Russia*. Viking Press, 1973.
Kostyrchenko, Gennady V. *Tainaya politika Khrushcheva: vlast', intelligentsiya, evreiskii vopros*. Mezhdunarodnye Onosheniya, 2012.
Kozachenko, Bohdan. "'... Gde tvoya rodina, brat?' Matveii Talalayevskii: mezhdu kosmopolitizmom i kosmosom." *Zerkalo nedeli*, December 27, 2008. http://zn.ua/CULTURE/gde_tvoya_rodina,_brat_matvey_talalaevskiy_mezhdu_kosmopolitizmom_i_kosmosom-55788.html.
Kozlov, Denis. *The Readers of Novyi Mir: Coming to Terms with the Stalinist Past*. Harvard University Press, 2013.
Kreidich, Assia Kovrigina. "Babyn Yar in Personal Accounts." In *Babyn Yar: History and Memory*, edited by Vladyslav Hrynevych and Paul Robert Magocsi. Dukh I Litera, 2016.
Kushnirov, Aron. "Di muter Rokhl." *Forverts*, September 30–October 6, 2011, 13.
Kushnirov, Aron. "Di muter Rokhl." *Heymland: literarish-kinstlerisher almanakh* 5 (1948): 36–40.
Kuznetsov, Aleksei. *Mezhdu Grinvichem i Kurenevkoy: pis'ma Anatoliya Kuznetsova materi iz emigratsii v Kiev*. Zaharov, 2002.
Kuznetsov, Anatoly. "Babi Yar." *Iunost'* 8–10 (1966).
Kuznetsov, Anatoly. *Babi Yar: A Document in the Form of a Novel*. Translated by David Floyd. Farrar, Straus and Giroux, 1970.
Kuznetsov, Anatoly. *Babi Yar: A Documentary Novel*. Dial, 1967.
Kuznetsov, Anatoly. *Babi Yar: roman-dokument*. Molodaya Gvardiya, 1967.
Kuznetsov, Anatoly. *Babi Yar: roman-dokument*. Posev, 1970.
Kuznetsov, Anatoly. *Babi Yar: roman-dokument*. Astrel', 2010.
Langer, Lawrence L. *Holocaust Testimonies: The Ruins of Memory*. Yale University Press, 1991.
Lekht, Naya. "Narratives of Return: Babii Yar and Holocaust Literature in the Soviet Union." PhD diss., University of California, Los Angeles, 2013.
Levitas, Feliks, and Mark Shimanovskii. *Babii Yar: stranitsy tragedii*. Slid, 1991.
Litvak, Olga. "The New Marranos." In *A Club of Their Own: Jewish Humorists and the Contemporary World*, edited by Eli Lederhendler. Oxford University Press.
Lowe, David. *Russian Writing Since 1953: A Critical Survey*. Ungar, 1987.
Lower, Wendy. *The Ravine: A Family, a Photograph, a Holocaust Massacre Revealed*. Houghton Mifflin Harcourt, 2021.
Maes, Francis. *A History of Russian Music: From Kamarinskaya to Babi Yar*. Translated by Arnold J. Pomerans and Erica Pomerans. University of California Press, 2006.
Mankoff, Jeff. "Babi Yar and the Struggle for Memory, 1944–2004." *Ab Imperio* 2 (2004): 393–415.
Markish, Esther. *The Long Return*. Ballantine Books, 1978.
Markish, Peretz. *Far folk un heymland*. Emes, 1943.

Markish, Peretz. *Milhome*. 2 vols. Ikuf, 1956.
Markish, Shimon. "The Role of Officially Published Russian Literature in the Reawakening of Jewish National Consciousness (1953–1970)." In *Jewish Culture and Identity in the Soviet Union*, edited by Yaacov Ro'i and Avi Beker. New York University Press, 1991.
Markov, A. "Moi otvet." *Literatura i zhizn'*, September 24, 1961.
Martinenko, Bohdan. "Babi Yar vehashmadat ha'am hayehudi beUkraina 'al yedei haNatsim." *Mikhael* 13 (1993): 85–91.
Mayzel, Nahman. *Dos yidishe shafn un der yidisher shrayber in sovetnfarband*. Ikuf, 1959.
Mazower, Mark. *Dark Continent: Europe's Twentieth Century*. Vintage, 2001.
McDowell, Edwin. "Brodsky Quits Arts Group over Yevtushenko Induction." *New York Times*, June 20, 1987. https://www.nytimes.com/1987/06/20/arts/brodsky-quits-arts-group-over-yevtushenko-induction.html.
Merridale, Catherine. *Ivan's War: Life and Death in the Red Army, 1939–1945*. Picador, 2006.
Merridale, Catherine. *Night of Stone: Death and Memory in Twentieth-Century Russia*. Basic Books, 2002.
Michaels, Walter Benn. *The Trouble with Diversity: How We Learned to Love Identity and Ignore Inequality*. Metropolitan, 2006.
Mikhoels, Solomon. "Eynikayt in nekome." *Eynikayt*, October 5, 1944.
Mintz, Alan. *Popular Culture and the Shaping of Holocaust Memory in America*. University of Washington Press, 2001.
Mitsel, Mikhail. *Evrei Ukrainy v 1943–1953 gg: ocherki dokumentirovannoy istorii*. Dukh i litera, 2004.
Mlotek, Eleanor, and Malke Gottlieb, eds. *We Are Here: Songs of the Holocaust*. Workmen's Circle and Hippocrene Books, 1983.
Murav, Harriet. *Music from a Speeding Train: Jewish Literature in Post-Revolution Russia*. Stanford University Press, 2011.
Nakhimovsky, Alice. "Yevgenii Yevtushenko." In *Holocaust Literature: An Encyclopedia of Writers and Their Work*, edited by S. Lillian Kremer. Routledge, 2002.
Nakhmanovich, Vitalii. "Rasstrely i zakhoroneniya v rayone Babyego Yara vo vremya nemetskoy okkupatsii g. Kieva 1941-1943 gg. Problemy khronologii i topografii." In *Babi Yar: chelovek, vlast', istoriya*, edited by Vitalii Nakhmanovich and Tatiana Evstaf'eva. Vneshtorgizdat Ukrainy, 2004.
Nekrasov, Viktor. *Arestovannye stranitsy: rasskazy, intervyu, pis'ma iz arkhivov KGB*. Laurus, 2014.
Nekrasov, Viktor. "Pochemu eto ne sdelano?" *Literaturnaya gazeta*, October 10, 1959.
Nekrasov, Viktor. "Zapiski zevaki." In *Kak ya stal shevalye: rasskazy, portrety, ocherki, povesti*. U-factoria, 2005.
Niger, Shmuel. *Yidishe shrayber in Sovet-rusland*. Altveltlekhn Kultur Kongres, 1958.

Nikolaev, P. A., ed. *Russkie pisateli 20 veka: biograficheskii slovar'*. Randevu-AM, 2000.
Nora, Pierre. "Between Memory and History: Les Lieux de Mémoire." *Representations* 26 (Spring 1989): 7–24.
"Notitsn for calendar." *Sovetish heymland* 9 (1966): 160.
Noy, Dov. "The Model of the Yiddish Lullaby." *Studies in Yiddish Literature and Folklore* 7 (1986): 208–35.
Olick, Jeffrey K. "Collective Memory: The Two Cultures." In *The Collective Memory Reader*, edited by Jeffrey K. Olick, Vered Vinitzky-Serousi, and Daniel Levy. Oxford University Press, 2008.
O'Sullivan, Emer. *Historical Dictionary of Children's Literature*. Scarecrow Press, 2010.
Overy, Richard. *Russia's War: A History of the Soviet Effort: 1941–1945*. Rev. ed. Penguin Books, 1998.
Pasternak, Boris. *In the Interlude: Poems 1945–1960*. Translated by Henry Kamen. Oxford University Press, 1962.
Pikhoya, R. G. *Sovetskiy Soyuz: istoriya vlasti*. Sibirskiy khronograf, 2000.
Pinkus, Benjamin. *The Jews of the Soviet Union: The History of a National Minority*. Cambridge University Press, 1988.
Pinkus, Benjamin. *The Soviet Government and the Jews 1948–1967: A Documented Study*. Cambridge University Press, 1984.
Pinkus, Benjamin. *Tehiyah utekumah leumit: hatsionut vehatenu'ah hatsionit biVrit-hamo'atsot, 1947–1987*. Ben-Gurion University of the Negev Press, 1993.
Polyan, Pavel. "Babi Yar v zhivopisi I skul'pture: ot Vasiliya Ovchinnikova do Vadima Sidura." August 31, 2022. https://lechaim.ru/events/babiy-yar-v-zhivopisi-i-skulypture-ot-vasiliya-ovchinnikova-do-vadima-sidura-2/.
Polyan, Pavel. *Glukhoye echo: poslesloviye k antologii*. Memorial Holokostu Babyn Yar, 2021.
Polyan, Pavel, ed. *Stihi o Bab'em Yare: antologiya*. Vol. 1. Memorial Holokostu Babyn Yar, 2021.
P'yanyh, M. F. "Yevtushenko, Yevgenii Alexandrovich." In *Russkie pisateli: dvadtsatyy vek*. Prosveshchenie, 1987.
Rabinovitsh, Sh. "In Babi-Yar vert geshtelt a denkmol." *Folks-shtime*, August 28, 1965, 1.
Reavey, George. "Yevgeny Yevtushenko: Man and Poet." In *Early Poems* by Yevgeny Yevtushenko, translated by George Reavey. Marion Boyars, 1989.
Richmond, Steven. "'The Eye of the State': An Interview with Soviet Chief Censor Vladimir Solodin." *Russian Review* 56, no. 4 (1997): 581–90.
Rimmon-Kenan, Shlomith. *Narrative Fiction: Contemporary Poetics*. 2nd ed. Routledge, 2002.
Ro'i, Yaacov. "Nehama Lifshitz: Symbol of the Jewish National Awakening." In *Jewish Culture and Identity in the Soviet Union*, edited by Yaacov Ro'i and Avi Beker. New York University Press, 1991.
Rollberg, Peter. *Historical Dictionary of Russian and Soviet Cinema*. Scarecrow Press, 2009.

Rosenshield, Gary. "Socialist Realism and the Holocaust: Jewish Life and Death in Anatoly Rybakov's Heavy Sand." *PMLA* 111, no. 2 (1996): 240–55.

Rosenthal, Nissan. *Hahayim haYehudiyim biVrit-hamo'atsot 1935–1958*. Hakibbutz Hameuhad, 1993.

Rosenthal-Shneiderman, Esther. "Itsik Kipnis, aza vi ikh ken im (tsu zany vern a ben shivim)." *Di Goldene Keyt* 61 (1967): 123–68.

Rosenthal-Shneiderman, Esther. "Itsik Kipnises 'Babi Yar.'" *Lebns-fragen* 347/348 (1981): 7.

Rosenthal-Shneiderman, Esther. *Oyf vegn un umvegn: zikhroynes, geshe'enishen, perzenlekhkeytn*. Vol. 2. Farlag Y.L. Perets, 1978.

Roskies, David G. *Against the Apocalypse: Responses to Catastrophe in Modern Jewish Culture*. Syracuse University Press, 1999.

Roskies, David G., ed. *The Literature of Destruction: Jewish Responses to Catastrophe*. Jewish Publication Society, 1989.

Roskies, David G., and Naomi Diamant. *Holocaust Literature: A History and Guide*. Brandeis University Press, 2013.

Rothberg, Michael. *Multidirectional Memory: Remembering the Holocaust in the Age of Decolonization*. Stanford University Press, 2009.

Rubenstein, Joshua. *Tangled Loyalties: The Life and Times of Ilya Ehrenburg*. University of Alabama Press, 1999.

Rubenstein, Joshua, and Vladimir P. Naumov, eds. *Stalin's Secret Pogrom: The Postwar Inquisition of the Jewish Anti-Fascist Committee*. Translated by Laura Wolfson. Yale University Press, 2001.

Rubin, B. "Uroki odnoi poeticheskoi biografii: zametki o lirike Yevgeniya Yevtushenko." *Voprosy literatury* 2 (1963): 17–45.

Rudy, Peter. "The Soviet Russian Literary Scene in 1961: A Mild Permafrost Thaw." *Modern Language Journal* 46, no. 6 (1962): 245–54.

Sakwa, Richard. *The Rise and Fall of the Soviet Union, 1917–1991*. Routledge, 1999.

Sallinger, Rick. "'Holocaust by Bullets' Uncovers Mass Graves, 1.6+ Million Victims." *CBS News Colorado*, November 6, 2017. https://www.cbsnews.com/colorado/news/holocaust-mass-graves/.

Service, Robert. *A History of Twentieth-Century Russia*. Harvard University Press, 1998.

Shapiro, Leon, "Soviet Jewry Since the Death of Stalin: A Twenty-Five Year Perspective." *The American Jewish Year Book* 79 (1979): 77–103.

Sheldon, Richard. "The Transformation of Babi Yar." In *Soviet Society and Culture: Essays in Honor of Vera S. Dunham*, edited by Terry L. Thompson and Richard Sheldon. Westview Press, 1988.

Shmeruk, Khone, ed. *A shpigl oyf a shteyn: antologye: poezye un proze fun tsvelf farshnitene yidishe shraybers in ratn-farband*. Magnes Press, 1988; photo-offset of the 1964 edition.

Shmeruk, Khone. "Sifrut Yidish biVrit-hamo'atsot." *Behinot* 1 (1970): 5–26.
Shneer, David. *Through Soviet Jewish Eyes: Photography, War, and the Holocaust*. Rutgers University Press, 2011.
Shneer, David. *Yiddish and the Creation of Soviet Yiddish Culture, 1918–1930*. Cambridge University Press, 2004.
Shneiderman, S. L. "Yiddish in the USSR." *New York Times Book Review*, November 15, 1970, 71–73.
Shrayer, Maxim D. *I Saw It: Ilya Selvinsky and the Legacy of Bearing Witness to the Shoah*. Academic Studies Press, 2013.
Shrayer, Maxim D. "Jewish-Russian Holocaust Poetry in Official Soviet Venues: 1944–1946 (Ehrenburg, Antokolsky, Ozerov)." Paper presented at the Annual Conference of the Association for Jewish Studies (AJS), Washington, DC, December 21, 2008.
Shrayer, Maxim D., ed. *Voices of Jewish-Russian Literature: An Anthology*. Academic Studies Press, 2018.
Shtern, Ludmila. *Brodsky: A Personal Memoir*. Baskerville Publishers, 2004.
Shternshis, Anna. *Soviet and Kosher: Jewish Popular Culture in the Soviet Union, 1923–1939*. Indiana University Press, 2006.
Shvarts, Solomon. *Evrei v Sovetskom Soyuze: s nachala Vtoroi mirovoi voiny 1939–1965*. Amerikanskogo Evrejsokogo Rabochego Komiteta, 1966.
Sicher, Efraim. *The Holocaust Novel*. Routledge, 2005.
Sidorov, E. *Yevgenii Yevtushenko: lichnost' i tvorchestvo*. Hudozesvennaya Literatura, 1987.
Silverman, Jacob. "Inside the FBI's File on Soviet Poet-Dissident Yevgeny Yevtushenko: What the Bureau's Decades-Long Surveillance of the International Celebrity Reveals About the U.S. Government's Cold War Pathologies." *New Republic*. September 21, 2020. https://newrepublic.com/article/159382/fbi-surveillance-russian-poet-yevgeny-yevtushenko-cold-war.
Smolyar, Hersh. "Di groyse shlakht tsvishn di geto-vent." *Sovetish heymland* 2 (1963): 131–39.
Snyder, Timothy. *Bloodlands: Europe Between Hitler and Stalin*. Basic Books, 2016.
Snyder, Timothy. "The Holocaust: The Ignored Reality." *New York Review*, July 16, 2009. https://www.nybooks.com/articles/2009/07/16/holocaust-the-ignored-reality/.
Spechler, Dina. *Permitted Dissent: "Novy Mir" and the Soviet Regime*. Praeger, 1982.
Spector, Shmuel. "Babi Yar." In *Encyclopedia of the Holocaust*. Vol. 1, edited by Israel Gutman. Macmillan, 1989.
Staiger, Emil. *Basic Concepts of Poetics*. Edited by Marianne Burkhard and Luanne T. Frank. Translated by Janette C. Hudson and Luanne T. Frank. Pennsylvania State University Press, 1991.
Starikov, D. "Ob odnom sithotvorenii." *Literatura i zhizn'*, September 27, 1961.
Stradling, Robert. "Shostakovich and the Soviet System, 1925–1975." In *Shostakovich: The Man and His Music*, edited by Christopher Norris. Marion Boyars, 1982.

Sutzkever, Avrom. *Selected Poetry and Prose*. Translated by Barbara and Benjamin Harshav. University of California Press, 1991.
Talalayevsky, Motl. "Ba yene rivn." *Sovetish heymland* 6 (1963): 66.
Talalayevsky, Motl. "Kiev." *Sovetish heymland* 4 (1962): 3–6.
Taubman, William. *Khrushchev: The Man and His Era*. W. W. Norton, 2003.
Teyf, Moyshe. "Zeks milion." *Folks-shtime*, April 16, 1960, 5.
Todd, Albert, ed. *Yevgeny Yevtushenko: The Collected Poems, 1952–1990*. Henry Holt, 1991.
Toker, Leona. "Anatolii Kuznetsov." In *Dictionary of Literary Biography*. Vol. 299, *Holocaust Novelists*, edited by Ephraim Sicher. Gale, 2004.
Toker, Leona. *Gulag Literature and the Literature of Nazi Camps: An Intertextual Reading*. Indiana University Press, 2019.
Toker, Leona. "Target Audience, Hurdle Audience, and the General Reader: Varlam Shalamov's Art of Testimony." *Poetics Today* 26, no. 2 (2005): 281–303.
Toker, Leona. "Toward a Poetics of Documentary Prose: From the Perspective of Gulag Testimonies." *Poetics Today* 18, no. 2 (1997): 187–222.
Tőkés, Rudolph. "Varieties of Soviet Dissent: An Overview." In *Dissent in the USSR: Politics, Ideology, and People*, edited by Rudolph Tőkés. Johns Hopkins University Press, 1975.
Tseitlin, Shmuel. *Dokumental'naya istoriya evreev Rigi*. Jerusalem: n.p., 1989.
Tumarkin, Nina. *The Living and the Dead: The Rise and Fall of the Cult of World War II in Russia*. Basic Books, 1994.
"Undzer veytik un undzer treyst." *Folks-shtime*, April 4, 1956.
Vail, Peter, and Alexander Genis. *Shestidesyatie: mir Sovetskogo cheloveka*. Ardis, 1989.
Vergelis, Aron. "Der denkmol in Babi Yar vet shteyn ledoyres." *Sovetish heymland* 6 (1975): 158–64.
Vergelis, Aron, ed. *Horizontn: fun der hayntsaytiker sovetisher yidisher dikhtung*. Sovetskii Pisatel', 1965.
Vergelis, Aron. "Mit vos iz lebedik di yidishe literatur." *Sovetish heymland* 2 (1967): 124–35.
Viguchin, Semion. "Babi Yar – uroki tragedii." In *Pamyat' Babyego Yara*, edited by Ilya Levitas. Evreyskii Sovet Ukrainy, 2001.
Weiner, Amir. *Making Sense of War: The Second World War and the Fate of the Bolshevik Revolution*. Princeton University Press, 2001.
Wiesel, Elie. "Bezokhrenu et Babi Yar: Ka'avor arba'im shanah." *Masua* 10 (1982): 28–31.
Wiesel, Elie. *The Jews of Silence: A Personal Report on Soviet Jewry*. Schocken Books, 1987.
Yevtushenko, Yevgeny. "Di malke sheynhayt." *Sovetish heymland* 3 (1961): 43.
Yevtushenko, Yevgeny. *Early Poems*. Translated by George Reavey. Marion Boyars, 1989.
Yevtushenko, Yevgeny. *A Precocious Autobiography*. Translated by Andrew R. MacAndrew. Dutton, 1963.
Yevtushenko, Yevgeny. *Shestidesyatnik: memuarnaya proza*. Zebra E, 2006.
Yevtushenko, Yevgeny. "Styd kak soavtor." In *Shestidesyatnik*.

Young, James. *The Texture of Memory: Holocaust Memorials and Meaning.* Yale University Press, 1993.

Young, James. *Writing and Rewriting the Holocaust: Narrative and the Consequences of Interpretation.* Indiana University Press, 1988.

Yushkovsky, Mordechai. "Ha-anusim shel hameah ha-esrim: hane-emanut haleumit et-sel sofrim Yehudim Bivrit hamo'atsot." *Ma'amakim* 34 (2008). https://www.daat.ac.il/daat/ktav_et/maamar.asp?ktavet=1&id=955.

Zakharchuk, Iryna. "Babyn Yar in Belles-Lettres." In *Babyn Yar: History and Memory*, edited by Vladyslav Hrynevych and Paul R. Magocsi. Dukh I Litera, 2016.

Zeltser, Arkadi. "Tema 'Evrei v Bab'yem Yaru' v Sovetskom Soyuze v 1941–1945.'" In *Babyn Yar: masove ubistvo i pamiat' pro noho.* Ukr. tsentr vyvchennia istorii Holokostu, 2017.

Zeltser, Arkadi. *Unwelcome Memory: Holocaust Monuments in the Soviet Union.* Yad Vashem, 2018.

Zubok, Vladislav. *Zhivago's Children: The Last Russian Intelligentsia.* Belknap Press, 2009.

# INDEX

*Page numbers in italics indicate figures.*

## A

Abramovitsh, Sholem, 179
abstract art, 84–85, 202n1
Adorno, Theodor, 139–40
"After the Storm" (Pasternak), 5
*Against the Apocalypse* (Roskies), 137
Akhmadulina, Bella, 58, 78, 209n1
Akhmatova, Anna, 165–66
Aksyonov, Vasilii, 202n1
*Aktionen* (mass shooting campaign), 4
Aleichem, Sholem, 179
Alexeyeva, Ludmilla, 192n26
Altshuler, Mordechai, 134, 181, 191n17, 212n15, 215n44, 221n20; on Kipnis, 135; on the Polish Yiddish press, 123; on synagogues, 27–28
ambiguity, 54–55, 65, 67–68, 71, 73, 85–86
ambivalence, 175, 181; of Khrushchev, 35–36, 120; of Nekrasov, 51; of Yevtushenko, 69, 71
American Academy and Institute of Arts and Letters, 69
amnesia, 7, 9, 200n37
"Among Jews" ("Tsvishn yidn") (Kipnis). *See* "Babi Yar" (Kipnis)
Anielewicz, Mordechai, 6, 221n13
anti-Cosmopolitan campaign, Soviet, 17–18, 26–27, 82, 104, 112, 122, 197n20, 198n10
antisemitism, Soviet, 2, 199n23, 202n48, 204n16, 215nn42–43, 217n72; Khrushchev dismissing, 37–38, 121; in Kyiv, 136, 151–52; Nekrasov on, 44–45, 50–51, 53; Stalinist, 33–34, 93, 97, 119–24, 146–47, 161, 165–66; Ukrainian Soviet Socialist Republic, 37; Yevtushenko on, 59, 63, 65–70, 73–74, 78–79, 81–89

Anti-Zionist Committee of the Soviet Public, 183
Arad, Yitzhak, 4, 190n13
Arendt, Hannah, 4
*Arrested Pages* (Nekrasov), 44
arrests, 26, 30, 57, 122, 146–47, 174, 214n35; of Talalayevsky, 161–62
artistic freedom, 56, 70, 72, 82, 84–87, 92, 113
assimilation, 3, 113, 129
Assmann, Jan, 6, 157
*At Babi Yar*, 159, *159*
"At Babyn Yar" (Pervomaisky), 219n9
atonement, 137–44
"At Those Ditches" (Talalayevsky), 162–63
Auschwitz concentration camp, 3, 5, 14, 76, 115
authenticity, 96–99, 149
authoritarianism, 185, 186
"authorized" memory, 16
"Avraham" (Holovanivsky), 22–23, 26

## B

Babat, Malvina, *2*
Babat, Polina, *2*
*Babi Yar* (Kuznetsov), 91–92, 101–7, 140; role of testimony in, 93–100
*Babi Yar* (symphony, Klebanov), 26
"Babi Yar" (Cherniavsky), 169–72
"Babi Yar" (Driz), 132, 145–52
"Babi Yar" (Ehrenburg), 21–28, 30
"Babi Yar" (Kipnis), 132, 133–44, 145, 162–63, 173
"Babi Yar" (Ozerov), 26, 61, 76–77
*Babi Yar* (Thirteenth Symphony), 18, 37–38, 80–90, *84*, *87*, 124–25
"Babi Yar" (Yevtushenko), 9, 56–59, 61–72,

"Babi Yar" (Yevtushenko) (*continued*)
75–79 *60*, 184, 195n13, 202n1, 204nn15–16; in *Folks-shtime*, 158–59; Jewish martyrdom and, 63, 74, 205n29; Mankoff on, 206n36; public recitations of, 59, 64, 73–74, 80, 84–85; set to music, 80–90, 124–25; Sheldon on, 206n39
"The Babi Yar Cradle Song," 146–52
Babyn Yar Holocaust Memorial Center, 3
Babyn Yar ravine, Ukraine. *See specific topics*
Bagerovo ditch, 207n63
Baltic states, 4, 218n1
Bauer, Yehuda, 52, 189n5
*Becoming Soviet Jews* (Bemporad), 180
Beider, Chaim, 146
Belarus, 4–5
Bemporad, Elissa, 180
Bergelson, Dovid, 135, 196n14
Berggolts, Olga, 17
Beria, Lavrentiy, 30, 36, 198n12, 198n15
Berkhoff, Karel, 1, 23, 210n23
Biblical Hebrew, 108, 157, 213n20
biblical prophecy, 142–43
Bilinsky, Yaroslave, 202n48
Birobidzhan plan, 111, 153–54, 217n71
*The Black Book* (Grossman, Ehrenburg), 21, 61, 194n3
black-hole, memory, 9, 42–43, 83–84, 129, 155, 159, 175, 183–84
Black Hundreds, 48, 67
"Black Years," 27–28, 174
Blake, Patricia, 73
Blobel, Paul, 201n43
*Bloodlands* (Snyder), 4
Bondarovskoy, Valentin, 61–62
bones, uncovered at Babyn Yar, *29*
Boyarsky, Riva, 145, 150
Brest Hero-Fortress memorial, 132
Brezhnev, Leonid, 17, 19, 31, 46, 92, 116, 125–27, 223n46; mini-Thaw under, 130–32, 215, 223
Brodsky, Joseph, 69–70
Brotshenko, Vadim, 164
Brown, Edward, 202n1
Brumberg, Abraham, 122, 132, 217n71

Brumberg, Joseph, 132
Bush, George H. W., 184–85
"By the Light of the Day" (Kazakevich), 202n1

## C

Carter, Jimmy, 14–15
casualties, Babyn Yar, 4, 10–14, 181–82, 193n37; Jewish, 14–15, 22–25, 67, 74, 89, 143–44, 161–64, 169–72, 173, 183–86; Jewish children, 2, 166, 170–71, 175, 190n8, 219n9; Khrushchev on, 37–38; Kuznetsov on, 100–102, 106; Nekrasov on, 42–51; non-Jewish, 1, 3, 11, 14–15, 66, 155, 157, 184–85, 189n7, 204n21; Yevtushenko on, 73–77. *See also* civilian deaths
censorship, Soviet, 194n3, 204n21, 209n5, 213n20, 216n65, 223n44; Brezhnev regime, 126; Glavlit, 176, 223nn45–46; Kuznetsov and, 18, 93–96, 103, 106; of Nekrasov, 39, 43–44; relaxed, 115; "Second Thaw" and, 56–57; self-censorship, 20; *shestidesiatniki* and, 58; Solodin on, 223n45; Thaw period, 194n46; by Vergelis, 176–80
Central Committee of Jews in Poland, 134
Cherniavsky, Shloyme, 19, 168–72, *169*, 175, 178, 181
children, Jewish, 145–52, 167–69; casualties, 2, 166, 170–71, 175, 190n8, 219n9
civilian deaths, 4, 10–14, 48–52, 172, 184, 190n8, 193n37, 195n8; non-Jewish, 1, 3, 11, 15, 155, 157, 184–85, 189n7, 204n21
Clark, Katerina, 202n1, 223n44
Clowes, Edith, 10, 28, 51, 61, 104, 197n18
Cold War, 3–4, 9–10, 16–17, 39–44, 65–66, 80, *177*, 184
collective memory, communal and, 5–6, 54, 80, 116, 137, 167, 172, 175–76
collectivization policy, Stalinist, 210n16
commemoration. *See* memorials and commemorations, Babyn Yar
communicative memory, 6 , 186
Communism, 103, 122–25, 157, 160, 210n7, 215n41, 220n11

# INDEX

Communist Party of the Soviet Union (CPSU), 10, 32, 157, 160–62, 173, 194n46; Evsektsia, 111–12, 135, 215n42; Nekrasov excluded from, 46; Shostakovich and, 83, 87–88
concentration camps, Nazi, 10, 201n39; Auschwitz, 3, 5, 14, 76, 115; Majdanek, 5, 97, 115, 208n5; Syrets, 48, 116, 189n7, 192n30, 201n43
counter-memory, 10, 65, 206n36
CPSU. *See* Communist Party of the Soviet Union
cradle songs (*viglid*). *See* lullabies
credibility, 32–33, 69, 96–102
Cultural Revolution, 83, 111, 165
Czechoslovakia, 94

## D

Daniel, Yuli, 31
*Dark Continent* (Mazower), 5
Darnitsa labor camp, 48, 50–51
Dawidowicz, Lucy, 1–3, 14–15, 104
death toll, Babyn Yar, 3, 43, 48–49, 189nn6–8
deep memory, 76
defection, 18, 91, 94–95, 99, 103–7. *See also* exile
de-Judaization of Babyn Yar, 14–16, 22–23, 27, 47–52, 116, 154–55, 157, 176–82
"Der zelber veg" ("That Same Road") (Khaykine), 166–67
Desbois, Patrick, 4, 190n15
de-Stalinization, 32–40, 56–59, 78, 125–27, 198n15
Diamant, Emmanuel, 62, 128–30, 174, 205n28
dictatorship, 38, 72, 103, 125, 176, 198n12
discrimination, 3, 38, 92, 181, 212n7
dissents, Soviet, 29, 39–41, 44, 50–51, 83, 91–92, 105–7; Brezhnev era, 126; Jewish, 10, 41, 172–76, 185, 192n26. *See also* permitted dissent
Dobrenko, Evgeny, 165, 222n30
documentary novel (*roman-dokument*), 91, 95–99, 105
Donskoi, Mark, 26, 197n20

*Dos Shvartser Vint* (Falikman), 223n41
Driz, Shike Ovsei, 19, 145–52, *146*, 175, 178, 219n4
*druzhba narodov* (friendship of peoples), Soviet, 66, 103–4, 117, 134, 141
dualism, 9–10
Dziuba, Ivan, 62

## E

Ehrenburg, Ilya, 17, 21–28, *25*, 73, 194n46, 199n34, 203n3, 206n39; criticizing Soviet leadership, 31–32, 57. *See also specific works*
Eichmann, Adolf, 52, 199n23
Einsatzgruppen (German special killing squads), 4, 10–11
*Der Emes* (journal), 112
emigration of Soviet Jews, 46, 126, 128–31, 185, 192n26
Era of Stagnation (Zastoi), 125, 223n46
erasure, 9, 15, 37, 42–43, 129
Erik, Maks, 109–10, 161
Estraikh, Gennady, 180, 220n11, 223n46
ethnic identity, 8–9, 27, 143, 157, 184–85
*eto ne dolzhno povtoryt'sya* (Never Again) (painting series), 159, *159*
European Jewry, Nazi extermination of, 2, 4, 7–10, 158, 164, 171–73, 183, 186, 189n5; Markish on, 119; Stalin on, 24; Vergelis on, 176–80
Evsektsia (Jewish section of the Communist Party), 111–12, 135, 215n42
exile, 126–27, 133–34, 214n35; of Kuznetsov, 18, 91, 94–95, 99, 103–7; of Nekrasov, 39, 44, 46
extermination centers, Nazi, 3, 14, 201n39
Extraordinary Commission, 43, 48–49, 51
*Eynikayt* (newspaper), 24, 113–16, 134, 137, 169

## F

factuality, 93–100
Falikman, Yekhiel, 223n41
famine, 96, 104–6, 186, 210n16
fascism, 3, 17, 24, 43, 155, 157, 183, 199n23
Fedenko, Panas, 68–69

Feferman, Kiril, 52–53, 199n23
*Di ferte strune* (*The Fourth String*) (Driz), 147–48
fiction, Holocaust, 6, 96–99, 223n41
Final Solution (Nazi plan), 5, 10, 104, 190n13, 201n39
flooding of Babyn Yar, 33–35, 40, 42, 46, 59, 103, 210n16; Kurenivka mudslide caused by, 62
Floyd, David, 209n5
focalization, 102–3, 140
*Folks-shtime* (periodical), 123–25, 158–59
*The Fourth String* (*Di ferte strune*) (Driz), 147–48
Frank, Anne, 63, 66, 205n30
freedom, artistic, 40, 56, 70, 72, 82, 84–87, 92, 113, 147, 223n46
freedom, literary, 40, 147, 223n46
freedom of speech, 70, 72, 126
friendship of peoples (*druzhba narodov*), Soviet, 66, 103–4, 117, 134, 141
*From Jewish Folk Poetry*, 82

## G

Gen, Tevye, 5
gender, 82, 117–18, 159, *159*, 165–68
generational divides, Soviet, 17, 28, 56–58, 76, 126, 144, 160–61, 174, 197n27
generation of the sixties, Soviet (*shestidesiatniki*), 57–59, 78, 91–92, 130, 144, 203n8
Genis, Alexander, 72–73
genocide, 2, 11, 14, 24–25, 66, 102, 104–6, 137, 164
German Democratic Republic, 22
German–Russian War, 120
German special killing squads (Einsatzgruppen), 4, 10–11
Gershenson, Olga, 87
Gessen, Masha, 95
ghetto mentality, 179
Gilboa, Yehoshua, 218n13
Gitelman, Zvi, 19, 181, 193n37, 215n42
Gladilin, Anatoly, 209n1
Glasnost era ("openness"), 13, 31, 183–84

Glavlit (Soviet central censorship body), 176, 223nn45–46
Glikman, Isaak, 81
Gluzman, Semen, 92
Gontar, Avrom, 124
Gorbachev, Mikhail, 184
Gorbatov, Boris, 26
"A Gravestone over Babi Yar" (Nekrasov), 44–46, 51–52
Great Patriotic War, Soviet, 3, 5, 10, 93, 102, 141, 190n13, 194n49; Babyn Yar associated with, 90, 133–34, 155, 158–59, 164, 171, 174, 180; de-Judaization of, 14–16, 27; Ehrenburg on, 26; master narratives around, 16–17; monuments, 33; Nekrasov addressing, 43, 48–50, 52–53
Great Terror, 57, 83, 110–11, 127, 161, 203n3
Grossman, Vasily, 21, 44, 103
gulag literature, 99–100
gulags, 30, 122, 133–34, 161–62, 201n39, 214n35

## H

*Half-Way to the Moon* (Blake), 73
*Heavy Sand* (Rybakov), 220n10
"The Heirs of Stalin" (Yevtushenko), 71
Himmler, Heinrich, 189n5
Hirsch, Marianne, 76
historiography, 3–5, 15–16, 27, 102, 180
Hitler, Adolf, 22–23, 52, 68–69, 189n5
Hofshteyn, Dovid, 141, 196n14
Holocaust. *See specific topics*
"The Holocaust" (Snyder), 4
*The Holocaust by Bullet* (Desbois), 4, 190n15
"Holocaust by Bullets," 3, 11
*The Holocaust in the Soviet Union* (Arad), 4, 190n13
Holocaust sites, 3, 6–7, 41, 51, 92, 129, 173–74, 207n63; Babyn Yar as a, 53–54, 62, 66, 115, 154, 157–58, 174, 185–86
Holodomor (death by hunger), 96, 104–6, 186
Holovanivsky, Sava, 22–23, 26, 28, 200n37
"Hometown" (Nekrasov), 49–50

*Horizontn* (anthology), 166
Hungarian Revolution, 39–40, 42, 56

I

identity, 37–38, 141–42, 150, 175, 178, 180; ethnic, 8–9, 27, 143, 157, 184–85; Jewish, 8–9, 22–24, 27–28, 102, 114, 129, 159, 161–63, 171–72, 181; Soviet Jewish, 19, 180–81
"Ikh bin dort oykh geven" ("I Too Was There") (Khaykine), 166–68
*Ikh muz dertseyln* (Rolnikaite), 177
Ilichev, Leonid, 84–85
illegally printed self-publications (*samizdat*), 50, 126, 197n18, 202n52
illegal works published abroad (*tamizdat*), 49–50, 59, 123, 202n52
imperialism, 157
indirect extermination, Nazi, 5, 11
Institute of Jewish Proletarian Culture, 109–10, 166, 212n5
intergenerational relationships, 81–88
internationalism, 101, 160–61, 212n11
interwar period, 109, 116, 160–68
*In the Trenches of Stalingrad* (Nekrasov), 49–50
Iron Curtain, 4, 15, 47, 58, 80, 123, 145, 174–75, 181
"I Saw It" (Selvinsky), 74, 207n63
Israel, 26, 52, 130–31, 176, 217n71
"I Too Was There" ("Ikh bin dort oykh geven") (Khaykine), 166–68
*Iunost'* (periodical), 91–92, 93–95, 99, 102–5
*Izvestiia* (newspaper), 189n6

J

Jesus Christ, 63, 205n29
Jewish Anti-Fascist Committee, 24, 25, 113, 115, 119, 162
Jewish attention to the graves of the dead (*yortsayt*), 136–38, 162
Jewish Fighting Organization (ZOB), 7, 221n13
Jewish dissents, Soviet, 10, 41, 172–76, 185, 192n26

Jewish Fighting Organization, 6
Jewish identity, 8–9, 22–24, 27–28, 102, 114, 129, 159, 161–63, 171–72, 181
Jewish martyrdom, 63, 74, 157, 164, 205n29
Jewish martyrs, 63, 74, 157, 164, 205n29
Jewish nationalism, 6, 127–30, 134–36, 145–46, 159, 179–80, 213n20, 221n20, 223n41; Soviet dissent and, 41, 61; of Soviet Yiddish writers, 109–10, 114, 133, 173–74
Jewish section of the Communist Party (Evsektsia), 111–12, 135, 215n42
Jewish sites, Babyn Yar as a, 19, 51–54, 128, 174, 184–85
Joshua, Israel, 179
*Judenrein*, 2, 101, 195n8

K

Kazakevich, E., 202n1
*kdoyshim. See* Jewish martyrdom
Kenez, Peter, 57
Kerler, Dov Ber, 219n4
Kerler, Yosef, 176–78
KGB. *See* Komitet Gosudarstvennoi Bezopasnosti
Khachaturian, Aram, 82
*Khadoshim un teg* (*Months and Days*) (Kipnis), 135–36
Khaykine, Dore, 19, 165, 165–68, 175, 178, 181
Khazan, Liubov, 39
Khiterer, Victoria, 37, 151, 186, 190n8, 201n43
Khrushchev, Nikita, 18, 199n34, 202n1, 208n15, 215nn41–43, 220n11, 223n46; ambivalence of, 35–36, 120; antisemitism dismissed by, 37–38, 121; Babyn Yar monuments vetoed by, 41, 46–47; denunciation of Stalin, 194n46; de-Stalinization by, 33–40, 56–59, 198n15; on Nazi atrocities, 25–26; Nekrasov on, 30, 47; ouster of, 88, 92, 125–26, 158; "Second Thaw" and, 56–57; Secret Speech by, 33–34, 40, 56, 58, 120–21, 194n46, 202n1; Yevtushenko and, 37–38, 61, 63, 72, 83–88, 90
Khrushchev–Malenkov duumvirate, 35, 125, 198n15

"Khrushchev's Thaw." *See* the Thaw period
"Kiev" (Hofshteyn), 196n14
"Kiev" (Talalayevsky), 163–65, 173
Kin, Ostap, 195n6
Kipnis, Itsik, 19, *134*, 160–63, 166, 168, 217n10, 221n20; Driz compared to, 145–46, 149–50; on memorials, 141–42; during the Thaw period, 133–35. *See also specific works*
"Kira Georgevna" (Nekrasov), 202n1
Kirschenbaum, Lisa, 17
Klebanov, Dmitry, 26, 197n19
Kochubievsky, Boris, 174
Komitet Gosudarstvennoi Bezopasnosti (KGB), 18, 39, 44, 94, 128, 130
Korey, William, 14–15, 65, 85–86, 155, 208n15
Kornblum, Zyame, 164
Korotich, Vitaly, 62
Kosolapov, Valery, 59, 61, 92
Kosygin, Alexei, 92, 125
Kultur Lige, 109
Kurenivka tragedy (*Kurenyovskaya tragediia*), 62, 103
Kushnirov, Aaron, 19, 115–18, *117*, 139
Kuznetsov, Anatoly, 29, 90, *94*, 140, 209n1, 210n11, 210n16, 210n23; on Babyn Yar casualties, 100–102, 106; censorship of, 18, 93–96, 103, 106; documentary novel by, 91, 95–107; exile of, 18, 91, 94–95, 99, 103–7; permitted dissent and, 91, 103–6; works published abroad by, 94–95, 102–3; Yevtushenko and, 18, 61–62, 91–95, 101–2, 105, 108
Kyiv, Ukraine, 1–2, 165, 192n30, 196n14, 197n28; antisemitism in, 136, 151–52; Babyn Yar commemorations in, 33, 184–86; City Council, 33, 42–43; German occupation of, 3, 13–14, 23–25, 49, 95–99, 100, 103–5, 179; postwar, 42–43, 116–17, 140–41, 173; Soviet takeover of, 22, 25–26; Yiddish literary scene in, 18–19, 109–10, 146–52, 153–73
Kyiv Art Institute, 146

L
labor camps, 14, 48, 100, 116, 126, 146–47, 161, 219n2
*Lady Macbeth of Mtsensk* (opera), 82
landfill, Babyn Yar treated as a, 61, 197n28
Langer, Lawrence, 76
Lekht, Naya, 92, 223n41
Lemkin, Raphael, 105
Lenin, Vladimir, 83, 94, 110, 168, 210n11, 212n11
Levitas, Ilya, 184, 190n8
*Lexicon of Soviet Yiddish Writers* (Beider), 146
liberalization, 29, 31, 35–36, 40, 42, 202n1
*Life and Fate* (*Zhizn' i Sud'ba*) (Grossman), 44, 103
Lifshitz, Nehama, 145, 150–52, 218n1
literary freedom, 40, 147, 223n46
*Literatura i zhizn'* (journal), 66
*Literaturnaya gazeta* (newspaper), 38–39, 41–44, 47, 92, 214, 221n21; Yevtushenko published in, 58–59, *60*, 61, 124
Liubov Khazan, 190n8
*Liven'* (Ozerov), 197n18
*longue durée*, 29–30, 76, 89
Lowe, David, 69
"Luftbalonen" (Driz), 148
lullabies, 145–52, 219n4, 219n10
Lysenko, Mikhaylo, *156*

M
Maes, Francis, 82–83
Majdanek concentration camp, 5, 97, 115, 208n5
Malakhovka, Russia, 48
Malenkov, Gregory, 35–36, 198n15
Mandelstam, Osip, 165–66
Mankoff, Jeff, 10, 48, 65, 193n33, 197n27, 206n36
marginalization of Babyn Yar, 14–15, 35, 125, 175
Markish, Perets, 19, *25*, 61, 115–16, 118–20, 139, 141, 214n36
Markov, Alexei, 66

martyrs, Jewish, 63, 74, 157, 164, 205n29
Marx, Karl, 110, 210n11
mass executions, 5, 11, 15, 41, 114
mass graves, 2, 201n43; Babyn Yar as a, 21, 28–29, *29*, 34, 37, 45, 61, 100–101, 124–25, 155, 162
mass shootings at Babyn Yar, 1–3, 5, 11, 15, 25, 143–44
master narratives, Babyn Yar-Holocaust, 10, 16–17, 19, 24, 118, 132, 150, 164, 178; around victimhood, 12–13
Maxim Gorky Literature Institute, 58, 91, 108
Mayakovsky, Vladimir, 73
Mayzel, Nahman, 213n22
Mazower, Mark, 5
"Melnyk Street" (Holovanivsky), 200n37
"The Memorial at Babi Yar Will Stand Forever" (Vergelis), 153
memorials and commemorations, Babyn Yar, 8–10, *42*, 154–55, 183–86, *185*, 197n27; dissent and, 29, 174–76; Khrushchev rejecting, 36–37; Kipnis on, 141–42; Kyiv City Council, 33, 42–43; literary, 17–18, 21, 127, 131, 133–34, 173–75; postwar, 127–28, *128*, *130*; Soviet suppression of, 136–37. *See also* monuments
memories, 5–8, 16–20, 139, 178, 181, 186; black-hole, 9, 42–43, 83–84, 129, 155, 159, 175, 183–84; coexisting, 134–37; collective, 5–6, 54, 116, 137, 167, 172, 175–76; counter, 10, 65, 206n36; de-Judaization of, 14–15; Jewish, 48, 146, 179, 185; multidirectional, 52–55, 201n39; Soviet, 35, 159; of Soviet Yiddish writers, 104–6, 137, 162, 164, 167, 169–70, 173, 175. *See also* collective memory
menorah monument at Babyn Yar, 184–86, *185*
Merridale, Catherine, 16
meta-narratives, 52–53
Mikhoels, Solomon, 115–16, 119
mini-Thaw period, 130–32, 147
Mintz, Alan, 14
Mitsel, Mikhail, 136

"Mit vos iz lebedik di yidishe literatur" (Vergelis), 178–79
modernism, 109, 165
Molotov, Vyacheslav, 23–24, 195n8
*Months and Days (Khadoshim un teg)* (Kipnis), 135–36
monuments, 34, 132; Babyn Yar, 8–10, 16, 22, *42*, 61, *128*, *130*, *135*, 154–55, *156*, 183–86, *185*; Holocaust, 6–7, 33, 36; menorah monument at Babyn Yar, 184–86, *185*; Nekrasov advocating for Babyn Yar, 40–41, 44, 46–47, 51–52; Yevtushenko addressing absence of, 9, 59, 63, 67, 75
Moscow Polytechnic Institute, 59
Moscow Yiddish literary scene, 116, 153
*Moskva* (journal), 46
"The Mother Rachel" (Kushnirov), 19, 115–18, 124
multidirectional memory, 52–55, 201n39
Murav, Harriet, 114–16, 118, 136, 181
Museum of the History of Polish Jews (POLIN), 6
music: lullabies and, 145–52, 219n4, 219n10; symphonies as, 18, 26, 37–38, 80–90, 197n19, 208n22; Yiddish folk songs, 145, 148–51, 219n10
*Music from a Speeding Train* (Murav), 181
"My Second Beginning" (Talalayevsky), 161

N
Nakhmanovich, Rafael, 61–62
Nakhmanovich, Vitalii, 15–16, 192n30
Nartova, L., 1
nationalism. *See* Jewish nationalism
nationalism, Ukrainian, 12, 129, 185–86, 193n33, 196n14, 221n20
Nazis, Nazi rule and, 22, 157, 201n43; Babyn Yar massacre by, 1–4, 10–14, 45–46; extermination centers, 3, 14, 201n39; Final Solution plan, 5, 10, 201n39; mass executions, 5, 11, 15, 41, 114; mass shootings at Babyn Yar, 1–3, 5, 11, 15, 25, 143–44; occupation of Kyiv, 3, 13–14, 23–25, 49, 95–99, 100, 103–5, 179; POWs, 139–40, 143;

Nazis, Nazi rule and (*continued*)
  Soviet repression and, 44–47; war crimes, 5, 11, 15, 45, 48, 181, 192n30, 201n43. *See also* concentration camps; European Jewry, Nazi extermination of
  neglect of Babyn Yar, 8–9, 28–29, 33–38, 59, 141, 170, 199n23
Neizvestny, Ernst, 85
Nekrasov, Viktor, 29–31, *41*, 61–62, 90, 201n45, 202n1, 202n54; advocating for Babyn Yar monument, 40–41, 44, 46–47, 51–52; on antisemitism, 44–45, 50–51, 53; censorship of, 39, 43–44; exile of, 39, 44, 46; KGB and, 18, 39; permitted dissent of, 39, 42–43, 47–48, 50–51, 54; Red Army service of, 39, 49–50, 53; Yevtushenko and, 61–62. *See also specific works*
neo-Stalinists, 36, 46, 126, 131
*Nepokorennye* (film), 26
Nepokorennye (Gorbatov), 26
Never Again (*eto ne dolzhno povtoryt'sya*) (painting series), 159, *159*
Niger, Shmuel, 135, 179, 213n22
*The Ninth Wave* (Ehrenburg), 26–27
non-Jewish Babyn Yar casualties, 1, 3, 11, 14–15, 66, 155, 157, 184–85, 189n7, 204n21
non-Jewish composers, 82–83
non-Jewish poets, 9, 73–74, 170, 195n13
non-Jewish writers, 29, 50–51, 124, 195n13
Nora, Pierre, 7–8
"Notes of a Bystander" ("Zapiski zevaki") (Nekrasov), 46, 49–51
*Novy mir* (magazine), 21, 27, 32, 38, 203n3
Noy, Dov, 149–51, 219n10

O

October Revolution, 17, 23, 87, 109–10, 126, 135, 160–61, 209n22
*Ogonyok* (journal), 62
*Oktiabr'* (journal), 26, 61
Okudzhava, Bulat, 58, 72–73
Olick, Jeffrey, 7, 191n19
*One Day in the Life of Ivan Denisovich* (Solzhenitsyn), 57, 100

"On hokhmes, on heshboynes" ("Without Thinking, Without Calculation") (Kipnis), 123, 134, 221n20
"On Sincerity in Literature" (Pomerantsev), 32
"openness" era (Glasnost), 13, 31, 183–84
Operation Barbarossa (1941), 4, 10, 22–23
Organization of Ukrainian Nationalists (OUN), 12, 185–86, 193n33
*The Origins of Totalitarianism* (Arendt), 4
Orthodox Christians, 113, 185–86
Ottaway, Hugh, 209n22
"Ottepel'" (*The Thaw*) (Ehrenburg), 31
OUN. *See* Organization of Ukrainian Nationalists
Ovchinnikov, B., 33, 36m 46–47
Ozerov, Lev, 26, 28, 61, 76–77, 197n18

P

Pasternak, Boris, 5, 165
patriotism, Russian, 68–69
Peretz, I. L., 179
permitted dissent, 38, 72, 102, 107–8, 123, 126; Kuznetsov and, 91, 103–6; Lifshitz performance as, 151–52; of Nekrasov, 39, 42–43, 47–48, 50–51, 54; Yevtushenko and, 63–71, 80, 82–83, 86–88
Pervomaisky, Leonid, 219n9
Pikhoya, Rudolph, 35, 198n12
pilgrimage, 61–62, 140–41
Pinkus, Benjamin, 27, 51, 110, 181, 212n11, 214n37, 217n72
Podgorny, Nikolai, 34, 36–37
poetry as testimony, 72–79, 148
poets, non-Jewish, 9, 73–74, 170, 195n13
pogroms, 25, 63, 109, 135–36, 151, 195–96
Poland, 4, 133, 158, 161; Communist Party, 122–25, 221n13; Soviet Yiddish literature in, 133–34; Warsaw Ghetto, 14; Warsaw Ghetto Uprising, 6–8, 50–52, 158, 177
Polevoi, Boris, 91–92, 94, 101–2
POLIN (Museum of the History of Polish Jews), 6
Pomerantsev, Vladimir, 32, 73

*Po moskovskomu vremeni* (poetry anthology), 169
popular memory, 10
postmemory, 76
post-Soviet era, 185–86, 193n33
Post-Stalin era, 33–39, 104, 110, 119–20, 173, 176, 178
postwar era, 16, 19, 22–24, 136, 162–63, 170–72, 178–80; commemoration of Babyn Yar, 127–28; Kyiv, 42–43, 116–17, 140–41, 173; Poland, 122–23
POWs. *See* prisoners of war
*Pravda* (newspaper), 26, 48, 71, 189n6, 195n8
President's Commission on the Holocaust, United States, 14–15
prisoners of war (POWs), 35, 48–49, *156*; Nazi, 139–40, 143; Soviet Union, 11, 14–15, 116, 143, 155, 184
Prokofiev, Sergei, 82
*Prolit* (periodical), 165
Pronicheva, Dina, 98, 100, 106, 210n23
propaganda, Soviet, 31, 69–70, 120–21, 131–32, 158, 165; Communist Party Propaganda Department, 194, 213n22
Prorokov, Boris, 159, *159*
publishing abroad, Soviet works, 123–25, 134–35, 137–39, 218n20; by Kuznetsov, 94–95, 102–3; *tamizdat*, 49–50, 59, 123, 202n52

Q
"The Queen Beauty" (Yevtushenko), 124

R
Radio Liberty, 103–5
Rappaport, Nathan, 6
Red Army, Soviet, 6, 89, 112, 136–37, 141, 157, 168, 207n63; Jewish soldiers, 24, 113–19, 134; Nekrasov serving in, 39, 49–50, 53; Talalayevsky in, 161, 164
repression, Soviet, 9, 28, 44–47, 169, 174, 181, 185–86, 198n15
Reyzen, Zalmen, 135
Riga Ghetto, 176–77

Rolnikaite, Masha, 177–78
*roman-dokument* (documentary novel), 91, 95–99, 105
Rosenshield, Gary, 220n10
Rosenthal-Shneiderman, Esther, 135, 141–42, 161
Roskies, David, 16, 137, 139, 167
Rothberg, Michael, 53–54
Rubenstein, Joshua, 198n10
Rubin, B., 204
Rudy, Peter, 202n1
Russian Civil War of 1918–1920, 109, 135
Russian non-Jewish poets, 9, 73–74, 170, 195n13
Russification, Soviet, 112, 185
Rybakov, Anatoly, 220n10

S
*samizdat* (illegally printed self-publications), 50, 126, 197n18, 202n52
"Sanctified Land" (Ehrenburg), 116
Second Thaw (1961), 56, 78, 86, 202n1
Secret Speech (Khrushchev), 33–34, 40, 56, 58, 120–21, 194n46, 202n1
self-censorship, 20
Selvinsky, Ilya, 74, 207n63
*Sequel to a Legend* (Kuznetsov), 93
Sheldon, Richard, 51, 67, 93, 202n54, 205n29, 206n39, 218n13
*shestidesiatniki* (generation of the sixties), 57–59, 78, 91–92, 130, 144, 203n8
Shmeruk, Khone, 114, 218n20
Shneer, David, 5, 22, 114, 165, 190n13
the Shoah. *See specific topics*
Shostakovich, Dmitri, 18, 29, 37–38, 80–90, *84*, *87*, 124–25, 208n22
*A shpigl oyf a shteyn* (Shmeruk), 218n20
Shrayer, Maxim, 61
Shtern, Ludmila, 70–71
*Der shtern* (Yiddish almanac), 160
Shternshis, Anna, 180–81
shtetls, 135, 146, 160, 179
Shvarts, Solomon, 65, 208n15
Sicher, Efraim, 106

silence around Babyn Yar, 16–17, 26–30, 92, 153–55, 158, 176–77; neglect of Babyn Yar and, 33–38; Nekrasov addressing, 46–47
Silverman, Jacob, 71
Singer, Isaac Bashevis, 179
Sinyavsky, Andrei, 31
Sinyavsky–Daniel Trial, 126–27
Six-Day War, 6, 128, 130–31, 223n41
"Six Million" (Teyf), 124
Skirda, T., 41
slave labor, 35
Smekhov, Venyamin, Venyamin
Smolyar, Hersh, 124, 158, 221n13
Snyder, Timothy, 4–5, 14
Social and Cultural Association of Jews in Poland, 122–23
socialism, 110–12, 160–61, 179–80, 212n11, 215n41; Thaw period and, 57; Zionism and, 131
socialist-realism, 6, 31–33, 61, 98, 162
"socialist romanticism," 78
Solodin, Vladimir, 223n45
Solzhenitsyn, Alexander, 57, 100, 126–27
Sosiura, Volodymyr, 195n13
*Sovetish heymland* (journal), 121, 123–24, 132, 150, 217n71, 223n41; Babyn Yar in, 153–55, 157–70, *159*, 172; Khaykine published in, 165–68; Talalayevsky published in, 162–65
*Soviet and Kosher* (Shternshis), 180
Soviet central censorship body (Glavlit), 176, 223nn45–46
Soviet citizens, 16–17, 24–25, 39, 53–55, 135; victims of Babyn Yar as, 37, 48, 154–55, *156*, 157, 183
Soviet Jews, 1–2, 9, 182, 193n37, 212n7, 215nn41–43, 224n59; Babyn Yar Massacre of, 10–15, 23–25, 28, 155, 157; "counter-memory" of, 206n36; emigration of, 46, 126, 128–31, 185, 192n26; evacuation of, 108, 136, 140–43, 167–68; identity and, 19, 180–81; synagogues of, 27–28, 48, 113, 121, 212n15, 215n44; Vergelis and, 152. *See also* Soviet Yiddish literature

Soviet literature, 9, 16, 22, 28, 59, 61, 73; literary memorials to Babyn Yar in, 17–18, 21, 131, 133–34, 173–75; Soviet Russian literature, 18–20, 30, 32, 39, 53, 104, 121–22, 181. *See also specific works*
Soviet Union (USSR), 66, 111, 120, 166, 198n12, 212n7, 215nn41–43; anti-Cosmopolitan campaigns, 17–18, 26–27, 82, 104, 112, 122, 197n20, 198n10; art, 28, 33, 57–58, 82–83, 85, 87, 89, 94; artistic freedom in, 56, 70, 72, 82, 84–87, 92, 113; collapse of the, 15, 25–26, 76, 126, 184, 206n36; complicity in Babyn Yar massacre, 5–6, 141–42, 186–87; dictatorship, 38, 72, 103, 125, 176, 198n12; "friendship of peoples" doctrine, 66, 103, 134, 141; generational divides in, 17, 28, 56–58, 76, 126, 144, 160–61, 174, 197n27; government, 9–10, 14–15, 195n8, 212n11; intellectuals, 10, 29, 31–35, 38–52, 57–58, 82–87, 90, 174; KGB, 18, 39, 44, 94, 128, 130; Khrushchev–Malenkov duumvirate, 35, 125, 198n15; liberalization, 29, 31, 35–36, 40, 42, 202n1; as multiethnic, 5, 13–14, 119, 160–61; passports, 217n69; POWs, 11, 14–15, 116, 143, 155, 184; repression, 9, 28, 44–47, 169, 174, 181, 185–86, 198n15; Russification, 112, 185; stance on Babyn Yar, 23, 33–39, 90, 155, *156*, 157, 168, 173–75, 183–84; synagogues in, 27–28, 48, 121, 212n15, 215n44; totalitarianism, 34, 38, 44, 105–7, 142, 165, 186, 198n12; Zhdanovshchina policy, 17–18, 26–27, 134. *See also* antisemitism; censorship, Soviet; Communist Party of the Soviet Union; dissents, Soviet; Great Patriotic War; propaganda, Soviet; Red Army, Soviet; suppression of Babyn Yar, Soviet
Soviet Union, Holocaust in, 1–6, 9–14, 66, 99, 155, 207n63; Nekrasov addressing, 40–41, 53–54; Vergelis minimizing, 176–80. *See also specific regions*
Soviet Writers' Union, 32, 65, 109, 119, 158, 165, 222n30. See also *Literaturnaya gazeta*

Soviet Yiddish culture, 19, 119–20, 153–54, 214n37, 218n13, 220n11
Soviet Yiddish literature, 18–20, 108–19, 154, 177–82, 213n22, 213nn19–20, 214n35–37; lullabies as, 145–52, 219n4, 219n10; mini-Thaw for, 130–32. *See also specific authors*; *specific genres*; *specific works*
Spechler, Dina, 38, 151–52
the Stagnation era, 125, 127, 133, 223n46
Staiger, Emil, 95
Stalin, Joseph, 16–17, 24–25, 82–83, 110–13, 194n46, 218n20; death of, 28–30, 31–32, 35–36, 49, 59, 65, 73, 194n46, 197n27, 218n1; famine under, 104–5, 210n16
Stalinism, 17–18, 112–19, 125–27, 133, 203n8, 214n35; antisemitism under, 33–34, 93, 97, 119–24, 146–47, 161, 165–66; collectivization policies, 106, 210n16; Ehrenburg portraying, 31–32; Holodomor perpetuated under, 96, 104–6, 186; socialist-realism during, 6, 31–33, 61, 98, 162; Soviet art under, 85
Starikov, Dmitry, 66
*The Storm* (Ehrenburg), 26–27
suppression of Babyn Yar, Soviet, 18, 25–28, 95, 133, 136–37, 178; post-Stalin era, 40–52; during the Thaw period, 29–30
survivors, 14–15, 25, 37, 76, 97, 100, 103, 106–7; Babyn Yar, 98, 118, 141, 210n23
Suslov, Mikhail, 103, 178, 214n37
Sutzkever, Avrom, 171
symphonies, 18, 26, 37–38, 80–90, 197n19, 208n22
synagogues, 27–28, 48, 121, 212n15, 215n44
Syrets concentration camp, 48, 116, 189n7, 192n30, 201n43

T
Talalayevsky, Motl (Matveii), 19, 160–68, *163*, 174–75, 221n20
*tamizdat* (illegal works published abroad), 49–50, 59, 123, 202n52
Tarkovski, Andrei, 216n65
testimony, 7, 15, 51, 93–100, 103, 106; poetry as, 72–79, 148

Teyf, Moyshe, 124
"That Same Road" ("Der zelber veg") (Khaykine), 166–67
*The Thaw* ("Ottepel'") (Ehrenburg), 31
the Thaw period (1953–1966), 6, 194n46, 197n20, 197n27, 210n7; Brezhnev era, 125; flooding of Babyn Yar during, 33–34; following the death of Stalin, 31–33; Kipnis during, 133–35; *Novy mir* during, 21, 27, 32, 38, 203n3; references to Babyn Yar during, 17–19, 28–30, 121, 158, 172; symphonies during, 80–90; Vergelis and, 154–55. *See also* Second Thaw
"Their Memory Is Alive" ("Zeyer ondenk lebt") (Mikhoels), 116
Thirteenth Symphony (*Babi Yar*), 18, 37–38, 80–90, *84*, *87*, 124–25
*A Ticket to the Stars* (Aksyonov), 202n1
*Time* magazine, 64, *64*
Todd, Albert, 204n21
Toker, Leona, 93, 99–100, 103, 201n39
Tőkés, Rudolph, 175, 199n26
Tomb of the Unknown Soldier memorial, 132
totalitarianism, 34, 38, 44, 105–7, 142, 165, 186, 198n12
"To the Jewish Fighter" (Markish), 119
*To the People and the Fatherland* (Markish), 141
"Toward a Poetics of Documentary Prose" (Toker), 99–100
translations, 75, 101, 124, 143; Polish, 133; Russian, 24, 150, 168–73, 178, 197n18, 197n27, 209n5
Treblinka concentration camp, 115
"Tsvishn yidn" ("Among Jews") (Kipnis). *See* "Babi Yar" (Kipnis)
Tumarkin, Nina, 16–17, 97, 132, 140
Tvardovsky, Alexander, 203n3

U
Ukraine, 1–5, 187, 225n7; government, 33, 184–86; Holodomor, 96, 104–6, 186. *See specific regions*
Ukrainian Academy of Sciences, 212n5

Ukrainian Central Committee, 34, 86, 142
Ukrainian Extraordinary State Commission, 24–26
Ukrainian nationalism, 12, 129, 185–86, 193n33, 196n14, 221n20
Ukrainian Soviet Socialist Republic, 37, 47, 155, 163
"undesirable elements," 2, 192n30
Union of the Russian People, 67
University of Kyiv, 160
*Unwelcome Memory* (Zeltser), 181
USSR. *See* Soviet Union

V

Vail, Peter, 72–73
vengeance, 21–22, 137–44
Vergelis, Aron, 153–55, 157, 164, 174, *177*, 183, 223n46; Babyn Yar de-Judaized by, 176–82; master narratives and, 19; on the Polish Yiddish press, 124
victimization, victimhood and, 16, 139, 143, 159, 162–64, 185–86, 199n23, 225n10; Jewish, 3, 101, 150; master narratives around, 12–13; Soviet, 138
*viglid* (cradle song). *See* lullabies
Vilna Ghetto, 177
Viner, Meir, 109–10
Vlasov, A., 33, 36, 46–47
Volgograd Memorial, 132
Voznesensky, Andrei, 58
Vysotski, Vladimir, 216n65

W

"A Wagon of Shoes" (Sutzkever), 171
*War* (Markish), 19, 115–16, 118, 124
war crimes, 5, 11, 15, 45, 48, 181, 192n30, 201n43
Warsaw Ghetto, 14
Warsaw Ghetto Uprising, 6–8, 50–52, 158, 177
*We Are Here* (song collection), 145, 219n2
Wehrmacht, 10–11. *See also* Einsatzgruppen
"Why Has It Not Been Done?" (Nekrasov), 31, 40–47, 49, 51, 54

Wiesel, Elie, 14–15, 97, 215n43
"Without Thinking, Without Calculation" ("On hokhmes, on heshboynes") (Kipnis), 123, 134, 221n20
witnesses, 14, 17, 37, 61–62, 72–77, 95–99, 201n43
World War II. *See specific topics*
*Writing and Rewriting the Holocaust* (Young), 96–97

Y

years of silence, 17, 46, 119–22
Yevtushenko, Yevgeny, 29, 56, *60*, *64*, 99–100, 178, 204n15; on absence of Babyn Yar monuments, 9, 59, 63, 67, 75; on antisemitism, 59, 63, 65–70, 73–74, 78–79, 81–89; Cherniavsky compared to, 169–70; critics of, 66–72; Diamant on, 205n28; Driz compared to, 145, 150; on Jewish martyrdom, 63, 74, 205n29; Khrushchev and, 37–38, 61, 63, 72, 83–88, 90; Kuznetsov and, 18, 61–62, 91–95, 101–2, 105, 108; in *Literaturnaya gazeta*, 58–59, *60*, 61, 124; Nekrasov compared to, 54–55; as a part of the *shestidesiatniki*, 58–59; permitted dissent and, 63–71, 80, 82–83, 86–88; as a Russian non-Jewish poet, 9, 170; Shostakovich and, 37–38, 80–90, *84*, *87*, 124–25; Todd on, 204n21. *See also specific works*
Yiddish almanac (*Der shtern*), 160
Yiddish culture, 145–50, 178
Yiddish folk songs, 145, 148–51, 219n10
Yiddish literati, 109–12, 124, 155, 214n35
*Yidishe shriftn* (periodical), 123–24
*yortsayt* (Jewish attention to the graves of the dead), 136–38, 162
Young, James, 96–97, 99
Yushkovsky, Mordechai, 224n59

Z

Zakharchuk, Iryna, 44
"Zapiski zevaki" ("Notes of a Bystander") (Nekrasov), 46, 49–51

Zastoi (Era of Stagnation), 125, 223n46
Zeltser, Arkadi, 16–17, 24, 181
"Zeyer ondenk lebt" ("Their Memory Is Alive") (Mikhoels), 116
Zhdanovshchina (Soviet policy), 17–18, 26–27, 134
*Zhizn' i Sud'ba* (*Life and Fate*) (Grossman), 44, 103

Zionism, 128–31, 174, 183–84, 217n71, 221n13
Zivs, Samuil, 183
*Znamya* (journal), 27
ZOB (Jewish Fighting Organization), 7, 221n13
Zubok, Vladislav, 78, 84–85, 203n8
Zuckerman, Yitzhak, 52

# ABOUT THE AUTHOR

SHAY A. PILNIK IS THE DIRECTOR OF THE EMIL A. AND JENNY FISH CENTER FOR Holocaust and Genocide Studies at Yeshiva University in New York City. Formerly, Pilnik was the executive director of the Nathan and Esther Pelz Holocaust Education Resource Center in Milwaukee, Wisconsin. He holds a PhD in modern Jewish studies from the Jewish Theological Seminary.